# ENDLESS WINTER

# ENDLESS WINTER

*The Inside Story of the Rugby Revolution*

**Stephen Jones**

MAINSTREAM
PUBLISHING

EDINBURGH AND LONDON

First published in Great Britain in 1993 (reprinted twice) by
MAINSTREAM PUBLISHING COMPANY (EDINBURGH) LTD
7 Albany Street
Edinburgh EH1 3UG

ISBN 1 85158 684 9

A catalogue record for this book is available from the British Library

Typeset in Baskerville by Saxon Graphics Ltd, Derby
Printed in Great Britain by Butler & Tanner Ltd, Frome

To Duncan Gareth Jones

# Acknowledgments

I would like to thank sincerely several people who helped in the production of the original edition of *Endless Winter* and also in this paperback edition. Caroline North, my agent, was also the book's editor and general pervasive influence for the good. At the presentation lunch for the William Hill/Sportspages Awards, she wore a nice hat.

Ian Robertson gave advice on what a cautious non-gambler should do with a £500 betting voucher from William Hill (answer: bung it on France to beat Ireland in Paris at 1-6 on; nearest thing to a certainty in sport. Cover yourself with £100 on Ireland at 5-1 and £30 on the draw at 16-1, and whatever the result you clean up about £500).

Thanks to the Institute of Contemporary Arts for inviting me to address it on 'New Sports Writing'. Bit difficult that, because if there is anything contemporaneously artistic about sports reporting then I haven't found it yet. By New Sports Writing, I think they meant that after Nick Hornby's *Fever Pitch*, sports journalism had apparently gone up a notch in public perception; that we as a bunch were no longer quite as disliked and that we could all look forward to a future when we were regarded as literary giants. Me, I prefer the dislike, the freezing press box, the nonsensical deadlines and the phones that don't work.

Thanks also to my dear family; to my colleagues on *The Sunday Times* – especially for the impetus of friendship and professional passion from Nick Pitt, Brough Scott, Chris Smith and Lauren St John. Lauren may be unaware of how her brilliant golfing book *Shooting at Clouds* influenced me. And finally, thanks to my friends and colleagues in the media on rugby's endless road and its byways. Our relaxed manner, and our warm fraternal welcome to new men on the touring circuit (especially to Mick Jug Ears Cleary and Paul Judas Ackford) are bywords in the sport.

**Stephen Jones**
**September 1994**

# Contents

# *Another Divine Madness*

## INTRODUCTION TO THE NEW EDITION

In any work of more than 120,000 words, there are bound to be some errors, something for which to apologise. Accordingly, many apologies to Dudley Wood and Eric Clapton, grievously wronged in the hardback edition of *Endless Winter*. Er, that's it. That's enough penitence.

I accused poor old Dudley's Rugby Football Union of constructing a gigantic concrete and steel-girder aircraft hangar instead of a rugby stadium. I suggested that Twickenham would lose its atmosphere. Then came the tumultuous day in November on which England beat New Zealand, that strange touring team of 1993 whose smile was only skin deep. The crowd went noisily berserk, the noise thundered around the new stands. I still stand by my claim to have discovered dinosaurs and fossils in and around Twickenham, but fair cop. I was wrong about the stadium.

And about poor old Eric. I accused the Great Axeman of losing touch, of playing 'White Room' and the rest of his repertoire by rote, while dressed in Armani; of failing those of us who came up with him from the days of the Yardbirds.

Then, in 1994, I caught him again. The omens were not propitious. He was at the Albert Hall, hardly the grimy, sweaty, beer-serving environment to reclaim his roots. I felt at home, though, coming from rugby. Half the people there were guzzling on corporate balconies, no doubt wondering who that bloke with the guitar was, making all that racket. But he came on be-Levi'd, on a spare background set, started with old Robert Johnson blues anthems then played the most shattering, seminal, storming version of 'White Room' since who knows when.

Lots of people who were kind enough to buy or steal *Endless Winter* wrote to say I was wrong about other bits. Tough. But as rugby has ploughed on in season 1993–94, it struck me more than occasionally that I had actually understated the strength of the processes, for good and bad, which are running in the sport at the moment. Certainly, no one in the past year found the catch-points for the runaway train. High-profile rugby matches piled in on one another and the game's profile continued to rise in quantum leaps. On one day in June 1994, all four of the home nations played major Tests around the globe – Wales in Canada, England in South Africa, Ireland in Australia and Scotland in Argentina. They did so after home seasons packed with major matches.

The Southern Hemisphere quickly took over. South Africa, Australia and New Zealand had their national teams in perma-camp – South Africa met England then toured in New Zealand; Australia, once their players returned from the heroic Super-10 series, met Ireland and Italy in Test series, then prepared for the Bledisloe Cup match against New Zealand. The All Blacks played a series against France, stayed together for the series against South Africa, then met Australia. Then all the Southern Hemisphere nations prepared to come north for our autumn; and all this, the whole endless season, is only a prelude for the World Cup of 1995. Madness, of course, but a divine madness.

The sense of the family expanding, the gurgle of new arrivals in sport's maternity ward, also filled the year. I can still see the astonishment on the face of Steve Tshwete, the new South African minister for sport, once a founder member of the Robben Island rugby team in captivity and a vastly impressive man. He had arrived in his car – chauffeur-driven, yet modest – at the sports field of the Soshenguve township, twenty miles to the north-west of Pretoria. The occasion was a mass coaching session arranged for black rugby players from the surrounding districts, to be conducted by members of the touring England team. Their team bus, followed by a long, snaking line of hire cars carrying a media army, went gliding through the township like the leader of a Toyota-borne friendly invasion force.

At the sports centre, the England players fanned out, each taking a group through various drills, and as far as the eye could see, the pitch was full of fun. The players were superb. Victor Ubogu took a scrummaging clinic, which quickly became a giggling shambles. Ubogu's scrummaging was a feature of the tour. It just seemed that Victor found it difficult to pass on his talents to others. Tshwete was almost staggered. 'I had no idea this was happening, that rugby among black people had ever started here,' he said, indicating the township itself but also, effectively, the Pretoria area. He was even shooed aside by Les Cusworth as he marched on for a little politicising when Cusworth was running a ball skills seminar.

Who could blame Tshwete for his sense of wonder in Pretoria? The high-veldt provinces, Transvaal and Northern Transvaal, have always been white temples of rugby. The game there has been seen as something of a monster, something which never touches black people. Tshwete was speaking only a few weeks after the elections and, more to the point, less than two years after the renegade playing of 'Die Stem', the white anthem, at the Ellis Park Test between South Africa and New Zealand, a day which was essentially a calculated snub and two fingers to any vision of a new South Africa. Yet here, at Soshenguve, rugby was reaching out. The Northern Transvaal Union, whose development officers were running the show, has injected considerable resources for development. The South African Rugby Football Union (SARFU) was to use 30 per cent of the proceeds of the England tour purely for funds for non-white rugby. At the fairly humble Soshenguve sports centre, there are three full-time rugby coaches, present every day, and paid for by the union. The advance is the same throughout South Africa.

Perhaps it is partly guilt-driven. Who cares? 'This is all a bit staged,' said a fellow traveller as we took in the Soshenguve coaching clinics. 'Of course it is,' I said. 'Do you think that 300 black players and the England rugby team would come upon each other by accident?' Later in the tour, England also took a seminar at the celebrated Dan Qeqe stadium, near Port Elizabeth. It was good to see the stadium improved yet again, standing proud and unvandalised in the middle of one of the least well-appointed townships, Zwide. It is high time, incidentally, that the South African squad made the same sort of trip.

A few days later, there was England's wondrous Test victory in Pretoria in the First Test. It was 32–15, with tries by Ben Clarke and Rob Andrew, and if it only provoked the South African team into a frenzied and winning response one week later (27–9 at Newlands), then at least it was a day to savour. So was the rest of it. The vast (white) crowd gave President Mandela a rousing reception; sang 'Die Stem' uproariously – Mandela had asked that the old anthem be played as a gesture of reconciliation – and then everyone stood in respectful silence as 'Nkosi Sikelele 'iAfrica', the new anthem was played. They had to be silent. They didn't know the words (although Stuart Barnes, long-time ANC supporter, had a crack at them). It was a wonderful occasion; it gave you a sense of attitudes changing.

Of course there is a long road to travel in South Africa. Of course rugby attitudes there can be as entrenched as any. But the cast-iron evidence, both circumstantial and factual, and gained first-hand, is that rugby is slowly reaching some of the non-white community in South Africa. It should. As I wrote in the first edition of *Endless Winter*, history has found few communities immune to rugby's appeal and essential goodness.

And the advance continues. In season 1993–94, another wonder was the qualification for the 1995 World Cup. All over the world, mini-avalanches of qualifying matches and tournaments took place, in Andorra, Berlin, Lisbon, Nuku'alofa, Santiago, Asunción, Montevideo, Buenos Aires, Tunis, Gdansk, Siauliai, Budapest, Suva, Nairobi, Den Haag, Apeldoorn, Amsterdam and Bermuda. And that was just the first wave. They gradually threw up qualifiers for South Africa 1995, and among them were Ivory Coast. They fought their way through a fiendishly testing African zone event, past Zimbabwe, Namibia and Morocco, and proudly take their place among the top sixteen. For yet another nation, rugby will never be the same.

And your country did not have to qualify to experience that uplift. In places as diverse as Latvia and Germany, Czechoslovakia and Chile, Sweden and Papua New Guinea and Portugal, the impetus of the World Cup, and especially the internationalism of Rugby World Cup, gave a boost. RWC's hard work in allowing so many countries the opportunity to take part, even in the early stages, is vastly to their credit. They must work, urgently, to teach the top and moneyed nations that the money derived from the final stages of the event is not to be touched by them for their futuristic new stands and lily-gilding. It should be handed on to the smaller countries to buy the essentials of rugby life.

Elsewhere, Italy played brilliantly in the First Test in Brisbane in June, and could easily have beaten Australia. In Australia itself, official Government figures revealed that youth participation in the sport has now increased by 54 per cent in three years. Canada beat both Wales and France during the past season; a triumph over logistics, a triumph of commitment and playing excellence.

In the British Isles, even if the standard of the Test teams is not to be compared, in general, with those of the Southern Hemisphere, at least the interest soars – the phenomenon called mini-rugby, which is now almost literally overwhelming the clubs running mini sections, is now the wonder of British rugby. In England alone, the RFU believe that over 100,000 children under eleven now turn up at clubs on Sundays during the season, and that their only remaining problem in securing future expansion of the game is coping with the sheer numbers.

The bank manager is blissfully free of anxiety. The sport, particularly in the major countries and especially in Britain, is more commercially successful than any other. The £7 million paid by Courage to extend their highly successful sponsorship of the Leagues, the untold millions paid by BBC to retain their contract to show domestic rugby, the enthusiasm of ITV's summer tour coverage and the fact that, with the arrival as a TV player of BSkyB, the prices will be driven up in the future will make rugby richer. BSkyB's weekly world rugby magazine programme was an outstanding addition to the sport's TV profile.

You see. Told you. The game's gone crackers. It was only six or seven seasons ago that we sports hacks used to spend half our season reporting on gentle strolling club matches played in front of 1,500 people. Now, it's hard to write a single report without overdosing on the words 'death', 'glory' or 'cash'. The sport needs a massive, non-addictive, can-be-taken-with-alcohol, easily digestible, not-tested-on-animals tranquilliser.

Yet all that is the good news. It is also possible that I slightly underestimated rugby's ability to handle all this – or, perhaps, grossly underestimated it. I felt, a year ago, sanguine in my original conclusions about the end result of the divine madness. The past year has made me anxious indeed, chiefly because rugby's administration has quite spectacularly failed to react to the pace of change. The higher you go, the thinner the air. Some examples: in the past year, the operation of the by-laws relating to amateurism has been an utter farce. Some countries, notably Canute-like England, still try to interpret them strictly, thereby disadvantaging and infuriating their own international players. A document circulated to the players recently summarising the views of the RFU amateurism sub-committee on the scope which players in England have to market themselves was numbingly neanderthal in tone, dangerously divorced from the reality of the sport in the 1990s.

There is no point debating the role of amateurism. It is like discussing the future of the Spitfire. The only discussion worth having is on amateurism's replacement. There is no earthly point in defending Rorke's Drift if the Zulus have all moved on. Elsewhere last season, other unions effectively gave up even reading the by-laws, or else found specious ways to get round them. Unprincipled, perhaps, but if you are demanding of your international players that they give roughly one-third of their whole lives to their national teams alone, then what else can you do but placate them with a few quid, or even a few thousand quid?

Then there is discipline. In this book there is a description of a typical incident in the life of team managements these days, when the team managements of the British Lions and Southland affected, to a man, not to have seen a gruesome stamping incident in the match between the teams on the Lions tour of 1993. Everyone else on the ground and watching on TV, and their wives, had seen it. There was a carbon copy when England met Eastern Province on their 1994 tour when Tim Rodber and Simon Tremain were sent off, allowed to escape unpunished; when a player (in this case, Jon Callard) had his face slashed by a boot and when yet again, anyone in authority appeared to be answering a call of nature, or to be seated behind a floodlight pylon, or else otherwise unsighted, just when their censure was needed.

The basis of this non-reaction is the growth of the non-whining culture, and also the perception of some people, the English included, that only dastardly members of other teams are violent, not our own nice chaps. The no-whining culture is reaching ludicrous depths. The fools who claim that kicking at prone players is all part of rucking had another field year. To clear up the game is so easy: it needs a few suspensions, and a little honesty. And a little image-mongering. Of course, the game is less violent than ever, but a fat lot of good that does if violence occurs, and if it goes unpunished, in the televised mega-matches.

The laws? There is ostensibly one set, printed in all handbooks. Effectively, there are about fifty sets; we are still in the nonsensical situation where players who spend many anguished weeks preparing for big games, smoothing the mind and body and tactics, now take the field with no idea of the interpretations which will apply, which thereby renders all their planning a waste of energy. 'We have to adapt to the referee during the match,' is the quietly despairing reaction of team coaches.

And the experimental ruck/maul law in particular? Nowadays, even the excited dreamers who greeted its arrival in 1992 as the saviour of the open game have slunk away. Even the likes of Laurie Mains, the All Black coach whose style the new laws ostensibly suited, have caved in to the evidence of their own, and the world's eyes; finally realised that tries, drama, movement, excitement, crowd noise, are drastically down. By the IRB meeting of 1994, when the law came up for either confirmation or obliteration, I could trace not one single leading player or coach anywhere in the world who was in favour of it.

What a tragedy then, that the International Rugby Board has been so slow to admit it. In March 1994, they abandoned the ruck part, once again giving possession to the team which took the ball in and, in the essential dynamics of the game, drove forward. Yet ridiculously, they have kept the law as it relates to the maul, killed the action – and given referees a fearful job in deciding when mauls became rucks, or simply fall over of their own accord. Will they ever realise, these men shying away from the game's public, smugly aloof from the views and advice of the key people in the game, that the only way they are ever again going to clear the clogged field for the game to run free is to consign the whole experiment to history? Instead, we are stuck with it for the World Cup and that tournament will be profoundly the worse for that.

But the mess remains – amateurism, laws, violence, interpretations. And with every notch of rugby's growth, they will be exacerbated. Where is the action? When is the urgent seminar on law standardisation? When is the urgent meeting on amateurism or, more precisely, on what form the new professionalism should take, so that every player in the world has a set code to follow into the next millenium? Who is coming clean on violence? Why have the IRB not introduced a flying squad of top referees, overriding the feeble local prejudices of individual countries simply pulling for their own, inadequate officials? Where are the emergency meetings of the IRB to deal with these urgent issues, these growing pains of the game? Where are the attempts to speed up the Board, to devolve some executive power so that decisions can be made? All I can hear is a deafening, dangerous, self-defeating silence. What is the point in having the fastest-moving game in the world if its officialdom is moribund?

Perhaps the extent of the shambles passed the average rugby follower by. I hope so. Some of the best letters I received from people who bought *Endless Winter* reminded me that those of us caught up in the whirl of top rugby are forgetting that the game itself goes on, is played and attended to with energy and unchallenged affection by men and women and boys and girls all over the world, and particularly, that the game still remains an escape, an outlet, a social diversion, to millions of people who care not a damn for unions and their machinations. They were preaching to the converted. Rugby, or any sport at its finest, is not just a vehicle for international glory and your bank balance. It is a diversion, an escape from the nine to five haul. And in the past year, through another endless season, there was so much fun and friendship to share, still a firm grip in the handshake of the largest freemasonry in sport and leisure.

Yet there were also the first signs of a drifting. Take the England tour of South Africa, significant and typical of a trend. There was so little contact between the tourists and their hosts, so little time off for culture, or even for shooting the breeze. After the matches, the players hardly had time to nod to their opposite numbers before they were hushed for the speeches, ushered on to the bus and driven back to the sanctuary of the team room, from where the vast operation of training and dissection was run. Touring in a vacuum is a denial of something which sets rugby apart. 'We are all becoming dull cabbages,' said Stuart Barnes on the tour. Things may not be that bad. In my experience, the average international player still has something about him; still, I hope, has some sense of proportion. But the severity of the age is worrying. Tours must continue, but they must have time for contemplation as well as for training and playing for your life. The preparation culture has gone mad. Coaches the world over suffer panic attacks unless every waking second is spent working on their men. They should lay off. They would improve their teams no end.

And if rugby wishes to remain true to itself, to preserve what is worth preserving from the game as it used to be pre-revolution, to ensure that to double in size is to be twice as good, instead of twice as confused, then it must act, call a few emergency meetings. Rugby at all the lower levels will thrive. But in the top echelon, I believe that there is no middle ground. The sport is confronted with two visions of its own self: either the anarchy and shambles already approaching – and no one who has followed the game around the world in the past two years will deny that – or, alternatively, a wonderful future as the world's second largest sport.

How fared the other heroes and anti-heroes during the past year? The rugby world had already lost Dr Danie Craven, that outstanding, baffling man; you never quite knew where you stood with the Doc. Was he a visionary liberal genius or just some old bloke who'd gone on too long?

At least there is no problem with his successor as head of rugby in South Africa. The advantage of Dr Louis Luyt is that you know exactly where you stand (about five miles away is believed to be about right). Luyt's tentacles stretch deep into the playing and commercial aspects of South African rugby and his influence is vast. This is all very well – a dictator or two in rugby is fine. But it is still to be proved that Luyt is the man either world or South African rugby is looking for. If he has a vision of rugby's future, if he has a sense of humour, and if he is less interested in commerce than in sport, then these qualities did not surface during our short stay. South Africa, in my experience, is split into two camps. One lot says of him: 'Well, at least he gets things done.' The other lot dish out all sorts of criticism about him, behind their hands, prefaced with: 'For Christ's sake, don't tell Louis I'm saying this.' But, as I say, at least the country itself, bathed in the post-election glow, has half a chance of coming through, and dragging our mate Louis with it.

Out on the field, where rugby occasionally strayed during the year, the England team continued to show the utmost courage and dedication; the likes of Ben Clarke, Tim Rodber, Brian Moore and Jason Leonard provided stout hearts and strong arms. Yet there is still so little élan about the whole sweep of English rugby; there is over-coaching, so little footballing wit and off-the-cuff genius – especially since Jeremy Guscott missed almost the whole season with a groin injury, and Stuart Barnes, brassed off with the sporting world at large, announced his retirement in June 1994.

Wales, on the other hand, advanced. Their team made progress once team affairs had again been entrusted to Alan Davies, Bob Norster and Gareth Jenkins, just when their positions seemed weak following a grim home defeat by Canada in the autumn. Here are three candidates to lead the next British Lions. Wales may not have been a wondrous team in 1993–94, but as they hammered through their World Cup qualifying matches in Portugal and Spain, and afterwards through Canada and the South Seas (where they were themselves hammered by Western Samoa), their new pride was obvious.

Ieuan Evans, the captain, has cemented a place in Welsh legend for his play, his authority, his Welshness. Yet Wales, too, lack the edge of star quality and may well come up short for the lack of one athletic line-out giant, one dazzlingly crafty back. But they played 1993–94 as a team, whole in body and soul. And, happily, after the sackings and the turmoil had died down yet again, yet another new WRU administration came shuffling back into the spotlight, with a QC, Vernon Pugh, as chairman. They managed to pick up the threads, and to their credit they kept on the wavelength of the players.

Elsewhere among the Five Nations, Scotland sagged alarmingly, were humiliated against New Zealand in the autumn and are still suffering from the demise of Gary Armstrong and Craig Chalmers, the half-backs who should be their core until 2000. Armstrong's motivation and Chalmers' form and fitness are weakened. Their tour of Argentina was a shambles; so was Ireland's visit to Australia, and it strikes me more firmly than ever that a squad of young Irish players is being let down for lack of high-class preparation, organisation and motivation. I believe that they have the talent, that they have the levers, but no one to pull those levers.

Rugby league? There were odd touches of realism here and there in the code, although Colin Welland, as ever, was blissfully unaffected by them. A few people I read about seemed to accept that if three blokes and a fax machine set themselves up in a foreign country and burble about rugby league, it does not necessarily mean that that whole country is then conquered, and queueing to knock on league's door. There is certainly a new realism from Maurice Lindsay, the Rugby Football League's chief executive. An article he wrote recently laid bare the bitter realisation in the game that what they all thought was a boom in the late 1980s not only petered out dramatically, leaving the sport impoverished, but in fact, hardly even took place at all. 'The simple fact is that we have thirty-five clubs chasing too few spectators.' He touched on the embarrassment associated with most of league's attempts to expand. Significantly, he wrote: 'Expansion has to be properly co-ordinated with grassroots development . . . in schools and boys' clubs.' Now he's talking. Now the game may realise that you cannot promote or market a game into existence.

Ultimately, however, I still gained the impression that league and league followers are still expending far too much energy on bitterness, especially on the incomprehension that rugby union should have so massacred it for popular appeal and commercial muscle in Britain and the world; on its multiplicity of anguished demands for a slice of the various cakes; and on the repeated, fulminating attempts to blame everyone, union and the whole world, instead of turning the spotlight around and searching among themselves for the answers. The lack of perception in the code about the recent revolution in rugby union is staggering. They are aiming at a point where rugby union actually left about sixty years ago; around seven or eight years ago, union rapidly moved on again. And still, league is aiming for the original target. When they get there, they are going to be a little disappointed.

One example: Lindsay, in the same article, looked forward to the Rugby League World Cup of 1995, in which there are – just – enough participating teams for the title 'World Cup' not to be an utter misnomer. 'I do not subscribe to the rugby union view,' he says of the World Cup, 'that you simply invite as many countries as possible, regardless of their playing ability.' Yet for his World Cup, Lindsay and his colleagues have had to dredge up participation from some countries in which the rugby league played is merely a few mates playing on a few parks, while rugby union's qualification rages on in seventeen separate countries, involving nearly sixty countries in all, just for the honour of reaching the last sixteen and the starting line. So *who* is inviting teams just to make up the numbers? Perhaps rugby league is waking up; perhaps it is still in its dream world.

Elsewhere, Bath celebrated the departure of Jack Rowell in the only way possible; with a Cup and League double. Rowell made a favourable impression as England manager in South Africa; still as relentlessly sharp as ever, still claiming not to read the papers then recalling word-perfect some article written a decade ago. It must be a warm feeling for him to realise that no club coach will ever win one quarter of what Bath won under him – and I somehow do not believe that Rowell will replicate that feeling with England. Not that he will not be successful; just that in many ways, to manage and coach and guide England is an exercise for the intellect and the technical gifts; to lead Bath, or any other successful community club, is something which comes from the heart, and is felt deeper.

The alarmingly short close season intervened before a new beast, season 1994–95, appeared on the horizon. I would love to know the number of players and officials who winced before they began their preparations; the number for whom it was all a desperate chore. Something on which we could all agree is that anyone brightly popping up these days and declaring that it is only a game should be carted off with a one-way ticket to the funny farm.

# Strange New Worlds?

All I wanted to do was play guitar with Bruce Springsteen's band. Fair enough, I never begrudged Miami Steve van Zandt the job in the early days. He and Bruce were thick from way back. But Bruce never came to me when Steve left. He drafted Nils Lofgren. The midget. Then what happened when he disbanded the E Street Band altogether? He bloody well takes on Shane Fontayne. Shane bloody who?

I needed a fall-back. It was called rugby. Imagine the reflected sporting glory of life as a teenager in Wales in the 1970s. If Wales won and yet scored fewer than five brilliant tries we had to hold an inquest. Glory days. Our Saturdays would be crammed full of the game. On Saturday morning, there was the school match, for Bassaleg. We used to run everything. When we toured Newton Abbot we thought we were on Mars. And on Saturday afternoons, the pilgrimage to Rodney Parade – we saw Newport beat the All Blacks, the Springboks. We saw them beat everyone. We watched David Watkins, for God's sake; and Keith Jarrett, the most talented player I ever saw. We saw the wondrous anti-heroes, Del Haines and Keith Poole, the bob-bank legends.

One winter's afternoon in the early seventies I was actually called up. I wore the black and amber for the first time when Newport United played Chepstow on the Glebelands, then Newport's second ground. John Jeffery, the massive number 8, was coming back after injury and was playing. He had to prove his fitness for the next match, against some people called the All Blacks. He was another hero. 'I'm John Jeffery,' he said in the dressing-room, crushing my hand in his giant mitt as he tried to assess the new schoolboy, which I still was.

I searched for a suitably macho reply, to give the impression I was underawed and ready to play. 'Er, I know,' I said. 'I've seen you on the television.'

In the evening, the ritual was usually the same. The bus to Machen and an evening in the Fwrrwm Ishta, the rugby pub then run by Jack Davies, the legendary WRU committee-man. Jack used to draw the odd free half from the barrel when he knew you were strapped. All night we pulled rugby apart, gnawed lovingly at the bones of the game. The arrival of the boy bearing the *South Wales*

*Echo*'s pink sports edition would herald mass movement all round the pub.

'Christ! Spikey Watkins got sent off for Crumlin.'

'Bedwas hammered Senghenydd, then.'

'That bastard Wally. He's leaving Machen and going to Newbridge!'

On dry nights, we used to walk home, right over the mountain from Machen, dipping into the next valley at Risca, gabbling about rugby. We were too young and inexperienced then to realise what a wondrous sport we had chosen, or rather, been born into. We took the love for granted. What did we know about rugby when we only knew about rugby?

We left, as people do. I knew not a soul on arriving at college in England. After the rugby club trials I knew half the college. I knew not a soul in the vastness of London on arriving as a tyro journo in the southern suburbs. One train to Richmond, change at Clapham Junction, and I was immersed in that oasis called London Welsh RFC. Branches everywhere, rugby. And all that stuff about the spirit and the friendships – it's true, all true.

That was then. The global warmth of the game is toastingly obvious to those of us with the ridiculous good fortune to be sent around it to report on rugby. But the game is different now. It has become formidably serious and a serious commercial concern. It has changed with incredible swiftness inside a few years, become bigger and vivid and, maybe, better.

For me, the passion remains. Journalists are a cynical lot. That is what we are paid for. Any non-cynical journalist is not a journalist. And yet there is not one man I can think of among my rugby-writing colleagues in the British Isles who is not, still, in love with the game.

But the smile on the outer face of rugby is no longer so wide. It would be a disaster of epic proportions if the new-era rugby banished the old, more innocent joys. If youngsters did not play and gabble about the game all day long; if even the World Cup winners did not keep it all in perspective. Has the old ambience survived? And if so, is it threatened? Rugby has always been a sport apart, no matter how fiercely the non-believers have tried to deny it. But has rugby now become just another sport? Has the current ferocious urgency, where the scoreboard is the first and last arbiter of rugby enjoyment, had a fatal effect? Does the end of amateurism mean the end of everything?

In the rugby season 1992-93, which began for me in South Africa in early August, rambled on through fury, fuss and frippery through almost a whole year, and ended in July, when the British Lions played their final match of the New Zealand tour, I had the perfect chance to find out.

But, Bruce, I'm still out there for you, man.

# CHAPTER 1

# *Rugby in the Nuclear Age*

## SIX YEARS THAT HAVE CHANGED THE GAME FOREVER

Panic, panic. On a drab winter Saturday six seasons ago, Barry Newcombe, the rugby correspondent of the *Sunday Express*, and I approached on foot the rugby ground at Franklin's Gardens, home of Northampton RFC.

It was less than twenty minutes to the advertised kick-off time of a match between Northampton and Rosslyn Park. There was not a soul about. A few cars pulled into the adjacent supermarket car park, but there was no flow of rugby folk. We walked past the turnstiles on the popular side – they were locked. We peered through the fence. Three people were mooching about near the clubhouse. 'There's nothing going on *here* today,' said Newcombe.

'Christ,' I said. 'Either it's off for some reason or we've got the venue wrong. It must be down at the Park. What the hell are we going to do now? Can we get to Leicester in time? Can we get to Bedford? What am I going to tell the bloody sports desk?'

We walked on, into the clubhouse. More promising. There was a small gathering of people in the main bar, a few Rosslyn Park scarves and a decent profusion of Northampton ties knotted neatly round middle-aged, middle-class, middle-minded Midland throats. Phew. Saved. There was a match.

People shuffled reluctantly out of the bars. Eventually, a few hundred spectators gathered and peered out from the gloomy main stand to where the floodlights were reflected in the pools of water glazing a typical Northampton pitch bog. The press box was almost empty. On the popular side, they stood one deep and mostly silent.

The Park won easily although Northampton, a team comprising chiefly local lads, played with spirit. It was a Division Two match in the Courage Leagues. In fact, it was the final League match of the first season in which leagues had ever operated in English rugby. The win meant that Park, already promoted, won the division.

Northampton, one of English rugby's giants but by then moribund, finished bottom. They won just one match in the season, finishing four points adrift of Blackheath, who were last but one. With a stroke of outrageous fortune they avoided relegation because for that inaugural season, there was none. The whistle went, a few Park men cheered, Northampton went for a beer. The club emptied, they turned out the lights.

Near the start of season 1992-93, Northampton were at home to Bath. At one o'clock, a full two hours before the kick-off, the ground was packed and seething. A jazz band toured the perimeter. All around the ground, in spanking new hospitality boxes, well-appointed verandahs and other new installations, people wined and dined in corporate feasting. The Saints Shop, where replica jerseys and all kinds of souvenirs were on sale, had a queue backed out of the door. From miles away from the ground there were signs for Saints Car Park, and fleets and fleets of cars nosed their way on to the back fields (where Northampton had set up a training head-quarters), pointed on their way by an army of attendants. Among the vehicles were coaches from the West Country bearing Bath followers.

Severe jobsworths, some with sergeant stripes from the corps of commissionaires, barred door-frames and stood aside only at the production of a fistful of tickets. The clubhouse, by now extended almost out of sight, was packed to the rafters. The Northampton team walked by en route from the hotel where they had met to the dressing-rooms. Immaculate in sponsors' tracksuits, they were a cosmopolitan bunch: West Countrymen and Northerners and Midlanders and Wayne Shelford, the New Zealander and one of the most famous figures in the world game. The gates were shut on a full house.

Inside, the ground looked magnificent. The pitch was pristine. The club had invested a small fortune on a sand-slitting facility. If they had mown it with the blades full down you could have played snooker on it. The pitch was bordered on one side by a high-tech artificial running surface, embossed with a sponsor's name; new wing stands overlooked the scene. The media were packed into the press box and into a substantial overflow area. Cameras bristled from the new TV gantry. Sponsored billboards smothered every installation. Before the teams took the field, hordes of youngsters pattered round the pitch in intensive mini-rugby and age-group matches with Barrie Corless, the club's paid playing director, in benevolent charge. The mayor of Northampton and his corporation sat in the committee seats.

Northampton beat Bath amid scenes of wild excitement. Nick Beal, the young threequarter who, until only months before, had played for High Wycombe, scored a try by hacking on the ball for eighty yards in a thrilling chase, and reaching it before Bath's Phil de Glanville.

When the team disappeared down the tunnel, chorus after chorus of 'When the Saints Go Marching In' saw them off. At that stage, Northampton were favourites to win the Division One title. The team was to lose its way a little: eventually, Bath came powering back, and were not to lose again in the league. They won the Courage Trophy for the third time in succession.

Yet Northampton, the old Midlands giant, was the new Midlands giant. Even as they watched the Bath match, the club's forward planners were looking straight past it — two, five and ten years down the development road for club and facilities and team. Never, you might think, has one sporting institution so utterly transformed itself in so short a time. You might be right. However, the processes which revitalised a decayed club were not at work only in North-ampton. They were working throughout rugby union. The game has changed more in the last six seasons than it changed in all of the rest of its history.

The late 1980s and the early 1990s, as a period, saw rugby change more abruptly, and completely, than any sport has ever changed. These have been the revolution years, the boom years; they have also been a difficult passage into uncharted territory. They have been gloriously heady, and they have caused no end of bother as well.

The growth of interest in the sport has been remarkable. Not that it was expiring through the lack, but it has reached a new league. For the Test matches, and even the major club matches, rugby provides the black market with bigger business than West End sell-outs, the FA Cup final and the Wimbledon Centre Court combined. The rapacious swirl of money-making riding on the back of the Five Nations Championship is such that were the championship taken away, then so would huge chunks of profitability for airlines, hotel chains, rosette-sellers, bar-owners and travel companies.

Twickenham international matches in particular are now sur-rounded by a vast unauthorised operation of corporate hospitality and ticket touting. The demand for match tickets is such that, the RFU believe, they could get rid of the 62,000 tickets three times over.

Even at club level the situation has changed. Most British and Irish clubs are watched by substantially increased numbers (though not to be compared with soccer's Premier Division); many clubs have become gate-taking, programme-selling, sponsor-kissing in-stitutions for the first time. Many, especially in England, have found their facilities suddenly outgrown, among them Bath, Saracens and Wasps. In Wales there are clubs whose gate stewards now exceed in numbers the total attendance for games in the mid-1980s. A few Irish clubs, especially in Limerick, have just entered an era of five-figure crowds for their top matches. At junior levels, some clubs are overrun by youngsters.

The new commercial activity in the game did not so much ride the recession as ignore it. Some examples: at the start of 1993, Courage invested over £7 million in their continuing sponsorship of the Courage Leagues, and there was hardly a sponsorship to be had in British rugby which did not have a waiting list of companies. ITV, who televised the 1991 World Cup, reported their biggest-ever uplift of advertising revenue during the period of the tournament. The gems of the game, the World Cup and the Five Nations, are now so coveted by the television companies in the UK that the competition between them to seize the rugby contracts has become fierce and bitter.

While the main changes have taken place in Britain the revolution is far-reaching. In 1993, the admission to membership of the International Rugby Board of Norges Rugby Forbund (Norway's governing body) brought membership of the IRB up to sixty nations. Six years ago, membership stood at less than ten. Yet a survey published in 1992 showed that the game is now played regularly in 110 countries, and rising.

The continued brilliant success of the Cathay Pacific-Hong Kong Bank Sevens in Hong Kong, a tournament of infinitely wider significance than its simple revelation of the world's best VII, has dragged rugby interest to new heights in the Far East and around the world. The first tentacles of interest are now snaking out into mainland China.

The established Southern Hemisphere nations, desperate for an equivalent to the benevolent monster that is the Five Nations Championship, illustrated the new confidence by setting up last season the Super-10 Tournament, a high-profile made-for-TV affair featuring the top provincial teams from New Zealand, Australia and South Africa together with Western Samoa, another boom country. It was a grand concept, difficult to stage and fund. But it went ahead and was a success. Transvaal beat Auckland in the final in Johannesburg.

In Australia, official figures showed that youth participation in rugby union rose by over 40 per cent in two years from 1991, when Australia won the World Cup. Of course, there are countries where the game is struggling. In the USA, the governing union had to cancel an inbound tour by England set for the summer of 1993 because of lack of funds. Yet that was simply a game giving best to the vast distances and logistics of having a team scattered over America's vastness. In terms of playing numbers, the game in America *is* growing.

There has even been an astonishing rise in women's rugby. From 1987 to 1992, the number of British women's clubs doubled every year. The inaugural World Cup, a heroic affair given the shoestring budget, took place in Wales in 1991 and was won by the United States, who beat England in the final. By 1993, the women's game was afflicted severely by the problems of its own success: the amateur officials could no longer cope with the volume of interest.

The most striking example of the new rugby and its impact in the fields of human interest and commercial activity is the season enjoyed by English rugby and the RFU in 1991-92. For the vast numbers, joyful and successful sport and heady excitement, no country's rugby has ever approached the long, high winter of that season. The union's income was massive. To the various companies sponsoring the competitions at all levels, and to all the official suppliers at Twickenham, could be added a long list of élite sponsors, who invested in exchange for packages of benefits around Twickenham. Much of the income was devoted to the development of the game, and the RFU made a rush of new appointments to the post of youth development officer. There are now thirty-eight YDOs round the country, fostering and liaising and coaching and sowing the seeds. In 1987 there were none.

On the pitch, that season was a sensation. No fewer than 606,400 people went to Twickenham to watch rugby. On eight occasions – for the England matches against New Zealand, the USA (both in the World Cup), Ireland and Wales, for the World Cup final itself (England v Australia) and for the Varsity Match, the County Championship final (Cornwall v Lancashire) and Pilkington Cup final (Bath v Harlequins) – the stadium was sold out. The suspicion grew that if the RFU had staged a match between two groups of old-age pensioners then Twickenham would have been full.

The stadium itself provided a faintly bizarre yet arresting backdrop: the towering, vertiginous new north stand, the first instalment of a stupendous rebuilding project, was open for business. It overlooked some glorious rugby. England won a withering Grand Slam, their second in succession as their hegemony over the European game reached its height. They cruised along, rippling with wellbeing and confidence, tuned to a T and ferociously motivated.

There was the World Cup itself, a brilliant success; Cornwall's appearance in the County final was wholly remarkable – probably nineteen of every twenty people in the ground were Cornish, bedecked in gold and irresistibly proud of themselves and their team and their county (country?). All morning long, a vast fleet of cars, coaches, broken-down old buses and charabancs made the pilgrimage up the M4. Cornwall lost to Lancashire, sadly for Trelawney's Army.

The same pilgrimage had descended the previous year; the same full-scale desertion of the county. On that occasion, in a fantastic contest (though a moderate rugby match), Cornwall had defeated Yorkshire by sheer, unbendable iron will. On the Sunday, the victorious team travelled back into the Duchy by coach. Their progress was monitored all the way, passed on by local radio stations and word of mouth. They were greeted like the conquering heroes they were at all points: at the border, in the main towns and hamlets. As the coach crossed the most deserted part of Bodmin Moor, the team saw a lone figure in the distance, standing on the back of a trailer and frantically waving a black and gold Cornish scarf. It was a lovely image.

Back in 1991-92, the seasonal finale was fitting. The Pilkington Cup final, between Bath and Harlequins, was in some ways the most remarkable match ever seen at Twickenham, Test matches and World Cup included. It was an emotional contest between two outstanding teams in which Harlequins, denuded of leading players for various reasons but playing superbly, took Bath, the mighty force of the British club scene, to the very wire. The match was won, with the very last kick of extra time at the end of the longest season in the game's history, with a drop-kick from Stuart Barnes, the Bath fly-half. It seemed that the trophy would be shared until Nigel Redman won a line-out and Barnes fired over the kick. It was unbelievable and yet, somehow, it fitted what had gone before in the English season.

Journalists should never be comfortable praising authority. My view is that rugby's media should actually go out of their way, on behalf of the millions of followers, to strip away smugness among rugby's administrators. Yet that season, frustratingly, there was only praise to shower. English rugby had it right. The RFU – save for their handling of the debate on amateurism, to which we shall come shortly – had it spectacularly right.

Season 1992-93 was bound to be an anti-climax because nothing could outpace the glorious bandwagon of 1991-92. England lost their dominance, retreated into the pack. Yet there was still the little matter of the vast £7 million Courage sponsorship of the Leagues for Twickenham to gloat over. A debenture scheme to fund the next stage of Twickenham's stratospheric development was, ostensibly, a failure in that a year after it was launched it was by no means sold out. Yet by April 1993 it had brought in £10 million. There are a few sporting bodies who would welcome failures of that magnitude.

And a few newspapers. The media coverage given to rugby in the last six years has grown to the level of wallpaper. For the 1987 World Cup, that innocent inaugural event held in Australia and New Zealand, *The Sunday Times'* preview consisted of an article written by me which extended to around eighteen paragraphs and which was placed on an inside page, plus a few paragraphs on the television coverage (the television coverage by the BBC in this country only needed a few paragraphs).

By the 1991 event, our preview had grown slightly. We produced a colour broadsheet newspaper of sixteen pages. We had never before produced a special of that size, even for the Olympics or soccer World Cup. It took over the lives of a few of my colleagues and myself for months on end. Almost every newspaper attempted something along those lines. Our special issue, we all modestly believed, was far superior to any others. But that is another story. We never got paid a penny for the extra work, either. Thanks a lot, Rupert. That, too, is another story. But the rise of rugby – now *that* is another story.

Most sports periodically proclaim a boom. How many activities have you heard described as the 'fastest-growing sport'? At various times, I have heard American football, basketball, ice-hockey, rugby league and golf (the latter with some justification) so described. Most of the 'booms' have been illusions, wishful thinking or self-delusion or simply an attempt to attract sponsors. Rugby's recent growth is set in concrete. There are participation figures, commercial balance-sheets and audience ratings to prove it, and to prove it as a quantum leap.

But where did it come from? These sort of changes do not come about by accident. The surge came from a profound and reverberating change in the whole culture of the sport, especially in Britain. That change was based squarely on the advent of club league rugby. All other theories are entirely subsidiary.

The comparatively simple manoeuvre of grouping almost every club in England, Wales and Ireland (Scotland began leagues in 1973) in peer-group divisions, with promotion and relegation, galvanised the game in this country. It was as if, after playing a long video in slow-motion for decades, someone had suddenly thrown the fast-forward switch without any transitional time at normal speed. In the late 1980s, the sport suddenly began to move with the fast, uncontrolled and jerky rhythm of a Keystone Cops movie classic.

Rugby was always a smug sport, with power in reserve which was never used. It was a sport which, whether in playing standards or self-promotion or commercial activity, never set out to discover its limits, or even, in many circumstances, to change and progress at all. We were all happy. Why change?

When leagues arrived, and club rugby and the whole ethos of the game suddenly leaped forward into a new pace and dimension, the prevailing motivation was unquestionably panic. Old lag clubs realised that within two seasons they could now lose all the status they had so smugly enjoyed for a century. And that the circle would quickly become vicious; that they might lose it forever. Take London Welsh. Many clubs have played well more consistently, but it is arguable that no club has ever attained the glorious, sweeping heights the Welsh reached in a period of four or five seasons around the end of the 1960s and the beginning of the 1970s. There were always going to be a few clubs simply not ready for leagues. London Welsh were one. They have dropped from the senior ranks like a stone. They play season 1993-94 in Division Five.

Northampton, who finished bottom in the inaugural season when there was no relegation from Division Two, were more panicky than most. Their old, loyal committee was suddenly faced, at the AGM of 1990, with a brash and breezy group of seven who tabled what amounted to a vote of no-confidence in the old guard. The new men included Geoff Allen and Jon Raphael, Northampton men and true but from outside the old inner core. They realised that overnight, rugby had become an unforgiving world. They realised that Northampton were tottering on the brink of what would, eventually, represent oblivion.

In that annual meeting, the essential new realities of the game were paraded in one room under a brutal spotlight. The new men swept to power. They immediately brought in Barrie Corless as paid administrator, one of a new professional breed of officialdom which had recently been permitted under amateur bylaws. They began the process by which a club of echoing corridors and cobwebs suddenly became teeming and gleaming.

Some of the old guard walked out of the meeting never to return. Don White, a wonderful old England forward and a cornerstone of the club, and still a member of the RFU committee, departed. So did others. 'These were good, solid Northampton men through and through,' said Gary Pearce, captain before and after the revolution. 'But perhaps they didn't realise that dramatic changes were needed.'

Inside two years, Northampton had a five-fold increase in membership. Corless, now admired throughout the game for his hard-nosed work for the club, and now departed to try the same magic at Gloucester, says: 'Sadly, they took it all as a personal attack. Yet, on the other hand, many people who had stayed away for years in frustration now came back into the fold.'

Rugby's smugness manifested itself in many ways. Ultimately, in rugby's culture no one was desperate to find out which team was best. At club level throughout Britain, there were no major leagues. Every match was a 'friendly'. However, it would be preposterous to suggest that they were meaningless: when Bristol played Gloucester, or when Cardiff played Newport, or when Garryowen played Shannon, the intensity was plain. Indeed, it was said of Welsh club rugby in its vintage years that leagues were a bad thing because the matches were charged enough as it was. But the guaranteed status meant that you could lose all your matches, maintain your position, come out next September and start again as if nothing had happened.

Steps towards a competitive structure were made in the 1970s when cup competitions were instituted in Wales and England. The Welsh Cup was substantially a success from the start, the English Cup became so when Leicester, a team with an enormous following and a wonderfully refreshing attitude to the game in a stolid era, won the Cup three times in succession. Yet even though the Cup was something to covet, you did not suffer long-term harm if you were dumped early on.

The inert background made rugby, if not lazy, unreceptive to change and dynamics. The cosy world of a rugby club could be maintained comfortably: status was assured, there was no real need for any rapacity in recruiting; costs were low and manageable and entirely predictable. They could be covered by the bar profits, a few pounds taken at the gate, a Christmas draw or two. Without the rapacious edges, without the insecurities of having to win matches simply to maintain existence, Northampton-style cobwebs enveloped many clubs; many were like comfortable fireside armchairs.

Some aspects of rugby culture were distasteful: the essential touring attitudes that rugby could not be enjoyed off the field without bawling out those agonisingly, appallingly dreadful sexist songs or without trashing a hotel had gradually fallen into disuse, but in many corners – notably in some Old Boys clubs in London – they were still practised.

I was horrified in the first season I played in English rugby, as a member of the Oxford Poly team in the 1970s, how rugby dragged into its orbit, along with members of the global brotherhood, a desperate horde of strap-hangers and fellow travellers who mistook rugby as an activity for damage and abuse rather than a sport. God, there were even British Lions who made the same mistake. Yet these were details of the old attitudes. They were not caused by the inertia.

Rugby has always had a large following in England, chiefly among the middle class; yet there was never any real need to pull in new ones to drag the existing followers from their armchairs to actually go along, and maybe to watch on the terraces. There was no promotion; very few spectator comforts. Even the biggest clubs made do with a small refreshment hut, pies and tea.

The game never struggled. It relied on a legendary and much-envied essential inner greatness, manifesting itself in a genuine and warm global brotherhood, and in an essential forgiving nature. It drew people because of a positive aura and vibe. To say that the game and its officials were not inclined to move onwards and upwards is not, at heart, a criticism. There was simply no pressure for change; there was no call, until recently, even in the Southern Hemisphere, for the game to abandon its essential, middle-class Englishness in approach and in amateur ethos.

The inertia led to top-heavy committees. Rugby today is still a little top-heavy with officialdom; in the days before the revolution it was choked with men in blazers with nothing to do except clog the channels, but who assumed that they were indispensable. As in a mismanaged company, the workforce becomes overloaded. In an overloaded committee, the status quo is preserved because you need too many people to vote against it. Forty-man committees existed at some clubs.

A graphic example of the attitudes towards drawing new people to the game came in 1986. Bath played Wasps in the Pilkington Cup final at Twickenham. It was a hair-raisingly tense day and Bath were trailing 12-4 with only ten minutes left. By that stage in the development of that wonderful club they were already drawing massive support from all around the West Country. When they scored the try that put them in front inside the last five minutes, there was a crowd invasion, mainly by youngsters. Two minutes later, they scored again and there was another invasion. The referee, Fred Howard, blew the match over, effectively abandoning the contest with a few seconds of injury time ostensibly still remaining.

The inquest was anxious. RFU people spoke in wounded tones of the damage to the turf. To anyone else, it looked the same after the hordes had left as it did before they rushed on. Twickenham has never grasped the fact that the green bit out there is actually a rugby pitch, not a bowling green or billiard baize. But the anguish was chiefly reserved for the invaders themselves. It was as if the sacred acres had been violated. As long as no one was injured I simply did not give a damn about the invasion. It was a sign of exuberance. It was a one-off.

'Do you know,' pointed out one old Twickenham contemptible, 'Some of them wore Bristol Rovers scarves.' My God, outsiders! How dare they invade our game? Rugby is only for rugby people, surely.

In *The Sunday Times* a week afterwards, I wrote: 'I seem to be in a minority in believing that we have not reached the end of the world ... Do people want the Cup final to be watched by 3,000 spectators, average age sixty-five, sitting in the stand? Should we introduce a card system, which says: "This is to certify that the bearer is a true rugby supporter?" Every year, Bath's success attracts more people to the final and more people to rugby.'

Amazingly, the telephone number of the Rugby Football Union in 1986 was still ex-directory. It was only the arrival of Dudley Wood, one of the first leading rugby administrators to have a real flair for the job, that persuaded Twickenham they might conceivably do a little business here and there, spread a little information, do a little PR good, sell a few tickets, if only you could actually reach them by phone. Wood was certainly worried about the safety aspects of the Bath invasion but nowadays he is firmly and fiercely in the business of promoting the game to outsiders – even those wearing soccer scarves.

On the field, prior to the late 1980s, nothing was taken to the max. Top players were dedicated; they spent long hours training, long weekends in squad sessions, thought about diet and sleep patterns and about not drinking too much with a big game on the horizon. There were many articles written about the unacceptable demands on players. I know. I wrote some of them myself.

At international level the culture changed abruptly. The Five Nations has done massive business for decades; victory has also been coveted with desperation even though most of the trophies on offer were mythical. But there was no World Cup to give extra edge or to give rise to long-term planning. The balance of power in world rugby was worked out artificially, by comparing the results of Test series on tour and drawing your own conclusions.

In terms of preparation it would still not be true to say that not a stone was left unturned. There was still a residual recognition that players' domestic and work commitments were sacrosanct; there was also not quite such an impetus to have them out there performing at every available opportunity because inert, non-ambitious aspects of the game had no need of funding for any playing push. Yet the advent of the World Cup, and changing attitudes in the game, jacked up the whole process of international rugby just as the advent of leagues poured icy water over British clubs. The changes, as the community of international rugby players of the world has found to its glory and also its heavy cost, have been equally profound. Demands on players are now stark, staring crazy.

The new severity manifests itself in many forms. First, in the decades of friendly matches we never really *demanded* to know which team was best in any area. Now, we are desperate to know. Through the Leagues, we demand the champions. There are 1,187 teams in the Courage Leagues alone, all fighting to be peerless among their peers, be it the mighty Bath in Division One, or Whitehouse Park in Division North-West West Three. We now need to know which is the best team in the world (in 1991 it was Australia) through the World Cup; the best sevens team in the world through the World Cup of Sevens (in 1993, England). Competitive rugby is taken to the ultimate degree.

We even need to know which are the best teams of the worst teams. In 1989, a cup competition was inaugurated in England for which qualification depended on finishing low down your division. The Provincial Insurance Cup was born and has proved a staggering success. It has revitalised the underclass of the English game to such an extent that tiny park-pitch clubs have derived almost an instantaneous development, with their own little local sponsorship deals and mini-marketing packages.

Yet if the spectre of relegation has panicked the old traditional clubs into action, then the prospect of promotion has been the most joyful release for every other club. The old élites in England, Wales and Ireland maintained a semi-formal and bitterly-resented fixture cartel from which the aspiring were firmly excluded – a perennial bone of contention, especially in Wales. There was nowhere for the thrusters to go. The senior Welsh clubs especially fought a long and bitter battle to stave off the threat of league action.

The Heineken Welsh Leagues have been running for just three seasons, and the break-out has been achieved. Dunvant, a wonderful club from a suburb of Swansea, won Heineken Division Two in 1992-93, only two years after promotion from Division Three. For 1993-94 they proudly take their place in the top flight, from which tradition excluded them for so long. Their fate is the opposite to that of London Welsh.

The surge in interest among the clubs released from the years of frustration is far-reaching. Robert Cole, the Welsh journalist, believes that in many towns and villages the status of the rugby club as social centre, and even village life itself, is revitalised. 'With the demise of the heavy industry, the docks, steel and coal, the emphasis has switched back to the rugby clubs as the social centres,' he says. 'Many of the more successful clubs in the lower divisions are taking paying customers for the first time. The interest is remarkable.'

Last season there were some epic inter-village battles. Tenby and Narbeth, two teams from Division Three, twice drew in more than 5,000 spectators when they met; Builth Wells, the mid-Wales club far removed from heartland areas, averaged crowds well into four figures; Treorchy, the splendid Rhondda club, drew 2,000 regularly and their battle with Mountain Ash drew more than 4,000 people. It was a warming revival in the faded concept of taking in live sporting action on a Saturday, forsaking the armchair and the supermarket. It was an indication that rugby's followers were powerfully in favour of meritocracy, leagues and of the new rugby. Even some of the smaller clubs are appointing full-time officials, building stands, appointing state-of-the-art medicos. The meritocracy is now galloping in all corners of the world game at national and all other levels of play. There is a drive to win and win and win. The drive has brought a passion for greater fitness and endurance and so for state-of-the-art training techniques; the need to make every club more comfortable for the member and paying customer; the need for better facilities for the players, better perks, better tours; better medical and technical back-up – all down the leagues. And obviously, the costs in running rugby have vastly increased. Hence, the avaricious drive to play for it all.

Rugby clubs and other institutions have come under severe pressure. Committees throughout the British club game have been pruned drastically the length and breadth of the country; the old inert bodies are now sidelined in favour of small executives; occasionally, a shadowy benefactor businessman lurks outside the committee, funding the buying-in of players or paid coaches outside the annual financial statements of the clubs themselves. Marketing has become frantic; match and season and local and ball sponsorships have proliferated.

Take Kingsholm, home of Gloucester. They appointed the legendary Mike Burton, their former player, as their marketing manager. Kingsholm is now wallpapered with sponsors and advertisements; hospitality complexes tower over the pitch; every week, the parents of a young rugby-lover shell out so that their pride and joy can lead on the Gloucester team as match mascot; and all this at a club until recently thought of as conservative, inward- and backward-looking. Junior Burtons now exist at junior clubs all round the country.

The explosion is, as explosions tend to be, uncontrolled. The most damaging fall-out on the club scene is unquestionably the dizzying whirlpool of poaching, illegal inducement, sharp practice and dishonesty which is the booming rugby club transfer market. In 1989, Sandy Sanders, then RFU president, saw the first signs of what was to come. 'I would appeal to the clubs,' he said, 'not to engage in over-ambitious recruitment schemes.' It was like letting loose a pack of hunger-crazed lions in a field of wildebeests and asking them to behave themselves. Sanders' plea was hell's snowball.

Clubs have always attracted players through rugby's freemasonry – a job arranged here, a bed made there. Especially in Wales, there have always been the brown back-handed envelopes. But these moves were chiefly low-key, to set the seal on the arrival of a player already bound in that direction. The current swirl is a different beast. It is, at heart, a process by which players can be brought to clubs in different localities, countries, even hemispheres, in which they have no other interest. The activity was such that when in September 1992 the team manager of Newport, the great David Watkins, announced that he was cutting any overblown perks and inducements for his players, the news almost took the game by storm. Watkins told me that his mind was partially made up when he was attempting to attract a famous British Lion to play for Newport and he received from the player a faxed list of demands.

Article after article in the media, plea after plea and measure after measure from the unions, highlight the grim flow. The RFU's response consisted chiefly of appeals for calm and measures whereby players had to sign for a club months in advance to be ready for the start of the season. Otherwise, they had to serve a qualification period. It curbed a little activity here and there, but not the worst abuses. Win bonuses now exist throughout Wales.

It has led, even at its most honest, to buying for the squad, a practice first highlighted by Bob Paisley, the Liverpool FC manager. Northampton already have two excellent fly-halves in Seb Tubb and John Steele, the England B player. Yet in January 1993 they announced that Paul Grayson, one of the most promising players in the north of England, would join them for season 1993-94. I am not accusing Northampton, whose approach I admire, of illegal inducements. But to hog three fly-halves is, on moral grounds, a shady procedure. It brings them to the point of signing players simply to deny them to other teams.

Harlequins bear the brunt of the criticism for their vast player-catching activities. Jamie Salmon, team manager, reacted strongly to the allegations of inducements and sharp practice last season. 'People forget that we do raise many of our own players. They also forget that players ask to join and not the other way round. They simply want to play alongside the likes of Carling and Moore.'

Among other clubs to attract raised eyebrows for alleged voracious recruiting recently are Moseley, Askeans, Rugby, Newport and Cardiff. However, there are perilously few innocent bystanders among clubs in Britain – other clubs poach, your club attracts through their atmosphere; one club pays illegal inducements, your club does not (but they can't speak for Mr Moneybags, the club benefactor). There are casualties. Take Saracens: at the end of 1992-93, for all their efforts in transforming a club with no natural resources into a highly motivated first-division outfit, they were relegated. Most of their leading players – Justin Cassell, Chris Tarbuck, Dan Dooley, Eric Peters and others – signed statements of intent to move on, just as the likes of Dean Ryan and Ben Clarke and Jason Leonard, three of the best forwards in British rugby, had moved on. For every outstanding young man captured by a top team, whether by fair means or foul, there is always a club left fulminating in frustration.

For me, the worst aspect of the whole new club culture is the almost total decline of club loyalty. It is blissfully easy for me to write, as I did in April 1993 in *The Sunday Times*, that Cassell and his friends should stay true to their club and put it back on its feet. After all, I am not a young player trying to break into the glamorous echelons. Everyone, especially in the modern era, wants to get on, to grab some of the Five Nations glory, to go to Hong Kong, to play in a

Twickers final, to share in the purse now proffered through the new freer bylaws and that provided by the new dodgy payments under the counter.

Yet as far as the aspirations of the acquisitive clubs are concerned, history backs my argument utterly. All of the truly great clubs in the history of British and Irish rugby have been based on the town and community in which they play, have taken strength from the support of the locals and have taken their players from the community too; or, if they have spread the net a little wider, they have at least imbued the outsiders with the spirit of that community. History tells us that great teams are not bought in and thrown together. Great teams, or at least their major components, grow up together. That rule has yet to be challenged. I hope that it never is.

Bath and Leicester have ruled English club rugby since the 1970s. They are pillars of their community; they thrive on locals. Orrell, one of my favourite institutions in any sport at any time, call a man an outsider if he is born more than five miles from the ground. Gloucester, another marvellous, marvellous club, call a man an outsider if it takes him longer than five minutes to walk to Kingsholm. Those are what I call rugby clubs.

Club rugby will never succeed on National Football League lines. It will never exist simply as a forum for the top level of players to fan out at random around the clubs without a nod to the localities. I have many rugby heroes, but none to be quite so revered as the giants who stuck by the team, stuck by their mates. David Waters, the astonishing Newport lock with over 600 games to his credit in the engine-room, and still sprightly enough last season at thirty-seven to switch from lock to back row, a man who has sometimes been Newport's only bastion in the bad years – now that is what I call a rugby player. That is also what I call a dying breed.

We are not merely bemoaning the passing of traditional practices at the top level. Some people suggest that the lower levels of the game are left untouched, still play their happy rugby and their coarse rugby with the old attitudes. I doubt it. The tentacles of the new game are almost of infinite length, and powerful of grip. They have reached everywhere.

The benefit to ambitious and greedy clubs of the lower echelons is that they do not even need the free fleet car or the flat or the holiday, or anything else from the paraphernalia of rugby's exchequer. One deal for steaks with a local butcher, or fifty quid in the back pocket, and they have lured the lesser local hero. In the end, there is no answer.

I have sympathy with the unions. They have all said they will act if they have hard evidence. That commodity is painfully difficult to come by. In the end they have to trust the clubs. The clubs of the modern era are not worthy of that trust. They will do themselves short-term good. In the long-term, especially if they neglect for one moment their responsibilities to nurture young players from tots to colts, they will be no good to anyone.

Many of the old comforts are gone. Traditional old fixtures have disappeared; tragically, the top England, Welsh, Scottish and Irish clubs never, ever meet in matches that mean anything. The first-string players are kept back only for league action; last season, Swansea sent a weakened team to play at Bath and conceded seventy points. If these two teams had met in, say, an Anglo-Welsh League then no club ground in the country could have held the numbers who would have paid to watch. Yet no league points, no contest.

And, unquestionably, many clubs are going to lose out spectacularly in the new rush. There are not enough titles for everyone, there is not enough sponsorship available. In past years, with income and expenditure both controllable and predictable, it was extremely rare for any club to report severe financial problems. It was always a few soccer clubs and a large number of rugby league clubs who seemed to be in the financial mire. But those union clubs sucked in over their heads, those clubs who over-extend themselves in a desperate search for playing success which does not materialise, will be left high and dry. There is absolutely no doubt that clubs will go to the wall; there is no doubt that the amalgamation debate will rage more widely. More and more clubs will have to make up their minds to throw in their traditions and identity, and to form a new club with a nearby outfit.

The evidence of many amalgamated clubs – Liverpool St Helens, Leeds (formerly Headingley and Roundhay), Bradford and Bingley, Birmingham/Solihull – suggests very powerfully indeed that the panacea is by no means instant; that in the maths of amalgamation, five plus five can equal three; that a new chemistry can take time to achieve. Yet the prospect of a Division One in the next millennium comprising, say, Bath, Gloucester and Bristol together with amalgamated clubs called Manchester, Birmingham, Thames Valley, Sheffield and Leeds is a live one.

The impetus of meritocracy has brought benefits in preparation and performance, pride in self and club and a dynamism in administration and marketing, gate takings and tension. Blessedly, the old sexism is long gone; so, too, is the old unwritten rule of membership that you have to be a card-carrying member of the middle classes to take part. New rugby is on the way to a welcome classlessness. Incidentally, we can forget here and now two of the most doom-laden predictions about the way the game would go under leagues and merit – that rugby would become more conservative in approach with the pressure-play bringing more kicking, and that violence would increase. The good news is that there has been no increase in violence and that, in fact, the game is far cleaner and less murky now than it has ever been and for that, the revelatory work of the press can take a bow. On the first point, there was a barrage of kicking in the game anyway. Leagues and the World Cup have not increased that barrage.

Yet the price has been high in terms of the old trust. Old warriors of the game have departed, at Northampton and everywhere. Some of them were willing workers who were turfed out. Most of the old innocence has been lost, the old elements of chance reduced . . . The sport is less comfortable and starker.

But is the game still, substantially, the same in ethos – forgiveness and respect, fun and honest competition? And can the very first principle of rugby union, amateurism, now survive this vast shake-up in the culture of the game in any meaningful and recognisable form?

# CHAPTER 2

# The Faded Shades of the True and the Blue

## THE AGONY OF THE BATTLE FOR AMATEURISM

Amateurism. The fetching old devil. As far as the principle applies to rugby it can be defined as follows: playing rugby and preparing to play rugby and therefore taking up vast tracts of leisure time (and more recently, biting chunks out of work and family time as well), while receiving not a penny in recompense, losing out financially, grinning and bearing it while beating yourself with birch twigs before retiring for a kip on a bed of six-inch nails – and then telling yourself that these are the days of your life. I love the whole idea. What heroism.

There is a central heroism in the whole concept, of course. It is only a guess, but by God, it is a good guess, that rugby's balance, its amicable fineries and global warming, stems from amateurism. The essence of the activity means that you go out and lay your reputation and wellbeing on the line and, perhaps in a match of vast significance before a global audience, you become a hero; and then, on the Monday, you work cheek-by-jowl with those people who revered you, grafting down the same pit, serving in the same shop, welding at the same factory, operating in the same hospital or broking in the same exchange.

And has this heroism of the ethos been enacted simply on the pitch? Good Lord, no. Rugby has a roll of honour of supremely dedicated amateur officials with which you could wallpaper the Pyramids. There are millions of the lovely little beaverers: club secretaries and treasurers and chairmen and boot-blackeners and line-markers and bottle-washers, mini-rugby coaches and tea ladies and tea men who vividly demonstrate their affection for the game and its ambience by spending every leisure minute in the exhausting process of providing the fitting backdrop for players at all levels to come out on to the rugby field and play. They still do, these heroes. Every week. For nothing.

Amateurism. It is part nonsense, of course: amateurism is like cricket – if you are involved you understand it but it is still impossible to justify to an outsider. Yet anyone who denies the impetus and the goodness it has given to rugby knows rugby not.

Some years ago, after I had written an article for *The Sunday Times* on the possibilities of the game leaving behind its true blue roots, the sub-editor surpassed himself. The heading he put on the piece was 'Rugby runs on love, not money'.

Ah, sub-editors. Dontcha just love 'em? Er, no actually. This is a breed who would never blink before leading your sympathetic article on why it would be entirely in the best interests of the over-burdened Will Carling not to lead the Lions, so that he could withdraw from the firing-line and hone his wondrous playing gifts, with something like: 'Drug-crazed child-molester Carling should be shot'.

But 'Rugby runs on love, not money' summed up exactly what I was trying to say. I believed that amateurism was valuable, even with a lick of the old birch twigs. I still do. But I no longer believe that amateurism as a strict doctrine is sustainable for one second; or that even the current drastically watered-down version can last for long. There is also the vast, completely unbridgeable chasm in attitudes between Britain and the Southern Hemisphere. That is the chilling prospect for the remaining depleted ranks of the true blue.

Anyone with the most perfunctory interest in sport will know that the debate on amateurism has lately grown burningly intense. How could it be otherwise when the first principle of the sport is being jettisoned? A Rubicon was crossed, after generations of Victoriana, in March 1990 when the International Rugby Board decided to allow earnings from certain ancillary activities. It might not sound much but it caused fuss and fury in spades, not least because, like most proclamations of the IRB, it was couched in terms as woolly as a New Zealand meadow.

Yet it is still important to remember that the impetus of the movement away from amateurism is very recent; that the debate, bitter and painful though it has been, is a recent phenomenon; that the Rugby Football Union, revered or reviled throughout the world as the truest and bluest of the true blue, has only really come under pressure since the late 1980s. And that the pressure corresponds precisely with the onset of rugby's bonkers years.

All right, there have always been brown envelopes; the likes of Andy Haden, the old All Black, always had some anti-amateur wheeze on the go to feed his love of jousting with authority. But here is some evidence of the newness of the problem. In 1986, David Cooke, that splendidly dashing Harlequins flanker, retired from the game and declared that he saw no reason why players should not be paid. Nothing remarkable about that – except that it was the first time I had ever heard a leading player or figure in the sport say such a thing.

'The age of rampaging commercialism had dawned before Cooke's statement,' I wrote in *The Sunday Times* later. 'But rugby always endured with serenity the views of those outside the game who thought that professionalism was inevitable.' In 1987 I still believed that rugby was immune to the harshness of the outside world's relentless pursuit of the main monetary chance.

It was only as recently as 1989 that a serious proposal was made that trust funds should be set up for top rugby players. The Queensland RU, pushed along by a group of their players, including Wallabies Bill Campbell and Jeff Miller, put up a plan to the Australian RU for possible adoption and onward transmission to the IRB annual meeting. The proposal never made it.

In January 1989, Ray Williams, then recently resigned as secretary of the WRU, declared himself in favour of ancillary earnings for players. 'If someone wants to pay players for opening a shop or speaking at a dinner, what business is that of the unions?' he said. Naturally, the freedoms had been floated. But this was the first time a leading official in the Northern Hemisphere had come out and supported that principle. As I say, the debate is a recent event.

It is also crucial to remember that the number of leading players who have ever called for the game to be professional in the formal sense of wages, is few to the point of non-existence, even today. No one should fool you that the players are demanding straight cash payments (or that the game at large could support enormous wage bills). Yet the pace is now rapid. The 1990 IRB measure, momentously, allowed players to accept proceeds from communication and appearances, or endorsement or advertising; provided that advertisements and endorsements were not rugby-related. So Will Carling could endorse a product but not while wearing his England kit; he could promote a squash vest but not rugby boots.

The woolliness caused appalling problems. Different unions interpreted them in different ways. English players, because the RFU accepted the changes with bad grace, were prevented from exploring some commercial avenues which were open to other players. Nothing was so calculated to cause discontent. But, however tortuously, the bridge had been crossed.

Later, the IRB put up communications allowances for players involved in the activities of national teams; introduced hardship payments for players losing money while undertaking their duties as members of national representative teams. At their meeting in March 1991, they increased payments for financial disadvantage for players in a national representative fixture from £20 to £40 per day.

Again, the RFU jibbed. They refused to apply the dispensation allowed to every union by the IRB that rugby-related communication for payment could be permitted. In other words, players could speak at rugby dinners and be paid. The RFU said no. They also, more seriously, originally refused to consider paying hardship allowance. All very well, except that if one union is given a dispensation to act differently, then their players are disadvantaged; and what on earth is the point of making laws in any case if people are allowed to opt out when they are miffed by them?

Last season, they were clinging to the novel idea that the game was still amateur. They have the highest of motives, even though it is undeniably easy for their committee's wealthy businessmen to call for amateur sport. They are not robber barons. Yet leave aside for one moment the vast and raging torrent of illegal inducement endemic throughout the game. The Rubicon had been officially crossed by the IRB, so the only way in which the RFU could claim that amateurism still ruled was by carefully massaging the definition. If their definition was that, despite all the payments made to players officially and unofficially, there were no monthly wage cheques, then, shakily, they spun a thin thread of justification. But not one which took the strain. They are deluding themselves.

But over the last few seasons, it has been abundantly clear that the players are becoming radical, and that whatever forces pushed the IRB into allowing certain earnings, those forces had not returned to barracks. They were still out there . . .

The *Rugby Union Who's Who*, a highly significant little annual brought out by Save & Prosper and Alex Spink, the Scottish-based English journalist, appeared as usual in September 1992 and, as usual, provided the potted biographies of every leading player in Europe. Not much of moment there, you might think. But the book is crucial because it provides a codified body of the opinion of the players. Almost to a man, they demanded clarification of the new regulations, and effectively, that as checks on ancillary earnings should be swept away, no one should lose a penny for time spent in rugby. The hounds are loose. The radical and high-earning plans announced in the summer of 1993 by which the Australian and New Zealand squads will market themselves is a massive thrust.

Where have the mighty forces to change the ethos of the game come from? The era is one of rampant commercialism, of course, but how much of that strain has been brought on themselves by the people who run the game?

The pressure on amateurism has emphatically not come from money-grabbing players. It has not come simply because the unions are raking in massive wodges of cash from gate takings and the furious activity of rugby's commercial sectors. It has not come from the grimy years when, so the rumours ran, teams put together in the shade were touring South Africa and being paid handsomely for their trouble. The fact that young men have agreed to accept large sums of money does not mean for one second that they are denying the amateur principle. It is just that they, like roughly 99.99 per cent of the population, are strongly in favour of receiving large sums of money.

Yet to blame the players for a new greed is the horrendous and demeaning error made by too many people. The drift from the high code is all part of the same process that has taken rugby itself into the stratosphere, for good or evil. The mistake of true blue officialdom is that they themselves fail to see it; or more pertinently, that *they* are the root of all the problems.

At a media briefing held at the end of the season in 1991, there were two main items on the RFU's agenda. Item 5 was an outline given by Don Rutherford, the RFU's technical administrator, of the programme he and the England hierarchy had mapped out for a development squad for the 1995 World Cup. For the players included, it was obvious from the severity of the programme Rutherford introduced that leisure time for the young players at the top levels was ruled out completely until 1995 and beyond. And players 'failing to attain the necessary standards for fitness', said Rutherford, 'will be ruthlessly eliminated'. Rutherford is not a man given to savage proclamations. He is no flagellator himself. Yet his words were an indication of what is now expected of leading rugby players, in England and beyond. Sacrifice yourself completely, or be ruthlessly eliminated. Sounds like the way the Black Dalek used to speak to old William Hartnell.

Item 6 was next. It was a ringing proclamation by Dudley Wood, the secretary of the RFU, that rugby should remain amateur. The IRB had recently announced that the £20-per-day reimbursement could be made to players who could prove that they were losing money when they were away at squad sessions. Wood said that the RFU were violently opposed to the measure and that a sacred principle had been breached. At least Wood saw the powerful irony of lumping the two issues together. He was decrying in passionate terms the drift away from the principle he and Twickenham held most dear, only seconds after yet again winding up the pace of that very same process. 'The Rugby Union is bent on running amateur sport as recreation,' he said.

Some recreation. Brian Moore, England's hooker and, with Dudley Wood, a major player in the rumbling controversies of the last few seasons, recalled his World Cup preparations as the 1991 event was about to begin. 'Eighteen months before the World Cup a giant scroll almost a yard long was pushed through my letterbox. That wallchart has dominated my life ever since,' he said. The chart was his training programme. 'We were also given [in the same envelope] a reminder by the RFU; amateurism [whatever that is] was to be strictly upheld.'

The commitments for rugby's leading players are now of terrifying proportions. At the April 1993 meeting of the International Rugby Board an Irish representative, Ronnie Dawson, said: 'I believe we have reached the point where we can demand no more of our top players. The demands on them are quite incredible. It is out of hand.'

No one escapes. The England players are now, seemingly, in perma-camp. Last season they were in camp to prepare for their early-season warm-up against Leicester; that was a warm-up for the match against Canada, which was a warm-up for the match against South Africa; which was the prelude to the Five Nations Champion-

ship; after that, some went with the Lions, the others to Canada with
the rump of the England squad.

They had to front up for club training in the new severity of
League action; they had to front up for training for the divisional
matches. They had to maintain a personal fitness programme
tailored to their needs by the vast ranks of the technological and
medical and psychological back-up men and women that dog the
squad. A pint of beer, incidentally, is now regarded with the same
derision as flared trousers and the records of The Archies.

And since all of the England squad are in full-time employment
of sorts, since many have wives and families, their whole lives have
become a juggling process, and the stakes are high. England even
spent New Year's Eve in Lanzarote, involved in the high-octane and
ferocious fitness-testing regimes.

It is only a matter of years since training was regarded as a
necessary evil between the match and a beer. Now, it is a matter of
intense pride, and rightly so. The performances in various fitness
tests are trumpeted throughout the game. The Welsh squad
followed England to the same Lanzarote camp and performances
were eagerly compared. These are men of dedication and pride
engaged in a po-faced business, but a business without the rewards.
'We are giving rugby players Olympic athlete's schedules to train
every day, or even twice a day,' says Dick Best, England's coach. 'It
has got beyond a joke.'

The twist of the fixtures ratchet is becoming vicious. Free
summers are now quickly crammed with tours, development tours,
any tours. No union can let a summer touring slot go by without
leaping on board a plane. The refreshing properties of an England
summer are apparently not part of the plan.

All over Britain, the league programmes are becoming larger;
home and away league matches begin in England in 1993-94. The
limited programmes of the inaugural league years have grown into
menacing clumps, like a group of Triffids. The odd mid-week
league match is sneaking back. Saturdays are hoovered into the
maw of rugby's hungry rush, spare time relentlessly pared back
until the commitments eat into the painful area where leisure time
ends and essential time begins. And not only in England. It is the
same the world over.

In the Southern Hemisphere, the new Super-10 is the latest twist.
The competing teams from South Africa, Western Samoa, New
Zealand and Australia have to travel vast distances, making mini-
tours whenever they do so. Every available nook and cranny of
every season is filled up.

The fact that major Test matches can gross £1 million from
primary sources alone is hardly guaranteed to diminish the
importance of international rugby in the eyes of the fixtures
secretary or the treasurer, either. Test cricket has been ruined by
sheer repetition – it is the repetition of a host country needing the
revenue of Tests, and so having to promise to make a reciprocal visit

for every inbound money-spinner. Rugby is now tumbling down that path.

For the rich rugby playboy the 1990s are a dream. Had he the motivation he could catch Test or top tour rugby in the world every week of the year. He could have started, for example, in August 1992 taking in the New Zealand visit to South Africa and ended almost a year later with the Third Test between New Zealand and the Lions. He could have taken a week off for Christmas. Otherwise, he could have watched mega-rugby every week.

He would also, given the standard of rugby under the experimental new laws introduced for 1992-93, have been stupefyingly bored, but that is not quite the point. The point is that we need to know the winners of everything; the unions and clubs and coaches are desperate that the winners will be their lot, the unions are desperate to grow and to pay for that growth. The colossal swirl is reaching the game's neck.

Some of it is not so much the fault of the unions as a reaction to the chain of events which they and the modern era have set in train. Yet they also take things too far. Indeed, the new preparation culture has gone bonkers.

I recently received a fairly low-key handout from the Midlands Division of the RFU concerning divisional matches. The annual divisional series around Christmas every year is, to my mind, a waste of time; not to mention a waste of money for paying spectators; and, if they had a free voice to admit it without putting the noses of the England selectors out of joint, the players would tell you that they hate them to death as well. It is the most soulless event in world sport.

'New Midlands team to test Under-21s', said the handout. It told of the formation of a Midlands B team (no doubt the team has its squad sessions and medical back-up and will drain the last semblances of spare time from another thirty-odd young men) to play a Midlands Under-21 team.

'The match . . . will allow us to assess our reserve strength below full level,' said Stan Purdy, chairman of the Midlands selectors. Why on this earth, Stan, would you want to do that? Why not guess about your reserve strength, if it means that much to you; and send all your B squad home for a nice rest and a cup of tea?

Alan Davies, the Welsh coach, also supported some sort of divisional event in Wales, or even a joint event with England's divisional teams. Surely a properly organised selecting system can judge from the top club matches? And if not, surely it is highly dangerous to base selection on what, in any English and Welsh divisional event, are going to be scratch teams? These are false rungs on the rugby ladder. I even heard an argument that all Test teams should now know their fourth and fifth teams. Why? Guess what your fourth and fifth teams are.

And while we are on the subject of false rungs, I remain to be convinced in any way that the new layer of Under-21 rugby imposed on the scene is of much use, or rather, if it is worth the effort. Earnest coaches will tell you that it is vital to the clubs and the national unions. Earnest Stephen Jones will tell you that it may well prove an artificial exercise worth neither the time nor the money. False rungs take up time and money. They should be the first on the bonfire when officialdom starts making a real effort to cut back commitments.

I am completely in favour of rugby's quantum-leaping and the part played by pride in preparation and performance. I detest the old fuddy voices complaining about coaching and preparation and the arch grins about arriving by train on the morning of the match, playing for England, giving three hurrahs for the jolly chaps in the opposition and setting off home.

For example, I am strongly of the opinion that Ireland's victory over England at Lansdowne Road on a mad March day in 1993 was to the detriment of Irish rugby's future because it may persuade them that their national team is well prepared when it is nothing of the kind. As Brendan Mullin, the great Irish centre, says: 'Those in authority in Irish rugby don't understand what is required to coach and manage a side in international rugby at the moment.'

Yet the culture has indeed gone mad. I have been, since he ascended to the post, a full-hearted admirer of Geoff Cooke, the England team manager. He has brought to the job a clever, adult, professional and inspiring quality. Yet he has not grasped that there are some occasions when it is better for the team if you cancel the seventeenth session and simply let them stay in bed.

And too many people are trying to slot too much into the structure; the English rugby ladder is the only ladder I have ever seen which has a rung every three inches. Why not a Midlands C squad, to assess the reserve strength of the B team?

The situation is not so advanced in Wales, but there is still the B squad, the national development squad, the East Wales squad, the West Wales squad, the Under-20 squad, the Under-21 squad. You cannot deny that Wales needed organisation and development to make up for the appalling decline in rugby in Welsh schools; but history's scoreboard will tell us if they are simply gilding the gilded lily. And the stand of the RFU and the Scottish and Irish unions on amateurism would be infinitely more convincing if, to add to the fusillade of fine words on the subject of paying attention to players' interests, they or any other union had actually taken any significant action on the issue.

Where is the first grand gesture, the first real reining-in of the madness, the first decision to be made purely with the interests of the players (and of amateurism – the two considerations go hand in hand), the first instance of the demands of the treasury being subjugated? Who is at the reins of the stagecoach shouting 'Whoa'? No one. It is all talk. Fair enough, flog the players. But don't stand, whip in hand, and talk about amateurism.

Nowadays, even the crannies of the crannies are being packed. One of the most striking features of the stupendous Bath-Harlequins Pilkington Cup final in 1992 was that in extra time, after the most rigorous season in living memory, the players were effectively out on their feet. Gone. I wrote at the time that every player has his limit and that it is vital for the future of the game that we never discover what those limits are.

The final blow may yet fall. Apparently, television companies wish to show live matches on Sundays. Rugby authorities have placed desperately few ring fences around the game, given players little protection. Yet there is a ring fence of sorts around Sunday. At least there is one day for the family (provided the players are not travelling back from some epic Saturday or squad session); at least there is a day to reflect before returning to work; at least there is the chance to blow steam on the Saturday night. If they take that away, if they start to play serious rugby on a Sunday and make Saturday yet another early-to-bed drudge night, then I'm afraid that the RFU's battle for the last vestiges of amateurism is over for all time.

The point is this. A completely professional ethic of preparation and demands has been imposed on the leading players at club, provincial and national level around the world. No one should blame administrators for a quest for excellence and for banishing the smug years. In concert with the players they have made rugby a success beyond its dreams. However, the excesses must be curbed. The players are being savaged. They are becoming ever more radical. It is those who have imposed interminable and even unnecessary regimes who have driven out their own true blue visions of the sport.

In this respect, Jonathan Webb, the Bath and England full-back, has always been a hero of Twickenham. Webb, often a brilliant full-back and with a burgeoning medical career, is held up by Dudley Wood as the living proof that you can progress in your career and still give time to top-level sport as an amateur. It is a stark view. When Webb was running the careers parallel he paid a hefty price. As he told David Hands of *The Times* in March 1993: 'I have hardly seen Amanda [Webb's wife] at all and I am certainly not seeing the children because I am away from the house before they wake and they're in bed by the time I get back. That is really stretching me as far as I want to go where combining the two is concerned.'

As David Hands continued: 'There can have been few more supportive rugby wives than Amanda, but even she is looking forward wistfully to the end of her husband's playing career. He never accepts invitations to extra-mural rugby occasions; even one night out would upset the delicate balance of his life.'

So that is the lifestyle on which the future of amateurism is validated. One day spoils the balance. It is a fragile basis indeed. At the end of season 1992-93, Webb could take no more. He retired. Webb is a pale man. As he left the game he looked positively white.

# CHAPTER 3

# The Dudley–Moore Show

## AMATEURISM 2: DAWN OF THE DINOSAUR

They told us in history class that no one man or woman makes history. For instance, even though Mikhail Gorbachev is recognised as the man who set free the Soviet Union, it was the underlying trends that were the real catalyst. Even though, as my politically correct English lecturer used to say, it was Othello who smothered Desdemona, the real killer was the murky force of racism embodied by Iago.

So Dudley Wood is not the sole bastion of amateurism on this earth, the living embodiment of the ethos. There are other blue forces at work. It just *seems* as though he is. There is no doubting the power of his beliefs and no doubting the discomfort with which he views the pace of the drive towards professionalism. There is no doubting, either, the courage of his convictions. As so many sports columnists have found over the years, the most blissfully easy piece to write on rugby is to decry its amateurism, to call Twickers all the reactionary adjectives under the sun. Dudley wavers not.

In 1991 in *The Sunday Times*, Robin Marlar took the opportunity of a secondment from his duties as our cricket correspondent to attack Wood. Robin, a wonderful commentator on cricket, is not known to hold back when he wields the pen as offensive weapon. This is the man who, angry at being sent in as nightwatchman to quietly play out the closing overs of a day in his life as a Sussex cricketer, was out, second ball, for six.

'That devoted anachronism, a dinosaur doomed to extinction,' wrote Robin. 'Out of touch with commercial reality,' said another paper. They were discussing Dudley Wood. I went to see him a few days later and if he was hurt then he hid his hurt beautifully. In fact, he could hardly stop laughing. The hide-bound old dinosaur had then been in the secretarial seat for five years. In that time, the RFU had changed more radically than any other organisation in sport and with breathtaking speed. It was Dudley Wood who jammed his foot on the accelerator and left it there.

As I wrote after the interview: 'Let us look at how little has changed since Wood became secretary. All that has happened is that the stadium has been transformed in stunningly quick time, with a new stand and final planning to extend it so that Twickenham will become a majestic bowl. There has been a fifteen-fold increase in marketing income from commercial activities alone; a profound revamping of Twickenham's relations with the outside world, including the media, local authorities and residents; the imposition, after more than 110 amorphous years, of a structure for English club rugby which has brought leagues and a massive increase in club attendances.

'Through the technical department, the RFU have woken up to the responsibilities of all sports and gone for the kids and for promotion.'

There was so much more. Wood himself was proud of his personal flourish, an elevated ramp which provides a glorious view of the action for the wheelchair-bound. 'I don't really appreciate being cast as unwilling to change when everything here under the sun has changed,' he said. 'As for being out of touch with the commercial world, I do find the criticism a little ironic. I have a certain amount of commercial experience.' His tongue was in his cheek. Wood had a stratospheric career with ICI. Some dinosaur, him. His longing for the true blue is based substantially on the examples of other sports.

'Nothing I have seen from the experiences of other sports persuades me that there is a case for professionalism,' he says. And who, taking into account the preposterously behaved superstars of other sports, the artificiality of competition induced by drugs, the denying of fair competition simply to preserve market value, can disagree?

Indeed, for me Wood is the most inspired administrator that rugby union has ever had – although the England players have a different view. He is certainly widely revered by rugby's media people, who have to deal with him sometimes on a day-to-day basis. As far as I know, he is revered, too, on the RFU committee, to which he reports. He is a devastating after-dinner speaker. He is lightning quick on his feet in debate. As I once wrote, if the IRB were disbanded tomorrow I would willingly support control of the whole game falling to Wood, Andy Ripley and Mike Burton, the perfect complementary trio.

There are two main categories of people who do not hold him in such esteem. The first category comprises the jealous, people from other unions and governing bodies who envy his talents, and I can report that such people exist in all the other European unions except the Welsh, in the IRB and in Rugby World Cup. The second comprises those who cannot stomach his views on amateurism and his adamant refusal to shelve them.

My view is that his stand is heroic but unsustainable due to sheer force of circumstances. Equally I have always feared the explosion of the transition period. That is precisely why I would prefer if Dudley bent a little with the prevailing wind – he is so talented as an administrator that I would prefer him to be still in the camp to manage the fall-out, not hoist by his petard of principle.

Wood absolutely does not see things that way. He chose an incongruous platform to say so. In 1991 the Rugby Writers XV, a gathering of writers on the game which makes occasional playing tours, visited Florida (we smashed Miami 7–4, and we would have smashed Fort Lauderdale, but that bloody referee . . .). Wood agreed to submit an article for the tour programme. After some initial pleasantries, he set full sail.

'Perhaps while on tour,' he wrote, 'you can all reflect and explain why it is that a knowledgeable, articulate bunch of writers who have seen plenty of action around the sporting scene and, as standards of performance have risen, have watched the steady deterioration of most games into a sort of pantomime, the sole purpose of which is to make mega-money for a few puppet-like performers and a tenuous living for an army of hangers-on, feel obliged to knock and change the one successful team game still played for the right reasons.

'My particular aversion is to those who claim the moral high ground of progressive thought, by virtue of their willingness to jettison the birthright of their own sport which has given them, if not fame, so much fun and enjoyment over the years. I suppose it reflects their craven unwillingness to stand up for what they really believe is right (someone else's job?) in their anxiety to be regarded as forward-thinking, when what they refer to as "the inevitable" happens. Sure, they may be able to say "I told you so". But do they really think the world they are advocating will be a better place?'

Phew. For God's sake, Dudley, say what you mean. I took his point about principle entirely. I recognised myself in the ranks of the people he was castigating. But does there not come a time when principle costs you the very values you are trying to uphold, and the unprincipled scoundrels such as myself, by our retreat behind the next barricade, actually do more to uphold valuable vestiges of the original principle under ferocious pressure?

It was inevitable that Wood would run into Brian Moore. With the greatest respect to rugby's officialdom, they have always traded on the fact that players were, generally, young men finding their way in the world who dropped from sight before gaining the maturity to demand some control of their own destiny. Moore is not of that ilk. Moore is a forceful man, an angry man, a singular man. He has grown into maturity in the team. I can tell you that large sections of the RFU committee are ticking off the days till Moore's retirement.

In seasons 1990-92, those of England's outstanding back-to-back Grand Slams, there was a running battle between the RFU and the team. The team were angry not so much at the bewildering lack of clarity of the new freedoms to earn, not even so much at the wasted opportunities as the bickering continued and the commercial interests faded. It was that Moore and his colleagues believed that Wood and his colleagues were being deliberately obstructive, using the IRB fog for their own brake-lining, if you know what I mixed-metaphorically mean.

It was a desperately murky episode. It is certainly true that the RFU, while the players were beavering fanatically on their behalf and on the behalf of the country, moved far too slowly. A few definitive pronouncements, a little leeway; even a green light for the odd advertising campaign pending later clarification – any of these would have placated the players a little.

The squad, led by Moore, moved under the umbrella of WHJ Promotions, a company run by Bob Willis, the England fast bowler; later, they split with them. The RFU issued a statement. 'Following the decision of the England players and the Willis Brothers Company to go their separate ways, the RFU . . . agreed to make available the resources of its own organisation, in an advisory capacity, to act as a clearing house for any commercial opportunities that arise . . .' Yet the move, as it turned out, was merely an excuse for the RFU to hold any offers in a clammy hand. The players, partly through no fault of their own, came out of the whole episode with image tarnished as well.

The players eventually linked with Parallel Media, who orchestrated the recent Run With the Ball campaign, in which various blue-chip companies allied themselves with the team. The outcome was not impressive: the original pay-out to England squad members was less than £1,500 – not to be compared with the amounts Will Carling and Jeremy Guscott earned from their individual ancillary activities. The breakdown in relationship was one of the most painful events of the Great Transition. The England team are still seething about the whole affair. And still, the RFU is not so much helping their players, as do most of the other unions, but standing square in their way.

If both sides, officials and players, all over the world had started on a friendly footing, then it could have been different. But at the top level, trust was missing. There is no question that unions and players all over the wide world of rugby had lost each other years before. Or that future episodes will involve the parties not so much thrashing things out, as thrashing each other.

The truth is that rugby's officialdom lost the sympathy of the players years ago and that they thoroughly deserved to do so. For years, leading rugby officials seem to have acted on the premise that rugby matches were the excuse through which they gathered and had fun. Still, even these days, there are far too many junketing officials descending on matches around which they have no role.

For many seasons the treatment of leading rugby players was an utter disgrace, made less so only by the familiarity of the travesties. The basis of the philosophy was that players should be seen on the pitch but not heard, or even treated like international athletes, or even like human beings, when they left the field. The stories are legion. Until very recently, top Test teams were crammed into the back of aircraft; until recently, every member of the RFU committee received almost double the allocation of international tickets to players. Is there anyone at Twickenham who dares justify that situation, even in retrospect? Spare me the one about trying to cut down players' black-market activities. Is there a member of the RFU committee who can put hand on heart and swear that no colleague supplies the black-market corporate hospitality industry?

It is only five years since the wife of Mike Harrison, then England captain, was unable to see her husband lead his country in Paris because she could not afford to go. It is less than four years since the Welsh team were boarded throughout a tour of New Zealand in a series of abject cabin motels; one, in Hamilton, was so cold that Jonathan Davies and his friends went to bed wearing jerseys and tracksuits. The international players and even leading club players around the world are now often treated regally. Yet a book of biblical proportions could not possibly do justice to the history of ill-treatment.

The old vestiges of an ignorance of the true status of players as the kings of the game still exist. The most graphic example in my experience was the official closing dinner after the World Cup final of 1991. All the players had been in camp and away from their families for more than a month, and that was for the tournament alone. The teams did the event mighty proud – indeed, they rescued it from administrative bogs, set it free and watched it soar.

They had to cram themselves into formal rig for the dinner, held at the Royal Lancaster Hotel in London. I was honoured to be invited myself; but I found the evening profoundly depressing and embarrassing. The players were all but crowded out by a vast, teeming throng of VIPs, not Very IPs and general hangers-on. The attendance rivalled that of Twickenham for the final itself. Needless to say, every national union of the world appeared to have their whole committee in attendance. Vast ranks of minor officials, largely unconnected freeloaders and huge sponsors' ghettos filled an aircraft hangar of a room. On a top table of thirty-seven people, not one single seat was devoted to a player, even though four squads – those of England and Australia, together with Scotland and New Zealand, the losing semi-finalists, were present.

The players' request to have their wives and girlfriends present was turned down. It's a stag dinner, they were told. Yet the sponsors' tables were mixed. The women were welcome, but pulled the rug from under the organisers' feet. The whole affair was so totally inappropriate, so completely against the wishes of the teams. It followed the normal course: splendid rich food (*terrine de Champignons, tranche de saumon, rosettes d'agneau, vacherin frappé*), dull speeches, stinking cigars and bawling cries of 'heeaarrr, heearrr', when people yackered on about the ethos of Our Game.

'Rugby World Cup,' we said in *The Sunday Times*, 'should have shoved the team and back-up men and families into the best restaurant/nightclub in London, signed a blank cheque and slipped away.' Perhaps it was the last blast of the old era of player abuse. The signs are that way, at least.

Yet the years of ill-treatment have left scars in the relationship. There is also the obvious fact that the years when Victoriana ruled in the amateur dispute, when the unions rigorously patrolled the amateur wires with snapping guard dogs, actually increased the pressure on the principle. To suffocate is no way to live. As I say, the fact that relationships were based on a guarded hostility counted against everyone when the freedoms to earn from ancillary activities were granted in 1990. There was neither trust nor machinery. So when so many aspects of the IRB ruling fell open to interpretation due to severe snagging woolliness, the grounds for aggravation were laid.

The deep distrust which unions felt for players at this time was illustrated starkly when David Sole, the Scottish captain, retired at the end of season 1991-92. Allegedly, this move was welcomed by a high official of Scottish rugby, who claimed that Sole had been 'a cancer at the heart of Scottish rugby' (presumably because Sole had led the Scottish players towards commercialism just as Moore had done in England). Sole, on the contrary, had been such a magnificent example, such an indomitable driving force, that he inspired his team to results that the strength of rugby in the country had no right to obtain. Sole will always figure in a shortlist of British rugby heroes. Not for everyone, it seems, not for the pompous Scot of the SRU. As long as the suspicion exists there will be no easy answers when the final fate of amateurism is settled.

What is on offer at the moment? Players in France and South Africa can unquestionably make a decent living without holding down another job. In this country, the rising and engulfing tide of inducements (a tide which began to flow years ago, of course) now offers leading players changing clubs a car and accommodation as a basic. There are the strongest rumours that at least two players in England earned a minimum of £750 per match last season as a straight cash payment from a club backer lurking outside the committee.

The other South African system, whereby players are paid inflated expenses in a lump sum, is now more prevalent in the UK too. South African provincial players, judging by a table of the expenses paid to them which was published when I was in the Republic in August 1992, apparently commute to games from Greenland. That is the only way they could actually incur the expenses they are paid.

And who can fail to have sympathy with the dying code of rugby league in France? The poor chaps quite savagely discriminated against for their decision to come clean years ago have to scratch a living in a semi-pro sport. Then they find that any union amateur player they might wish to sign could not possibly consider coming across due to the enormous pay cut he would have to take.

The sideshows are also more and more lucrative. There is the Italian connection. A massive number of Australians and New Zealanders now play highly lucrative seasons in the Italian Championship, an overwhelming commercial operation in which the sponsors rule. They do not so much add their name to that of the club, as supplant it. Benetton versus Pastajolly, that sort of thing. Reports in New Zealand in June 1993 stated that £18,000 per season was the going rate.

Every major national team now runs a ticket pool. The whole allocation is thrown in and the ticket-master allocates them at the going rate. The identities of the ticket-masters are well known within the game. Patrol the foyers of the team hotels in the days prior to international matches and you will spot them, negotiating avidly. The Australians are far more easy to spot than that. You will always see the dirt-trackers lurking outside grounds flourishing wads of tickets. When Australia toured in the UK last season, they set up decent-sized stalls flogging tickets, T-shirts and even their own books. 'I'm sure our players don't do that,' an RFU committee-man told me huffily last year. Dream on, I thought.

On the legal side of the laws, so to speak, the various commercial schemes are still largely in their infancy. In England, all collective activities come under the banner of Playervision, the players' company, and all deals are done in conjunction with Parallel Media. The proceeds have been small, yet the schemes laid down until the 1995 World Cup promise more – perhaps the squad might earn £5,000 per man per season if their profile remains high – but of course, the earning power of individuals such as Carling, Guscott and Moore would be many, many times that amount. Carling has featured in an expensive campaign advertising a camera; Guscott in innumerable marketing campaigns and modelling shoots; Moore in a striking poster campaign for Nike – he generously pooled the proceeds.

The activities of the Welsh players cause far less domestic fuss because they have the firm backing of their own union, in marked contrast to the sniffy response of the RFU. A typical deal was struck last season. When the South Wales Electricity Board entered into a four-year agreement with the WRU to sponsor what is now the SWALEC Cup, they lobbed £60,000 into the players' trust. Jonathan Price, the WRU commercial executive, believes that even the lowliest squad member will earn a minimum of £3,000 in any season. Hardly a fortune, but by no means a negligible end-of-season bonus. In return, the players take part in the Electricity Board's rugby promotions. 'It is the ultimate solution,' says Jonathan Price, currently in dispute with the WRU. 'The WRU are happy because we have a major sponsor, the sponsors are happy because they know that their investment is protected and the players are happy because they are being paid for promotional activities.'

Heineken, Volkswagen and the WRU itself add to the players' pool and other long-serving sponsors of the game in Wales make similar donations. The winning advantage of the Welsh proposal is that the players are not seen to be running around trying to market themselves in isolation. No one could accuse the current England squads of money-grabbing, yet that is sometimes the image that comes across, because they have been cast adrift by the RFU.

The Scottish players have been amongst the most hawkish; they have been sufficiently badly advised to ask for and even demand payment for straight media interviews. The view of newspaper editors is firmly that the articles increase the profile of players, and that there is a world of difference between a feature in their own words written in their own name and a straight profile article written by a journalist.

The patience of the Scottish players with the slow pace of incoming deals is wearing thin, although they do have the same freedoms as the Welsh players to obtain secondary deals with major SRU sponsors. The Irish players' initial earnings amount to not much more than £1,000 per season, but again, the number of sponsors prepared to lob in for secondary deals is growing and the Slattery PR Group of Dublin have begun to market the players more aggressively. And as Tom Kiernan, the old Irish full-back, said when announcing the setting up of the players' trust, 'Whatever they get, I wish it could be made retrospective.'

Down Under there are far more freedoms. After every match on the recent tours of South Africa by Australia and New Zealand, the players would fan out in groups to attend lunches, dinners, product launches and the like; all carefully overseen by representatives of the unions. Both sets of players have far more empathy with their officials, and the officials are far more inclined to put their own shoulders to the wheel.

Two explosive announcements in summer 1993 blew away some last vestiges. Nowadays, all marketing income derived by the Australian team goes to something called Wallaby Promotions and Marketing Pty Ltd. In May, the Wallaby Company revealed a barrage of plans, including a massive gala dinner which would earn each Wallaby squad member at least £15,000 per year. The ARU approved.

It is entirely possible that the All Blacks, for one group, have become a little too mercenary in some respects. They have a head-start in their marketing skills because they kind of 'anticipated' the later freedoms in any case. As long ago as 1987, you could turn on TVNZ and there would be Andy Dalton waving happily in a tractor advert, or open a newspaper to see Steve McDowell downing some body-building supplement in a newspaper ad.

They set the ball rolling by driving a coach and horses through the spirit of the old amateur regulations. Both Wayne Shelford and John Gallagher set up their own companies in the late 1980s. The laws stated, basically, that you could earn money from the game if you were fulfilling your bona fide occupation. Andy Haden, therefore, took the proceeds from his book in the mid-1980s because he claimed that when he wrote the book, he was a bona fide author (which came as news to New Zealand's literati, but Haden's idea was cheekily ingenious for all that).

Shelford and Gallagher reasoned that their jobs were promoting themselves, so they could be paid for all marketing activities: speaking, flesh-pressing, posing in the makers' kit, and so on. There was the wondrous sight of Shelford, a player in a game which still then called itself amateur, finding rugby so lucrative that he signed up with the International Management Group, one of the world's most famous sports marketing organisations.

Then in June 1993, the other announcement. The All Blacks and the NZRU announced the promotion of the All Blacks Club. Companies and members of the public were invited to join, swelling the coffers for direct onward passage to the national team.

The earnings of the international players of the world are already, therefore, providing extended pocket-money – enough for one extravagant holiday for the family, for example – and if you play Test rugby south of the equator, considerably more. The first stirrings of local sponsorships are also being felt down the scale at club level. And for the very top strata, the cream, rugby can become a very lucrative game indeed.

In 1983, I asked IMG what they felt the future held for rugby players in the commercial marketplace. They were disparaging. 'We don't see ourselves getting involved. I suppose we could market Bill Beaumont as a sort of British bulldog figure.' IMG have changed their tune. Neither they nor anyone else believe that rugby players are about to take over from Michael Jordan, or golfers or tennis players, as millionaires in the ancillary fields. The overwhelming majority of players will need regular jobs still. In that sense, time spent on ancillary activities will eat even further into their own time.

But IMG are now involved in rugby at various points, and recently jumped in with both feet when offered a slice of the game – they are now joint commercial partners in Rugby World Cup. The new profiles of the game, as well as dragging on the punters, galvanising (and knackering) the players, have attracted the circling money men of the sport. And buried amateurism, in its original form, comprehensively and forever.

There is no ring fence around the game now. There are some woolly laws but they are being bent and ignored throughout the world.

There is no reason whatsoever to believe that the overwhelming pressures which breached amateurism's once-mighty wall have lessened in any way. How could they, when the whirlpool is ever more dizzying, demands are still escalating, the beady and the businesslike are creeping up in greater numbers? There may be a lull in the non-World Cup years, but only a slight lull.

What are the next steps, to what does the RFU now have to address itself as it reorganises its defences? I would be astonished if, within the next five years, the pressure to abandon every check on ancillary earnings does not become intolerable, if all commercial operations, rugby-related or not, do not have to be allowed.

I would be surprised if, within that same timescale, the game does not, however reluctantly, come round to the views of Bob Dwyer and Nick Farr-Jones, those two marvellous rugby statesmen of Australia and the world. Both believe that, such is the vastness of commitment asked of international players, there must be retainers paid to Test squads. 'I am not encouraging pay-for-play,' says Farr-Jones. 'But I think that the players should be put on a retainer [by their unions]. The retainers would be consideration for the ever-growing demands on top players and their time spent away from work.'

Dwyer's timescale is less frenzied than mine. He predicts retainers by the end of the century. 'There is only one attraction in the game – the players. Money should go into consolidated revenue with the players required to do certain things to support the game. We are not talking about match fees, but for us in Australia, the cricket model is easily attainable, where players are put on a retainer.'

Retainers, trust funds, unlimited access to commercial deals. The benefit would be that everything would suddenly rise from the groping under-the-counter deals and be fair and square, and in the end-of-year accounts. There is also an important check on the process: even if it should continue its present upward course, rugby will never drag in enough to make everyone rich, or to make full professionalism and pay-for-play a proposition – at least, not unless there is another giddy, partly terrifying quantum leap in the game.

And who, when the bylaws relating to amateurism finally settle, will sit forward and say to the other party 'I told you so'? Will the RFU and all the defenders of the faith be proved right? There must be a danger that the worst excesses of sports and sportsmen on the make will run rampant; that the team ethic will suffer because the grafters are grafting for peanuts, and by default to project the image of the pretty boys; that the lesser, teeming, good-old-boy ranks will split, in jealousy and distaste, from the top tiers; that the heroic amateur officials will turn away. 'Why should they spend so much time organising and running rugby when it is only for the financial benefit of a privileged few?' asks Dudley Wood, pointedly.

Or will they all have fussed in vain? Will it be proved that rugby's amateurism, after all, was merely incidental to rugby's inherent greatness and balance as a part-time game? That money is merely the root of all progress, not of evil? The Southern Hemisphere no longer give a damn.

It is too early to be categoric about the answer because we are only in the early stages of the debate, anguished and protracted though it has been. Amateurism as the Victorians knew it is long, long gone. A sanguine view of the replacement is utterly impossible to take.

# CHAPTER 4

# *Fantasy! Rugby at the Fairgrounds*

## THE PITCHED BATTLES IN THE NEW LAW WAR, 1992–93

It was the most frantic season. The Springboks were back in the paddock, the Wallabies wounded but still bounding, the Lions filing their claws. There was so much rugby going on that most people missed something else – the rugby itself was appalling. The action in the Northern Hemisphere rugby season was slow and dreadful, the worst season's rugby for twenty-five years. The rugby played in the Southern Hemisphere season was lightning fast – and almost equally dreadful. The average match score in New Zealand domestic rugby seemed to be 66-42, which sounds a world better than it was to watch. 'I would prefer some of the matches I've seen that ended 3-0,' said the *Scotsman*'s Norman Mair, one of the sharpest rugby writers covering the sport. The season as a whole contained some of the least exciting, most shambolic rugby ever played. It was an endless winter.

There was one reason for the shambles, and one reason only: the law relating to rucks and mauls, introduced for the season originally as a one-year experiment but which now remains, still as an experiment, until the end of 1993-94. It has been watered down a little, but the apologists for the law will ensure that it stays and is confirmed into the law book in 1994. They have staked their reputations on it.

When the laws committee of the International Rugby Board sat down for their deliberations at the IRB meeting in Wellington in April 1982, they were faced with an enormous batch of proposals from member unions for changes in the laws. The Australian representatives on the laws committee, Dr Roger Vanderfield and Norbert Byrne, in particular had fistfuls of suggestions to mess around with the laws. It was in line with the current – disastrous – thinking of both the New Zealand and the Australian unions that huge batches of changes should be brought up at every opportunity. They are completely overreacting to the end of the hegemony of the four Home Unions in the government of the game. They are abusing their new-found power.

There were three powerful reasons for the game to await the results of the meeting in a cold sweat of fear. First, the IRB's record as law-makers and law-changers in the game is disgracefully bad. Some of the changes they have made over the last twenty-five years have been completely counter-productive. Others have been a complete nonsense and have been reversed. Others have been completely forgotten; when was the last time you saw a prop penalised for scrummaging with his shoulders lower than his hips? Did you even realise that the law still applies? If the laws committee had been the board of a major company they would all have been turfed out by incensed shareholders decades ago. Worst of all, they have completely and utterly failed in their responsibility to achieve uniformity of interpretation.

Second, what exactly was broken that needed such frantic efforts to repair? The game was well established in a boom phase; crowds in many of the major centres were dramatically rising. Third, the inside intelligence was that some of the proposals were worryingly radical.

When the fax of the press release of that April meeting beamed up from Wellington I almost tore it out of the machine. On the basis that the fewer the changes, the smaller the probable cock-up, I was encouraged. The try was to become worth five points – a measure which was to have no effect on anything, incidentally – and there were other minor and not unacceptable variations. There were also some experimental variations. I was struck by one in particular: 'In a maul or ruck, when the ball becomes unplayable or the maul becomes stationary, the team NOT IN POSSESSION [their capitals] at the commencement . . . will put the ball into an ensuing scrummage.'

Since previously the possession was given to the team driving forward as the ruck or maul was whistled indeterminate, my immediate anxiety was that the essential dynamic of the game was being removed. As Richard Best, the England coach, said when his first reaction was sought: 'It seems to be against the first principle of the game.'

It is important here and now to contrast the wholly malign effect that the new ruck/maul law was to have within the Northern Hemisphere with the different effects in New Zealand, because the contrast was total. In law, rucks and mauls have to be blown dead, to generalise only slightly, once the ball is out of sight in a ruck or the instant a maul stops moving. In the Southern Hemisphere and France, again to generalise only slightly, they never bother with half the laws.

The first matches I saw under the new ruck/maul law were in South Africa when the New Zealanders and Australians made their tours. The laxity in refereeing ensured that the new law rarely applied. Referees merely waited ages until the ball emerged. They hung around patiently filing their fingernails long after rucks had collapsed; they waited long after mauls had stopped moving or allowed them to stop and then meander off again. Then, the ball eventually trickled out. The matches were shapeless blobs, because even if you rarely turned the ball over you could still only have one scrum per attack, and all the other mini-disasters affecting flow (to which we shall come shortly) still applied. Yet there were few turnovers (the ball reverting to the other team).

The cold reality dawned when the Northern Hemisphere season began with the match between Leicester and an England XV at Welford Road. Two weeks earlier, even on a muddy day at Newlands, there were only three turnovers. At Leicester, there were eighteen. Not surprisingly, the effect on the game was catastrophic. There was no continuity, no excitement of pressure building. There was no rugby. There were eighteen turnovers simply because Ed Morrison, the referee, applied the laws. It was not a question of strictness. He was being neither strict nor lax. He was simply applying the law. If he could not see the ball he blew his whistle because that's what the book says. Suddenly, that day in Leicester, the season seemed to stretch interminably ahead.

The effect was different in New Zealand, but that is hardly the point. Even with the ball re-emerging with such regularity I was still profoundly against the principle and practice of the ruck and maul law. I could see why Kiwis disliked it less than we did up north because they at least had some action, albeit to me a sickly quasi-basketball with unsatisfying basketball scoring. They also, like Australia, have a nonsensical obsession with rugby league. They think that union should be created in league's image; they seem to believe, for instance, that because a two-second wonder called the Auckland Warriors are about to start up and play rugby league in New Zealand in Australia's Winfield Cup, it means that in two years the league game will sweep away rugby union for good. If I had a pound for every country which was about to be swept off by rugby league but which survived rather well then I would be the richest journalist in Christendom.

As I say, under the anarchic interpretations of New Zealand referees the law was just as disastrous; as I say, it was a different kind of disaster. Instead of the referee slowing up and fracturing the game as they did up north by being so inconsiderate as to apply the laws of the game, we had in New Zealand a furious headless chicken.

Back at the start of the Northern Hemisphere season, the effect was appalling. Players in defence no longer had to commit themselves to stopping the opposition drive. If the ball failed to emerge they won the ball anyway. The powerful wrap-up tacklers, players like Dean Richards of Leicester or Jon Hall of Bath, could stop a move and win the ball with one bear-hug. Where did the forwards go who, under the old law, were sucked in to stop the opposition drive? They stood out in the backs. Formerly, if you could carry on a move through four or five phases, your chances of scoring increased with every phase; now, the longer the move went

on the more fatso props and lurking locks stood around to snuff out
the move. 'I have never been tackled by so many props,' said David
Campese.

A theory evolved that you had to tie in the fringers. The theory
had it that you simply drove and drove again, thereby clearing them
out of the way. It was so much drivel. If you drove at a group of
players, others detached themselves. If you drove at them, the first
lot were lurking. At its worst, it meant that a small group of players
from each side would come together to contest the tackle while the
rest of the team would fan out in two lines and await developments.
And yes, it has been tried before. It is called rugby league and Ellery
Hanley and his friends play it a good deal better. The Divisional
Championship match at Gloucester between the South and South
West and London was almost pure rugby league.

And that was when the ball actually emerged. The law was meant
to curb those teams, not nearly as numerous as the apologists
reckoned, which had indeed evolved a negative game in which they
drove with the ball locked up in the wedge and picked their spot for
the next scrum. Foul play? Of course not. In any case, Australia, the
most glorious attacking rugby team of the past decade, did it all the
time. They picked their spot for the scrum, worked their way to that
point on the field and attacked devastatingly. 'Under the new law,
we can never set up the kind of attacking scrums we based our
moves on,' said Nick Farr-Jones, their captain.

To me, one of the disasters of the new law was that unless the
opposition knocked on or infringed in some other way, you could
never have more than one scrum in succession. If the whistle went
and the ball had not emerged, you lost it. There was also the truly
appalling sight of teams attacking brilliantly through a succession of
rucks and mauls only to lose all the ground gained to one massive
hoof after the next scrum. There was a vast increase in the amount
of kicking in Europe. Why should your team take the ball into
contact? Kick it to them, let them bring it into the ruck or maul and
then lose the next scrum.

Attacking scrums are the perfect platform. Furthermore, a
succession of attacking scrums is the most galvanising experience
for the crowd, especially when you can see that the opposition are
gradually caving in. The rugby in 1992-93 flitted all around the
pitch, going nowhere. Spectator noise was way, way down. And
pressure rugby, those long passages when you really put the finger
on the opposition, really drain their leg muscles and their morale in
an extended period, challenging them to lift the siege, was no more.

'It allows inferior teams to stay in the game,' said Bob Dwyer,
Australia's coach, the brains behind the most entertaining and
effective attacking rugby of the era, who was profoundly against the
law change. 'You can't play as precisely in impromptu situations as
you can in rehearsed ones. It is inhibiting the game. It is a disaster.'

It also forced teams to set the ball back as quickly as possible.
Especially in Britain and Ireland, the rugby match became a
zigzagging mess. Unquestionably the most asinine and simplistic

pronouncement of the whole sorry season was that from the
apologists that the new law kept the ball in play longer. People
solemnly took out their stopwatches and earnestly proclaimed the
new law a success because there were 2.75 extra minutes of action in
each half. So what? The ball is in play for hours in snooker. In
rugby, it is what is happening to the ball that counts.

I felt too that the IRB's laws committee were being deeply
patronising to the punters by telling them what they wanted. Of
course they wanted open rugby. But they also wanted the crunch of
the collision. Rugby is not basketball. It is a contact sport. You know,
tackling and all that. The candy-floss rugby which took the place of
the real thing left the quiet crowds not applauding, but heaving. If
you mess with the basic culture of a game then you are off down a
slippery slope. If you pander to every passing whim then you will
certainly disappear in the precise direction of your own backside.

Players had to run around a little more but they had energy to
spare – they were saved the sapping physical collisions of the scrum
and the driving into rucks and mauls to make them go forward. The
early months of the season were aptly summarised by two British
rugby magazines. 'Death of the game', said *Rugby World & Post*. 'A
law made by asses', said *Rugby News*.

The hidden impetus behind the new ruck/maul law was essentially refereeing failure. Too many rucks and mauls had ended
indeterminately, not specifically because the team in possession
wanted the next scrum, but because the laws relating to action in the
aftermath of a tackle were too confused, were applied with a
frightening lack of uniformity around the country and around the
world. When the new law arrived, referees started to pay close
attention to the tackle law because it became vital not to let
defending teams kill the ball in order to win the next scrum. The
tackle law, the requirements of the next man in to remain on his feet
– indeed, all aspects of the game situation – were endlessly
discussed.

There were two massive ironies here. First, if as much attention
had been paid to the tackle and its aftermath under the old law then
no new law would have been necessary. The ball would have
maintained a respectable flow. Secondly, there was the screaming
injustice of it all. Fair enough, if you simply took the ball into a maul
and held it there passively you lost the ball. But you lost the ball if
the other team wrapped it up either legally or illegally. You lost the
ball if it simply failed to emerge: for example, if too many bodies
toppled on both sides and trapped the ball. Either way, you could
easily fail to recycle the ball through absolutely no fault of your own
when there was simply no way that you could have cleared it.

This gave rise to another of the peculiarly asinine expressions
with which the apologists policed their new toy. 'Use it or lose it!'
became their cry. It was as if, in the frantic surge of activity in the
microseconds when a tackle became a ruck or maul, in the very
instant when the flankers or nearest players were arriving to secure
possession, everything was in perfect order and whether or not you

re-won the ball was entirely in your own hands; that there could be no extenuating circumstances (say, sheer ill luck, accidentally blocked channels, the ball bouncing off a stray foot from the arriving patter of huge feet, opposition skulduggery, etc., etc.) whereby the ball could fail to emerge, other than your team's own incompetence.

In the majority of turnovers in the season, teams losing possession after indeterminate rucks and mauls were penalised for no offence. Sure, you could reduce the percentages slightly if you practised techniques of recycling the ball until you were blue in the face. Teams did so in every training session throughout the season. But there were still too many imponderables, too many matters out of their own control. That is the simple and unavoidable truth and the desperate injustice of the whole thing. The International Rugby Board's ruling was based on the unsustainable assumption that rucks and mauls were formed in careful, orderly, polite ranks in which it could *only* be your own fault if the old leather pill was never seen again. It was rubbish.

The campaigns fought throughout the season and all over the world by the apologists and the abolitionists amounted by a street to the most fervent debate in the history of rugby law-making. *The Sunday Times* led the abolitionists in the country. 'When are you going to stop this campaign against the law?' asked Denzil Lloyd, then the Welsh representative on the IRB laws committee. 'On the day you get rid of it, Denzil,' I replied. I was proud of the campaign we launched to have the whole thing consigned to history's smelliest dustbin (although privately I agreed with those who grimly forecast that the IRB's credibility was at stake to such an extent that there was no way the law would be repealed. Among them, incidentally, were two people on the IRB itself).

'Rugby's rulers must rid us of this crazy idea', ran the heading on our main campaign article. I and the researchers seeking opinions of people throughout the game were soon so swamped with people savaging the whole concept that we had to decimate the gathered views just to fit them on to the page. The views we retained give some idea of the strength of feeling.

Alex Wyllie, retiring All Black coach: 'What a shambles. An absolute madness. It cuts across everything we believe rugby to be about. They talk about continuity. What happens is that possession is changing hands more often. That is not continuity, that is movement for movement's sake.'

Will Carling, England captain: 'I do not like it. It has put pressure on referees by making their interpretations more important than ever and interpretations are varying wildly. Why don't they sit down with leading players? At the moment, the people changing the laws are not the people playing the game.'

Mark Evans, Saracens' coach: 'A terrible law. It has ruined the whole game and made it impossible to coach. It is almost totally counter-productive.'

John Williams, then South African coach: 'It makes the game far more difficult to plan properly. It is doubtful whether it will have the effect intended.'

Fergus Slattery, former Irish flanker: 'It will get worse, not better. Nobody has abused the law as yet but it is open to widespread abuse. It will be a deliberate ploy for the defending side to go for the scrum by keeping the ball in.'

David Campese, Australia wing: 'They have got to change the law back to what it was. This season, even in the third and fourth phase of play there are still four or five defenders to beat.'

Des Seabrook, Orrell coach: 'Recently the game has become very marketable. But the new law is cheating the public.'

Bob Dwyer, Australian coach: 'If anyone wants a champion in the fight against this law then I put myself forward. It makes it impossible to plan the game properly. It is a great leveller, so poor teams benefit. They say it is an Australian idea. Nobody asked the Australian team or coaches. It is a disaster.'

Andy Cushing, London Scottish coach: 'You may have taken the ball fifty yards upfield; you may have won six rucks in succession, but if at the seventh ruck you cannot get the ball then you lose it. The opposition get it back and kick it back fifty yards. Who has played the better rugby?'

The criticism quickly became almost wall-to-wall. I wrote in *The Sunday Times* in the middle of the season that the only respected voices I had heard or read praising the new law (I had obviously not heard or read everyone, I hasten to add – I am not a particularly voracious reader of newspapers) were those of Gerald Davies and Alan Davies (who was later to change his mind on procedural grounds). Geoff Cooke and Richard Best, the England management team, came out strongly against, as did Don Rutherford, the RFU's technical administrator. The majority of club coaches in the top three divisions of the Courage Leagues were against.

Eventually, the opposition at the level of national coach was to become widespread. *Rugby World & Post* conducted a survey among leading coaches and summed up the results in one damning cover line as their reaction to the new law: 'SHOVE IT'. Of the major national unions, Dwyer, Best, Ian McGeechan (Scotland), Alan Davies (Wales), and Gerry Murphy (Ireland) all came out against while Pierre Berbizier of France expressed profound reservations. McGeechan's reservations were significant. Scotland were regarded as the style of team which could most benefit. 'You can be positive and dynamic in your attack and through no fault of your own lose the ball,' said McGeechan, although he also expressed reservations about the old law.

Laurie Mains, the New Zealander, was the only national coach in the survey who expressed support. He admitted that the interpretation of Kiwi referees helped.

Significantly, Mike Ruddock, the splendid Swansea coach whose club played brilliantly for a long period of the season, was unconvinced. Tony Russ, the Leicester coaching director, came out in favour and also – in my view, completely erroneously – claimed in *The Times* that the successful English clubs had been those which were coached by men in favour. Leicester were a tremendous young side but they played, for them, rugby of humdrum style.

Jack Rowell, the Bath coach, pointed out, correctly, that Bath could succeed under any law but his support for the new law surprised me: Bath have a varied main armament but one of their staples is the ability to drive a team back to their own line, and hammer and hammer away until they eventually collapse. If Ben Clarke or John Hall didn't get you with a back-row drive, or if Richard Hill and Clarke didn't combine to score, or if Jeremy Guscott and Stuart Barnes didn't manage to work anyone clear, or if Tony Swift could not quite manage to make the line, then they could always have another scrum and Gareth Chilcott and his mates would push you over. They had a perfect and absolute right to all those attempts. It was up to the defending side to get rid of Bath and drive them away. That part of the Bath machine has been dismantled in a committee room.

Glenn Ross, the Northampton coach, produced such a rose-coloured and delighted report on the new law that it made you wonder with a sense of urgent disbelief where on the planet he had been watching his rugby in the season. Possibly Ross was in that significant group of people who deemed the new law a success because of the principle and the intention and the *intended* result. They were high-minded, sure. But the actuality was dramatically different.

The statistics confirmed the rampaging counter-productivity of the new law. Tries were down massively, the proof that the pudding was rotten. Steve Bale of the *Independent* was just one writer to produce statistics. He wrote that in the Five Nations tournament, 'tries have not been as hard to score since the 1962 and 1963 Five Nations produced just sixteen each'. In all the major leagues, tries were dramatically down. Except in Wales. The apologists seized on the uplift in tries in the Heineken League Division 1. Llanelli, especially, scored them by the barrowload. Again, it was a false reckoning. Newport, in mid-table, were good enough in the season to thrash teams below them by fifty and sixty points. They played Llanelli twice. On each occasion, they conceded seventy points. The truth was that in Wales, the standard of club rugby and the breathtaking gap in class between the top and bottom – even the top and middle – made massive scoring a certainty. It was not the law, it was poor standards.

Even I was amazed at the depth of feeling. In this era in rugby, with the need to market the game as never before, there is contempt for those who are deemed to be dragging back the appeal and who are not 'positive' about the game. The apologists' buzzword cry was that we should all be 'positive' about the ruck/maul law. I was positive. I was positive that it was a monumental cock-up. I was also certain that the best way to be positive for rugby's future was to campaign against it. But it was easy for me. I had to answer only to my sports editor. The coaches who came out against often had to risk the wrath of their unions; those referees who spoke out against (it is quite staggering how disastrously meek and mild referees are when it comes to fighting their corner) had to risk a rap from their own hierarchies. We all had to run the risk that the trendies would deem that we were not 'positive'.

Yet not even the most fervent proponent of the new law could possibly deny the sheer extent of the opposition or at least, the profound disquiet – or could they? Probably the most sensational single aspect of the whole debate occurred when the International Rugby Board gave a press conference to announce the fruits of their interim meeting in November 1992. The new law had run a whole season in the Southern Hemisphere and up north had run for nearly three months. The press conference was probably the blackest day in the history of relations between the International Rugby Board and the rugby press, and by God, that takes in a few. On any number of subjects the IRB fudged, hedged, hid and refused to give a straight and honest answer to a straight question. Journalists may not always lay true claim to the moral high ground but they left the meeting seething with rage, especially at the performance of New Zealand's Russell Thomas, who gave evasive answers to questions regarding Rugby World Cup; at Ireland's Sir Ewart Bell, formerly a high-ranking civil servant in his country who nevertheless has an impenetrable delivery and a fudging style, and apparently little grasp of the question, let alone the answer.

They were also furious at the responses of Dr Roger Vanderfield of Australia. Vanderfield has spent years in the service of rugby. An administrator in Australia's health service, he has sat on the IRB since the 1970s and been chairman of the laws committee for ten years. He looked the world of rugby in the eye at the press conference. 'The new laws are achieving their desired objectives,' he said. Of coach Dwyer's belligerent opposition, he said: 'Perhaps Mr Dwyer should stop complaining and be more positive.' For me, that was the most insulting statement I have heard directed from officialdom to anyone in the real game. Perhaps Vanderfield should have swallowed his pride, driven to Dwyer's home on the front at Coogee, knocked on the door and learned something of how people at the sharp end saw it all. At the IRB press conference, Vanderfield appeared to be seriously suggesting that there had been no opposition. Senior IRB members quickly and privately backtracked and apologised for the PR disaster of the whole meeting.

In a sense, of course, what Vanderfield was saying was perfectly true. No opposition had been recorded from the IRB channels. Outsiders might think that leading players and referees and coaches are given either a formal say or a direct advisory input into law-making. They are not. The last time any of the IRB laws committee played the game was before Will Carling was born. The whole thing is run on channels of communication set up by each union. Some unions have some rudimentary framework for players to have input; others have nothing except the views of their own technocrats and bureaucrats. Others have representatives who carry union policy to IRB meetings and then, once ensconced in the clubbable atmosphere of the IRB gatherings, and not being mandated, simply cave in to the room's view.

The opposition of Alan Davies to the ruck/maul law was partly based on that situation. 'What I think about the new law is not the real issue. What I object to is the lack of consultation before the law was approved . . . Let's acknowledge the contribution we all have to make. I would like nothing better than to have a three- or four-day international workshop with some players, coaches and referees. We could study a proposed law, go away in groups to discuss it and then have a practical session, by which time you might have a better idea of the whole thing. Because of the lack of consultation in the present system the end product is always likely to cause disruption. As it is, because I'm not happy with the process, I'm not happy with the consequences.'

The one-year experiment came up for review in April 1993 at the annual IRB meeting. By the time the delegates met, the apologists were rattled, were no longer smug as some had been at the IRB interim meeting. For a start, England had sent up their reservations through the normal channels; secondly, the fierceness of the debate shook out the smugness. One official of the Australian Rugby Union, clearly a little put out, approached me at the Rugby World Cup Sevens in Edinburgh. 'We in Australia are determined to press ahead with the law, you know,' he said.

'Who, I asked, is "we"? Your national coaches have opposed the law from the start; so has your captain, Nick Farr-Jones, who is one of the wisest and most erudite rugby players in the world. So has David Campese, the greatest attacking player the game has ever seen; so, to a man, did the touring party to the UK before Christmas; so do John Connolly, the coach of Queensland, and Greg Smith, the coach of New South Wales. On whose behalf is the Australian RU going to vote to continue with the law? Who is left? With respect, are you sure you are representing the game in your country properly?'

He went a little quiet.

The supreme arrogance of those men in committee rooms who think that their opinions should always carry more weight than those in the shop window of the game is a perennial wonder of the sport.

Some of the apologists became just a little anxious. In response to the campaign in *The Sunday Times*, the Australian Rugby Union dispatched a letter to the editor attempting to refute our view that the law was a shambles and that Roger Vanderfield might at the very least have acknowledged the possibility that not everyone was delirious with joy about the law. The letter was signed by Joe French, the ARU president and chairman. It was one of the weakest letters we had received in the sports department for months. It was too weak even to rescue a paragraph or two for publication. I respected Joe French almost without reservation but his letter, for me, revealed the weakness of his case. Among a host of non-sequiturs and irrelevancies, Joe presented his list of the people who, he claimed, had 'voiced their support of the new ruck and maul law'. The list consisted of Andrew Slack, the former Australia captain, Dick Marks, the ARU coaching director, Nigel Starmer-Smith, Dr Danie Craven, former All Black Bob Stuart, Roger Uttley, the former England coach, and Alan Davies.

I was staggered by the list and wrote back to Joe to tell him so. As for Slack, Marks, Craven and Stuart, while they were hardly operating at the time in the stratosphere of the game occupied by Dwyer, Campese, Carling and Ian McGeechan, at least I took Joe's word for it, not having heard their view either way. I had to point out to Joe, however, that:

a) Nigel Starmer-Smith dynamited the new law in an editorial in *Rugby World & Post*, the magazine which he then owned, and that the magazine had called on the law-makers, as we have already established, to 'SHOVE IT'. Not quite, shall we say, unreserved support.

b) Alan Davies, if he was once in favour, had backtracked furiously.

c) Roger Uttley had recently written a long and passionate letter to *The Times*, which had been used as the lead letter at the top of the letters page, in which he castigated the whole thing. With supporters like those, I thought, Joe French had no need of enemies. French claimed Uttley as a supporter!

When the IRB met in April there were stirrings of sanity on several fronts, if not substantive saving graces. Geoff Cooke, the England team manager, had bravely arranged, around the Hong Kong Sevens, a gathering of all the major national coaches to discuss the laws. In order not to offend proper procedure, he had to undergo a long period of forelock-tugging, apologising and the like. He insisted that he was keeping England's IRB representatives, Albert Agar and Denis Easby, fully informed, that *of course* he wasn't trying to have the ruck/maul law abandoned, that he apologised for being alive but that he and his fellow coaches were just going to have a nice little chat, that they might drop the IRB a line outlining their chat and that the IRB might find some spare time in their crowded schedule to glance at it, begging their pardon. Ian McGeechan, the Scottish coach, received what was described as a 'flea in his ear' for attending. Disgraceful.

The meeting was a great success. And lo and behold, the IRB acknowledged it. Seated facing the press in the New Balmoral Hotel in Edinburgh, with the whole IRB obviously wary of another PR disaster, Dr Roger Vanderfield praised the document that the coaches produced. It was well presented and constructive, he said. Would you now take the coaches' forum on board as an official consultative group, I asked. That was travelling far too fast. 'We have our own procedures,' said Vanderfield. 'We'd like to hear from any group.' It was a start, a step down the staircase from the ivory tower. It was to the credit of Cooke that he set up the meeting and to the credit of Vanderfield and the IRB that they listened.

There were other heartening items. The ruck/maul law was not inked in but continued as an experiment for another year, so comes up for final review in April 1994. It was also watered down. Now, if a maul which was formed immediately a catcher took the ball from a kick ends indeterminately, then it goes to the side which took the ball in; if the referee cannot sort out which team took the ball into a ruck or maul then the scrum is given to the team going forward. This made the whole thing a dog's breakfast of different philosophies and laws. So much was still open to the referee's interpretation. But at least someone had acknowledged the problems.

There was a slight drawback of course. The damnable law, essentially, still existed. The ruck/maul law will, almost beyond question, become full law in April 1994. Pride is at stake; the Southern Hemisphere unions (if not all their coaches and players) want to keep it and their power in the IRB now is awesome, their word final.

And rugby will never be the same. Until the blessed day in the future when the law is repealed and the essential driving dynamic returns to the game, it will be suffering. The sport as physical contest will be diminished; the attacking team emasculated, the superior team emasculated; the rhythm of the game changed, the appearances of the game changed, the build-up of excitement lost.

If differences in law interpretations continue to be as prevalent (and the gaps are becoming chasm-like through three-quarters of the rule-book. If you disagree you were not in New Zealand with the Lions), then the game north of the equator will continue fractured and false and unfair, and the game south of the equator will continue fast but unsatisfyingly frothy. You might go home with the vague impression that you enjoyed bits of the game but for the life of you, you will not be able to remember what they were. So much effect from a few words inserted into a law by a few committeemen, who told the players how the game would be instead of asking them; who may have stilted rugby's box-office boom; who tried to mend something that was never broken.

If rugby learns that to pass laws for the modern game it must consult, rigorously, the leading practitioners, then perhaps not everything is a waste. If rugby takes more care before it breaks with its own ethos, then it has learned a valuable lesson. Laws should evolve. There is never a need to force the pace, and especially not in a desperate bid to inflict on the paying public something that they may not even want. Faddism should be damned to hell. Look what happened to flares and skateboards.

'What will you write about now that the fuss about the new law is over?' asked a friend and coach of a Gwent club who had corresponded with me about *The Sunday Times* campaign. 'But it has only just started,' I said.

# CHAPTER 5

# *Free Nelson Whassisname*

## SOUTH AFRICA RETURNS TO INTERNATIONAL RUGBY

I had that dreadful sinking feeling when I was walking down the aisle, carrying my cabin bag. When I looked down at my boarding pass, and up at the seat row number, I knew it had happened to me again. I had drawn the Fat Bastard. He must be in every airline's frequent flyers club because he always turns up in the seat next to you on the long haul. He drinks all night, blathers loudly through the film. And with low cries of phwooaarr, with small masterpieces of overstated unsubtlety, he tries to pull the stewardess.

Worse, he actually thinks he is making progress. He never realises that when the poor girl disappears behind her curtains, she is actually working out the financial implications of her summary dismissal for shoving the *rosettes d'agneau farcie au romarin* down his throat, balancing the loss against the fleeting moments of unadulterated joy she will experience.

'Whaddyer do for a living then?' he asked before I had even opened the peanuts.

'Er, I'm a journalist.'

'Journo eh? Don't trust 'em. Haar, haar. Whaddyer write about?'

'Er, mostly sport; mostly rugby.'

'Jesus. Did you see that World Cup? I watched that World Cup on the telly. Load of crap. The Springboks would've taken it, piece of piss. There is no way they will not beat the Kiwis and the Ozzies. No way.' We took off. Only twelve tortuous hours left before we would land in Johannesburg.

We were on the blue and white aircraft and in the dung-brown seats of a South African Airways flight on a beautiful English summer day in August 1992. In the company of several colleagues from the British sporting media and one porky Afrikaner, I was en route for South Africa to cover the return of the Springboks. Short and yet potentially momentous tours by New Zealand and Australia were to mark the official end of the long isolation of South African rugby.

In the years of boycott, practically all the South Africans had seen were furtive rebel squads ('Course we weren't paid, guv. Never saw a bean') or dredged-up, scratch groupings. 'It was all we had at the time,' Naas Botha, the South African captain, told me once. His eyes said that it was never enough. Naas, at thirty-four, was just young enough to continue his grievously interrupted Test career.

The return of South Africa had profound implications for rugby and for its fast-moving revolution. With one of the triple pillars of the old world restored, it was inevitable that the boom would gather yet more pace; that major matches and tours would be ever more numerous and glamorous and pressurised; that demands on players and the faltering ethos of amateurism would become ever more ferocious. Rugby was welcoming back a supreme practitioner. But in its pariah years, South African rugby had never been a stout defender of the amateur faith. Expenses for players in the Currie Cup were enormous. So it was all grist to the whirling mill, it was typical of the fast yet fearful progress which the sport was making.

The dam-breaking visits by New Zealand and Australia promised the highest drama on the field. The All Blacks were finding their feet again after booting out the tired Auckland old guard after the 1991 World Cup disaster (they only reached the semi-finals, poor dears). South Africa–New Zealand in any era is probably rugby's most titanic clash.

The Australians, meanwhile, saw the Springboks as their final frontier. A gang of South African supporters paraded a banner round some of the World Cup grounds in 1981 which bore the inscription: 'You aren't the real world champs till you beat the 'Boks.' It may have been tiresome and fatuous. 'Look at those prats,' we said. But it struck something of a chord, even in flinty Wallaby hearts. They focused on South Africa with beady eyes.

In the meantime South Africa had already been awarded the privilege of staging the 1995 Rugby World Cup. These tours would give us a clue as to whether South Africa would measure up to the task – would the event be properly staged, did the infrastructure exist to put on an event of that magnitude? How were the buffet facilities for the media? And more important, given the widespread and daily reports of appalling atrocities in South African society, by no means all of them confined to non-white areas, would the thousands of inbound spectators expected in 1995 be safe?

The harbinger of this new rugby dawn of 1992 was the rapprochement and amalgamation early in the year of the South African Rugby Board and the South African Rugby Union. It happened in a brief and beguiling period of optimism in which the white South African voters gave President F. W. de Klerk a referendum mandate to follow his reforming path; when the Codesa (Convention for a Democratic South Africa) talks were proceeding, with the main parties together.

Nelson Mandela was out and free, sparing us those appalling mass concerts in which bands on their uppers revitalised their careers before a global audience and made outrageously simplistic speeches about er, Nelson Whassisname. Best of all for many, the Springboks, those gleaming national icons, were in training again.

The SARB, the old white-dominated governing body led by the old white bulldog, Dr Danie Craven, had finally joined SARU, the South African Rugby Union, a far smaller body which oversaw some, but by no means all, of the black rugby. SARU, which had turned down repeated entreaties from Craven over the years, had always been politicised under the banner of the African National Congress (just as the SARB had been politicised, to some degree, under the banner of the Broederbond). Ebrahim Patel, SARU's president, became joint president, with Craven, of the new body.

It had been nearly fifteen years since an initial burst of amalgamation saw the South African Rugby Federation, which organised rugby for coloureds, and the South African Rugby Association, which dealt with the non-SARU blacks, merge to form the SARB. That was a movement of sorts, but it came in an era when South African rugby regarded the appearance of two non-whites in a white team as final and incontrovertible evidence that society was now integrated. The amalgamations in themselves deserved praise, but the SARB never realised that they were protesting too much, that it all proved the opposite; that there could, indeed, be no normal sport in an abnormal society.

The 1992 amalgamation, which formed the South African Rugby Football Union, enabled the sporting arm of the African National Congress to give its blessing to the resumption of rugby. South Africa's cricket team had already re-entered the wider arena and had struck a chord with everyone. Steve Tshwete, the ANC's sports spokesman, had been incarcerated for a long stretch on Robben Island. He confessed that he had never cried on Robben, but had finally burst into tears of joy when he saw the South African cricket team take the field. It was a revealing aside from an impressive man.

The rugby amalgamation was well meaning. People on each side had to file away old enmities. We were later to find, on our travels, that it was very far from being a root and branch amalgamation. But for the time being, it did the job.

However, by August and our outward-bound flight, the heady optimism of earlier in the year had completely evaporated. The Codesa talks had broken up, with fierce accusations on both sides that they were being undermined. Massacres at Boipatong, a town in the anarchic Vaal Triangle, and in the Ciskei, the nominally independent homeland, had stalled the peace processes and had raised the unthinkable spectre that it would all be sorted out with a fight to the death. Both massacres, and so many of the other atrocities that were taking place, illustrated the painful difficulties of transition and the malevolent input of those who wanted no compromise. Quite obviously, the Government, the ANC and Inkatha all had shadowy elements under their banners which they could not control. It suited those in the shadows to foment discord and death. If any one group suffered a massacre, were the perpetrators the obvious enemy, or men from their own ranks who could blacken that enemy's name so grossly?

Even the parties were sub-divided and then sub-divided again. Every side to the argument had a hawk wing – the quasi-Nazi AWB for the loony right, the Pan-African Congress for the no-deals left. The atrocities grew ever more sickening, the townships ever more anarchic, the argument ever more fragmented. Indeed, for a long time in the Northern Hemisphere summer, it had seemed as if both tours would be cancelled; that the ANC, having left the Codesa table, would pull the plug or that the inbound teams would simply deem it too dangerous to tour. Nick Farr-Jones, the Wallaby captain and a wonderful statesman of the game, publicly expressed his fears. 'What is the point of a rugby tour if we have to go everywhere with security men and guns?' he said.

The tours proceeded. It all made the organisers of the 1995 Rugby World Cup wake up at night in a bath of sweat. Not to mention every South African citizen. And every visiting journalist.

The tours marked the end of an era which rugby had found unbearably traumatic. The first time that the issue really socked rugby between the eyes was in 1967. The All Blacks were due to tour South Africa in that year but then they found that they had to be All Whites. The South African Government declared that the All Blacks had to tour 'under the old arrangements'. This meant that their Maori players could not tour. Full stop. In the olden days, New Zealand would simply have left the Maoris at home and taken only *pakehas*. But this was the 1960s. The pennies were beginning to drop. They told South Africa to shove the tour. So, one year later, did the MCC when they were told that they could not bring Basil D'Oliveira, the Cape coloured all-rounder.

When it came to the iniquities of discrimination, even the sporting stories defied belief. I found that with the D'Oliveira affair, the Maoris affair and the other rotting garbage of sporting discrimination, you were never immune from incomprehension. Take poor Papwa Sewgolum. Papwa was an outstanding golfer. They would never let him play in big South African tournaments because he was of Indian descent. Eventually, they allowed him into the 1963 Natal Open. The South African Broadcasting Corporation cancelled coverage. How could they be expected to cover a golf tournament with a black guy in it, for God's sake?

Papwa won the Open. Now for the trophy presentation. Papwa stood in pouring rain outside the window of the Royal Durban Golf Club. The trophy was presented to him by an official standing inside the window. There were Indians allowed inside the clubhouse, but only servants to serve drinks and clean the mud from the whitey spikes. Papwa was banned.

In 1966, Papwa was paired with the great Gary Player in the first round of South Africa's PGA Championship. Government inspectors accompanied the large gallery to keep Indian and coloured spectators apart from the whites. And to think some people, even now, try to apologise for the old South Africa, try to insist that we should have played sport with them. Until recently, there were people who believed that sport and politics did not mix, even though they are one.

The bandwagon demanding South Africa's expulsion began to grow. The focus switched to Britain in 1969 when the Springboks made what was to be their last trip to this country for nearly twenty-four years. There were frequent demonstrations, and a particularly violent one at Swansea, where protesters fought with what were essentially rugby vigilantes. Yet at no time was the tour likely to be abandoned. It was simply a high-profile inconvenience.

The ragbag of opposition groups on that tour were unified by the Stop the Seventy Tour campaign, which practised on the rugby tour for an assault on the proposed Springbok cricket tour of Britain later that year. The group's acknowledged spokesman, Peter Hain, was an exiled South African and a young Liberal. He was to become, in 1992, the Labour MP for Neath. Back in the late 1960s, he infuriated the conservative sports-loving public.

The cricket tour was cancelled because of the threats. It was fairly easy to guard a rugby pitch for eighty minutes but a more exposed cricket arena for a three- or five-day match was unsealable. If that was a success for the SST group, and for Peter Hain, then it is astonishing to recall the naïveté of it all. The protesters complained that most of them were portrayed as scruffy, long-haired students. There is one rather sound reason for that. Most of them were scruffy long-haired students.

Ah, the naïveté. Hain, in his book *Don't Play with Apartheid* recalls a gutsy operation when, unarmed, he secreted a packet of powdered dye into a game. 'Now Mr Hain, you wouldn't be doing anything silly like taking a packet of dye in with you?' asked a police commander whom he knew, as Hain passed police lines on the way into a stadium.

'Now Commander, you know I wouldn't do a silly thing like that,' Hain replied, walking boldly into the stadium. He threw the dye on to the field. What courage! What radicalism! What leadership! The Vorster Government back in South Africa must have come close to scrapping apartheid on the spot. A whole packet of dye.

Yet the anti-South Africa operation became vastly more sophisticated. Rugby was the highest point of contact, and rugby began to collide ever more painfully with protesters and frequently with its own responsibilities.

The British Lions did tour South Africa in 1980 and England toured in 1984. The Springboks had toured Australia in 1974, their last external tour till 1992. There was a tour of Britain by the South African Barbarians, a brilliant exercise in counter-productivity. There were twenty-four players – eight whites, eight blacks and eight coloureds. As an exercise in propagating the truth that South Africa was a society of deep divisions, the tour simply could not have been bettered. Yet the frequency of tours declined; the tempers of the rugby men who hated this meddling, who spouted about bridge-building, the need not to give in to blackmail, the need to keep politics out of sport – all the wagonload of rot, in fact – rose steadily.

The rise of the South African Non-Racial Olympic Committee provided another impetus to the fuss. They busied themselves tying any rugby contact between any country and South Africa to wider questions. Particularly, they demanded that countries who had played ball with South Africa should be excluded from Olympic or Commonwealth Games, and in the meantime encouraged other participants to boycott the Games.

The All Blacks toured South Africa in 1976. It was a bitter tour and it had a bitter aftermath. SANROC and the Black African countries demanded that New Zealand be withdrawn from the Olympics in Montreal that year. New Zealand refused, and two days before the opening ceremony, twenty African countries withdrew from the Games.

And yet SANROC were to become, as far as the rugby question went, the most counter-productive force in the debate. Sam Ramsamy, the SANROC mouthpiece in London, was in private a reasonable man. His public utterances, which were hawkish, unfeeling and bullying, caused rugby men to dig in their heels. Rugby did not take to being threatened. Ramsamy unquestionably, if indirectly, considerably strengthened rugby links between South Africa and the outside world. He resurfaced as the head of delegation for South Africa's Olympic team in Barcelona, still occasionally barking intolerantly in what he thought was the cause of tolerance.

The most appalling fall-out of rugby's determination to proceed in the face of protest, world opinion and morality, came when the Springboks made a tour to New Zealand in 1981. The tour almost caused New Zealand society to disintegrate. Families were split between pro and anti. There were massive demonstrations at every game and public order was seriously compromised. There was far more discussion about the tactics of the riot police than those of the Springboks. The tour was a complete farce. It did reach its conclusion, but only after the tourists had had to subject themselves to overwhelming security precautions – they often spent the night in the dressing-rooms where they would change for the match next day. It was a negation of the principle of rugby tours. The final tour match, the Third Test, was probably the most bizarre rugby match in history. A light aircraft buzzed the crowd, throwing flour bombs on to the field. One bomb felled Gary Knight, the All Black prop.

There was even a painful footnote. The Springboks stopped over in America on the way home and played a Test so affected by security precautions only a handful of people made it to the match. Even leading officials of the game in the host country had no idea of the venue.

*Dudley Wood, secretary of the RFU and the only revolutionary dinosaur in captivity*

*The Springboks, and the packed stands at Ellis Park, belting out 'Die Stem'. It was the gesture of defiance which almost ended South Africa's comeback*

*James Small, the excitable Springbok wing, excitably launches a pass towards Wahl Bartmann in the Ellis Park epic*

*The words to it are ludicrous, the threats dangerous, but the Haka must prevail against the abolitionists. The All Blacks give it the final leap at Ellis Park*

*The late Dr Danie Craven, mesmeric and confusing as ever, addresses a hushed tent after the All Blacks beat the Junior Springboks in Pretoria*

*Nothing new here. On show are the Australians' immaculate public relations and the line-out lifting endemic in the South African game. Fun and politics on a township visit at Uitenhage, near Port Elizabeth*

*No longer the nasty booter. Nice Naas Botha kicks South Africa to victory over the abject French in the First Test in Lyons*

*Naas Botha on his inter-planetary trip, pressing the flesh as the stilted Springboks trained for world opinion in Nyanga Township, near Capetown*

*Wem-ber-lee! Canada's Scott Stewart hounded by England's Tony Underwood in the Test at Wembley. Should all Tests be played there? Should Twickenham sit gaunt and empty most of the year?*

The tour dragged New Zealand into the modern era. For the first time, police wearing visors were seen on the streets, carrying batons and canisters and all the paraphernalia of riot control. In staid New Zealand society, it was as if aliens had landed. The country was shaken rigid. Welcome to the twentieth century, Kiwi.

In fact, public opinion in Britain was never much moved by the South African question. There was never, in any survey, over-whelming feeling for or against sporting contact. But New Zealand's experience shook the rugby authorities. It was six years before New Zealand recovered. Many people believe that the wounds were finally healed only when rugby reunified the country in 1987, when the All Blacks won the inaugural World Cup, beating France in the final at Eden Park. Even then, members of the same family did not speak.

Incongruously, perhaps, the two most bitter tours, by the All Blacks to South Africa in 1976 and by the Springboks to New Zealand in 1981, gave rise to two of the very best books in rugby literature. Terry McLean's *Goodbye to Glory*, on the 1976 tour, certainly seemed to derive a little of its anti-South African passion from the fact that the Springboks had won the Test series, yet it is still a wonderful read. Don Cameron's *Barbed Wire 'Boks*, on the disasters of the 1981 tour, is a remarkably frank account of Cameron's own near-incomprehension of what was happening to his country and his sport.

Rugby's most profound weakness in the whole era when South African contacts were such a burning issue was that the game worldwide turned up not one official of stature, hardly a single figure who did not cringe behind the untenable tenets, or lurk behind the curtains drumming up players for scratch or rebel tours. The prevalent pronouncement of the era was: 'We all abhor apartheid, but . . .'

I had first visited the country once before the 1992 trip – for six weeks of sensory assault when the ill-fated 1984 England tour had struggled and subsided. The manager of that 1984 tour was Ron Jacobs, a former and bandy England prop, then the RFU president and a square and solid Cambridgeshire farmer. He was imposed by the RFU over the head of Derek Morgan, who was then the England team manager.

Was Ron an inspired choice to deal with the painful political questions from the hovering media, to take through South Africa the message that the South Africans had to begin to deliver emancipation in exchange for the tour? After all, that bargain was what most rugby people had in mind when they droned on about bridge-building, keeping communication open, and so forth.

No, he was not. He was sent out to plant his foot down the track, to play the deadest dead bat in the history of sport, a forward defensive that would have frustrated Michael Holding till the second new ball; to stop every question with even the most innocent political undertone. 'We are here to play rugby, not to discuss politics,' Ron said, day after day. England played so badly, were lacking dedication and were so completely wiped out in the Tests, that Ron never had much sport to talk about, either.

But what about the bridge-building? What about keeping channels open? The *raison d'être* behind the continuing tours disappeared completely once the tours themselves arrived. I never once heard any rugby official talk to a South African on any aspect of apartheid. There was no need to keep channels open. The channels were off the air. Get off the plane, play on and forget it.

Another illustration of the standards came when that England party was pool-side at the Elizabeth Hotel in Port Elizabeth, sunning themselves at the glamorous beach-side location and sipping cool drinks. A high official of the Rugby Football Union had arrived on tour. He was actually an extremely nice man. He had come down from Johannesburg on the famous Blue Train, the sedate suites-on-wheels which is the pride of South African Railways. He climbed out of his suit and into some Victorian bathers. He stood on the pool deck, gazing out to where the Indian Ocean lapped the beach, sipping a drink cool and stiff. 'Do you know something,' he said. 'I believe the problems of South Africa have been exaggerated. When we came down on the Blue Train we waved at blacks in the fields, and they all waved back. They seemed happy enough.' Er, yes.

There was just one political statement emanating from anyone in the party during the whole tour. At a press conference the day after England had disintegrated against the Springboks at Ellis Park and were preparing, thankfully, to fly home, Derek Morgan was asked how he found a trip to Soweto, which some of the party had joined. It was the Government-run trip, as much a part of visiting South Africa at the time as a gawp at Windsor Castle is for Yanks touring Britain.

Morgan was an honest man. He had a think. 'It doesn't make everything right,' he replied in his rasping Gwent accent (he was a dentist in Newbridge). 'But there are far worse places on this earth,' he said of Soweto, the seething city. True, Derek, I remember thinking. But are there far worse places on this earth in countries with the gross national product of South Africa?

The tortuous questions obviously put pressure on every individual conscience. I felt that pressure particularly because rugby journalists simply had to Say Something, had to come down on one side of the argument or the other. My first inclination was to say play on. I was always (and am still) in awe of rugby's power as a force for good and for friendship. All that stuff about rugby's legendary forgiving nature, the global brotherhood, the lasting friendships, all that stuff about rugby being a sport apart, is true. All of it is true. I have met rugby people on impoverished Fijian islands, in Prague nightclubs, at Romanian dinners organised by the Securitate, on Florida beaches, in South African wilderness huts, at New Zealand outposts, at the fantastic Hong Kong Sevens. The common language, the sense of belonging, the benevolent freemasonry, the concept of the universal rugby man: all these take only minutes to be firmly established and re-established. I love rugby and what it can achieve. There was the temptation, therefore, to say that we should not turn our backs on the South African arm of the brotherhood.

Of course, other countries were more vicious to elements in their populations, frequently on racist grounds, than South Africa was to its people. 'Ah, but in South Africa that racism is enshrined in the constitution,' anti-apartheid groups used to say. The distinction was a nonsense. As if persecution, discrimination and murder sprang only from a constitutional basis. 'Dear madam, we are sorry that your son was recently tortured and died but you will be glad to know that this was unconstitutional.'

I also heard some appalling apologists for the antis. In 1985, together with Ian Robertson of the BBC, I had an audience with David Lange, then New Zealand's prime minister. We were joined in our discussion of the South African question and the problems it caused New Zealand by Chris Laidlaw, the former All Black who was an adviser to Lange. We pressed Laidlaw, chiefly as the devil's advocates, on why the Government condoned contact with Soviet teams and yet not with South African teams. Laidlaw went into a long and rambling explanation that since at certain local canton levels some Soviets had a vote, then the Soviet Union was actually a prime and free democracy. Robertson and I played back his tape at length afterwards, trying to work out what on earth he was talking about. It just showed that there was weakness in both sides of the argument.

Ultimately, the temptation to keep contact was swamped utterly for me by realities. I simply could not support the continuing contacts. If rugby was to remain true to the famous goodness and morality then the answer was to shut out South Africa, not to encourage them. You see, South Africa did not practise what rugby preached. Rugby had to compromise its own standards to tour there just as the Olympic movement and the Olympic charter were compromised. If you play rugby you need the package. You must be able to play with anyone at any time, to socialise with your opposite number – even to sleep with his sister – to invite him back to your hotel for a beer, to have him make a reciprocal visit. South African society did not enable you to play to those rules. It burned the rule-book of rugby's supposed humanity.

The discrimination, the inhuman discrepancies in funding for education and health, the vast apparatus of Acts that erected the wall of apartheid, the shocking horror of the signs of petty apartheid, blacks in here, whites in there – how could they be ignored? The inhumanities were not visible from the tourist traps of a rugby tour – they were around the corner, over the hill, and always in the mind. I could support people travelling to South Africa who simply wanted to see for themselves – on the grounds that to see apartheid in the flesh is surely to have your mind made up for life. I could never condemn young men with inducements dangling before their eyes if they went to play. But I hated the rest of rugby for its blindness.

The other problem, of course, was the disastrous PR image that rugby portrayed as its officials ham-fisted their way through the problems. In my experience rugby is the least racist pastime I have ever come across. Racism is simply not a factor in the sport. Rugby never brags, as other sports do, about black representation, black opportunity, the first black man to do this or that, simply because it has never been otherwise, never been something worth remarking on. Indeed, in all the years I have followed the old game, only once have I come across a racist incident. Glen Webbe, Bridgend's wing, was briefly abused by one spectator at a Welsh village club in a Cup match four seasons ago. That is it. And yet . . . given the association of rugby with racist South Africa, the true picture of the game was submerged by a powerful and inaccurate image. Not even among the most conservative apologists in rugby officialdom did I ever detect any overt racism. But a fat lot of good that did the sport if the public perception was something else.

I had no answers. I accepted that a demand for some sort of immediate smooth switch from apartheid to democracy, and of power from white to black, was an utter nonsense. I hated the bullying of outsiders. I hated the Hampstead bleeding hearts who castigated rugby over champagne flutes – and by God, my newspaper employed a few of those. I hated the absence of the mighty Springboks. I understood the views of old players who had formed warm friendships.

Yet in the final analysis, that case was overwhelmed by malevolence, inhumanity and disgrace. There was no question in my mind of resuming contact until the Government in South Africa moved substantially, until the non-white people felt able to start to forgive; until normality beckoned. Until, for practical purposes, the African National Congress said so. Then rugby could resume its role as a force for rapprochement and good fun. Only then.

What of the victimisation of South Africa's white rugby players and followers? Sad, of course. Yet the assumption has always been that South African rugby men represented not the victims of the apartheid years, but the vanguard of the perpetrators. That intolerance was ingrained in their echelons as powerfully as in any other group in the country. This suspicion was, incidentally, to be ringingly confirmed during the tours I was flying out to cover, especially in the Transvaal.

How many sportsmen actually stood up to be counted on the issue? In the whole period of the pariah years, desperately few. Eddie Barlow and some Springbok cricketers staged a significant demo at a cricket match once; Danie Craven made the odd brave call for freedom; the Watson brothers, heroes to every non-white South African sportsman I have ever met, stood boldly above the parapet, and even played for black SARU clubs (and had their property torched for their pains). But few others, few rugby players, broke cover. It would have been courageous for them to have done so, of course, in a conservative and even vindictive section of society, but it could not be compared in terms of personal danger with, say, the dissident voices in the old USSR.

The 1984 England tour lasted six weeks, but you hardly needed six weeks to be dazzled by the country. I found it a haunting, spectacular, gigantic and strange land. Obviously, it was two countries, and two countries divided by vast chasms of constitution, mistrust and wealth. What astonished me as a first-timer in the Republic was how infrequently that chasm was breached. All right, there was no vote for the non-whites. They could not even live alongside the whites – when day ended and dark fell, all but hotel waiters and domestic servants and the like slipped back to the townships.

There was my Western bleeding heart to negotiate. I vividly remember standing by the cable car station at the foot of Table Mountain, in Cape Town, trying desperately to find the bottle to go up the mountain. I stood and watched a large family of blacks. They had the bottle to go up – their problem was finding the money. They pooled their resources, and found enough for about half the children to ascend. The lucky few set off, cackling with glee. The others stood sadly, and waved.

What was I to do? Shell out a few rand from my expenses, give them all a trip, pat their heads and go back to my five-star room in a five-star hotel, where a room-service order for one hamburger was served by four blacks, and tell everyone about my blow for human rights, my ceaseless work for underprivileged blacks? South Africa was a gorgeously comfortable country. People were nice. And it was a profoundly uncomfortable country too.

To pander to opinion, the South Africans magnanimously created the status of honorary white for black sportsmen crowbarred into white teams, or for groups such as the rebel West Indies touring party. Some of the crowbarred non-whites could play, like Errol Tobias, the black diamond fly-half or centre who played against that England side. Others were useless, a sop to Western media and public opinion. But even Errol had to go back to Caledon, his township, when the match was over, sport and politics in indivisible operation again.

But there was more than the forced geographical separation of the races. It was the lack of contact at any point. Two parallel lines with no transversal. If you spent time in one community you were given no reminder that any others existed. The lack of cross-pollination in any walk of life was astounding. White South African popular music was a prime example. In 1984 it was quite stupendously anodyne. It made Radio 2's middle of the road sound like safety-pin-in-the-nose punk music. It lacked soul, black soul. It lacked the glory that black musicians had given to Elvis and everyone who followed him and wielded a guitar. There was no integration in music, not even a note of the music of the other groups. There seemed no exchange of literary cultures, or artistic cultures or culinary cultures. Imagine music without blackness; imagine our athletics team without Linford and Kriss and Daley and Tessa and the others. Imagine what South African society missed out on for so long. South Africa was a place without soul in the music or gold in the medals. As well as the injustice, there was the desperate, desperate waste.

As Fatso began his sonorous snoring and we neared Johannesburg, there was time to contemplate and to dream of an idyll. Would there be evidence of the communities drawing together, of whites and non-whites hugging in the streets? Or at least, evidence of a genuine cross-pollination as well as movement towards political change?

Would there be new blackness in the music? In 1984 you could find no black music in the downtown music stores, and this in a country with a phenomenal musical heritage. I am a fervent follower of South African Mbaqanga music, the driving township rock, and had searched South African shopping malls for it without success in 1984. Would I find it now integrated into the high street and consciousness, as an allegory for life itself? Perhaps a scratchy old classic on the shelf from Sipho Mabuse? Or a long-buried original from the glorious Mahlathini and the Mahotella Queens? Or perhaps an early forerunner of the township compilation classic, the Indestructible Beat of Soweto?

Crucially, would we now see evidence that the South African rugby authorities were making up for lost time and ploughing millions of rand into the development of rugby among the non-white population, trying to come between at least some of them and their passionate affair with soccer? Because if there was greatness in sheer numbers, then greatness beckoned for the Springboks.

I took an unfond farewell of Fatso at Jan Smuts Airport. 'Here's my address,' he said. 'Come over for dinner one day.' Yeah, sure.

Jan Smuts was dull and unprepossessing and we all felt the first tug at the lungs as the thin air took effect. Some of us in the travelling press were staying at a hotel in Sandton, in the northern suburbs. As the courtesy bus, quiet with first impressions, circled Johannesburg we passed enough razor wire to circle the world, fencing off shopping malls and residences, surrounding grilles where stood security guards and howling dogs.

The enforced geographical separation of the communities had ended with the passing of apartheid; only economic factors separated them now. You could hardly move from a shanty shack in Soweto to an affluent house. The law allowed you to, but your pocket banned you just as surely as the old law. Yet those economic factors also drew them together in violence. They meant that crime was coming out of deprived townships, creeping towards white areas. Razor wire was the thing to be in.

We learned from a friend about the Gafia, a group of black gardeners working at prosperous white households in Johannesburg who were able to tip off their employers when their district was to be hit. We learned that in the townships, you could hire an AK47 rifle by the hour.

The Junior Springboks were training on the very day we arrived, for their match, two days ahead, against New Zealand, the third match of the tour. I had missed the first two in an unscheduled departure from my planned itinerary. One week previously, packed and loaded and about to set off to drive me to Heathrow, my wife had taken one last call. It brought the news that her father, a man I liked and admired as much as anyone I have met, had died. He had made par at a par-5 on a golf course in Welwyn, a feat which would have tickled him pink. He had walked to the next tee and there suffered a massive heart attack. It brought home the savage shock of sudden death, and gave even a rugby tour of South Africa a perspective.

New Zealand had already beaten Natal in Durban, and the Orange Free State in Bloemfontein – two convincing victories, achieved in the strange and false-war atmosphere of the experimental law change. This gave possession after indeterminate rucks or mauls to the team which did not have the ball when the ruck or maul began. It was a change I profoundly distrusted before I ever saw it in action. A full season under the law only heightened that distrust. *The Sunday Times* ran a long campaign against the law, a campaign most of rugby joined and of which I was ferociously proud.

We immediately felt at home as our hired tin can pulled into the car park of the Loftus Versveld stadium, vast Pretoria home of the Northern Transvaal, the Blue Bulls. The global brotherhood of rugby writing has representatives on perma-tour and there were familiar faces from all countries at the ground. Even more familiar, it was obvious that large areas of Loftus Versveld had been torn out and replaced by the guzzling galleries of corporate hospitality suites – at least South African rugby was up with the rest of the world in one respect. As the blessed Frank Keating said, at the end of a TV programme in which he gloriously sent up and tore down the striped-tent ghettos: 'Corporate hospitality? It's the end.' Very soon, there will be a rugby stadium in which the number of corporate tiers outnumber the ranks left for rugby supporters, the people who put the game where it is. Don't worry. Me and Frank will torch it.

We waited on the touchlines for training to start. Now, at last, we would see some Springboks, could prepare the superlatives. We had heard so much about these giants, how they would come back into their own with an irresistible surge. I had read in a London paper, for example, that South Africa's leading Currie Cup teams would hammer teams in the Five Nations; I had read the contention in the excellent *SA Rugby Writers' Yearbook* that South Africa were ranked second in world rugby, ahead of England and New Zealand. I had read in the same book the contention that one Adolf Malan was the greatest mid-line jumper in the game. 'South African players are massive, athletic and explosive,' said an article in *Rugby World & Post* in 1992, and it was the universally held perception that even their scrum-halves would be sprinting giants. As for their locks

– God, even Big Wade of England would need a ladder. Now, at last, we would see these gleaming specimens in the flesh.

The Junior 'Boks straggled on to the field. The session was one of the most desultory I have ever seen. And the players, they were something else. They were, by the standards of modern-day Test rugby, tiny. We looked for the locks but could see none. It was as if they had not turned up and reserve flankers had been drafted. Eventually, the local writers pointed them out: Kobus Wiese and Drikus Hattingh. Next to, say, Wade Dooley or Martin Bayfield, they were short. Hattingh was bulky enough. No wonder – he had recently served a suspension from athletics after a positive drugs test. But Test locks – nah! The only way they are going to win the line-out on Saturday, said one Brit onlooker, is if they lift them every time (and by the blessed memory of Denzil Forklift Williams, the old Welsh prop, they had a darn good try, too.)

Still, these were only Junior 'Boks. We'd find giants soon, surely. We never did. Every South African pack, up- or down-country, was the same. Most of the props were porkers in the old style of the years before the conditioning penny dropped. They tied their shorts just underneath the nipples and they came down to the knee, voluminous like yacht sails. There were some sizeable guys, but no lighthouses.

Adolf Malan, it turned out, was a brave player but hardly won a ball in the Tests that month and hardly won a ball on the entire tour of France and England later that year. He was a trier, but too spindly.

The surprising lack of height and the misapprehension held in South Africa that their men were giants taught us a highly significant early lesson. It was the first indication that South African rugby had not kept up. There was no hype, no lies, in their excited revelations of monster Springboks. They genuinely believed that they had giants. They did not realise that forwards in the outside world had grown and grown, and at a far faster rate. While the likes of Nigel Redman, the splendid Bath lock, could win a cap as England's mid-line jumper in 1984, by 1992 he was too small even for the front of the line-out. When South Africa last played a real Test Match, in 1984, you could be six foot three in the line-out and get away with it, but by 1993, six foot four was nowhere.

As the tours by New Zealand and Australia wore on, the truth dawned clearer. The South Africans had access to video, to books, to television. They had contacts with coaches and referees. But it was never, ever enough. Their misapprehension about size was only a small symptom. There was also their failure to see that their standards had slipped, that then, most of their Currie Cup teams were, say, lower Division One and upper Division Two in the Welsh and England club leagues, at best.

Their style was slow and set-piece orientated. At the end of the Australia Test to come, John Williams, the angular and austere professor who coached them from the wilderness, said: 'We no longer play rugby like the rest of the world. They are playing a different game.' We were to find a game dominated by kicking, and in which backs and forwards never combined.

Some of the old strengths were still there, especially in the upper body and tackling. But South African teams, we were to discover, were not even quick enough and fit enough to play with passion. You can snort and breathe fire but if your legs don't carry you to the action then you are a paper dragon. John Robbie, the former Ireland scrum-half now domiciled in South Africa, had written before the tour, in a column for *Rugby World & Post*: 'The 'Boks are either the true world champions or a collection of dinosaurs, hopelessly out of touch with the modern game and in for a rude awakening.' It was the latter.

The machinery of technical progression had not become so rusty that such a magnificent rugby country did not have every chance of catching up in the medium term. The excellent performances of the South African teams in the inaugural Super-10 Series was a testimony to that. But realisation was a salutary experience. Bombast was replaced by harsh self-appraisal. The news is that isolation hammers your game.

The full conclusions were still weeks ahead as my colleagues and I drove up to Pretoria for the match on the Saturday, on a clear and crisp afternoon. But there was a pilgrimage of sorts to be made en route. As you pass Pretoria on the six-lane motorway from Johannesburg, the Vortrekker Monument looms out of the veldt. You see only the top as you circle up the mountain which it commands, but when you arrive at its foot you find that it is square, grey and massive, over fifteen storeys high.

We drove into the car park underneath the monument expecting to be revolted. We assumed it would be merely a celebration of racism, and racism in the name of religion; a celebration of the stoic, dour, racist Boers who drove into the heart of the country on their trek from Cape Town, starting in 1835; the men and women who did not so much found the modern-day South Africa as hijack it.

We were wrong. The monument was unbelievably impressive. The story of the Vortrekkers was the story of a simple heroism. The Dutch had landed near the Cape of Good Hope in the seventeenth century to establish a glorified watering-hole for ships of the Dutch East India Company on the trade route between Europe and the Far East. By the 1830s their ancestors had had enough of conflict with the black tribes, who had migrated in a great sweep southwards, towards the Cape and confrontation. They had had enough of the insufferable colonial British, who had arrived and were busy creating a Little England complete with nineteenth-century equivalent of paperclips, trying to shape an alien country into British form. So they set off into the heart of the country.

A stunning marble frieze around the base room of the monument depicts the main events of the Great Trek, the dogged nose-down persistence with which the puritanical trekkers and their ox-wagons met all the obstacles of the harsh environment and marauding tribes. The first two parties that struck out into the interior were almost wiped out – van Rensburg's people by the Shangaans, and the Trichardt group by fever.

As the various Vortrekker groups met the Xhosa, Shangaans and the Matabele, they took heavy losses. Piet Retief, probably the most famous Vortrekker, led a party as far as the Drakensburg mountains and modern-day Natal. He negotiated land rights for his people with Dingane, the Zulu king. At what was supposed to be a celebratory piss-up, Dingane's men brutally murdered Retief and his party. Apparently, they used the same method as did the murderers in Marlowe's *Edward II*. Suffice it to say that it ruins a good pair of underpants.

The Vortrekkers established themselves at the Battle of Blood River in 1838, in the immediate aftermath of the death of Piet Retief. A small group were besieged by vast numbers of Zulu and drew their wagons into the classic defensive *laager*, the same sort of configuration adopted by Randolph Scott and Hoss Cartwright whenever the Indians attacked. The Vortrekkers' steadfastness, their resigned courage, their tactics, and the way that the wagon circle was sealed, kept their losses remarkably low considering that they were so outnumbered. They endured waves of attack over a considerable period; eventually, they changed tactics. Every now and again, a small Vortrekker commando would emerge to make lightning raids from the *laager*. Outmanouvred at every stage, the Zulus suffered massive losses. Blood River became a victory.

The frieze and the monument represented a justified celebration of heroism and sacrifice. It was unfortunate that white South Africa took the *laager* mentality to heart, that the search for living room and the wish to avoid the other tribes, black and white, was eventually to turn into an aversion for any tribe but their own. That is why the monument is a holy place for the hard-line Afrikaner.

The monument commands the surrounding country. On the way up the motorway we had watched a light plane perform unbelievable manoeuvres at what was obviously an air display a few miles from the motorway. As we looked down from the monument, we could see a pall of smoke back down towards Johannesburg, at roughly the point where we had seen the plane. Sure enough, we read next day that South Africa's leading aerobatic pilot had pulled too late out of a spectaular dive, and crashed. He died a day later.

We left the monument, and drove down to Pretoria and to a mere rugby match in a country where the new *laagers* were marked out not by wagons, but by razor wire.

CHAPTER 6

# Danie and the Juniors

## THE DOCTOR SPEAKS, TO MEN ONLY

New Zealand beat the Junior Springboks by 25–10, coming to life effectively yet only occasionally. The crowd was large yet not capacity. The spectators were almost all white. The hawkers and sellers, the men with Coke and *biltong*, were almost all black.

The rugby All Blacks looked exactly what they were – a team in transition, in which some parts worked and some parts didn't. At least they unveiled their latest dark gem. John Timu, after understudying the wing positions for some time, had recently established himself at full-back. He played brilliantly at Loftus, making memorable tackles in each of his corners to keep out tries. And he added the electric dimension to New Zealand back play that had been utterly absent since John Gallagher made his ill-fated move to British rugby league.

The Junior 'Boks were undercooked, undersized. They had a meaty goodness about them but nothing electric. They were also, and amazingly, lacking in passion – especially surprising since this was the first foreign opposition most of them had ever met, and the Springbok team to play New Zealand was being announced that evening.

The local press had built up the confrontation between Richard Loe, the fierce All Black prop, and Piet Bester, a pugnacious and squat tight head from the Free State who had already crossed moustaches with the All Blacks in Bloemfontein. It was a damp squib. 'A disappointing absence of shoe', was the summary of a British journalist who normally devotes high-minded columns to highlighting foul play. Gerbrand Grobler, the full-back, often brought the crowd to their feet with some dashes and Jacques Olivier had a turn of foot on the wing. Chris Badenhorst, the other wing, scored for the home team, blasting on to a chip from Jannie de Beer at fly-half, but Timu scored late in the match, overlapping outside John Kirwan on the wing in his best Gallagher style.

The most striking feature of the match was the line-out performance of Drikus Hattingh, or rather, the line-out elevation of Hattingh. He won some beautiful clean ball at the front of the line-out – chiefly because he was hoisted upwards by his props, poised expectantly in mid-air waiting for the ball to arrive, like some sort of circus tableau. 'We don't call it lifting. We prefer to call it supporting,' said John Williams after the match. 'It seems to us a way of ensuring clean possession, which must be for the good of the game.' He had a point, but he missed a more important one. Another symptom of the wilderness years was that refereeing interpretations had lost standardisation (not that much standardisation existed in the outside world anyway, but that is another story). South African referees allowed jumpers to be lifted bodily into the air by supporting players gripping them round the shorts and hoisting them like a human forklift truck.

In the rest of the world, some referees played to the letter of the law and allowed no real contact between the supporter and the jumper. But most allowed support after the jump – in other words, you could keep the jumper up in the air after he had jumped under his own steam. The variance was a few micro-seconds, but the interpretation was significantly different. Albert Adams, the referee at Loftus, allowed the lifting because that was the way he always played it. In the forthcoming Test Matches, the Springboks would pay dearly for their failure to accept that neutral referees would see it all differently. It was not the interpretation that John Williams preferred that was important: it was the interpretation that the visiting referees would apply in the Tests.

After the match, in a massive marquee in the grounds in a glamorous throng of players, ambassadors, scene-makers, high officialdom and journalists raiding the tables, they called for silence for the formalities. Dr Danie Craven took the podium, together with Professor Daan Swiegers, convener of the South African national selectors. 'We are going to hear the team to play New Zealand on Saturday. But first, a word or two from Doctor Craven,' said the announcer. There was a vast and adoring cheer.

Craven cut it all short. 'They don't want to listen to me,' said Craven. 'They want to hear the team. Read it out now.' Craven exuded authority. The applause redoubled, then they announced the men who would make South Africa's re-entry burst. Professor Swiegers, in what was for we British an impenetrable Afrikaans accent, solemnly read out the team. It was an emotional moment. The green and gold blazers could come out again. Good old Franny Cotton and Steve Smith back in England had signed up to supply the jerseys. It never said 'Cotton Traders' on the jersey when Danie was wearing it. Come to think of it, nor did a dirty great red splodge bearing the words 'Lion Lager' figure prominently in Danie's day. Nevertheless, the Springbok green was back.

There were wild cheers, especially for Naas Botha, the idol of Loftus; and especially for Danie Gerber, the centre. Gerber was by now thirty-five and must have lived for years with the anguish that he would be too old when the call came again. He had waited so long, and was in chiefly because Brendan Venter, the Free State centre, had suffered a serious ankle injury against New Zealand in Bloemfontein and missed the Test, and the rest of the season. There was still time, just, for the saturnine and talented Gerber to fulfil himself – and with any luck, to put a little more trade the way of 'Danie's Man About Town', a clothing concern advertised in the Test Match programme. 'Danie's washable leisure slacks are real comfort.'

Then Dr Craven stepped up for his say. When he spoke the tent fell silent. For other speakers, the buzz had remained. The players came out of their broad-shouldered huddles, even the media forsook the buffet tables. As he spoke in the marquee it was obvious that he still rolled some marbles. He was a short man, but had a presence, a jutting jaw, a mock-irascible delivery which could hold the attention. Craven was then eighty-two, and had been president of the SARB/SARFU since 1956. The term of presidency was to end only on his death, which came early in January 1993. There is surely no justification for one man holding such a post for so long. No one can retain freshness, no one should maintain that degree of absolutism. Even benevolent dictators eventually find themselves surrounded only by sycophants, and outside that inner circle, a void. Independent thought is lost.

He was the Albert Ferrasse of South African rugby. I can vividly remember attending a dinner with Ferrasse, then the long-reigning president of the French Rugby Federation, in Auch some seasons ago. A long line of flunkeys and hopefuls paid court to him all evening. They would approach him one by one, whisper something in his ear while he kept his head down and his eyes on his plate. There might be a curt nod, a curt shake of the head; then it was the next man's turn. It was a portrait of power, a portrait of a constitution in a shambles. It was a little revolting and fascinating. I have always disliked the inherent and gross weakness of the alternative to the autocratic style of rugby government – the over-use of the committee system which so paralyses the progress of rugby in the home nations, especially in Wales. That style is democracy paralysed by democracy. But even that is superior to the ways of the old absolute monarchs, Craven and Ferrasse, for all that their hearts were big, and correctly situated.

When Craven died, barely six months after we saw him at Loftus, his status as the most famous rugby administrator who ever lived was beyond question. At least you could say that for the rash of obsequious obituaries which appeared. He had also been a gen-uinely innovative rugby thinker. To his eternal credit, he was the one man I have come across who saw rugby as a science while recognising that heart and soul always come before science and techniques, even at Test level. He had been a great player, coach and selector, a formidable academic at his dearly beloved Stellen-bosch University, and had had a successful career in the Army PE wing.

In his later years he still had bursts of sharpness. Yet, as John Robbie wrote so tellingly of the obituaries of Craven: 'It's all rather sickening . . . Eulogy follows upon eulogy and the impression is given of a man who was universally loved, who was ahead of his time and who had no weaknesses or enemies . . . Now we know better. In the late days he had become a shadow. He was indecisive, suspicious, grumpy and . . . muddled.' Old men are allowed to be all of those, but hardly when still in the process of guiding a vast organisation through a political, social and sporting minefield, hardly when wielding the sort of power that Dr Craven still wielded, hardly when the stakes were so high.

Some of that muddle surfaced, almost hilariously, later in the tour. At a function at Newlands before the Test against Australia, he rose to the platform to address the throng, mostly people from the burgeoning media party. After a preamble, he set off. 'I would urge you not to have anything to do with women journalists,' he said, apropos of nothing. 'They cannot be trusted. We all know what they are after.' He ranted on in similar vein. The initial reaction of those present, women included, was to dissolve into fits of laughter.

Arrie Oberholzer, the SARFU's chief administrator, eventually snatched back the microphone. 'Some people say you are going senile,' said Arrie, to his credit. 'Perhaps they are right.' That night at dinner, with the brutality that only the press can muster, we dubbed him Doctor Gaga. We actually sat down and tried to select a whole team of leading rugby officials who had gone, er, a little wonky. We had two teams of gaga officials plus replacements and a referee before even the bread rolls arrived.

Later that year, Craven vetoed the appointment of a female fitness adviser for the Springboks' tours of France and England, on simple sexist grounds. Eugenie Shaw, formerly an athlete of repute, had trained up the Springboks for the home Tests. 'A woman has no place in the Springbok camp or in the camp of a rugby team,' said the good Doctor. He brought in Bokkie Blauw. Bokkie was from Stellenbosch. He was a man. Little did Craven know that in the Northern Hemisphere there is hardly a team nowadays that does not have female physios or other medical staff. It is now a major news item if a male physio runs out to attend to a player, with lots of haw-hawing when he squeezes the magic sponge down the front of someone's jockstrap. 'One of the last bastions of female domination fell today when attractive father of three Arthur Bloggs took the field at the Recreation Ground . . .'

When we stopped laughing at Craven's attack, we wondered if it were really possible to be a genuine liberal in the field of race and violently conservative in the field of sex.

At least Craven lived to see South Africans play rugby abroad. He was invited by the French Federation to Bordeaux for the match between French Espoirs and South Africa in October 1992. It kicked off their first tour on foreign soil for eighteen years. He still had the energy to perform a ceremonial kick-off. He had the energy to negotiate, the day after the match, a tortuous homeward journey which involved Bordeaux, Gatwick, Heathrow, Frankfurt, Johannesburg, Cape Town. He was not well enough to return to Europe for the Test against England at Twickenham and that homeward journey could not have helped. He did not ever leave his home territory again.

Ultimately, and putting down the sexist attack to his great age, his reputation as a liberal and reformer inside South African rugby rests on whether or not he made one notorious pronouncement. He is reputed to have said, in the 1970s, that 'a black will play for South Africa only over my dead body'. That statement haunted him. I have met people who insist that he did say it. I am more inclined to believe Craven's vehement denials. 'It was an utter fabrication by the dirty tricks department of the security services,' he once said. If he did indeed have an inbred aversion to a black filling the Springbok jersey, then most of his actions in the pariah period become a sham, undertaken purely to bring back rugby at any price, including the price of his own conscience.

If not, then history will justifiably see him as a brave and fighting liberal, a stroppy and contrary one, but still a liberal. A man who took on heavy and shadowy forces and fought rugby's corner. He attacked the South African Government's policies as early as 1969, when his union was still, almost certainly, dominated by members of the Broederbond. Later, he even engineered a ban on Broeder-bonders on the SARB executive. In 1978, he was the engineer of the first amalgamations, when the SARF and the SARA joined the white body.

In 1989, before semi-clandestine meetings with the African National Congress had become chic and scene-making for any businessman worried about his investment in post-apartheid South Africa, he went to Harare to discuss the future with ANC officials. He won their respect. He led the SARB delegation at unity talks. When he died, Steve Tshwete, the ANC's sports spokesman, generously called Craven 'a great visionary'. There were other tributes in similar vein, and play in a cricket Test between South Africa and India was interrupted for a minute's silence.

There is also the view that he kept in order the more extreme elements in South African rugby – extremists not in the political sense, but in the sense that they cared not a damn about the principles of the game and would gladly have ended South Africa's rugby isolation by paying up-front money to anyone they could find. That 'devil-you-know' view of Craven certainly has a validity. Ferrasse was alarmed at the void. 'I am afraid that South African rugby may never recover. Behind Danie there were a lot of ambitious people. He was the only one capable of taming them.'

Yet the impossible, contradictory Craven was never far below the surface. For example, if he was allowed to criticise his Government's policy and the apartheid and problems of his country, then he was damned if anyone else was so allowed. He would hardly hear a word against his country. You would think that if his liberalising drive was as powerful as he said, then he would welcome external opinion, world opinion, to help him in his quest.

No way. He once reacted angrily to a line of questioning from John Hopkins, the British journalist then of *The Sunday Times*. 'Look, you are not going to touch my country. It is the only one I know . . . and you are not going to do damage to my country. Don't look for stories in South Africa that you could find in England. You don't have to come to South Africa to find stinking ghettos. You don't have to come to South Africa to find riots. You've got them in your own country. Why pick on us?' Surely, no hard-line right-winger could better have put so mock-eloquently such a feeble and irrelevant apologia.

Craven also tried desperately to break the boycott. He was always blithely proclaiming that this country or that group or that scratch selection was about to tour. If I had a pound for every team that was supposed to make a triumphant visit to South Africa, but which never did, then I would be a rich man.

The point is that he allowed his desire for live rugby, for the smell of embrocation in South African nostrils, to blank out any other considerations. In London in 1986, he promised the International Rugby Board, which had heard rumours of the rebel tour by the New Zealand Cavaliers, that he would cancel it.

Only a few days later, he sat happily in the stand and applauded the Cavaliers, newly arrived in contravention of all the ethics of the sport. There were overwhelming indications that the Cavaliers were handsomely paid. Craven never visited London again.

The SARB and Craven promised that there would be no repeat. There was. The South Seas team, containing Fijians and Tongans among others, and again travelling without the permission of their home unions, arrived for a tour in 1988. Again, there was massive circumstantial evidence of illegal payments to the tourists. They even refused to come out for one of the tour matches till money due was actually handed over.

Even the centenary tour officially sanctioned by the IRB went spectacularly sour. The South African Rugby Board celebrated the landmark in 1990 and the IRB gave permission for them to invite top players from all member countries. Hardly any players accepted. The concept faced disaster. Then, suddenly, people in British rugby became aware that strangers were among them, bearing gifts. In about three days flat, hordes of players around the world suddenly became available. A short tour by a World XV took place – it was a scratch team, a weak team, but at least it was a team.

This time, the allegations of massive payments were even more widespread. This time, again, procedural etiquette went out of the window, especially in Wales, where the Welsh Rugby Union found itself completely undermined by people working behind its back to spirit Welsh players away to South Africa. It reflected appallingly badly on the SARB, on whoever had provided the money and the shadowy agents to buy in players; it reflected badly on the four Home Unions organisation, led by John Kendall-Carpenter, a former RFU president. It was that body which helped to undermine the Welsh Rugby Union. A Welsh Rugby Union inquiry into allegations of payments concluded that at least one player had earned £30,000 from the tour.

The abysmal lack of statesmanship in world rugby and the double standards of Craven were sharply revealed in these tours. The

IRB's founding ethic is to defend amateurism. They were desperately keen to do this when, for example, they landed from a great height on some unfortunate wretch who had once taken a few pence for a book and who was then found playing in some godforsaken charity match. They were not nearly so keen to act on widespread abuse of the ethic in the South African arena. All sorts of people solemnly and pompously devoted to amateurism suddenly sank their principles without trace when it came to dragging on the playing relationship with South Africa.

What swingeing action did the IRB take after receiving reports of the South Seas rebel tour, and this only a year after they had issued a final warning to South Africa over the Cavaliers tour and after Craven had given 'a solemn and irrevocable guarantee' that no such tour would happen again? They banned for life from the game Arthur Jennings, the Fijian-based manager of the tour party. As if Jennings could possibly have done it all off his own bat – the arrangements, fixtures, sponsors, travel, accommodation, marketing and promotion inside South Africa – without help and complicity from the SARB and other South Africans.

Craven certainly held principles and applied them to try to get South Africa re-accepted and, at least in sport, integrated. That was to his credit. Yet he never let those principles interfere with the prospect of a good game of rugby, either. I am prepared in many senses to go along with the gushers who found Craven a magnetic man. He was certainly, if you take the game out of its context, one of the greatest rugby men who ever lived. But like so many others, he refused to accept that you simply could not take rugby out of its context. Along the deep Craven furrow, the plough often seemed to meander infuriatingly off course.

Craven's speech ended in the marquee. The evening broke up – not, these days, for the players to group together and celebrate. There is a new severity of sacrifice in that, especially on tour, late-night revel after late-night revel is now regarded as mediaeval behaviour.

Yet there is also a new commercialism. There is no longer a single major Test team which does not, for the right rate and on a rota basis, farm itself out to a range of sponsors' functions, club dinners and company launches, and photo opportunities; not a team which does not add to the communal pot by flogging off its allocation of tickets. If your union believes to the contrary then I have to tell you that you are fooling yourself. All non-rugby related, of course.

The All Blacks are particularly clued up. On a recent tour to Ireland, they played in Galway and then, two by two, spread out to certain pubs in which a sponsor sold his product. They smoothly rolled up, sunk one or two, pressed the flesh and smoothed out. On that trip, they failed to show for a major dinner for which places were laid, food lovingly prepared by the womenfolk of a club, a warm welcome guaranteed – what was not guaranteed, however, were the readies.

On the drive out of Pretoria, we became hopelessly lost. Colin
Elsey, the most famous British rugby photographer, sat in the back
and began to bark a stream of directions. Big C is a familiar figure.
He has stood, walrus-moustached and immovable, in front of most
of you on the touchline of the major rugby grounds of Great Britain
and the world. He took the Fran Cotton 'mudman' picture, surely
the most famous snap ever snapped in the sport.

He also has difficulty finding his way out of a phone box. A few
days after the Lost in Pretoria experience, he navigated a media car
on the drive out to Potchefstroom for a match. Easy, he said,
turning away offers of a map. One hour later, driving straight
through the middle of Soweto, way off the route, approached by
massed ranks of the beady-eyed at traffic lights, and having
unwittingly taken part in a black demonstration outside a Soweto
hospital, Big C was forced to admit that the map might not have
been such a bad idea after all.

In Pretoria, we played a hunch. We turned in the opposite
direction to the way Elsey suggested. If he said left, we turned right,
to his exasperation. And vice versa. It worked a treat. In that
fashion, Elsey negotiated by default the unfamiliar darkened
streets of Pretoria's suburbs and we drove back, in a violet sunset of
indescribable beauty, to Johannesburg.

# CHAPTER 7

# *Anthem for Doomed Louis*

## THE DRAMATIC TESTS OF ELLIS PARK AND NEWLANDS

Dear old Auntie. You cannot, in my experience, remain abroad for any period of time without developing a new fondness and even a fervent admiration bordering on lust for that maligned institution, the British Broadcasting Corporation. It is only when you are deprived of the good old Beeb that you realise how well they toil on our behalf compared to the television stations of other countries. A few weeks in South Africa was a case in point.

Romanian TV did have an inbuilt disadvantage when it came to scheduling in that every programme had to celebrate the glorious achievements of the Great Facilitator and Enormous Nutcase, Nicholae Ceaucescu. The service improved no end after Nicholae was shot. 'We now have an English classic serial direct from the BBC,' a Romanian lady told me in Bucharest on a recent trip. 'It is called *The Life and Progress of the Dynasty Howard.*' After about twenty blank seconds, dredging my memory of English lectures for a sympathetic echo of this English classic, I realised that she was glued to *Howard's Way*, the dreadful seafaring soap.

Nor will you be uplifted in the spirit by television on any tour of Australia. Unless you find an endless procession of harness racing and up-and-down rugby league particularly cerebral and unless you share the misconception of Australian current affairs producers, and indeed, Australians in general, that anyone in the outside world cares what they think.

Australian TV reached a new literary peak in 1989 when the British Lions were in the country. There was a slot on one of the stations every Saturday mid-morning when they showcased semi-naked women's mud-wrestling, mixed in with nude tug-of-war. Strangely, the public rooms of the hotels always seemed to be hack-free when the wrestling was on. Probably researching in their rooms, I expect.

The Barcelona Olympics ran concurrently with New Zealand's rugby tour of South Africa. The South African Olympic team's return to the Games was supported fervently by all sections of the community and indeed, when the team paraded at the start it brought tears to the eyes of many people. Anyone still dry-eyed was soon blubbing when they experienced SABC's coverage. It was abysmal. The highlights came on South Africa's day of days: when South Africa's darling, Elana Meyer, was to run in the women's 10,000 metres, for which she was favourite. Meyer, a squeaky-voiced running automaton, shouldered the hopes of so many South Africans because, apart from the fact that they were actually there and competing, the Games for South Africa had been a disaster.

The drum-beating and publicity and Meyer's squeaking had so turned off the British rugby writers gathered in a Johannesburg hotel room that we were fervently praying for Liz McColgan, another major contender. That is another incontrovertible rule of touring: you want the host country's athletes to lose in any sport at any time. Meyer and our Liz had conducted a fairly terse battle of words in the press.

The programme came on air. 'My heart has been beating since early this morning,' said the anchorman, which was hardly a first. They wavered through a tortured build-up. The kick-off approached. 'Elana, South Africa is with you. And now we go over to our Canadian commentators for the big race.'

It was true. SABC had obviously not shelled out on commentators; they were taking sound from elsewhere. A couple of unknown and unnamed Canadians began to blabber over pictures of the race and off the runners went. Suddenly, SABC went to an advertisement break.

'How can they do that? It's the big moment for the whole country and they've gone to a bloody break.'

Cringingly, they broke for ads time after time. A few laps of darling Lizzie, tracked by baddie Elana, and off they would go for ads. Suddenly, after one break, they lost the Canadians. Completely unheralded and unannounced, we suddenly heard the familiar and even nostalgic voices of Coleman and Brendan Foster, and the professionalism of David Coleman threw the whole thing into sharp relief. Suddenly, between ad breaks, we saw that Liz was struggling.

'——— it. That bloody Springbok is going to win.'

'Turn if off. Let's go for a beer.'

'Hang on a minute. Who's that black girl? She's going well.'

We switched allegiance from Scotland to Ethiopia. Derartu Tulu, a frail youngster, swept past Meyer and on to a glorious victory. Afterwards, Meyer caught up with Tulu on the lap of honour. The white South African and the black African, according to the papers next day, had made a lap of honour of powerful symbolism. It seemed to me, especially from Tulu's reluctant body language, that Meyer had simply hijacked Tulu's big moment and Tulu's right to run around on her own. At least they didn't go to a break in the last lap of the race, or when Elana was on the podium for her richly deserved mdeal. Ah! dear old Auntie, back in dear old Britain. Good old Colemanballs.

The live rugby was shown, not on the national station but on M-Net, a satellite station. They obviously knew their rugby and their commentators. No Canadians for them. They brought down, from Hawick, only the voice of the sport. Bill McLaren is such a homely home-lover that he is an incongruous sight in foreign countries, South Africa, New Zealand, England and the like. He looks somehow out of habitat, a bit like a Scottish flanker on his own side of the offside line.

But if you want professionalism and one of the nicest men on the circuit, then you call for Bill. I was in on an Ian Robertson prank played on McLaren during the World Sevens at Murrayfield. Robertson, seated alongside McLaren in the BBC commentary box, was talking live to the studio about prospects for the event while a minor group match took place for which McLaren was not providing live commentary. Suddenly, one of the unknown Latvians broke away on a long run.

Robertson broke off his interview. 'I see that Latvia are on their way to score and I'm sure Bill McLaren can tell you all about it,' says Robertson. If he expected a shuffling of notes, some coughing and a few seconds of embarrassed silence he was disappointed. McLaren glided off into commentary like a Rolls-Royce. 'Thank you Ian,' he said, taking the surprise cue instantaneously. 'And this is Silovs, the twenty-four-year-old from Riga, six foot two and all fifteen stones of him; a bank official in Riga. He scored three tries in the qualifying round against Russia; and his dad, Vladimir, who also played six times for Latvia and scored three tries and a dropped goal, will be delighted with that.' Astonishing.

There was Bill on the South African touchlines at training, grappling with the Afrikaner names, not to mention the Afrikaner nicknames. It always seems to me that the Afrikaner never has enough Christian names to go round. Everyone has a nickname and that, essentially, becomes the official Christian name. For example, no one actually calls Ian Hattingh, the Central Unions flanker, plain old Ian. Oshkosh Hattingh – now we all know who they mean. Bill managed to keep a straight face when negotiating Cheese van Tonder of the Free State, and never even batted an eyelid during the front-row collision in the main warm-up match for the Ellis Park Test, when Bongo van der Merwe packed down against Wimpie Otto.

The All Blacks drove to Witbank, 100 kilometres from Johannesburg, for their next match, a flag-waving exercise against the Central Unions selection in Witbank. The need to crush the two tours into a short period meant that the game took place on a Monday, just two days after the Pretoria match against the Junior Springboks. They drove down from Pretoria on a cold, dazzlingly clear and sunny day, typical of high veld weather, and people sat in masses munching the traditional rugby stadium snacks, *biltong* (tastes like rotting old bootlaces) and *boerewors* (decayed gerbils).

The gap in class between the teams was massive. The Central Unions had the usual porky props and talent-free backs of South African junior provincial outfits. Yet the final score was only 39-6. There were two tries from Terry Wright, the slightly built wing who was out of the first string. There was high promise from Marc Ellis, the young Otago centre, and from Matthew Cooper, the Waikato full-back. The final result was strange because the score was 22-0 at half-time and, given the supreme ruthlessness of the All Black nature, those who had sixty points and more in the sweep seemed handily placed.

The penny dropped quickly. Under the old laws which gave scrum possession to the team driving forward, teams with the superior driving pack could really drive the legs from under the lesser, less fit and less durable pack. Yet the Central Unions did not have to drain themselves – they could stand off and have a blow now and again, could even tackle the odd All Black back if they had a mind. Andre van Wyk and his Central men had cause to thank the law-meddlers for their free pass from oblivion in Witbank.

Still, who cared about that technical stuff when Campo was in town. The Australian touring party were in the country, were acclimatising and, as usual, their public relations machine was whirring nicely. They even tour these days with their own PR director in Greg Campbell, formerly a rugby writer with *The Australian* newspaper.

The Australians were due to start with a match against Western Transvaal at Potchefstroom, 120 kilometres from Johannesburg. Campo was already in full voice. Wherever he went that season he lambasted everything in his path. The Irish were still living in the past; the English were boring; the All Blacks likewise. As soon as he landed in South Africa, he was calling South Africans 'arrogant'. And why was he in South Africa at all? 'We are the world champions. Why should it be us who have to travel? The Springboks should have come to Australia.' Naas Botha, he added, had never tackled so much as a hot lunch.

The South Africans soon got their own back. Rugby marketing is now at a different level. In Australia, they have massive posters of lions sinking their bloodied fangs into a ball to promote British tours; in Wales last season, the TV showed a sequence of Jon Webb blunders to whip up fervour before the match against England. In South Africa, they produced a poster ostensibly of a wallaby skin stretched out to dry between six pegs. On the skin was the number 14, Campese's number.

Yet, as usual, Campese got clean away with all his fulminating. How can you bite back at him? Potchefstroom, the first point of contact with real South Africans, is redneck country. Would the rednecks grow restive about Campese's 'arrogance' jibes, which were stratospherically widely reported? Would he need an escort? The great man was besieged, all right. He was borne around the giant Olenpark stadium before and after the match like visiting royalty, obviously a hero to every white, red and black-necked person in the vicinity. How does he do it?

The Australians won 46–13, even though they had not accustomed to the altitude, to the extra glare and the extra bounce. Terence Stewart did manage a try for Western Transvaal but there were six tries for the Wallabies, and even if the fatso props took advantage of the new laws to tackle His Eminence Campese on occasions, it was a satisfactory run-out in every way. Warwick Waugh, Andrew Blades, Tim Gavin (two), David Wilson and Garrick Morgan were the try-scorers.

The Australian forwards were mostly second-stringers. They were massive and gleaming. Waugh and Morgan were two battle-ship-sized locks; Blades and Matt Ryan two huge props. Later events were to prove that it was the weakness of the home teams which caused us to overrate the young Wallabies, because on the evidence of the later tour to Wales and Ireland, some of the gleam was false, and wore off under pressure. But still, not bad for reserves.

And after the game, as the short dusk of South Africa fell, all the party, even those who had played that day, were out training, urged along by Bob Dwyer, Bob Templeton and the others.

The contrast in the PR operations between the All Blacks and the Wallabies was evident up-country. The mayor of Witbank hosted a magnificent reception in the Town Hall after the Central Districts match. Witbank, like the rest of South Africa, had waited a long time for a live glimpse of the rugby heroes of the world outside. The mayor gave a short speech and announced the vast buffet open to the vast throng. Yet as soon as he had finished speaking the All Black duty boys were moving urgently among their men, tugging at sleeves. They craved their own *laager*, the privacy of their own coach back to Johannesburg. Off they went, leaving behind enough to feed a whole army of humanity, or at least ten of the media convoy.

When the Wallabies filed into their post-match reception in Pootchefstroom, they were taken aback. 'We were told it was a quick buffet-style thing and we were expected to stay for half an hour,' said Greg Campbell. 'Then we found it was a formal sit-down function, speeches and everything.' Even worse, there was every rugby team's nightmare: the Wallabies were not seated together, but were spaced out around the hall, among the old contemptibles telling tall tales of sepia-edged tries. They blinked, spaced them-selves out, stayed the whole night and gave an outstanding impression.

I caught up with Nick Farr-Jones as the Wallabies prepared for their match against the Blue Bulls of Northern Transvaal on the following Friday. He was approaching what he saw as his final frontier, the Test at Newlands in just over a week's time. As ever, he was patient, clever, sharply focused. Even off duty in his Levis, there was always an aura of authority and leadership about Australia's captain. 'If we win the Test match I would probably give it away, pack my bags and retire gracefully. It is not really another stage on from the World Cup. We won that and we will still be world champions for four years whether or not we beat South Africa. But it would be nice to beat them. If we did lose, I might keep on playing until the Springboks come to us next year [1993].'

I did not test him by asking why it should be that a brilliant player, the engine of the whole Australian rugby operation, a man who stood squarely in the ranks of the great rugby statesmen, and who was having the time of his life, should wish to chuck it all over the fence when still at his peak. I assumed that it was just part of the general and unnecessary tizz into which players descend as they approach their thirties and become obsessed with the notion that they are about to fall apart as players and men. I sensed enough doubt in him to dream of a comeback – and Farr-Jones duly reappeared for the Bledisloe Cup and the South African Tests in Australia, and played beautifully.

Australia lightly barbecued the Blue Bulls at Loftus Versveld, a match dragged forwards to Friday to allow space for the mega-match, the South Africa-New Zealand Test at Ellis Park. Australia won a poorish match by 24-17, helped by two tries from Campese. Gerbrand Grobler, the fierce Northerns full-back, and Jacques Olivier, the left-wing, were the most impressive of a meaty and ponderous Bull bunch. Hannes Strydom scored their try. Farr-Jones barked and burrowed his way along and the Wallabies were working up nicely. Then even the world champions were relegated to the sideshows.

The South Africans had trained during the week at the Rand Afrikaans University in Johannesburg, and for many people watching, it was their first contact with live Springboks in the flesh. The pack were squat, looked a little small and slow. Adolf Malan was the tallest; he would lock the scrum alongside Adri Geldenhuys, who too often, we were told, made up for what he lacked in height with flashes of temper. Uli Schmidt, by the testimony of all of South Africa the greatest hooker in the world, was in the front row between Heinrich Rodgers and Lood Muller. Wahl Bartmann, the old fox flanker, Ian MacDonald, the tall open-side, and Jannie Breedt were the back row.

Naas Botha and the tall Robert du Preez ('the new Terry Holmes', said his publicity. Holmesy, sue immediately) were at half-back, Gerber and Pieter Muller in the centre. James Small and Pieter Hendriks were on the wing with Theo van Rensburg at full-back. Eight of the team had never played a Test match, not even the scrappy affairs against scrappy teams which the deprived South Africans were forced to call Tests for so long.

The training was old-fashioned, antiquated even. The major gesture to what was perceived as the modern era came in the team warm-up. Eugenie Shaw, formerly an international hurdler, conducted an aerobics routine armed with a ghetto-blaster. The sight of grown young men cavorting like Gay Gordon himself at the beck and call of a mere woman was too much for Dr Craven, who banned

Eugenie from the South African tour in Europe later in the year on the grounds that she was a woman.

John Williams, the coach, and Abie Malan, the team manager, hovered uncertainly as the gigantic media scrum hovered uncertainly. Williams angrily remonstrated with a photographer who had come a little too close as he took the session. He was asked afterwards why he had made such a fuss. 'If anyone is obstructing me or preventing me doing my job, I'll settle it there and then,' he barked. This is an era of mass photographic intrusions. Big John was lucky there were none in his shower when he went back to his hotel.

The match loomed as an occasion of massive significance. I have never reported a game in which the stakes, the significarce (playing, political, sociological) were so high, or at which the sense of occasion was so overwhelming. 'It is the magic moment,' said Jannie Breedt. Donald Woods, the former fugitive dissident newspaper editor, had a wide beam on his face. He was a rugby-lover from way back. 'It will be a great day, a great day,' he said. 'It is almost eighteen years since I last saw the Springboks play a Test match.'

I have never reported a game in so massive a stadium, either. Ellis Park is a towering, intimidating bowl, home to Transvaal rugby and to the Moroka Swallows soccer team. On the day of the match we bade a fond farewell to the *Daily Mail*'s Peter Jackson when he discovered that his press ticket was for the top level of the stadium, not for the normal press benches halfway up. He disappeared into the lift to ascend to his rightful perch. About two minutes later, the lift door opened again. Jackson was still in the lift, green-faced and reeling against the back wall. The top press box, we gleaned as we sat him down and fanned him with towels, hangs out from under the roof of the monolith, and you watch the distant dots below through your feet. 'There is no way I am going back up there,' said the poor man weakly. That was the scale of Ellis Park.

There was another nice touch: Ellis Park, like many sports stadia in the country, can supply (for a charge) a small receiver and set of headphones through which you can hear the official – referee, umpire – talking to the players. It provided a fascinating insight into decisions. It is something which some enterprising businessmen in Britain should emulate immediately. Generally, the referees I have asked love the concept.

There was one figure whom neither tour party had encountered as yet. The president of the Transvaal RFU is Louis Luyt, the powerful and deeply controversial businessman who tries to put his imprint on everything in South African rugby. His business career has been every bit as controversial as his sporting career, and as far as his political inclinations go, it is unlikely that you will find Luyt ladling out succour in the soup kitchens of the townships. So there was endless fascination. How strong would the Springboks be and how fierce their approach? How would the followers react? And above all, how would the match sit as a pointer to the processes of emancipation? Would there be obvious bitterness, now that the wilderness years were over; or would there be relief, evidence of whites and blacks in the country forgiving and forgetting, and of whites welcoming non-whites into their rugby temple, into their sport? How would Louis behave?

The stirring of trouble began in the days before the game. The SARFU and the ANC had put their heads together well before the tours and set a price for the ANC's green light and support of rugby contacts. At the Tests, the South African flag was not to be officially flown, 'Die Stem', the national anthem (if only to the white minority) was not to be sung; there was to be a minute's silence at the Tests for 'all victims of violence in the country'. There was to be a message in the programme expressing the SARFU's support for peace and democracy in South Africa.

As outsiders we had no way of knowing as yet how South Africa's white rugby followers would see it all. But we soon found out. Conservative leaders all over the country angrily denounced what they saw as the insult to their right to bellow the anthem and wave the flag. All week long, there were unctuous appeals for the followers who had tickets to bring along the flag and to sing the anthem unofficially, if the band were not going to lead an official rendition. It seemed appallingly insensitive at a time when everyone in South African rugby, players and officials and followers, was on trial in so many senses and when the world would be watching.

On the drive to Ellis Park from Sandton, we must have passed fifty groups of people furiously waving flags, furiously flogging flags. We parked in one of the new phenomena of the country – an area inhabited by deprived whites. We were told not to return to the car unless in groups. And, walking to the stadium, we passed others begging everyone to sing their lungs out for the old (white) country.

When we took our seats the crackle of static electricity around the whole occasion made hairs prickle and skin crawl. Then, as packed tier upon tier of Ellis Park sat ready to grin and cackle at the show, Naas Botha led the Springboks on to Ellis Park in a fury of noise and anticipation. There had been some flag-waving, though no concerted demo. There was a good deal of ad hoc singing of 'Die Stem' in pockets of the crowd although nothing too loud. But when the minute's silence for the victims of violence was announced, the ad hoc songsters sang on. It was an ugly moment.

Then the teams lined up and after playing the good-natured old dirge 'God Defend New Zealand', the band struck up a tune which was unfamiliar to me. But not to any South African. It was 'Die Stem', played officially by the band, sung officially by the team in full-throated roar, sung uproariously all around the stadium. In front of me and a little below, on the camera platform, were perched the main cameras of SABC's operation. The cameramen were holding the cameras with one hand and with the other, to a man, they were conducting gleefully.

'What happened? They weren't supposed to play that,' said pressmen of all nationalities. What had happened, we found out only later, was that Luyt had simply ordered the band to play 'Die

Stem'. Up in his hospitality box, Louis sang on lustily – accompanied by the sound and the splat of something very nasty indeed hitting the fan.

For the moment, there were other matters to consider. The rugby contest was thunderous. It was flawed and loose but still titanic. New Zealand won 27-24 and there were vapour trails hanging over the stadium at the end.

South Africa might even have won. They came close and had to suffer along with James Small, the over-stressed and rather ham-fisted wing, who dropped the ball when completely free and clear in the second half. Yet the match was nothing remotely as close as the result suggested. Towards the end, when they trailed 10-27, South Africa began to spin the ball in desperation. Botha started flinging out long passes to his midfield and, surprisingly, they temporarily flummoxed Walter Little and Frank Bunce in the New Zealand midfield. Perhaps it was the shock factor of Botha passing the ball instead of hoofing it into the middle of next week.

In the late rush when the Springboks were carving out some splendid moves, Muller scored after a blatant knock-on by du Preez had gone undetected by Sandy MacNeill, the referee, and then Gerber scored deep into injury time, finishing off a superb attack with a slashing burst down the right. Danie still had a little under the bonnet. Botha kicked both goals to bring his team to within a point.

The All Blacks had asserted themselves powerfully. Little and Bunce hammered hard through the midfield after a line-out and when the Springbok centres came up offside to try to snuff out the next phases of the move, Brooke grabbed the ball, took a little tap penalty to himself and hurtled on to score. Bunce and Timu also scored later in the match, Fox kicked twelve points and, if one Test match can be a series, which it really can't, then New Zealand had won their first-ever series victory in the country. As far as the match as a sporting event was concerned, honour was satisfied and South Africa could talk with excitement about building on this victory. For me, not the least astonishing aspect on an astonishing day was that this first-up effort by the Springboks remained their best perfor-mance for many months. They played more sustained and more mobile rugby on this first venture than they were playing months later. So much for improving with every game.

When the teams left the field, the remainder of the twin-tour programme, including the Newlands Test against Australia, not to mention South Africa's impending tour to France and England, was already in the melting pot. Steve Tshwete of the ANC, who had so much been looking forward to the day, was furious. 'Verwoerd will not be allowed to rule this nation from his grave,' he said. Tshwete knew as well as anyone that the playing of the anthem, token gesture though it was, would simply drag the rug from under his feet, and let loose the hawks in the ANC.

Luyt eventually tried to justify his actions. 'Just as the ANC are free to play their own anthem, sings their own songs and hoist their own flags, so they should allow others to do the same.' It was, in any broad context, drivel, and insensitive drivel at that.

For a start, it was a rather cowardly scrapping of a solemn agreement. It completely ignored the raised sensibilities of all parties in South African sport and all non-white South Africans just when rugby had a glorious chance to acknowledge those sensibilities. Luyt ignored the weight of world opinion – even during the Olympic Games the spotlight was on the Test and the day. The world was watching Ellis Park to see if times had changed. Above all, it provided, in one afternoon, in one song, clear evidence that whatever movement South African rugby in general had made towards liberalisation, it must simply have been for the sake of returning to the rugby fold, simply cosmetic, and that they were prepared to go not one inch further in substance than it took to get the world to come to them.

The white temple of Ellis Park, ringing out with the verses of the national anthem, a ditty regarded in every note by the non-white population as a symbol of white supremacy, stood as a monument to a past that was still the present. Among the dignitaries present at the match had been President De Klerk and Chief Mangosuthu Buthelezi of Inkatha. Had they stood and sung along? They refused to say.

The ANC declared that they would meet as a matter of urgency to discuss the whole affair, the reneging on the agreement by SARFU and their appointed agents, and especially, the appalling attitude of Louis Luyt. The New Zealanders departed for home (though not without a last-night celebratory party which ended in a ferocious and snarling set-to between Jamie Joseph and Andy Earl, a shirt-ripping ritual gone mad).

The Australians moved on to Port Elizabeth, a resort obviously fallen on tough economic times, for the match against Eastern Province, but for forty-eight hours after Ellis Park it seemed that the game would never take place. The Australians were outstanding in the crisis. 'If the ANC, say, withdraw their support we will understand and we will by flying straight home,' said Joe French, president of the ARU. Indeed, it was neither the South African Government nor the SARFU which was primarily involved with saving the tour and healing the new wounds. It was the ANC, the Australian ambassador and the Australian team management, working together.

The ANC, quite obviously enjoying their status, enjoying the undeniable hold they now had on the aspirations of South African rugby and the right to continue the comeback, hummed and hawed and dragged out the process. For much of the time, the Australians sat in their hotel with all their cases packed. They took time off to visit the Zwide township, where they delighted hordes of youngsters with some training drills, a few happy photo opportunities. They saw the Dan Qeqe stadium, a facility essentially built by people from the township and all the more revered and maintained for that.

Eventually, the ANC decided to allow the tour to proceed, or at least, not to withdraw their support, which amounted to the same thing. They paid tribute to the statesmanship of French and the Australians and indeed, the maturity of Farr-Jones and his team was a treasure. The ANC issued a press release in which they stated firmly that the authorities and the crowd at Newlands, the venue for the forthcoming Test, held the immediate future of South African rugby in their hands and vocal chords. 'They can make rugby a reconciler of people or they can use it as a ritual that celebrates conquest and domination of black people.'

They said that they had been impressed by the sincerity of most officials of the SARFU, by the number of calls they had received from white followers expressing dismay at what the ANC called the 'barbarism of the events of Ellis Park'. They also attacked Luyt: 'He will have to live with the consequences of his actions.'

The shopping list for Newlands was set out. There should be a statement in the programme expressing the SARFU's support for peace and democracy. There were to be no official flags, no official anthems and there should be a minute of silence for victims of violence. All in all, it was a moderate statement. Yet among us outsiders, given what we had seen and heard at Ellis Park, there seemed the chance that the statement would focus opposition; that once again we would hear the strains of 'Die Stem'. 'If spectators go to the Test not to watch rugby but to challenge the new South Africa, the ANC will oppose all future tours to and from South Africa, including the 1995 World Cup.' The stakes were as high as that.

Yet there was a different atmosphere in Port Elizabeth and around the Cape. When you leave the plane from Johannesburg and the thin air, and emerge at sea-level, the air tastes of champagne. The oppressiveness of Johannesburg, where parts of the city centre were no-go and dangerous, was left behind. On the Cape, too, there is a liberalism in the air, in life and sport. Rugby is a bigger game to non-whites there than it is in Johannesburg and Pretoria (although whether South African rugby in the high veld deserves anything else is open to massive doubt). There were even non-whites at the Boet Erasmus stadium who had come to watch the game rather than simply to serve the cold cans.

The Australian win was routine. They won 34-8 with tries from Peter Slattery, Darren Junee, Paul Kahl and Tony Herbert. Eastern Province, sinking in Currie Cup ranks a little, fielded two players with renewed Springbok aspirations – Michael du Plessis, the centre who did not shine even against the second-string Australian centres, Tombs and Herbert; and the captain, Frans Erasmus, a bearded porker and a throwback to the days when props were never expected to soil their hands with the leather of the rugby ball. Frans was a fiery leader and in any Harry Secombe lookalike contest would have been a bigger contender than Harry. Eastern Province

also fielded the only non-white player either Australia or New
Zealand met, Christie Noble of the PE Harlequins.

That night, five of the media from Britain were invited to a
meeting of an organisation called the Eastern Cape Veteran
Players' Association. We were met in the town centre and driven out
through the suburbs into the townships beyond. The association
comprised former players from the ranks of SARU, the old black
rugby organisation which had been absorbed on amalgamation. We
were taken out to a darkened township and a battered school where
the veterans had gathered. A few onlookers were deputed to look
after our hire cars.

There, in the classroom, sat rugby men of all ages, including sixty-
year-olds who had played for the SARU representative decades
before. Some of them brought faded cuttings and even faded
framed photographs, obviously family icons. The only team which
SARU were ever allowed to play, since they had neither the
authority nor the money to travel abroad, was the SARF, the
Federation team which contained coloured players. We knew
immediately that we were in a gathering of rugby-lovers, and we
knew immediately that we were privileged.

Malcolm Klassen, the convener, explained why the association
had been set up. It was to try to rescue rugby in the townships
around Port Elizabeth (the association later expanded to include
most of the Eastern and Western Cape). Since amalgamation,
township rugby in the areas had suffered badly. The Eastern
Province Union's various policies had positively harmed the non-
white game, caused it to diminish and wither; caused amalgamation
of clubs and therefore a reduction of facilities. The veterans had
approached the EPRU to seek their approval of their activities.
'Within two minutes, we were told that we should disband our
association,' said Klassen. 'We were not even given a hearing.'
Klassen was a driven man, a rugby-lover and politically a radical. He
and his colleagues hoped to re-fire rugby in the school and clubs.

They were not dismissive of all the efforts of the white-dominated
union. Eastern Province had employed a development officer for
that season, none other than Lyn Mustoe, then the Pontypool prop.
Kenny, one of the association, said: 'Lyn is a nice bloke but what
does he know about the townships, the way people think round
here? In the townships it is not so much the famous players like
Campese who are the heroes, even though the kids love them. The
real heroes are the sportsmen of the area themselves, the people
whom all the youngsters look up to. It is to them that the
encouragement and the funding should be directed. Our members
have instant credibility, they can go into any school never mind their
political affiliation.'

They, and many non-white rugby men we met, were powerfully
dismissive of the amalgamation itself. It was transparently obvious
that it was an amalgamation of officialdom and of convenience. As a
root-and-branch coming together, it did not exist. The veterans
were scathing about the role of Ebrahim Patel, formerly president

of SARU and by then the joint vice-president of the SARFU. They were certainly suspicious of other officials of the former SARU. 'There is no point in handing funds out to some of them. Those funds will simply disappear,' said the vets with feeling.

Some of us joined Malcolm, Kenny and Bomza Nkohla for a drink. Bomza, barrel-chested and completely bald, was a heroic number 8, at his peak in the 1970s. 'Danie Craven came and asked me to play against England in one of the matches in 1972,' he said. 'I was offered money by others to play. How could I? How could I look my people in the eye if I took part?'

Both Bomza and Kenny mocked Malcolm Klassen's stances and voluble energy. 'He never shuts up,' said Kenny, gesticulating in Malcolm's direction. Malcolm was a critic of President De Klerk. The others were fans. 'At least he started the process and stood up to the right wing,' said Kenny.

Later in the week, the three wound up their old car and drove the vast distance to Cape Town to watch the Newlands Test. They linked up with a touring group of supporters from Sport Abroad, the firm run by Mike Roberts, the former Welsh lock. On the Friday before the Test they played for Sport Abroad's ad hoc team against a local selection, and afterwards, both the visiting Brits and the home black fanatics brought tears to each others' eyes with their own rugby songs. 'I've never had such a day,' said Bomza afterwards.

On the Sunday morning after the Test match, Kenny, Malcolm and Bomza came to the hotel where the Australian team and the media were staying to say farewell. They arrived at seven in the morning, and this after everyone had put in a hard night's celebrating. Kenny rang my room at what felt like pre-dawn. 'For Christ's sake, Kenny, buzz off,' I said. 'I'm all for the progress of non-white rugby but not at this time in the morning.' We had a quiet breakfast and eventually they all went chugging off along the Cape to Port Elizabeth.

They had provided valuable evidence on two counts. First, that the theory that non-whites in South Africa are not keen on rugby, are not part of the family, is complete, utter and dangerous balderdash and is offered simply as an excuse not to set up development programmes in the non-white areas. Here were men infected with the game to the same, terminal degree as anyone else in the world. Secondly, they showed that hardly anyone in white South African rugby apparently felt the need to reap that fascination, and to at least make up in some ways for the years of total neglect. Here was a way in which rugby, the Great Satan in so many black hearts, a status reinforced by 'Die Stem' and Ellis Park, could mediate, show willing and could bring the races together a little.

It was increasingly obvious that rugby was not taking that chance. That week we also met Ngcondi Balflour, appointed recently as the SARFU's director of development. Balflour, previously a prisoner of the white-dominated Government, had almost resigned on the day he started, such had been, so he said, the lacks of funds and

programmes and intent. He did not exactly pull his punches. 'The
attitude of white South Africans is too much to bear. The Springbok
emblem embodies everything I hate. They are only interested in
their history, not their future.' No prizes for diplomacy. Months
and months later, the SARFU announced that they were going to
plough millions of rand into the development of non-white rugby.
Welcome, but belated. Did they really need the nudge of Balflour,
of the likes of Malcolm and Kenny and Bomza, the bad publicity of
Ellis Park, before they started?

Cape Town is a glorious city, bordered on one side by beaches and
the Atlantic, and on another by the towering, awesome Table
Mountain. You could feel relatively comfortable in the city, even
after dark, although terrorism and death came to the city when a
church congregation was attacked in July 1993.

The Australians decided to play David Wilson on their flank and
not to draft Troy Coker. Otherwise, their team bore a familiar look.
South Africa eventually retained the same team. On the day before
the match the Springboks wound themselves up for a publicity
stunt. Amazingly to me, they had never before ventured into a
township to train or press the flesh. Some had conducted clinics but
any attempt to use their massive profiles to show willingness for the
unification of their country, or to help raise grass-roots funding,
had been non-existent. Solemnly, Abie Malan announced that the
Springboks would train at Lagunya Rugby Club in nearby Nyanga
township. A vast media army gathered and travelled in convoy with
the tracksuited Springboks, out of Cape Town down the airport
road.

It was planet to planet inside a few minutes. One minute we were
passing affluent suburbs, the next we crossed a motorway exit and
around the corner we were driving through unnamed roads in the
criss-crossing block system of a township. Caspirs, the huge police
vehicles, rumbled to and fro. We lost the convoy at one stage and
were left lost in the middle of the township. We had no way of
knowing how friendly the locals were and we nervously began to
finger the laminated cards which identified us as members of Her
Majesty's press. We drove through desperate areas where people
huddled under corrugated sheeting. Eventually we found the
pitch, and the team and the media army tumbled off.

It was a remarkable occasion. A large crowd of residents cheered
when Botha and his team disembarked and Naas and others had a
few photographs taken with them. Of course it was staged, but no
more so than any politician's baby-kissing stunt. Morné du Plessis,
the former Springbok captain and a firm ally of the non-white
sportsmen, was angry that the police presence was so marked, but
many of them, armed or not, simply wanted to watch the training.

A large group of schoolchildren arrived, shy and nervous, and
sang a moving song of welcome. A tall, elegant Jean Brodie of a
schoolmistress hectored them along and it was transparently
obvious that here was a community heroine, a woman who had

battled proudly through privations and lack of funding. Here, too, were some of the depths of human forgiveness. For God's sake, they were all citizens of the same country but here they were meeting as aliens, strangers; as people from either side of a great divide. It was a warming occasion but the perfect, upsetting demonstration of the awesome malevolent power of apartheid. The coaches and hire cars revved up, the Springboks and the media reboarded in a cloud of dust, and we returned to sumptuous hotels on the other planet across the road.

The teams withdrew, if only a little, from the political spotlight and returned to the build-up for a Test rugby match. The day before the match three of us drove out of Cape Town for the Cape of Good Hope itself, the southernmost point of the country and the continent. So much had happened that there was the subconscious need to gain perspective by distance.

My companions were Chris Jones, of the London *Standard*, and Nick Cain, then editor of *Rugby World & Post*. Neither was having all his expenses covered by his organisation. There was simply too much rugby happening in too many countries worldwide for the accountants to agree to every trip. Indeed, both were touring at a financial loss. 'We just had to be here,' they said, frequently. It was the basic instinct of a journalist to be on the scene for the story, or at least for the background to future stories, to greater under-standings.

We drove out past Sea Point, along a coastal route of glamorous houses and countryside, and eventually past Hout Bay, cutting between spectacular cliffs and beaches, and into the Cape of Good Hope nature reserve. For the final leg you park next to the souvenir hut and a roaring old bus stuck in first gear, called *Flying Dutchman*, takes you up a steep hill for a few hundred yards. You step out, negotiate more steep steps and, suddenly, you are on the promontory overlooking the ocean below.

From the look-out point you can see a few rocks below marking the end of the continent. Most people believe that the oceans meet at that point. In fact, the Indian and the Atlantic meet further east. But let's not let the facts get in the way. It was a calm day, no problem for seafarers out on the sea, although we had passed the odd rusting hulk along the coast. There were sudden mists, and the odd baboon. We looked north, back towards Cape Town, imagining from the solitude of our vantage-point the anguish and turmoil in the country we were visiting, not only then but throughout history; and not only in South Africa, but in the whole of the land mass that is Africa. For a few blessed and for some reason, moving minutes, before we took the bus back to the city and the rugby, we were the last men in Africa.

'Let's have a pasty at the souvenir shop,' said Nick Cain.

The Test Match was a marvellous day in almost every way. The weather was filthy but the atmosphere was healthy. A few members of the AWB parked themselves outside the stadium and barked angrily at supporters, and there were a few flags waved. But there was no anthem, either official or ad hoc. There were some moments of doubt when they called for the minute's silence but the 42,000 people packed in Newlands subsided into quiet. When the silence period was over they applauded. It was a sound of sanity and hope.

Steve Tshwete was beside himself. 'The crowd behaved beautifully. There were 42,000 saying they recognise the need for peace and democracy in our country. That moment of silence united South Africa.'

It was a great Test Match. Australia won 26-3, making light of the mud and the new laws with a display of awesome commitment and control. They led only by 8-3 at half-time but the control they displayed in the second half was staggering. Put together that half of play with their first half in the 1991 World Cup semi-final against New Zealand and you have something approximating to the perfect match.

Tim Horan in the centre and John Eales in the line-out gave brilliant performances, Horan in all-round, centre-flanker-superman role. The Springboks battled away, but Naas Botha's non-kicking foot slipped on the surface and his kicking was shaky. Wahl Bartmann in the back row was apparently playing the tackle law as it stood pre-war (Crimean). They were too slow and too worthy. The back row as a whole never worked in concert. Indeed, almost twelve months after this match and after seeing many more Springbok games, I still could not quite work out how Ian MacDonald on the flank and Small on the wing really added to the national team. Not surprisingly, Geldenhuys and Malan, the two locks eclipsed by Eales and Rod McCall, did not last the year.

Australia led by 11-3 towards the end of normal time when Tim Horan took another hand. He made a brilliant break out of deep defence and kicked on cleverly when tacklers converged. He caught Gerber in possession, rewon the ball and passed beautifully out to his right. There, lurking on his wing, was Campese, and the greatest attacking rugby player in the world motored over for his fiftieth try of an astonishing career.

Carozza had already scored a clever try earlier, set up by Farr-Jones and Phil Kearns, the rampaging hooker, and he scored his second soon after Campese's Horan-based effort. Carozza went slithering over in the corner for a try which would hardly have been possible on the bone-hard surface of Ellis Park on the previous Saturday. Michael Lynagh, who had kicked badly, put over a penalty and the conversion of Carozza's try and not even the most pedantic follower of the game in South Africa, or any other country, could deny that Australia's status as world champions was secure.

The refereeing certainly helped the occasion. David Bishop, as we could all hear on our headphones, was in beautiful control. Once, as he stood apart waiting for a kick at goal after a fast burst of play, he said, ostensibly to himself: 'Cor! Great game, great game.'

Fair play to you, mate, we thought. To hear a referee revelling in the occasion was a valuable insight.

The drama continued afterwards. Naas Botha and Nick Farr-Jones spoke of retirement in the dressing rooms – Farr-Jones probably because he felt a life's work was accomplished; Botha probably because he suddenly realised the volume of work needed. Both, happily, changed their minds. Dwyer and his men sat back in the realisation that nothing could feel so good again. Dwyer, who worked ferociously hard, stayed behind when the team flew home. He had set up a programme of coaching in townships around the country. That was Dwyer. Great man.

And that was South Africa; the most bewitching, aggravating, glorious, dangerous place on earth. Obviously, the races were edging together on the fringes and there was a growing middle ground inhabited by people of all colours. Yet there were still appalling entrenched attitudes, and very few substantive changes that you could see with the naked eye.

'What was South Africa like?' people asked us when we returned home to the new Northern Hemisphere rugby season.

'Have you a month to spare?' we asked, with feeling.

# CHAPTER 8

# *The Blue and Golden Wonders*

## THE BRITISH ISLES DOMESTIC SEASON, PART I

### *(I) Jack? Jack!*

Stuart Barnes yawned. It was a quiet moment on the British Lions tour. 'Ah well, I suppose that I'll have to go and see old Lofty when I get back to see what we can learn from this trip.' It sounded from his tone of voice as if he regarded the Lofty interview in the same vein as a trip to the personnel office in a recession.

'Who's Lofty?' he was asked.

'You know,' he said. 'The Long Bloke.'

I knew who old Lofty was. I knew that Barnes, whatever impression he gave to the contrary, regarded Lofty as the most influential rugby man he had ever met.

Last April, eight minutes from the end of the Courage Leagues season, Lofty was a little agitated. Gareth Hughes, the classy Saracens fly-half, dropped a goal. It took his club into a 13-11 lead against Bath. The West Country club needed to win the match to take the Courage League title for the third time in succession. Suddenly, the title was slipping away. The Saracens spectators, at home but vastly outnumbered, were beside themselves.

Down on the Bath bench, where their medical people sat glumly in their blue and white tracksuits, Lofty, the angular giant, otherwise known as Jack Rowell, stared expressionless. Afterwards, he spoke in admiration of his team's priceless ability to absorb any anguish on the scoreboard and in the inner game, and to come back – for that is what Bath did. They defended their destiny wonderfully well. They stormed the Saracens line, scored a penalty through Stuart Barnes, a try through Jon Callard after Philip de Glanville and Jeremy Guscott, the centres, had made the running. The sponsors presented Bath with the Courage trophy in a low-key ceremony in the humble surroundings of the Saracens' tiny stadium.

It was their fourth title in the six years in which leagues have operated in England; they have also won the Cup an incredible seven times in the past decade, enriching the day of the final with the fervency of the team and their supporters.

It was impossible from Rowell's demeanour after the presentation to tell whether he had been as sanguine about the eventual victory as he appeared, but I was certain that he had been anything but. In the 1970s, the middle years of his career as Bath's coach, he used to disappear from the ground, unable to watch the tight moments. Once, memorably, he found the opposition coach out there too.

Bath have defied the wheel of fortune and very few individuals or teams in sport ever do that. Their turn should have ended, just as the turns of Liverpool, West Indies, Steve Davis, Jahangir Khan and Sergei Bubka – the people we thought would never lose – have ended. Yet the processes by which Bath have regenerated themselves every September are remarkable. For me, there is an endless fascination in the way they have refreshed their own sated inner men, even when they have to thrash themselves ever harder simply to win what they have already won before. Theirs is the greatest club rugby performance the world has seen.

They impose formidable peer-group pressure among themselves ('No one dares be the one to let Bath down, either in training or in the match,' said Andy Robinson, captain last season). Perhaps the best gauge of their potential for the future is that Steve Ojomoh, the explosive athletic back-row man with the potential to become one of the world's great forwards, will have to fight like crazy to win a regular spot. The team has been built around core figures, influential kings of the club, men like Roger Spurrell, Gareth Chilcott, Simon Halliday, Robinson, Barnes, Jon Hall, the new captain, and many others. The club's contribution to the national squad is unsurpassable. Their record in accepting raw talent into their mill and baking out glorious finished products – Ojomoh, Ben Clarke, Phil de Glanville, Jon Webb, Jim Fallon, all of whom maximised potential – is also awesome.

Their success is not measured by the memories of their victories, as much as memories of their defeats. There have been so few in important games over the last decade that they sit like boulders along the harsh trails of their successful seasons – and they all still infuriate. There were the two silly Cup defeats, against Moseley in 1988 and against Waterloo last season, which ruined Barnes' year because he opted to play for the Barbarians that day against Australia. There was the more convincing defeat by Leicester in 1991, in the league; that shoddy effort a few years ago at Saracens and another at Nottingham. There are a few others, but not many.

Whenever sport is played this well you recall the favourite theory of Brough Scott, the great sportswriter. It deals with the importance of realising your achievement at the time, not waiting for history's perspective. Only then, with the realisation that things may never be so good again, can you properly maximise the warm feelings.

Rowell has been there through everything. How much of the monument is his? Some people try to deny the credit, ascribe his input as ingredients in the mix. Others, even insiders, have found him too intense, even angry. To me, it is far more than that. Rowell is not the ingredients, he is the stirrer, the Keith Floyd. He is the man with the perspective; the re-motivator, the man who nudges on the club when the technical hounds in the club threaten to catch him. He is unsurpassed, in my view.

Barnes could write a book on him. 'He is just a staggering bloke. He is the most intense person I have ever met. He is a great man-manager.' A great coach too? 'It is not as simple as that. Some of his sessions are not great. But he is good at pulling together bits and pieces from other rugby cultures and coming up with fresh ideas. He also has the confidence to ask people their opinions. He asks Coochie, Robbo, Hally and others what they think. Not all coaches have that confidence.'

It is more than the technical lead. 'He is the motivator supreme. Some people don't like him. Someone like Jerry [Guscott] pretends not to like him but deep down, I think he does. But others don't because he is too abrasive for them. He says what he thinks, which is why he has never coached England. But Jack is highly Machiavellian. He does not actually *want* to get on with everybody.

'Sometimes, after he has given someone a bollocking, they will go out and play with fury. They might come up to me afterwards and say, "There, that showed the old bastard." I don't say anything. Jack has had the desired effect. He likes people who stand up to him, like Hallers [Simon Halliday] and myself. Some of the others he riles up to go out and play.'

'But how does he do it? Why does he need to keep doing it?' I asked Barnes. After all, Rowell is an increasingly major figure in the business world, with the Dalgety company.

'Yes, and the bugger's just been promoted again. He has to travel all over the place. He may be in Amsterdam one day, somewhere else the next. But if we've won he'll be in the nightclub till five in the morning then next day he'll be back in Amsterdam. Staggering bloke.'

In all the best rugby clubs, you see, there is a Rowell or sub-Rowell. There are no wages to dock if the players play badly. No contract to enforce or other weapon to throw. So there must be a figure in each club to answer to, someone that you know to your disquiet you will have to face, man to man, at some time in the evening, if you have bottled your assignment. It might be the coach, or the team manager, or the soul of the club, or the most powerful presence, or even the stroppy bastard who is always complaining in the dressing-room; someone for whom you hold a respect in spite of yourself – or it might be Jack Rowell, all those characters in the same man. Rowell keeps his methods under wraps. Occasionally, he might venture an anecdote about how he had helped Ben Clarke just after Clarke joined. 'He did not start too well. I had a word with him at Orrell. I told him it wasn't good enough.' Clarke remembers the chat. He never looked back.

He is not exactly in the dark as to the extent of his achievements. He has been known to take issue with people he supposes are devaluers. 'He doesn't like the reflected glory to be too reflected,' says Barnes, prior to thrashing out with Lofty a few Kiwi-tinged ideas for the annual regeneration and the fervent march of Jack's fervent men.

In fact, there was not quite such an all-consuming sweep about Bath in their league programme last season. Rowell expressed his support for the radical ruck/maul law and I am pleased to say that I disagreed profoundly with him. He said that Bath's pacy game was well suited to it, and of course, it was. But it also took away a staple of Bath play: the ability, and indeed, the God-given right, to hammer away from scrums near the opposition line until they crumble and you score. I felt that roughly one-third of Bath's armoury was removed by the law.

They began their programme by hammering Harlequins and thrashing London Irish. They lost in an emotional contest at Northampton but won all the remainder of their games; most pertinently, they won at home against Wasps, who put up a courageous battle for the title and lost only to Bath's vastly superior points differential. Yet the match between the two teams was halting, rough and disfigured; was affected by the sending off of Fran Clough, the Wasps' centre, on a day when vertigo affected some of those who had never been so high before.

There were major issues in the English domestic scene which did not involve Bath. For a long time, as the Leagues worked out, it seemed as if Gloucester and Orrell might be relegated. Why not? They had no more divine right to stay up than any other club. Yet I must confess to sweating on their behalf. They represent what rugby was always supposed to be (your town against their town) better than almost any other clubs. Gloucester's team are Gloucester men; Orrell, the richest shoestring club, call a player an outsider if he does not come from the tiny village that is Orrell. If the rugby genie appeared one day when I was cleaning my binoculars, my one most fervent wish in the game, bar none, would be that Orrell had won the Division 1 title they deserved before the great Eric Smith, their wonderful committeeman, died.

At least Eric, with gruff delight, saw the arrival of his tiny club of dreams in the very top flight. 'It is like the black tulip. You nurture it. You see it grow. You get used to two backward steps for every one forward. When everything is realised it is almost wondrous.' I am afraid that anyone who does not share that view of club rugby, anyone who simply sees Britain's club teams as a direct part and parcel of their beloved development plans and squads, instead of an end in themselves, will have to get past me first – and Lofty, too.

The typical Bath home match has become an event experience. In the pre-League days the media could spread their favours. Now we have to chase those chasing silver. The traditional Bath day kicks off with a one-course lunch at Papa Capetti's excellent Italian establishment. Bath, on a sunny winter's day, is a beautiful, beautiful place, yet the Recreation Ground itself is pitifully inadequate and so, if the annual shenanigans of Bath's committee are any indication, are some of the people who would like to be in authority at the club.

Yet there is always fascination in reading the team lists over lunch; there is never a visit without the tingle of anticipation. Guscott can drift into freelance activities during club games, but there is something gloriously watchable about the man; there is the old maestro, Tony Swift, as good over the last two seasons as at any time in his high-scoring career on the wing – and they still take the piss out of him unmercifully; there are the stark, steely attitudes of Robinson, the aggravating flanker, and the booming power of Hall, standing tall on the drives as none of the textbooks recommend.

They may dip occasionally but plans are well advanced to carry the dynasty. They will have to replace Barnes, the master tactician and craftsman, in the next few years. That would be the most integral worn part they have had to deal with for years. They will be working on it, today.

And after the match, the illustrious players of the most successful rugby club the world has seen fan out on the grass in front of the clubhouse, PR immaculate and accessible. Perhaps they like meeting their followers, or revelling in their efforts as Brough demands; or perhaps it is the best place to avoid Jack Rowell.

At the end of the previous season, when Bath had thundered to a marvellous double of Courage Leagues and Pilkington Cup, thanks at the death to a dropped goal from Stuart Barnes in the last second of a fantastic final against Harlequins, I received a letter from a Bath supporter who had enjoyed the *Sunday Times* coverage of the epic feats of the club. And at the end of her kind letter she thanked me 'for all my support of the club during the season'.

It was such a kind note that in my reply, I did not mention that I had not supported Bath that season and nor was I ever likely to. It isn't my job. What I might have added, however, is that there is no rugby institution which I admire more, especially for their inch-perfect demonstration of everything that the wonderful world of club rugby is supposed to be.

## *(II) The Last Supper of the Natural Game:*

### *Rugby's Search for an Alternative to the Classroom*

I am not being ungrateful. But by the time you have been to your twentieth rugby function of the season and met there the same movable feast of guests who were, with a few replacements, at the other nineteen, drunk the same rather niggling mulled white wine and heard all the speeches, all based on Mickey Burton's 1982 repertoire, in the same male chauvinist washroom, then your appetite for the next event might be rather jaded. Especially for the 'nobby' events. I enjoyed, say, the annual bunfight at Shipston-on-Stour RFC far more than the Rugby World Cup final dinner.

There was no question of where the finest livener for a jaded palate was provided last season. The menu for the forty-first annual rugby dinner at Caldicott School, the celebrated prep school near Slough, was breathtaking:

*Saumon Fumé Dominique le Saint*
*Crevettes Aberdures*
*Sauce Martinique*

*Boeuf Rôti Nicolas le Patron*
*Pudding de York Tristecrase*
*Pommes de terre Jaconquiennes*
*Chouxfleur Gratiné Façon Jacques Poulet*
*Petit Pois Alexandre*

*Salade de Fruits Jacques Culotte*
*Bombe Glacée Laurentienne*

*Choix de Fromage Granmère*
*Celeri Paulomme*
*Biscuits Trainé*

*Café Maxwellien*
*Chocolats à la Menthe Guillaume*

But this is not the story of food and drink and dinners. It is the story of the future of the game. The boys at Caldicott, obviously, are overwhelmingly fortunate with their food and their surroundings, with the financial backing at their disposal and with the marvellous facilities they have to play sport.

Yet whatever your views on the philosophy of education, rugby is extremely fortunate to have establishments like Caldicott, ridiculously fortunate, in fact. Under the influence of Peter Wright, their recently retired, long-serving headmaster and a legend in education and rugby, the school have a wonderful rugby life. They have five senior teams and two colts teams, and last season, under the leadership of Nicholas Kinder, who spoke with formidable composure at the dinner, the first XV lost only three of their eighteen matches. Their record in the Prep Schools Sevens at Rosslyn Park is magnificent.

The contribution of the public and prep schools of England to rugby simply cannot be underrated. The scene at Caldicott, where everyone plays the game, everyone apparently wants to play the game and where the masters are providing the perfect balance of sympathetic rugby coaching and perspective, is warming but also a throwback. It is hardly hot news that, because of the decline of rugby in schools, that sort of introduction to rugby is now available to far, far fewer youngsters.

Or, as Bill Samuel puts it, the rugby education of children is better left to 'trained educators; and physical education is taught better by those who studied it for at least three years, not those who have attended the Welsh Rugby Union's one-week coaching course at Aberystwyth'. Bill Sam, mentor of Gareth Edwards and one of the most famous teachers of physical education in Wales, believes that professional educators provide a significantly more rounded training than those who merely teach the children the techniques of the game at the rugby club. He is correct. He also believes that, except at places like Caldicott, 'rugby has ceased to be the *natural* game to play. Now, from the age of eight onwards, children are *organised* to play.'

The game has been working furiously hard to fill the enormous vacuum caused by the fact that, due to cutbacks, changes of timetable and emphasis and priorities, their ready-made pool of young people has been drained. Every club worth its salt runs mini-rugby sections, many others spend hours and resources in running colts and youth teams. Every national union has created development officers – the RFU alone has regiments of them – some of them trained in education, to take the game into schools, to attract children at first through gaudy images in the game's primary colours. On all these people, on the parents and enthusiasts who spend Sunday mornings away from the fireside, a colossal responsibility lies. Some of the aspects of the age-groups game are out of balance, too competitive and too unsympathetic to defeat and to the lesser standards; too inclined to put the interests of the club before those of the boy or girl.

I must confess to feeling distaste for the mini-rugby games I watched last season, for the jabbering, bawling parents and coaches pressurising gaunt-faced little tots who should have been revelling in the match, not being anxious about the trophy at the end. As so many mini-rugby coaches have admitted, the biggest danger in the new age of rugby's self-help is the number of parents living out their frustrated sporting careers through their offspring.

There are heroes in the fight. Alan Black, the national development officer at Twickenham, has everything in perfect balance, if only it would rub off through the country. Rugby authorities at clubs and county and national level have to impart the same warmth to the all-round development of youngsters – we used to take it for granted but it is now restricted to the schools which have managed to maintain their old glorious standards. If they are successful then we will all feast at the neglected high table of rugby education.

## (III) A Consultation with Scott

Was it the prototype twenty-first century rugby player who was marching through the foyer of the hotel in Swansea? Scott Gibbs was in his formal number one tracksuit, immaculately turned out, bang on time and wearing those kind of moon-shaped spectacles which the National Health Service used to fling at any poor short-sighted devil whether he wanted that style or not (and he didn't), only to find that the world and his wife and Elvis Costello suddenly found them *de rigueur*, whether they were short-sighted or not.

This was early last season when Scott was only potentially a centre of true world class. He was to become that animal, with extra horns into the bargain, with the British Lions, where his play was an unmitigated joy. But here in the foyer he was still promising. He was also blazing a new trail. Gibbs had turned down a massive offer several months before to play rugby league with Wigan. To this day, they and other clubs are still snuffling around, and in late summer 1993, Wigan and St Helen's flourished the massive cheque again. He was originally able to turn it down, all £250,000 essentially, because interested parties in and around the Welsh Rugby Union were desperate to keep him, desperate to stop the life-draining flow of their greatest players to the north of England.

They suggested after the first refusal that he set himself up as a 'sports consultant'. It meant that, as Wayne Shelford had done for some time in New Zealand, he was now trading on his fame as a player and taking the proceeds for the resulting commercial activity. He was allowed to do so because the activities constituted his full-time job. Technically, he could not have augmented his income with rugby-related activities if he held down another job.

He already had the security of various retainers: he was retained to put together a conditioning programme for the employees of one firm; he was available for personal appearances, product launches and all promotional activity. It was not an easy time to start, because not only was the Welsh economy in depression, but the Welsh game was at a low ebb. It was only just over a year after the Welsh national team had effectively ceased to exist in the dire debacles of Sydney and Brisbane on their tour of Australia. But with the squeeze on players' time becoming agonising, with the profile of the sport growing, if not exactly to the commercial heights enjoyed by a Michael Jordan, then the precedent set by Gibbs will be keenly followed and evaluated by other players.

When we met he was twenty-two. Beside him, with briefcase, was his agent; not an understudy for the title role in *Jaws*, but a young, blonde girl. They did not survive long in tandem. By the end of the season, Gibbs was fighting out of another stable. His prospects were helped by his successes in New Zealand and yet probably hampered by his conviction for serious horseplay, driving over the limit in a temporarily borrowed taxi.

He was no gauche innocent when we met in Swansea. 'To project our image for commercial opportunities, we obviously have to play well, to find that extra five per cent on performance. I have to have flexibility in my day. I can train as often as I like. I can pay attention to diet and relaxation and fitness schedules. The improvements I get are relatively slight, but crucial.'

He was working hard on improving his Welsh. A Welsh-speaker has opportunities in two languages. Sure enough, between the ceremonial taking of the picture and the interview itself, he broke off to attend a studio in Swansea for a Welsh language interview.

Afterwards, we adjourned to St Helen's, home of Swansea. Chris Smith, the brilliant photographer, set up a few flagposts and told Scott to swerve in and out of them. Smith has taken some photographs for *The Sunday Times* so outstanding that your words can only spoil the effect. This time, he did not want Scott posing at sunset on the Mumbles. He wanted him weaving through the corner flags. Scott obligingly swerved, and we got a smashing pic (which the office then, due to an overwhelming need in the public interest to run a story on two blokes falling down a mountain in a hollowed-out dustbin, decided not to use. Thanks, lads).

A few days earlier, St Helen's had been packed and seething with excitement. Swansea, beginning the season superbly, had beaten the world champions, Australia. Gibbs had played brilliantly and had scored a vital try, bursting over from short range after taking a short pass on the blind side from Robert Jones, Swansea's scrum-half.

It was only afterwards that he realised he had missed a massive marketing opportunity. In the background as he scored, as he celebrated with his team-mates, and as the endless replays ran in slow motion, was the advertising board for the Crest Hotel in Swansea. 'I ran into the manager afterwards and he was absolutely delighted,' said Gibbs. 'He said that his hoarding was on TV for thirty seconds after the try.'

Curses. If only Gibbs had done the deal beforehand, he could have brushed his hair, instructed Robert to give the optimum pass for camera angle, and dived ceremonially over in front of the hoarding. I predicted at the time that nothing else would get past Gibbs in the season. I was right. And there may be many players who come after him, trading on their famous names.

## (IV) No Roads Lead to Malawi:
### Easy Life in the Fourth Estate, 1993

Everything was in place for the Ultimate Wind-up. All the others had been done. It had started small. One person had received breakfast room-service prunes at 5.30 am. I had been served with a kosher meal on a long flight. They insisted that I had rung requesting it. I had opened the door of my Sydney hotel room in the early hours one day on the 1989 Lions tour and found there Daphne from the Thundercats Escort Agency. Where did she want to escort me to at that time of night, I thought, as I firmly closed the door (honest).

Clero had rung his sports editor from Edinburgh at 4.00 am. 'But I've got this message to ring you,' he said feebly, trying to cut off the blood-curdling abuse from the other end. Newks, also a tennis writer, had stayed in his room all morning one day waiting for a call from Peter Graf, father of Steffi, and therefore the certain scoop about Steffi, as per Peter's message left at reception. He had also reacted to a bogus fax by preparing a speech to deliver at the opening ceremony of the revamped Orrell clubhouse, a function to which he was not even invited.

Nick Cain, until recently editor of *Rugby World & Post*, is not only one of the most respected figures on the circuit but a famously well-travelled member of the media. He is especially fortunate with invitations from organisers of the burgeoning spring sevens circuit, and has been to Portugal, the West Indies, Spain, Catania and Hong Kong. The organisers can get good mileage from a colour spread in the mag.

He was fascinated by a faxed invitation to report on the Malawi Sevens. The fax gave all the details: Air Malawi were sponsoring the event, to be held in the Lilongwe National Stadium over three days. Should Mr Cain do them the honour, then he would fly over business class on Air Malawi, staying for five nights at the Lilongwe Hyatt. Among the competing teams were Zambia, Malawi, Namibia, African Barbarians, Wanderers from Dublin, the Zebras, and from England, Bath. Would Mr Cain let Air Malawi know of his decision at the fax number given? All tickets would be waiting at the Air Malawi counter.

The fax number was a safe house in southern England. The Bath reference stood up brilliantly when a perfectly primed Andy Robinson called across to Cain in the Bath club after the England B–Italy B game last season. 'Hey, Nick! I hear you're going to these Sevens. See you in Lilongwe'. The noose tightened. Other journalists apparently invited and named in the fax confirmed that they were attending, too. 'Sounds a great trip.'

The conspirators then called a meeting to see how far we would go. The original intention was to mass at the Air Malawi desk at Heathrow, if there is one, to see our man, all ready to fly out, vainly demanding his tickets. We even began research into the actual cost of a ticket so that he would actually fly out to cover a non-existent tournament; and the cost of a local photographer to snap Cain as he wandered the terminal in Lilongwe vainly looking for the officials of the tournament who had promised to meet his flight.

Disaster struck when we learned that he intended to feature the Malawi Sevens in his column on rugby around the world in the *Daily Telegraph*. With regret, we had to wind down the wind-up. The *Telegraph* would not have been amused.

You need a sense of humour to work on covering rugby almost every day of your life. You need a sense of humour for the rugby itself, and for its never-ending cycle. The Great Recorders, people like David Hands of *The Times*, John Mason of the *Daily Telegraph* and Steve Bale of the *Independent*, to name the London men alone, produce thousands upon thousands of words per week, still entranced and, when necessary in copy, furious about the old game; but far more for the journalism itself.

The era of fire-on-sight employers is with us. There is also the perennial, teeth-gnashing confrontation with Them, Our Lot, Those Bastards – those are the polite terms for our sports desks and for the endless struggle. Sorry, they have no space for the feature you spent a month on; sorry, but the sub stuck on an inflammatory heading and now all the players are after you. And all their memos saying how much they enjoyed your piece? Lost in the post.

That is the wonderfully enjoyable, viciously unfair, onerous and endless and unmissable world of life on journalism's rugby circuit. 'I bet you talk about anything but rugby and writing', someone said on the Lions tour as a few of us were having dinner after work. Wrong. Apart from what you might call the normal healthy pursuits, we talk about nothing bar rugby and writing – endless mock cynicism about the old game; endless real cynicism about some of its authorities; endless revelling in the great moments; and also endless, recycled anecdotes, still fresh as the day they were first coined and exaggerated, about old media men, old subbing howlers, the pomposities and affectations of the icon writers.

The strange thing about the media in rugby, love them or hate them, is that very few people in the game have the remotest idea of what the press is, how it operates, what it needs to feed on, how requirements differ radically; how good the job can be and how pressurised, especially with the loneliness of the empty laptop screen. Probably the biggest misconception is that the press are cheerleaders rather than dispassionate observers. It is not a question of 'getting behind the lads', as some people, gratingly, demand. Sometimes, you are able to perform the dispassionate function and still give people exactly what they want to read; sometimes not. Tough. Anything else would be an abrogation of responsibilities.

No one has a clue about deadlines. They think all the Sunday reporters chill out with a few beers, wander into some warm office attended by hostesses and chisel out a few leisurely paragraphs to waft by uniformed pigeon to the office. The reality is a grey-faced, frozen-fingered panic. When the final whistle blows, you pick up the phone and file. Not in ten minutes, now. The age of portable phones has eliminated some of the old brawling as hacks on deadline wrested phones away from others in full burble. Shame. It was good for release of tension, unless you stole Big Clem Thomas's phone. That was good for release of head.

To the poor devils like the Lions management, cooped up, trapped in the hot seats of a press conference, the barrage of cameras and notebooks would be one lump, indistinguishable. But every person there wants something completely different. Jack, Super Ted, Bas and Chris, the Sunday heavies need a general impression of the management's views – not for quoting, for their papers want their own opinions, not reportage of those of someone else, thank God – but they wouldn't say no to some pithy quote, if you'd be so kind, Geoff, which would resoundingly confirm the thesis of their feature article. Jack Butch needs straight-up solid facts, injury news and clarification of scorers, for his agency reports. The tabloid men, Jacko, Shambling, Kenny Ball and Iguana, need some ringing proclamation or stinging aside from which, as they lurk later, they can tease up their story, their line; to which they can add a little top-spin. Norman and Midlothian want to ask Geech where on earth all the Scots have disappeared to on tour for their Scottish readers. Ned and Semi need the Irish angle: 'Why did Poppie go off, Geoff?'

Foulmouth needs his Cardiff angle, 'Geech, how would you assess the performance of the Lions centres today?' He means could you please praise Scott Gibbs to the skies to give me a booming intro. Huw needs anything as long as it's in Welsh. He tends to prod the microphone into the faces of Ieuan and Robert, rather than, say, Galwey and Carling. Beast needs something colourful for his magazine article, Roche needs no mention of Jerry at all so he can save up the nuggets for his Jerry column. Polecat, stuck at home, needs some major news to boost his Carling biography. Jack Tension grimly hangs on for something that will hold for two days, to give him his evening paper story. Never mind how the team go – we assess the management on the number of unguarded blasts they deliver at the target of their choice.

The photographers are a race apart; apart, that is, from when they are standing in front of you at press conferences wielding one of their bazooka lenses. There was an incident on the Lions tour when one of them attended an official function near the end of the tour wearing a tie. He was immediately summoned before the Photographic High Council. There were even wild allegations that he had washed his jeans before the function and he asked for two offences of not wearing dirty training shoes to be taken into consideration. I think they had him shot.

Generally, the Lions team were a delight. Gavin Hastings apparently suggested to the Lions at the early gathering in London that the press might chip into a kitty for interviews. Thankfully, different counsel prevailed. It is all very well for the television people to lob in something, as ITV did, to oil some wheels, but fundamentally, they have to show the game with criticism only skin-deep. The written media has different and more analytical responsibilities. That is the essential superiority of journalism of the written word.

Players can now be paid for writing their own columns and, haunted by ghost-writers, at least ten of them did so from new Zealand. We had a hilarious evening setting out an imaginary match commentary substituting the paper for the players. *The Sunday Times* (Moore) throws in; the *Manchester Evening News* (Dooley) has won the ball with support from *The Sunday Times* Irish edition (Popplewell); he taps it back to *The Western Mail* (Robert Jones), out to *The Times* (Andrew). A short burst from the *Mail on Sunday* (Carling), and now it's *Today* (Guscott) breaking through. Up comes the *Daily Express* (Hastings) from the back. But why oh why don't they pick the *Daily Mail* (Barnes)? But ethically speaking, there should be no question of money changing hands for interviews. And to be fair, the Lions, almost to a man, were a pleasure to deal with.

Some of them take their column duties very seriously. For Brian Moore's columns in *The Sunday Times* over the last few years the paper has received substantial reaction. After the South African match last autumn, we even carried in our first edition a piece by England's hooker sensationally savaging the RFU, the president and some of his fellow players. Unfortunately, Moore knew nothing about it whatsoever. In the fury of Sunday newspaper production, someone had pressed the wrong button and inserted Moore's byline on a piece written by my colleague, Chris Jones. It was instructive to see how certain RFU committeemen tried to make a mountain of that molehill, and how certain of their number simply did not believe our explanation, thinking that Moore had gone over the top, that we were trying to protect him and that here, at last, was their chance to get him.

Other Lions players appeared as the 'second voice' on the ITV match coverage from New Zealand. Many of them, apparently, were very poor. My friends watching back at home were scathing. 'They never *say* anything,' they said. They exempted Rob Andrew. And before I get caught in the crossfire of the bitter, niggly battle currently raging between ITV and the BBC for the next domestic contract, I should say that my unpaid but outspoken TV monitors did not exactly go a bundle on some of BBC's summarisers, either.

There is a major trend throughout world sport (one hardly dear to the hearts of those who have reached a summit of sorts after years of absorbing all the lessons of reporting and layout and editing, graphics and journalistic law and history and principles) in which papers and electronic media take on former participants to fulfil certain journalistic functions. The trend thrives even though, as general rule, you read or hear very few insights that you could not possibly have gained without participating yourself at their level. Which completely defeats the object.

The success rate in most sports of former brilliant players performing well and earning the respect of journalists is about one in fifty. James Hunt was brilliant in motor racing; so is Richie Benaud and several others at cricket , but many of the other cricket conversions are just the dreadful 'in my day' bores. Soccer? Nah, unless you sit bolt upright whenever Trevor Brooking is in full, er, flow. Perhaps Jim Watt in boxing; certainly Brough Scott in racing. This is by no means an exhaustive list, of course. But you would hardly exhaust yourself with the full list.

Probably the greatest broadcasting vignette I have ever heard on sport was contained in Sport on 4's Grand National preview some years ago when Richard Pitman recalled the day when he had taken Crisp miles into an apparently unassailable lead in the National; how he fought desperately to keep Crisp running on as Red Rum gradually ran him down. Pitman described the rising panic, described the rising drumming in his ears as Red Rum's hooves came closer; then the snort-snort of Red Rum's breathing as he came alongside. I was driving to a rugby match with a colleague and we both found the hairs rising on the back of our necks. It was such a brilliant, evocative piece, only a jockey could have produced it. We almost stopped the car. That sort of thing is what you desperately need if you pay a former participant instead of a career journalist.

In rugby, the strike rate is far higher, though not exactly a strike every time. Clem Thomas, John Taylor, Gerald Davies and more recent retirees such as Eddie Butler and Paul Ackford command vast respect; Ian Robertson and Chris Rea were so successful that they became first voices. There is some good stuff from some old players on Welsh radio. In Ireland Mick Doyle's often brutal columns are wincingly readable although the players resent personal abuse. Norman Mair is a delight. Who else could begin his rugby preview for a Murrayfield Test with an anecdote about Tom Weiskopf, take seven paragraphs before he ever mentioned rugby, give the impression that he is merely rambling amiably and readably and yet still, at the end, leave you with a probing insight?

Yet so many of the old sportsmen in the media, even in rugby, would still qualify for a first-class honours degree in the Art of Stating the Bleeding Obvious at the University of the Sacred Sinecure.

No wonder they want to get into the media. Conventional wisdom is that it is the life of Riley, and provided Riley can put up with the atrocious hours and being away half the year, it is. Rugby is a marvellous world in which to work. We love it to bits, almost every second. We never need to be told how privileged we are. And, as every bar-room authority knows, all we do is live off the game then go for a drink.

Easy life, easy life. Recently, we took a random sample of twenty-five of the top rugby journalists. Of the twenty-five, how many had not either gone through at least one divorce, had at least one heart attack or suffered at least one stress-related illness? Three. Funny that. Must be a coincidence.

# CHAPTER 9

# The Inconceivable English

## THE BRITISH ISLES DOMESTIC SEASON PART II

### (1) Rugby World Cup – Sevens and Bungles

They really had to work hard to pack it all in because the inaugural Rugby World Cup Sevens lasted just three (cold) days in April in Edinburgh. At the end, they had just about managed it. They squeezed in every last cock-up. Never in rugby have so many people, organisers, hosts, media, referees, made such a resounding pig's backside of so many aspects of a major occasion.

That is the glorious legacy this event handed on to the next host city for the second World Cup of Sevens, if there is one. The new hosts can bask in the knowledge that they could not possibly get so much so wrong. On the other hand, if they have to run it under the secretive, bungling, bickering, labyrinthine organisation called Rugby World Cup, they might well return to shambles. The only people who performed well in Edinburgh were a few young men from various countries, and in particular, ten young men from the Old Country, led by a Nigerian-born flash of forked lightning called Andrew Harriman.

It was not a bad idea of Rugby World Cup, the body entrusted by the International Rugby Board (and indeed, the two bodies have members in common) to run World Cups, to hold a Sevens tournament. Good start, pity about the rest. They got the venue wrong, the ethos, the balance, the format. As far as the ethos went, most of the competing teams failed, too, including England and Scotland, respectively the winners and the hosts.

What are sevens? Rugby at international level is a deadly serious business which, as it descends through the scales of ability, becomes a bit of fun. Sevens started as a bit of fun, and has, ridiculously, been allowed to become a desperately serious business. A World Cup of Sevens is a perfect promotional vehicle for the game; good for the TV and the sponsor's slice; good to drag in youngsters with an endless succession of tries – or at least, good enough to form the initial bond to draw them towards the sport itself – where those killjoys called the back row are still around to tackle you after you make the initial breach.

A World Cup of Sevens can bring together, as it did in Edinburgh, parts of the family of the game, and among them at Murrayfield, the glorious Latvia. They had qualified by beating Russia in a qualifying tournament, and were not so much babes in the wood in top rugby as embryos in the wood. However, they scored tries in their group matches against Romania, Wales, South Africa and Japan, running the ultra-trained Japanese to 14-21, waved goodbye to thousands of new admirers in the crowd at Murrayfield and departed for a night of celebration in Edinburgh pubs which should still be giving them a sore head today. Holland, Taiwan and Spain were some of the other lesser-known rugby nations to stand grinning on the stage before a wider audience.

But what the sevens emphatically should not be is some deadly serious event held simply to decide the top team in world sevens. The Murrayfield event was so overblown, so full of its own importance. Heaven save us, it even by its misplaced severity caused some of the competing nations to spend valuable time and resources and even to hold warm-up squad sessions and tours. That is pure, unbalanced nonsense. In one sense, I was delighted at the complete and utter demise of Scotland, who played abysmally. Their sevens squad high-tailed it all around the world to warm up, even robbing London Scottish of key players for the latter stages of Courage League Division 1, an event which, in itself, is twenty times more significant.

Scotland finished a crashingly embarrassing fourth in their group, below such noted sevens non-specialists as Argentina. In the semi-finals of the Bowl competition, the lowest of the three separate events into which the teams tumbled for the final for the three days, they managed to beat France, a country which spends more time on cricket than rugby sevens; and in the Bowl final against Japan, which roused the Murrayfield crowd to new troughs of silence, they were beaten by Japan. Served them right for misinterpreting the whole event. Why not gather the day before, have a run-out and a turn up and start? Anyone who tries to tell you that there is more to learn of sevens than you can pick up on after a canter around and a brief chat is dreaming.

Indeed, the event and sevens as a whole did far more damage to rugby in the USA and Fiji. Those two countries now spend dangerously too much of their finite resources messing around with sevens. Both have had their triumphs, especially Fiji, with their wonderful victories in Hong Kong. But look out for those roosting chickens again. The USA Rugby Union are so short of cash that they could not even host the England tour in the summer of 1993. The USA leg was cancelled. That begs two questions for the fervent rugby men of that vast country. It they can't stage an England tour, then who will they ever be able to host again? Secondly, what on earth were they doing shelling out on a sevens trip to Scotland when their main game was in trouble?

As for Fiji, they have become so obsessed with sevens that they hardly now play fifteens. When it came to the qualifying tournament for the proper World Cup, held in the South Pacific in June and July 1993, they couldn't hack it. They lost at home to Tonga and even though they won the return it was not good enough. They miss the next World Cup. That is a tragedy for a country in love with the game; and will, unquestionably, give rugby league the excuse to bribe Fijian players and enter them in the 1995 Rugby League World Cup in Britain. Furthermore, I am convinced that if they stopped putting their eggs in other baskets, Fiji actually have the all-round talent in their nation to make the top six in the world. Yet, like so many others, they mistook the easy glamour of Murrayfield for the real thing.

But that was by no means the limit of the nonsense. Rugby World Cup decided to impose on the players a ridiculously convoluted format. It meant, if you wanted to reach the finals, that you had to play ten ties of sevens inside three days, including five on the last day. The first two days were set aside for qualifying in pools (and were low-octane), then the main event devolved into another pool format. It was not until the semi-finals that we had some knock-out punching. It meant an intolerably severe programme.

I should have expected it. I attended the qualifying competition for the main event in the previous year in Catania, Sicily. There, Rugby World Cup, an organisation which, at least in principle, is there to organise rugby for the benefit of the players, subjected the hopefuls from all over the world to a murderous three-day programme of qualifying and parked the teams miles and miles away from the stadium in a complex with negligible creature comforts or leisure facilities.

On the day after the Catania sevens I shared an aircraft out to Milan with the Hong Kong team. Their ten-man squad took an age to board. Two were on crutches and had to be dragged on by the cabin staff. Others were assisted to their seats by old ladies. They looked half dead. That was the kind of event it was.

Why the savagery? There was a clue in the justification of the format for Edinburgh from Marcel Martin of Rugby World Cup. 'With this format, it means that we shall truly find the best sevens team in the world at the end,' he said. What he meant was that with such extended qualifying in pools their would be less left to chance, less chance of a superior team being beaten. With great respect, Marcel, it was complete and utter claptrap. It ensured that to an extent, the teams who came through to the semi-finals were those who had the most luck with injuries and were furthest from total exhaustion. By the final day, Western Samoa, Fiji and Australia were all fielding at least two players in every match who were not fit to play. (Although, to be fair, the alternative was to draft a member of an all-Scottish back-up squad available to all teams. Perhaps the teams with injured players had taken one look at the first-string

Scots and decided they would be better fielding their own men on one leg.) Anyway, who gives a damn if one of the lesser teams goes through on a freak? Sevens is a game of chance, of freak results and major upsets.

And the venue? If there is one thing that the old world of rugby officialdom detests it is someone else having a brilliant idea. The whole problem with the brilliant idea known as the Cathay Pacific-Hong Kong Bank Sevens, held every year in Hong Kong, is that Hong Kong have made a great success of it and neither the IRB and the RFU nor anyone else can get their clammy fingers on it.

They awarded the inaugural sevens to Scotland because Ned Haig, a Scottish butcher, is regarded as the founding father. Fair enough, but in fact, not appropriate. Over the last twelve years, the Hong Kong Sevens have become the jewel in the crown of world rugby, a marvellous, gaudy, theatrical tournament; it is something about which any other sport could only dream. The winning of the trophy is deeply coveted, of course; but the event exists on many other levels. Until the IRB moved into gear in their role as guardian of the world game, the Hong Kong Sevens were by far the most significant meeting-place of the game for the exchange of ideas, gossip, contacts; and indeed, with the congress of national coaches held concurrently with the tournament in 1993, that value is still high.

They are also a garish festival, a riot, a good-time thrash; they reduce the twenty-four teams to two, then one, inside two days without taking years off the lives of the players. It is a perfect disgrace that the RFU, against the express wishes of their team manager and players, have failed to enter an England seven. They always plead packed schedules, even though it is they who have done the packing. For the 1994 tournament they have no excuse. There is no World Sevens and so Hong Kong is the perfect place to put their reputation back on the line; and because so few of their sevens squad players are in the full national squad, there is no excuse of pressing commitments. If they do not enter an England seven in 1994 they will stand firmly accused of petty jealousy.

So, while a Scotsman invented sevens, it is beyond dispute that modern sevens are the child not of Scotland, but of Hong Kong. It was Scotland, and not Hong Kong, who deserved the tribute of the inaugural world event, not least because, with sevens dying in England and Wales and in other parts of Europe (have you *seen* the Middlesex Sevens lately? Did you stay awake?), it is Hong Kong which has kept the smaller game alive. Murrayfield was cheerless, half-empty, half rebuilt; the catering was extremely poor (not the fault of the SRU, say the SRU). There is no question that when Murrayfield is completed it will be a magnificent stadium: even half-finished for the Sevens it looked potentially imposing, and when the bowl extends around to meet itself it seems that the balance between essential homeliness and futuristic design will be perfectly met. But that is not to say that the 1993 Rugby World Cup of Sevens should not have been held in the Government Stadium, Hong Kong.

But as I say, there were disasters all around. Poor ITV, whose technical coverage of the event was outstanding and who were hoping frantically to use their sevens coverage as a plank of their argument when next the domestic rugby contract came up for discussion, made a resounding *faux pas*. People tuning in for live coverage of the later rounds on the Sunday found studio discussion of past matches droning on, while visible behind the interviewees' shoulders in the ITV pitch-side studio were snippets of dramatic live action. I cannot remember any piece of rugby on television which attracted the same volume of comment and criticism from the armchair legions than that.

The infallible, however, were a little thin on the ground. After two days of competition, in which Western Samoa, that remarkable rugby nation, Fiji (ditto), New Zealand and Australia had been way out ahead as the most impressive teams, I recorded solemnly in *The Sunday Times* on a page devoted almost exclusively to a sense of wonder at the strength of the game in the Pacific Islands, that 'it is inconceivable that the winning World Cup Sevens team will not come from the Southern Hemisphere, and there is a high proba- bility that the title will go to one of the Pacific Islands'. Next day, when England carried all before them in an astonishing victory and my colleagues thoughtfully blew up my article to wallpaper size on a copier and pasted it on the wall of the media centre, I briefly contemplated blaming the copy-taker.

There was, in my article, a tiny footnote tucked away concerning England. 'They . . . were hammered by the Samoans in their pool matches and have relied almost completely on the burning pace of Harriman. One heavy cannon can do terminal damage in the shortened game so England cannot yet be discarded.' But I could not hide behind that summary either, because on finals day, even though Harriman was achingly brilliant and Linford-quick, it was very far from a one-man band blowing away out there in English white.

Whatever you think of sevens the final day's action was a treasure. In quick succession, every grudge match and every historically or sociologically charged confrontation imaginable was fought out. Western Samoa-Fiji, Australia-New Zealand, England-Australia, Tonga-Fiji, South Africa-New Zealand.

And it was obvious from the first whistle of the morning that the southern sides had dipped. England were gathering strength in every tie. In their final-day pool they beat New Zealand 21-12, South Africa 14-7 and lost to Australia 21-12. Australia had scraped past South Africa, one of the most unlucky teams on show, and had been savaged by New Zealand 42-0, and so their win over England saw them squeeze through. Australia, despite their inferior com- parative results, somehow topped their pool, another tribute to the behind-the-scenes shambles.

The other final-day pool saw Fiji and Ireland come through, the Irish after a marvellous dawn win over Western Samoa and another over Tonga. They lost to Fiji, so the semi-final pairings were Fiji-England and Australia-Ireland.

By this time, the pace of Harriman had taken the tournament by storm. He needed a pass and a yard of room. It mattered very little how many defenders he had in front of him. He was so blazingly fast that he could outflank them all. Possibly only Nigel Walker, the former Olympic high hurdler now with Cardiff, could run so fast on a rugby field.

England beat Fiji by 21-7 with two dazzling Harriman tries. Fiji were not themselves. Waisale Serevi, the genius fly-half, showed some touches of arrogance (snide arrogance, not the arrogance of assurance) and Meli Rasari, the six-foot-five sprinting forward, had been palpably unfit since the start of the whole event. Australia beat the heroic Irish when Willie Ofahengaue scored in the last seconds of the match to overhaul them, and all over the pitch Irish heads were in Irish hands. The final was therefore to be a repeat of the 1991 fifteen-a-side event.

For Englishmen, it was a joy. They surged into a 21-0 lead, but were pegged back to 21-17 as Australia dragged tired minds and injured bodies into the contest. Yet England held on. Their team-work, their tackling and their sheer will served them superbly. For the first try, Harriman took the ball in space near the start, with David Campese shadowing and Ryan Constable, the young Aussie back, covering across. Campese knew it was all up seconds before Harriman came level with him, and made a token chase with a resigned air. Constable, with the impetuosity of youth, chased and chased. Harriman simply cruised away from him. It was like arriving at 10.00 am for the 9.00 am train. Harriman scored at his leisure.

The other try-scorers were Tim Rodber, who had a fantastic last day, with blasting tackles and superb footballing ability, and who sprinted in to score from way out; and Lawrence Dallaglio, the young Wasp not even a first XV regular. The other superheroes were David Scully, the tenacious Wakefield scrum-half, and the wonderful Chris Sheasby, the omnipresent Harlequin whose energy and optimism served his men beautifully. Adedeyo Adebayo and Nick Beal, of Bath and Northampton, were the other backs and Justin Cassell of Saracens came on as replacement for Rodber. Matt Dawson, the Northampton scrum-half, and Damian Hopley, the Wasps back playing in the forwards, were the other squad members and not one man in the whole squad failed to distinguish himself. Les Cusworth, who with David Watkins and Serevi is the worst line-out man and the greatest sevens player I have ever seen, was the coach.

It was great stuff. Argentina won the Plate competition, beating Spain in the final, and this after Spain had beaten Wales in the Plate semi-finals. It was not the defeat which must have hurt Welsh supporters as much as the lack of real rugby class and pace from the country which is supposed to have invented those commodities. Japan, giving credence to the cynic who told me the day before the tournament that they would manoeuvre themselves into a competition they could win rather than go all-out for the main competition, duly beat Scotland to win the Bowl.

Next morning England's victory counted for precious little in the global scheme of things, which as far as sevens goes is exactly as it should be. But for the inconceivable English, it meant the world.

There was an air of self-congratulation when Famous Grouse threw a celebration lunch on the Monday after the tournament. Another triumph for Rugby World Cup? No. Just as many aspects of the success of the 1991 World Cup came about precisely in defiance of their cock-ups, so the Sevens were something of a success in spite of them.

Indeed, the general consensus among professional commentators on rugby is that Rugby World Cup is the most worrying body in the game, a body with so much of the game's destiny in its hands which has signally failed to live up to that calling, and yet has proved secretive and sensitive when many of us have drawn attention to that fact. It may surprise you to know that this view of RWC is held in the national unions of almost every major country around the world. In the corridors of power at Twickenham, Cardiff, Auckland and Sydney you hear the same expressions of anger and amazement. And it is the unions' fault, for their inertia, if matters become worse.

RWC comprises a chairman, currently Sir Ewart Bell of Ireland, and directors: Keith Rowlands, also secretary of the IRB, who at least tries to communicate; Nick Labuschagne of South Africa, Leo Williams of Australia, Marcel Martin of France. How many of this lot would the rugby man in the street actually know from Adam? And yet do the rulers of the game not owe it to the millions of followers of the game to be outgoing, to keep them posted? They are quasi-autonomous and therefore not completely accountable, which is a disgraceful state of affairs.

When I asked Bell recently whether the IRB had a power of veto over RWC, and through the IRB the individual unions, he went into a rambling reply. As he droned on, someone behind me muttered: 'For Christ's sake don't ask him a difficult question.' When Bell finished his monologue, after which we gathered that the IRB could intercede over a few areas but not in most areas, he looked out balefully at his audience like a latter-day Quelch. 'And do I make myself clear,' he asked, rhetorically (he hoped). As mud, we thought. An amazing profile of Bell appeared recently which said: 'His handling of press conferences . . . employing virtually impenetrable civil service jargon won him the grudging respect of the media.' Did it hell.

The secrecy is alarming. On the day after the 1991 World Cup ended, I asked Russell Thomas, then chairman, if and when full accounts would be published. It was especially pertinent because of the massive criticism copped by the CPMA Group, RWC's commercial partners. They were charged with setting up a commercial blueprint and it did seem from the meagre £5 million profit the tournament made that they had offended a good number of people and made next to nothing.

A tournament making very little money but which remained sweet and light and visibly above board would have been acceptable. So would a tournament making millions upon millions, which was what RWC and CPMA promised many times, but which lost the thread of sweetness and light and even became money-grabbing, because at least the money could have been sent across the world to the many impoverished unions who needed it. Soon after CPMA's appointment for the 1991 tournament their managing director, Alan Callan, spoke loftily of the need to 'ensure the future of rugby around the world'. An International Settlement Trust was to be set up which would make disbursements of unions around the globe – perhaps, says, to the Fijian Union, where hundreds of clubs are serviced in a ramshackle hut; or other outposts of fanaticism where the price of a set of kit or even ten rugby balls would galvanise the game. Appallingly, those disbursements have so far amounted to the price of a packet of peanuts, or nothing.

I hope that RWC can live with themselves for that and also that the major unions who had not received a larger slice of the action are ashamed of themselves. Gilding the lily, adding a few refinements to a massive stadium, is one thing. Climbing a frayed shoestring in the lands the other side of Calais is quite another.

To fail on both counts demanded that full accounts be published to reveal what had gone wrong. No one was suggesting anything shady but that was not the point. Would they publish full accounts? 'Definitely,' said Russ. 'I can assure you that everything will be published.' Nothing happened. In 1992 I asked Keith Rowlands whether full accounts would be published. 'Yes, because the game demands it,' he said. Those accounts have never emerged in full so the performance of CPMA, and of all the other companies they licensed to market aspects of the tournament, can never be assessed independently.

That is public relations of medieval proportions. The continued entreaties from within the game for RWC at least to appoint someone who can divulge progress to the press and rugby public at large have been roundly ignored.

The desperately ponderous nature of RWC, made unwieldy by all its arms and by the partnership with CPMA (for the 1995 tournament, CPMA are now allied to International Management Group), is showing no signs of acceleration. The 1995 tournament, correctly awarded in the first place to South Africa, is now fraught with doubts. Not only is there the volatile political situation. There is also the fact that, when you marry CPMA/IMG to the commercial elements in South Africa and add to the mix the rapacious hordes from both sides of fair business practice all needing a share of the action, you have the recipe for something sick-making.

It is now a matter of extreme urgency that the whole organisation should be simplified; that the current RWC be disbanded as soon as possible to allow the drafting of more inspired officials more sympathetic to the present-day player; of more PR-conscious officials, people who are at home in front of the cameras and who have clarity of explanation; of people with a sure grasp of the commercial realities of the current game. With respect, the appointment of Sir Ewart Bell as RWC chairman was a step in the wrong direction for each and every one of those goals. Above all, a new body should be returned to the day-to-day control of rugby unions around the world.

RWC's explanation for their involved set-up, with offshore companies dotted around the globe, is that they can avoid tax. As one of the game's leading officials told me recently, the game at large would far rather pay all the tax the Inland Revenue could possibly demand if it meant that the whole World Cup business was simplified and brought to order.

No wonder so many people gloried in the Lions tour. Here was a simple event, of global significance, yet something accessible; an event in which the players could thrive from the start, not wait months and months for an unsuccessful framework to be set in place before they could begin; an event true to rugby tradition which made the money available in the game without imposing layer upon layer of marketing men, licensees, agents, hangers-on and twisters. It was an event which did not shut out, as does the World Cup, so much of what gave the game the impetus for a World Cup in the first place.

More than anything, RWC have cause to kneel down and offer a prayer to rugby players. The players saved their skins in 1991 when, in an event unforgivably scattered round half of Europe, with which many people were sick to death before it started, they exploded on to the pitch and created a masterpiece. They were baled out again at Murrayfield, when Andrew Harriman saved their bacon, and sent it streaking down the touchline at high pace.

## (II) Wembley's Way With Rugby

I saw two major events at Wembley during 1992-93. The first was a concert by Eric Clapton and the second a rugby match between England and Canada (England won 26-13), held at the stadium in which some of the major events, such as the soccer and rugby league cup finals, are now uncomfortably close to elements of self-parody. Why on this earth do they sing 'Abide With Me', the old funeral dirge?

There was something incongruous about both Eric and England. For those of us brought up on a devotion to the dazzling guitarist, on 'Eric is God' banners and on the hauntingly recognisable first notes of 'White Room', his legend is unsurpassed. Yet at Wembley here was this trillionaire in an Armani suit, still admittedly, outrageously nifty with his axe playing 'White Room' from habit rather than conviction. 'White Room' and Eric is something which should be dresssed in old denim, not Armani.

And here were England in one of the capitals of professional sport, miles north of Twickenham (where rebuilding work was proceeding), driving up Wembley Way and coming up the long tunnel into the daylight of the stadium. Incongruous.

Yet ultimately, one felt more comfortable than the other. I felt that Clapton and the concert was ultimately a pastiche, almost a self-send-up, no matter how good it all sounded. I thought that I could get used to England not playing at Twickenham very easily indeed. I even considered launching a campaign for the RFU to flog off Twickenham to a developer, cut their costs at a stroke and so be able to devote all their income to the grass roots of the game instead of spending it on the upkeep of an expensive installation which is packed to the rafters a few times per year and otherwise sits toweringly and sulkily empty, as much use as a giant empty vessel.

The rugby at Wembley was riveting. One of the delights for us neutrals lies in the tweaking of noble noses by emerging nations. Canada's effort in the World Cup was magnificent. Given the powerful and inbuilt geographical disadvantages and the lower funding, it was the performance of the whole event.

At Wembley they were smashing. It was probably the biggest day in their rugby history and yet some of the squad could not even get time off from work to attend, an indication of some of the difficulties which beset them. Yet Norm Hadley, their enormous and engaging captain, one of the best locks in the world when fully fit, gave a marvellous performance in the line-out; they had a splendid and mobile front row in Dan Jackart, Karl Svoboda and Eddie Evans. They were competitive, optimistic, athletic. With eight minutes left, they trailed by only 21-13 after John Graf, the scrum-half, scuttled through for a try and then Gareth Rees, their power-hoofed fly-half, missed an easy penalty which would have taken them to within a score of England in a period of sustained Canadian pressure.

It took two tries from Ian Hunter and one each by Jerry Guscott and Peter Winterbottom to subdue them. It also took a splendid effort around the field by Winterbottom to keep on the correct route a team which did not fire. Early-season stodginess? As it turned out, more like the signpost to decline. Yet both live and on the box, the spectacle and the backdrop was superb. The England players were delighted with the fast, close-cropped surface. Will Carling wondered aloud why Twickenham was not given such a short-back-and-sides. The length of grass there is something of a rueful joke among everyone who plays there.

So why not play all games at Wembley? Of course it is difficult to get to. Of course the surrounding area is largely devoid of creature comforts. Yet for four-fifths of Britain it is no more difficult to get to than Twickenham; and the environs of Twickenham are hardly themselves festooned with everything the discerning, feasting and drinking rugby man or woman might ever want.

All right, all right, let's not cause coronaries. Only joking, colonel. It was an article by the great Ian Wooldridge which opened the eyes

of the game to its own raging good fortune a few years ago. In a
piece called 'Cathedrals of the Game', he pointed out how much
other sports coveted the glorious backdrops, facilities, base camps
and unique focus provided by the mega-stadia, Lansdowne Road,
Cardiff Arms Park, Parc des Princes, Murrayfield and Twickenham; how reassuring and comforting they are, how powerful an
article of confidence in the future they represent; how much we
adore them.

Never mind the more severe considerations, that Wembley rake
off their share of everything, for a start. Never mind the ease of
access. When you take part in a pilgrimage then a few extra miles to
meet your maker and his mates is neither here nor there. They
should crop the grass at Twickers. There are people who have
watched their rugby there for forty years and have never realised
that the players were wearing boots, or socks. But the RFU and all
the other unions can be counted upon to jealously preserve these
vast, living monuments to their own successes, the trademarks
peculiar to rugby.

Having said that, there was a growing feeling last season that
Twickenham was becoming something of a peculiar trademark.
When you look at the old-new ground, with the gigantic stands
circling the edges of the arena like a giant bear trying to creep up
unseen on the camp fire; when you see what the stadium has
become and how it will be when the bowl reaches round to cup the
whole edifice to the South Stand, you simply cannot stop yourself
using the adjective 'majestic'.

Do majestic stadia make great rugby stadia? The energy and
ambition and money-making capacity of the RFU to mount such a
major rebuilding project, their deftness in opening the ground
throughout the process save for the Canada encounter, is remarkable. (Even though in many respects and in all conscience they really
might have considered taking the Canada Test to a major soccer
ground in the north of England, where smugness about union's
future is misplaced.)

But there is no doubt that the new Twickenham will take years of
getting used to. You can dust off 'majestic', of course. But you can
store away for all time in your descriptive box 'homely', and perhaps
even 'user-friendly'. And 'close to the action' is gone for good, too.
Around the pitch there is a strip of green surrounding the rectangle
itself; then, in most parts, a tarmac track; then some flat rows of
seats. Then the seats start to bank gradually up to the top of the
stands, way up above Middlesex with views to all corners of the
shires.

The banking is very shallow and so, significantly, it means that to
accommodate the numbers, the top of the stadium is very high
indeed. I graphically remember the day I was shown around the
half-completed stand. Halfway up I started feeling queasy. So the
top of the three Twickers tiers is very far removed from the action.
It is the opposite in degree of pitch from the Millard Stand in

Wellington, which is so steep that you can use the shoulders of the poor bloke in front of you as a foot-rest.

Small wonder that the media, for example, while initially welcoming the siting of their seats at the back of the middle tier on being shown plans before the stands were built, suddenly found themselves divorced from the action and atmosphere. Small wonder that Gerry, my mate for whom I scraped together some tickets for the Welsh match in 1992, should write thanking me and saying how much he had enjoyed 'the match between the white ants and the red ants'. I have heard many comments in a similar vein.

The culture of being at the match but not quite so near or so involved as in the old wooden ground is a different culture. It will be fascinating to see how deeply the Twickersgoers and the debenture-holders grow to love their new futuristic stadium. There may even be the odd sideways glance of longing for dear old Wembley. And don't expect Eric Clapton to play at Twickenham. It would hardly give him the sense of club-room intimacy needed to play the essential version of 'White Room'.

## (III) *The New Era Strangled by the Old: The South Africans in France and England 1992*

Vincent Moscato, the fierce French hooker who was sent off at Parc des Princes by Steve Hilditch in the warlike match between France and England in 1982, has a popular city-centre bar in Bordeaux, called, with cunning Gallic wit, Bar Vincent. For some reason, an old red British phone box lurks inside. Mine host usually pulls the demi-litres himself. Philippe Gimbert, his tight head at Bègles-Bordeaux and occasionally for France, occasionally works there too. They are not the sort of men to whom you return demanding that your short measure be topped up.

Vincent had some new customers in the autumn of 1992 as the season in France swung into its stride. They were the South African rugby team. The vast majority of the party were making their first overseas tour of any significance and it had been over a decade since the Springboks had played a serious match abroad. They were to play the French provinces, the England divisions, two Tests against France and one at Twickenham against England.

At first, Vincent found them poor trade, a little dour and shy. Then, as some of the ice melted, they began to dip their hands into their pockets, to slacken off at the shoulders and to fade into their surroundings with all the utter lack of success of any touring national rugby team of fit young giants anywhere in the world. 'It will be a learning process and a new era,' said John Williams, the coach. It was a learning process, but not in the way that Williams had hoped. It was not a new era. The tour, almost unrelievedly unsuccessful, rang down the curtain on the old era rather than ushering in another. It showed that the Springboks were moving with hidebound slowness in their attempt to re-scale old peaks.

For a start, the tour exposed Williams and the management team. It saw off Williams himself, saw off Botha, the captain; proved that first-string locks like Adri Geldenhuys and Adolf Malan and Drikus Hattingh were not the men to construct the line-out of the Springbok future; that the lack of pace and will in the SARFU's efforts to develop non-white rugby at home still spelled danger for the progress of their national team on foreign fields; that the old guard which selected and surrounded the team was too rooted. It is always useful in the long term to glean negative information about your players and structure. It is the best way to learn. And so in that sense and that sense alone, it was a tour of glorious success and long-term usefulness.

The tour was dogged in places by old echoes of the apartheid years. You would imagine that the Springboks, and especially their great players, would be simply bursting to tour and to make up for lost time. Instead, Uli Schmidt, regarded by many South Africans as the best hooker in the world, simply refused to tour. He complained that he did not believe the party would be welcome (which was complete balderdash). He also hinted strongly that he objected to the stance the Australians had taken in the 'Die Stem' bother.

It seemed for all the world that here was an unreconstructed South African, and some of his colleagues who did tour had no time for his view. Schmidt did tour Australia later, playing conspicuously although probably less effectively than his showy style at first indicated.

Jannie Breedt was another who never appeared. The talented number 8 had spoken of the 'magic moment' of South Africa's return. 'And it will be magic again when those picked to tour board the aeroplane in their green blazers to go to France and England.' Passionate words. However, the magic quickly faded for Breedt himself. He simply turned down the tour and departed for a stint in Italian club rugby amid a barrage of cynical nodding from those familiar with the alleged rates of bung available in that country.

The echoes continued, through no fault of the Springboks', as soon as they arrived in Bordeaux to begin the tour. Frédèrique Bredin, the French sports minister, complained bitterly when the party arrived that there was no non-white player. She suggested that one might be flown over. It was a monumentally stupid reaction, and briefly I imagined some inadequately talented black player arriving at Charles de Gaulle as the lone and token black to satisfy the warped conception of Bredin as to what really constituted multi-racial rugby.

There was even an echo of the old days of hairy protest. At the start of the English leg of the tour there was a flurry of publicity given to complaints of some activists in South Africa that the promised avalanche of funding for non-white rugby had not been forthcoming, and indeed, that the amount devoted to those areas to date amounted to not a deal more than a handful of peanuts. The ANC issued a warning that if the will and funds did not appear soon then they would pull the rugby plug, although they did maintain support for the tour and for the English Test. There was no suggestion from them that the tour be stopped.

However, that was not good enough for some. Out of musty old closets came small groups of superannuated beardies, last seen in the sixties and seventies, who called rallies and demos and demanded that the Springboks fly home and never darken our doors again. Before every game, local beardy chiefs promised mass rallies and, until the penny dropped, the police spoke of rings of blue steel around the place. Eventually, after a few two-men-and-a-dog mass rallies, everyone disappeared back into their musty closets and the police realised that a couple of local bobbies were all that was needed.

The only unseemly echo remaining came at Twickenham. The RFU got themselves into a desperate and wholly unnecessary tizz. They realised (the liberal devils) that 'Die Stem' could not be played before the Twickenham Test and therefore became obsessed with the view that 'God Save the Queen' was out too, in order to safeguard South African sensibilities and protocol – even though many host unions play the home anthem and no other. The RFU should have torn up the music to 'Die Stem' without a solitary twinge of conscience. The announcement that 'God Save the Queen' was not to be played gave every rose nationalist, every newspaper, every attention-seeker and everyone who simply liked bawling out the anthem at Twickers the excuse to mount a campaign. Had the union not caved in then everyone would have sung the anthem in any case.

Even then their consciences prickled. For some reason, and as a substitute for 'Die Stem', the RFU revved up Sir Peter Yarranton, the past president, to deliver to the crowd just before the start a cloying and utterly unnecessary welcome which, between the lines, seemed to suggest that the long absence of South Africa was in some way a travesty. Neither in sport nor in life were the months and years of post-apartheid to run smoothly.

One man emerged from the tour with his reputation profoundly gilded and with his eminence in the world game vindicated. Naas Botha, at the end of a career of unending controversy, had decided to revoke his pending retirement to bring the callow party. And if ever the cards were stacked high against any tour captain they were stacked against Naas. For a start, any major tour of France is a minefield, every match a potential snarling disaster and every stopover potentially fraught with cultural and language problems – especially for the unworldly new Springboks.

He had precious little back-up. The management team was a monumental carve-up. The original choice for tour manager had been Johan Claassen, the great old Springbok forward. It was a dreadful appointment, one greeted by observers like Deon Viljoen, the fine South African writer, with utter disbelief. Claassen had managed the 1981 Springboks on their disastrous tour of New Zealand and had impressed no one with his ham-fistedness. He was quickly shunted sideways to a non-post on tour as 'SARFU representative', and Abie Malan, a little more avuncular than Claassen, though hardly a global communicator and card-carrying man-manager, took over. That all led to a few fixed smiles, as did the appointment of Ian Kirkpatrick as assistant coach to Williams, since as a pair they had never been famous for finding the same wavelength. It argued powerfully that there was no one back at the ranch making clear and far-sighted decisions and that everyone was forced to tread on inter-provincial sensibilities.

Botha, as the one man who had travelled, the one man with a self-confidence in the European theatre, had to hold all that lot together. As he said himself, there were many other problems, many other fissures to worry him. 'There is the tour itself. In South Africa we leave for a match on Friday night and we are back home by Sunday. Suddenly, these guys are away for seven to eight weeks, which for some is a shattering experience. Besides, this is a young side, not only age-wise but also experience-wise. Some of our so-called veterans have played only one or two internationals.

'Another factor is the tribal structure of South African rugby. For many decades we have been divided into provincial entities. There are guys who left Northern Transvaal because they hated me and who are now touring with me. For years, players in Natal, Transvaal and Western Province regarded me as their foremost enemy. It is very difficult to change their mentality overnight and to make them think now, I like Naas Botha.'

Botha coped brilliantly. The party was harshly criticised in France and at home for breaches of etiquette: leaving dinners early, moaning about French food and practices. I think that given the whole package, the massive culture shock, Naas and his men actually managed rather well. I caught up with him in Bordeaux just as they were preparing to face French Espoirs in the opening tour match. He and his fellow countrymen had been on the back foot for so long in the PR innings, partly because of the lack of real movement and liberalisation in South African rugby. But Naas no longer felt the need to apologise.

'If you came across someone on a bus talking about South Africa, you felt it might be better if you just kept quiet,' he said. 'But this is the start of a whole new era. I am South African and I am not shy about it. We no longer have anything to hide. Our rugby is integrated, our touring team was chosen on merit and I am not being arrogant when I say that we are here, you accept us and that is it. There is no other story.'

Botha was spot-on, and courageous. If only the flourishing of old icons would stop pulling the rug from under his feet then he and the Springboks would be well set. He was a jewel against the Espoirs next day, when South Africa's re-emergence began with a cere-monial kick-off by Danie Craven, on his last visit to Europe. Craven was in too frail a state to return for the Twickenham Test at the end of the tour.

The South Africans, frighteningly for their tour prospects, were beaten by 24-17 by the Espoirs. Thierry Lacroix, the glorious talented back from Dax, orchestrated a succession of attacks which led to two tries from Pierre Hontas. There was a desperate lack of speed and inventiveness in the visiting ranks and only the meaty forwards and some soaring generalship and kicking from Botha kept his men together. As at Ellis Park and Newlands a few months previously, it had been obvious that they still had no line-out to speak of and no back-row balance, either.

They struggled on, scraping past an Aquitaine XV in Pau by 29-22, past an under-prepared Midi-Pyrenées XV by 18-15 in Toulouse and, more comfortably, against a Provence-Côte d'Azur XV in Marseilles. Remarkably, they won the First Test at the Stade Gerlaud in Lyons. Danie Gerber and James Small scored tries and Botha kicked ten points. Their tackling was gutsy, their scrummaging was solid and their upper-body strength wrapped up the ball for long periods – helped by the inclusion of three props: the four-square Willie Hills was switched to the middle of the front row between the five-square Johan Styger and the six-square Heinrich Rodgers. Wahl Bartmann, Adriaan Richter and Tian Strauss put together a decent back-row effort. Irresistible, however, it was not.

Yet France and the match itself were twin disasters. They tried to run the ball on a soft pitch. Alain Penaud at fly-half allowed the game to run away from him, Aubin Hueber at scrum-half, struggling with scrappy possession, had a day to forget and the whole, unbalanced, badly selected French team subsided in inverse ratio to the fuss and bother and back-stabbing in committee rooms which traditionally greets any French shambles.

The Second Test in Paris was a watershed. At last, Pierre Berbizier chose a balanced team, with the outstanding Abdel Benazzi to take the pressure from Olivier Roumat at lock, with Philippe Benetton to give the back row some power. The French were fifteen points better or more, and crushed the Springboks with tries from Roumat and Penaud, with a brilliant performance by Laurent Cabannes on the flank. The Springboks had no continuity, no line-out, little inspiration behind the scrum. They played without discernible passion. They were hammered, and with morale dipping and thoughts turning away from France across the English Channel, they lost, embarrassingly, to a young French Universities XV in Tours and to an old French Barbarians XV at that smashing stadium, Stade du Nord in Lille.

The culture shock lessened in England, where they understood the language, the menus, the referees. Inspired by Gerber, they thrashed the Midlands 32-9 with late tries from Gerber and Oosthuizen, even though, against a curiously disappointing Midlands of hard forwards and featureless backs, they fumbled for three-quarters of the match.

They scraped past England B at a teeming Memorial Ground, Bristol, with what was, with the possible exception of the first match of their return at Ellis Park, their best performance of the whole year. It was a marvellous match in which, for a change, continuity ruled. Hattingh, Richter and Jacques Olivier scored their tries and the England B midfield of Stuart Barnes, Phil de Glanville and Damian Hopley did their aspirations nothing but good. The momentum was maintained at Elland Road, Leeds, in the week with a 19-3 victory over a disappointing North Division.

The finale took place on a dungeon-dark and wet day at Twickenham. The Springboks led 16-8 at one stage, with a try by Strauss and some Botha kicks stretching them away from England, despite a breathtaking try by Tony Underwood. Yet the England forwards reasserted themselves. Rob Andrew began to loft kicks into the leaden skies – and South Africa began to drop them. Jeremy Guscott, Dewi Morris and Will Carling scored tries in the second half, and the final score was 33-16 – in many ways, it was England's most satisfying effort of the whole season.

The remainder of the year, as South African rugby busied itself in banishing the years of inaction, were mixed and salutary. The South African provinces, in general, played well in the Super-10 series and Transvaal squeezed past Auckland in the final. Yet somehow they allowed the weakened French to escape with a series victory in the Southern Hemisphere winter, with a draw, 20-20, in the First Test and a remarkable French win by 18-17 in the Second Test in Johannesburg. Theo van Rensburg, the home full-back, missed a kickable penalty in the last seconds and France, with an assortment of kicks but no tries, had won an unlikely victory – under an unlikely captain. After Jeff Tordo had had his face lacerated by the boot of Gary Pagel of Western Province he was able to take no further part in the tour and Olivier Roumat, previously a little moody, temperamental and inconsistent, was appointed in his place.

The French are not, as a historical rule, the best travellers. For South Africa to lose this series, again with inbuilt problems in the line-out, back row and in the fields of continuity, was a bitter disappointment. They flattered to deceive, too, in an emotional, competitive and hugely enjoyable series in Australia. They took the First Test at the Sydney Football Stadium under floodlights. Yet Australia, playing the whole series without John Eales, Willie Ofahengaue and Michael Lynagh (arguably their three key players) found themselves winning at Brisbane in the Second Test and, by 19-12, back at Sydney in the Third. In the Second Test, James Small became the first Springbok ever to be sent off in a Test when he gave Ed Morrison a big piece of his mind and Morrison, one of the referees of the year, waved him on his way to the dressing-room.

During the series, the Australians assimilated into their squad another Pacific sensation in Ilie Tabua, the former Fijian international, who made an astounding debut game in Brisbane. Significantly, the attendances for the series and the tour as a whole were enormous. Less than six years ago, Australia could sell only 17,000 tickets for their own appearance in a World Cup semi-final. Against the Springboks in the series decider, the Sydney stadium was sold out, with 42,000 supporters attending. Significantly, too, David Campese ended the series in wonderful form and Nick Farr-Jones with retirement, circling the pitch in a lap of honour at the end.

The Springboks toured under Ian McIntosh, their new coach, and François Pienaar, the blond flanker, who was captain. Still they were bedevilled by lack of line-out possession and Messrs Hannes Strydom and Nico Wegner, the jumpers at the end of the long year, were no more successful than Geldenhuys and Malan at the start and Kobus Wiese against the French in the middle. We were still searching for the athletic giants we had been promised.

The volatile political situation in the latter part of 1993 – the World Cup is in dire jeopardy – rather overshadowed the success or otherwise of the SARFU's development programme. It was launched in earnest in March 1993, and present were Steve Tshwete, the ANC's 'minister of sport', who is something of a rugby nutcase and who played for Robben Island's rugby team when in captivity; and Morné du Plessis, the old number 8 and a symbol, through his liberalism, his vision and his good sense, of a better future. It really would be the best step forward for a century if du Plessis could gain a position of power on the SARB. He also made the valuable distinction between doling out money and, in effect, bribing people to play, and actually changing moral stances.

Tshwete was categorical. 'A breakthrough in rugby could lead to a breakthrough in attitudes in society. Rugby can defuse the menace of the right wing,' he said, which is a heavy, heavy responsibility. The attempts of the South African rugby technocrats and players to raise and reform their rugby, another slow process, is a responsibility of a different sort. Both tasks were carried out with surprising slowness during the long year of the return. To have them back was a kind of aggravating and angry joy.

## (IV) Bob and the Bag-Snatchers: The Australians in Ireland and Wales

If it is possible for the World Champions of rugby to make a low-key tour, and if it is possible for any team containing David Campese, history's most astonishing player, to proceed in a predictable fashion then the Wallaby tour of Ireland and Wales in a damp autumn was relatively low-key and predictable. Relatively.

And yet it was also epoch-making. In the wet and under pressure from injury to men of vast influence, Australia did not dazzle. They had to graft and battle their way through. But neither were they threatened in either of the Tests, and it was the tour which signalled Australia's arrival as one of the pillars, as a rugby nation now regarded in the British Isles as on a par with the two more traditional giants, New Zealand and South Africa. Previously, to beat Australia when they toured was a source of satisfaction, a major fillip to your club or province, but it did not shift the history of your club or province on its axis; did not have the tilt of heritage. When you beat New Zealand or South Africa you knew, that day when the final whistle went, that you were in history, would be glowing at the fireside in your later years with the breathtaking memory. It completed the education of the Australian players to go through the threshing-mill that comprises the great Welsh clubs and the unquenchable men of Munster.

You could tell from the celebrations in Cork, Swansea and Llanelli that times have changed and that Australia's marvellous success during the tour and their style have made them a dish worth munching. Munster, Swansea and Llanelli all beat the Australians and the emotional scenes afterwards, the body language of the winning teams, the souvenirs produced to wear and to treasure later, were all a tribute to the winners – and even more, a tribute to the status of the losers. It was a significant shift.

There was nothing quiet about the Munster match, which the fierce Munstermen won by 22-19. It was a ferocious confrontation during which Garrick Morgan, the towering young Australian lock, was sent off and Bob Dwyer, the Australian coach, fired volleys of anger at Peter Clohessy, the war-like Munster prop who, claimed Dwyer, had started all the fuss and bother.

Swansea were conspicuously better on the day, winning 21-6, thrashing the Australian scrummage and thriving in their fast style, which served them well until the calf muscles seized a little at the end of the season. Llanelli were helped on their way through a glorious back movement which launched Ieuan Evans over at the posts. They won 13-9 and afterwards, Rupert Moon, their splendid captain, was carried from the pitch, punching the air in what was almost a paroxysm of delight. It recalled with wondrous haste the sight of Delme Thomas, sleeves rolled and biceps flexed above him, bellowing at the skies as he was borne from Stradey Park across a scarlet sea after Llanelli had beaten the 1972-73 All Blacks.

For me, the Australian teams of the last four years have been glorious, at their best one of the four greatest teams I have seen; for entertainment value and ambience in their work, among the most compelling. For me, they are an identikit of how a modern Test team should play, should conduct themselves, should entertain and should portray themselves to the outside world. If you graft on the indescribable Campese then you have the team of a lifetime.

They are in many ways a manufactured team. The attention paid to their team's inner welfare, conditioning and diet is staggering. It is based on the techniques of the Australian Institute of Sport in Canberra, and while by no means all of the squad have been through the Institute, the inch-perfect guidance culture which exists there has been taken on board the team bus for every journey. They never travel, it seems, without their doctor, physiotherapist, aromatherapist, dentist, and so many other -ists that they must nearly have to leave half the players behind to get them all on.

Even the aggression in their game is largely fed into the team mainframe well before match day. They are, even in the forwards, a team of fresh faces. They would pass for a bunch of college boys retaking exams for the fourth time. They have in their forward squad, with the possible exception of the exceptional Viliame Ofahengaue, no core of rough-hewn manual workers bringing natural toughness and power. Their forwards are the *nouveau* fit, scientifically matured into hard nuts. Phil Kearns, the strapping hooker and faithful disciple of the Institute, is as fresh-faced as any. But are you going to tell him so?

Dwyer is a giant of the game in the modern era. I spoke to him before the Irish Test, his fiftieth in charge. As ever, he was needle-sharp. Whether or not he was anxious to talk to me on a rare night off, providing at least temporary respite from the intensity he brings to his coaching post, he gave the impression that he was. He was at that time engaged in a long and bitter battle to reverse the experimental ruck/maul law, a law which dynamited every Australian game plan. There were three massive ironies. First, it was regarded as an Australian idea even though all the leading coaches in the country hated it; secondly, it was meant to create more open play, and yet as his team were the most attractive in the game by a street, why did they need it? Thirdly, as an answer to the lack of reference-points on the pitch Dwyer was forced to develop long rolling mauls, the very thing that the law was supposed to stamp out. 'If you want a champion for any campaign,' he said in his team's Ulster hotel, 'then I put myself forward.' I took him up on his kind offer.

By his success in welding together a talented young team to win the World Cup, and to elevate for all time the status of rugby union in his country, he deserved to be called the greatest coach in the game. But to produce a team which had not only such intensity but also such vision and gifts, not all of them the individual province of Campese, was another triumph. He even took apart the side on the French tour of 1989 (in mid-tour, mind you), pitched in the likes of Phil Kearns, Jason Little, Tony Daly and Tim Horan, and they all spread themselves into the team for life. Dwyer can be stroppy when things are going against him. He still bawls out the 1989 British Lions, who, he reckons, used the strong arm to drag his team out of the series. I suspect that he was rueing the fact that the Lions were doing to Australia exactly what he would dearly love to have done to the Lions; that the series sorted out a few Wallaby softies and that Australian forward play, courtesy of the Lions, improved in leaps and scrums.

Dwyer's attention to detail was amazing. I knew from past conversations that he regarded Tim Horan, the pocket battleship of a centre, as his core player. Yet when I spoke to him he was fretting about Horan. 'He is probably not so great at creating space for others. We have been working on it. He is a sensational player but has a little extra to work on.'

Before they arrived in Ireland they had lost Nick Farr-Jones, the team's infallible engine, who had petered out into semi-retirement. During the Irish Test, they lost Michael Lynagh, a little more diffident than Farr-Jones and significantly less consistent, but their new captain and play-maker. Also before the Welsh Test, they lost

John Eales. When Dwyer said during the 1991 World Cup that the youthful Eales, the wonderful athlete and line-out man, was 'close to being the most important player in world rugby', he was considerably understating the case. Eales missed the rest of the tour, the Bledisloe Cup match against New Zealand and, indeed, the series against the touring South Africans in August.

These were chilling blows. The tour did illustrate the one weakness of the Australian national squad: they lack depth. In almost every position, there is a significant fall-away between the top dog and his underdog. Indeed, even though Dwyer spoke bravely at the start of having thirty interchangeable players he was not himself fooled. Neither of the two young giants, Warwick Waugh or Garrick Morgan, came storming through as potential Test locks. Morgan played well against Wales with Eales missing but neither he nor Waugh played as well as someone of that size and potential should have played.

Peter Slattery, the barking terrier trying to emerge from the shadow of Farr-Jones, began well but suffered in temperament and efficiency later; so, emphatically, did Paul Kahl, the reserve fly-half who lacked the composure of Lynagh. Most of the other reserves were journeymen. There were even scrummaging problems later in the tour, when both Tony Daly and Cameron Lillicrap had been invalided home and neither Andrew Blades nor especially Matt Ryan were on the pace. Ryan, simply, was a slowcoach, unusual in a team of athletes.

Yet even if the problems caused Dwyer, the ultimate worrier, to grimace a little, the framework of the team, in morale and pride and personnel, remained. The Wallabies took direct hits below the waterline in Cork, Swansea and Llanelli, but were never to lose again, were never going to drop a Test. They thrashed Ireland by 42-17, despite giving what was probably their worst Test performance for years. They could easily have scored fifty points; they lost their captain, Lynagh, with a serious shoulder injury at half-time and yet still won easily, at a canter. The best of their five tries was scored by Jason Little. Campese led a break-out, the Australian front row took the ball deftly on and Little appeared down the left wing for the try. Campese, Ewan McKenzie, Kelaher and Horan were the other scorers.

The Welsh match was more stern and was closer than the 23-6 result reveals. The Welsh tackling and passion served them well. They even shaded the line-out battle because Tony Copsey and Gareth Llewellyn had the better of Morgan and Rod McCall. It was a staggering contrast to the match between the teams in the pool of the World Cup a year earlier, when Wales, after a recount, were deemed to have won two line-outs all afternoon. It was half a good performance by Wales.

But they did not score a try, never really came close to one and did not capitalise on possession. And no wonder. They ran straight into one of the greatest tackling stints that Cardiff Arms Park can ever have seen. It was led by Horan and Little but the blaster-in-chief was

Ofahengaue. His hitting was awesome. He often picked up Welsh players and dumped them yards back up the field. David Wilson, the improving flanker, McCall and Campese scored tries, Campese after a sprint down the right-hand touchline towards the end, when a mis-kick by Little popped obligingly into his path.

The rest of the tour was routine, with relatively easy wins over Leinster, Ulster, Connacht (on a filthy West of Ireland day), Wales B, Monmouthshire (a match which, with respect to Mr Smith of Ireland, contained the most abysmal refereeing I saw all season), the Welsh Students and ultimately, thanks to endless driving mauls, the Barbarians.

Yet of all the games, perhaps the most newsworthy was that against Neath. Australia won 16-8, but only after Neath had put up fierce resistance and only after both teams had descended into a nonsensical shoving, bickering and even head-kicking mass. It was a shameful match.

And it was at the Gnoll that Australia's superb off-field public relations came into their own. They are not a dirty team, and afterwards, Dwyer sat down and attacked Neath's approach. 'This place must be the bag-snatching capital of the world,' he said angrily. We looked at each other. What was he talking about? Had someone stolen his kitbag, or his handbag? The penny gradually dropped. He meant that Neath players had grabbed Aussies by the testicles. It was such a newsworthy quote and such a new concept and new description that the home media had a field day with the whole issue. Dwyer went on to decry everything dressed in a Neath jersey.

And because Dwyer's approachability and quotability has the world eating from his hand, and because in the war of words afterwards Neath could only field the quietly-spoken Gareth Llewellyn, who was not inclined to complain about things, the whole world and his wife left the Gnoll that day in the unshakable belief that Neath had initiated a one-way, one-team punch-up. In fact, Australia's approach was uncharacteristically appalling. Slattery, captain for the day, lost his rag under pressure. An Australian forward kicked Brian Williams, the Neath prop, in the head. It was a one-off match (thank goodness), but it showed how useful Dwyer's consummate skills in claiming the moral high ground in the name of Australia could be.

On the other hand, he often does not even have to bother. It would be a notion too ridiculous for words to say that Australia, for their approach, are a team to whom it is a pleasure to lose. But in their visits of late they have inspired great affection from followers in the British Isles. When Campese ran down the touchline to score in the last seconds at Cardiff, I am positive that there were Welshmen willing him on. There were certainly about 50,000 applauding him back to halfway.

Australia briefly lost some momentum as the season wore on. They lost the Bledisloe Cup to New Zealand in Dunedin, a match for which New Zealand had thirsted for months and in which

Australia were without Lynagh, Eales and Ofahengaue, bulwarks of the team. They welcomed back for that match, and for the subsequent series against the touring South Africans, the great Farr-Jones. Why, oh why do players make such solemn formal announcements about retirement, then have to negotiate a potentially embarrassing comeback song-and-dance when they unretire? Farr-Jones was apparently following the Paul Ackford theory: get out before some two-bit kid puts one over on you. I much prefer the Paul Rendall method: play on till you drop, as long as they still select you. And that is exactly what Dwyer and Australia would like the marvellous man to do. But he gave it away again after he saw off the Springboks in Australia.

The Bledisloe Cup defeat was Australia's first of any significance since the World Cup, and with their injury problems and the fact that the All Blacks have been thoroughly shaken down in the three-match series against the Lions, it is most certainly not evidence of long-term decline. They dropped the First Test of a superb series against the touring Springboks, but still without their Big Three, recovered to win in Brisbane to take the series back in Sydney with a glorious try scored by Horan. They even discovered another storming flanker in Ilie Tabua, from Fiji.

For a team as good as Australia have been, it takes years for the fires to die, especially if they keep together the core men – Gavin, Kearns, Eales, one or two others – for as long as possible. It will also take a long time for the wonderful memories of what Australia have done for their own rugby and the game worldwide, in their play and in their behaviour, to pass into the recesses of the memory.

CHAPTER 10

# The Hunt for the Green Lion

## (I) THE 1993 FIVE NATIONS TOURNAMENT

You only notice your favourite furniture when they take it away. Likewise, we take the Five Nations Championship so much for granted. Take it away and there would be more than a comfy armchair missing – three-quarters of European rugby would be gone, too. For excitement, the profile of the sport, the funding and well being of the sport; for well-balanced sportsmanship amid the deep hunger for victory, the winter weeks of the ten Tests stand utterly alone.

The burning questions to be answered in the 1993 event were: who on earth are going to beat England? Will Scotland be as weak on the pitch as they look on paper? Will Ireland seek modernisation instead of harking back? Will Wales be competitive now that their structure is sound, and will France stop bickering long enough to put a team on the field? Above all, will anyone come through to stop the British Lions choosing, say, twenty-six Englishmen, and will there be any Irish Lions whatsoever? Irish rugby players have found more glory in a red jersey than in the emerald green, and in January 1993 it was difficult to see who on earth was going to tour from Ireland to accompany the one secure, and potentially lonely, Irishman, Nick Popplewell. Enough, in the cold midwinter, to be going on with.

As it turned out, as an aesthetic and technically impressive Championship it was a disappointment. And it was also as fascinating, enjoyable and even mesmeric as ever. Tell me which team sport would not kill for their own Five Nations?

We soon knew about England. They took the year off. They still have more depth in key positions than the other countries but they lost their balance and their continuity, and also their famous and possibly overrated ability to keep their shape under pressure. Against Wales their attacking machine was quite easily contained by the home defence and the lurking Ieuan Evans swept past the dozing Rory Underwood for the vital try. They had been lucky to beat the French at Twickenham, where a flicked left-foot dropped goal from Jean-Baptiste Lafond cannoned back in-field off the crossbar when it could have given the French a win.

They did recover at home against Scotland. At last, they admitted to themselves that if they were serious about back play and maximising the return then they needed the sharper, more direct approach of Stuart Barnes at fly-half. Sure enough, the little Bath scuttler showed the men outside him in the best light for some seasons. Barnes made one electric break which sent Jeremy Guscott away and the unbelievable burst of pace which Guscott injected, and the wondrous sleight of hand with which he drew the defence and gave a try on a plate to Rory Underwood, were the individual glories of the whole season.

Scotland had begun with half a decent performance in a 15-3 victory over abject Ireland and another half in Paris, where their policy of choosing for their squad Scots, semi-Scots, arriviste Scots and plain old Sassenachs paid off. Andy Reed, until recently a Bath reserve lock from Cornwall, became a first-string lock for Scotland, and against the French he won some life-giving line-out ball. It was hardly a commodity which has frequently come the way of Scottish scrum-halves in recent years. Yet Scotland could build nothing on their platform and, not for the first time in the past five years, they produced precious little from their threequarter line. The annals of glorious Scottish tries have been a little thin of late. Coach McGeechan made strenuous efforts to fill in the holes and they were striving and assured in easy home victory against Wales. They finished second in the table, an admirable effort given the mediocre basic materials at their disposal.

That leaves France and Ireland, who both enjoyed amazing seasons. France's season was astonishing because it was astonishingly quiet. They eventually decided to stop backbiting and to concentrate on their rugby. Pierre Berbizier managed to survive the monthly coup after the French had contrived to lose at home to Argentina in the autumn. And he still supplied enough bone-headed thinking to keep the plotters on the go, notably in the indefensible decision to leave some senior players behind for the tour of South Africa. But when the Five Nations began, under the eerily quiet but nobly effective new captain, the Cleo Laine-haired Jeff Tordo, they made quiet progress. Berbizier, at last, had reintroduced Abdel Benazzi at lock, found a punishing scrum-mager in Seigne at tight head, and rationalised the back-row balance by shunting Cleo to hooker.

They could easily have won at Twickenham but did not; they could have lost at home to Scotland but came through with a try from Thierry Lacroix. They won easily in Ireland, 21-6, with tries by two of the backs of the European season – Philippe Saint-André and Philippe Sella (the former had already scored twice against England). They polished Wales off at home with three tries and a 26-10 victory – and without fuss, fratricide or rough play, without anger at the Anglo-Saxon referees, they had won the Five Nations. They deserved to. They were the best team. Who can begrudge them? The brilliant, teeming, argumentative and gloriously talented mass that is French rugby deserves to rule the roost. They also deserve, if they had the bottle to bid for it, to host the next Northern Hemisphere World Cup in its entirety.

Ireland's graph of progress for the season consisted of a vertical line. They were abject in the summer of 1992 in New Zealand, where they were massacred on Saturdays and in midweek. They were awful against the Scots, and thrashed by France at home. There was the astonishing sound of jeering and restiveness from the Lansdowne Road crowd, normally the most supportive spectators in the game.

But the feature of the season was a fierce and anguished debate off the field about the preparation of the Irish national team. The knee-jerk reaction whenever Ireland lost was to invoke the spirits of old forwards, to wonder where the fury and passion had gone, to assume that once the fire returned the team would begin to win again. There was much talk about new-fangled means of preparation not suiting Irish temperament or players. Moss Keane, the glorious charging lock, was a member of one of the most effective and passionate Irish teams of all time. He was disparaging about the current methods. 'The players nowadays remind me of battery hens,' he told Sean Diffley of the *Irish Independent*. 'Personality is not welcome in the system.' Keane complained about sponsors, new physiological trends of preparation, regimented training. He, and dozens of others, bemoaned the lack of the old irreverent spirit, and demanded successors to the pounding hooves of Phil Orr, Willie Duggan and the others.

They were all wrong. That Irish team of the late 1970s and 1980s were not simply chasers and harriers, did not play on spirit alone. They included men who played a certain kind of game at world class and could short-cut lack of preparation and conditioning through experience. The truth is that the dismal Irish record of eleven successive defeats (which ended when they won in Cardiff) was not due to lack of the old spirit. It was not, primarily, due to lack of quality players, either, because there are more in Ireland than many Irish people think. It was because they became seduced by the old days, appointing as their managers and coaches for too long people who were simply old playing greats, not always clued-up assets as man-managers or coaches in the modern era. Some people realised it – notably a major figure in the teeth-gnashing crisis months in the early phase of the last Five Nations season, David Walsh, the sports writer from the *Sunday Independent* in Dublin, who is certainly one of the very best writers on sport currently word-processing in the British Isles.

Walsh suggested that instead of invocations to Moss and his thundering ilk, Ireland would do themselves far more good by moving aside Noel Murphy, the manager, and others from the hierarchy, and instead installing a new high-tech and all-embracing package of man-management, organisation, fitness testing, first-class treatment and inner sustenance such as that already employed by England and Wales. On all those counts, the performance of those in charge in Ireland was decidedly fitful. Players like Brendan Mullin and Ralph Keyes and others, all of whom had the talent to be key players, simply turned away from the Test scene, driven out by frustration and lack of sympathetic back-up. Walsh used as his evidence some brave views from Simon Geoghegan, the wing who was simply brassed off with defeat, with lack of planning and direction, and said so. For his pains, Geoghegan was temporarily suspended from the Irish squad. Walsh also, perfectly correctly, raised the Neil Francis case. Francis, the rather irascible lock with elements of the prima donna about him, was vilified last season for what people saw as a lack of application and devotion to the cause and for languishing with injury.

I have news for them. Paul Ackford and Wade Dooley regard Francis as far and away the best forward of the era in Ireland. So do I. He should be the core of the whole team. Francis is partly to blame, but surely, in a wise management team, there should be scope for a difficult individual and also the talents and the persuasive qualities to make him less difficult and more useful? I once asked Francis how high on his list of life's priorities was a career in the Irish national team. 'There is no list,' he said. 'That is the only priority.'

So, in view of my fervently held opinion that no Five Nations without a strong Ireland is ever worth a light, I secretly hoped that they would lose all their games, and that the shock of the bucket of whitewash descending would galvanise them into action and into the modern era.

How were we to view, therefore, the end of the Five Nations? Ireland beat Wales in Cardiff in typical storming style, helped by a try from Brian Robinson, the fine number 8, and with some clever kicking at goal and into space from Eric Elwood, the newest of the new fly-halves. Hmmmm. There was only one way, however, to view Ireland's teeming victory over England at the very end, when England were still seeking the Five Nations title – as a glorious afternoon of typical Moss-like pounding. Ireland won 17-3, reducing England to a gibbering wreck of a team. Mick Galwey scored a thunderous try and Elwood, again cool as a cucumber, rifled over two dropped goals and two penalties. The reaction of the Dublin crowd contained exactly the same elements as the reaction of the Cardiff crowd after the Welsh victory over England: sheer, long-suppressed joy and release from seasons of purgatory.

How would this affect the Irish approach? I hope that, along with their invocations to the spirit, they will modernise, get their planning act together. Otherwise the Dublin experience will be a waste. But the main question raised by the Dublin weekend, as thousands of us sat down to discuss our Lions selection, was how far would it affect the Lions choice, and would Popplewell, after all, have company? Suddenly, it seemed that Elwood, Robinson, Clohessy and others were now bound for Kiwiland.

They stayed at home. The final noises of the Five Nations were unjustified complaints from Irishmen. They forget that Elwood and the others were, in effect, two-game wonders. They may well develop into great players, but that could not be taken on trust. As a sop, they sent Mick Galwey alongside Popplewell, but as a tight flanker and not a fine lock. It looked a bad choice and so it proved. Gavin Hastings, to the relief of a tired Will Carling, was chosen instead of him as captain. There were hundreds of English, and given their lack of visible power, a worrying number of Scottish tight forwards.

So the Five Nations wound up for another year. On the day after it ended there was a vast void. Nothing to argue about in Lions selection; nothing to chew over in one of sport's biggest and more enduring festivals. Still, January comes around once a year.

## (II) Wales – Accelerating into Reverse

At the start of the 1992-93 season Welsh rugby finally engaged a forward gear and after a few miles of devoted chugging the Welsh Rugby Union at last arrived somewhere which, after a recce, they recognised as the twentieth century. Their paid officials at their Cardiff offices, Denis Evans, the secretary, and Jonathan Price, the marketing executive presided (and in many cases, inspired) a full-scale revolution in every aspect of Union affairs. The movement was so far-reaching that, after years of black despair at the small-minded and secretive bungling of the Union, I at last managed to feel sanguine about the future of the game in Wales. Later in the season, on a day of high emotions at Cardiff Arms Park, Wales beat England to end England's hegemony in the Five Nations Championship.

By the end of the season and the summer off-season, Wales had been plunged into utter administrative chaos and bickering and, in many respects, the playing glow of the win over England had faded too. It seemed that a sorely-needed revival had accelerated, then slammed itself into numbing reverse. At the start of the season, the WRU were widely admired. By the summer, they were regarded as a joke.

The basis of the original change for the better was that Wales, finally, gave up on rugby as a natural sport. Youngsters had stopped regarding it as the only pastime; so had some followers; so had the business community, whose investment was needed. Recruitment into the game tended to be moribund and the major clubs were dying of apathy and of small-town resistance to change. Rugby, in the shape of players, technical lead, sponsorship and sheer numbers, no longer arrived well packaged for Wales to use, as it had done in the blessed days when Wales could be successful merely by waiting smugly in the wings. There was also a profoundly disturbing lack of natural talent. The bitter and ironic truth was that Wales had not produced a fly-half of true international quality since the departure to rugby league of Jonathan Davies.

The affairs of the national team and the various feeder teams were placed under a special Union planning committee and, day to day, under Robert Norster and Alan Davies. These were inspired choices. Norster was a player who had commanded the utmost respect, Davies an undemonstrative planner and far-sighted coach. The affairs of the Welsh team had for too long been dogged by poor coaching, non-existent techniques of man-management and miserably bad public relations. On the field, where the pair earned the vast respect of the players, and off the field, where they revolutionised the preparation of the team, they were very impressive, too. All aspects of conditioning, diet, mental preparation, technical improvements – even domestic welfare – came within the orbit of a range of coaches and professional advisers. In other words, Wales had belatedly got serious, had begun to catch up with the likes of Australia and England, who had left nothing to chance for the past five years. 'If you are in a company and you assume that things are going to happen then you go out of business,' said Davies. 'That is what happened to Welsh rugby.'

They also made an inspired choice of captain. Ieuan Evans, the Llanelli wing, had had a chequered career. His suspect shoulder had a habit of giving out under the stress of the tackle and Evans, the proudest Welshman who ever bestrode the wings of the game, was never thought of, because of his position and nature, as a natural leader of his country. He challenged that perception. By the time of the Five Nations, he had grown rapidly into the post. 'The most encouraging thing for us,' said Davies, 'is that way that Ieuan has developed as a person. You could see him beginning to grow into the role. We needed some stability and the way he has provided that has been outstanding.'

A costly but wholly necessary technical department was set up under Jeff Young, the former Welsh hooker. The department initiated many recruiting drives and operations to teach basic skills and employed development officers all around Wales. Denis Evans, not a natural communicator and not without outbursts of gruffness, was gradually won round to a new world of media relations and PR. Jonathan Price, the prime mover, helped to open the affairs of the Union, and especially team affairs, to the press, and therefore to the demanding Welsh public, in a way which impressively banished the suspicious, small-minded years when hardly an official in Wales knew what a journalist was, and how, if they showed a little of their hand, both could help them.

These revolutions were costly. Just as other major unions had to treble and quadruple their income in a short time, Price set about doing the same for the WRU. He succeeded. His manner did not impress everyone. He was in a hurry. 'Too big for his boots,' someone told me gravely. I disagreed. He was simply a shock to smug Welsh systems in which a committeeman made a call to his middle-management chum and brought in a few quid for the coffers. Anyone who still thought that it was possible to fund the enormous operation the WRU had become in that way was living in a gentler past.

Perhaps his most controversial move was flogging off the Welsh jersey. The old red icon re-emerged with the logos of the manufacturer, Cotton Traders, and with green flashes, collars and cuffs. Codgers fulminated. I never gave a damn. I preferred the new jersey to the old plain scarlet get-up in any case. For a start it was free and easy money. The exclusive deal and the patent which existed ensured that only Cotton Traders could make the official replica jersey and that they had to pay a percentage of their sales to the WRU in addition to the sum they had paid for supply and exclusivity. It meant that the WRU was now cut in on the profits which, previously, any old Tom, Dick or Ianto could make and keep by running up the old scarlet number and unpatented jersey in their back room, sticking on three feathers and knocking them out. These proceeds were not for gold taps in Union bathrooms. They were for lifeblood.

The disintegration, the arresting of progress, began just before Christmas. Glanmor Griffiths, the Union treasurer (and formerly one of the most powerful men in the Union, for he was one of the Welsh IRB representatives and held other key posts) resigned. A poll of clubs suggested overwhelmingly that they did not feel the need for a treasurer, anyway. Eventually, Griffiths issued a vast document which made serious allegations against Denis Evans and others. Griffiths suggested that Evans had short-circuited procedures, had wrongly authorised spending, had used the WRU janitor as a personal chauffeur while he served a ban from driving, and had also been personally abusive. He toured the country campaigning against alleged skulduggery until the WRU stopped him with an injunction.

The WRU countered with a bigger document which rebutted all the allegations. To many of us, it seemed not only a classic personality clash between two men trying to hold sway, not only an inevitable collision between a paid official (Evans) and an amateur committeeman (Griffiths), but also a case of classic Welsh predilection for everything being sieved through the onerous committee system so beloved of Welsh people everywhere.

Events moved quickly and became ever more bitter. The Evans camp drew people who realised that he and his administration had broken a log-jam and burst into real progress and, given the bottomless pit into which playing and administrative matters had sunk, did not much care whether Genghis Khan was in charge. The Griffiths ranks were swelled by a good few people who held personal grudges and who had felt the undeniably rough edge of the Evans tongue. He is not a patient man. The neutral ranks and the players could hardly believe that bickering was taking the place of improving a dismal run of Welsh results dating back six years and more.

When a special general meeting was called in what amounted to a straight battle between Evans and the WRU committee on the one hand and Griffiths and his followers among the clubs at large on the other, Griffiths had some priceless help. When they came to formulate their opinions the clubs had more reasons to drive themselves into a fury. First, it was discovered that the Union had suppressed the Pugh Report, which revealed the shadowy bungling of some members of the Welsh Rugby Union when South African sources, disloyally aided by some members of the Four Home Unions, had spirited away Welsh players for the South African celebration matches in 1989. Second, the long-promised constitutional reform of the Union had still not taken place. The anti-Evans bandwagon was swollen also by some major clubs. It took a disgracefully long time for some of the old élite to agree to take part in league rugby, and it was Evans who eventually helped to cut through their filibustering and posturing and dragged the Heineken Leagues into existence. They immediately started performing wonders for the game, but the ranks of the dispossessed merely sat on the sidelines waiting for their chance.

Ironically, Evans had come out of the South Africa incident with his reputation enhanced and had anyway been a prime mover in the drive towards reform. Yet at the SGM the vote of confidence fell, all members of the WRU resigned and less than half were re-elected later at the AGM, when Vernon Pugh QC became a kind of executive chairman, a new post leaving the president as a figurehead, and at which, among the new intake, came Ray Williams, formerly an inspired coaching director.

The events now took a more lurid turn. More serious allegations were made by Griffiths and others against Evans and Price. It was also revealed, rather histrionically, that the Union's trading year had gone badly. It was never properly publicised that many of the costs had been put into valuable investment and marketing programmes (though other funds did go into unsuccessful ventures). Evans and Price were suspended on full pay while an inquiry committee, the traditional Welsh port in any storm, was convened to look into alleged misconduct. Evans' solicitors pointed out that many of the allegations against him had been discussed and dismissed by properly constituted committees of the WRU. The whole affair dragged into the autumn of 1993. It was unsightly, a blight on progress and demeaning to the wholehearted efforts of the Welsh squad to pull around their results.

Of course, if malpractice by Evans and Price is proved then it will be a sad disappointment to those who trusted them and admired the pace of their reforms. If not, then it may still be impossible for them to remain in office – as it clearly should be, incidentally, for all complainants against them. This one, sadly, is still running strongly.

One of the first actions of the new regime under Vernon Pugh was to concede home advantage to Spain and Portugal for the qualifying pool for the World Cup in May 1994. The idea is to boost the sport in those countries. So, after a ferociously long season, the

Welsh players have to try to safeguard their World Cup future in heat and alien conditions abroad when they could have played at home.

I am fervently for the development of rugby all around the world, but there is a time and place. It was a rank bad decision by the WRU. That, and the grisly events of a season fought harder off the pitch than on it, made you despair that the day will ever dawn when Welsh rugby consistently gets the administration it needs and deserves; that officialdom in our country will ever grow up.

The playing season was a desperate search for good news, occasionally rewarded but not consistently so. The victory over England was something which Wales, and every other participant in the Five Nations, needed desperately. It was achieved by all of 10-9, and was greeted with as much euphoria in Cardiff and the rest of the country that evening as any previous Welsh victory in history. It was an heroic affair, with some astounding tackling from Richard Webster, Emyr Lewis and Stuart Davies in the Welsh back row and especially from Scott Gibbs in the centre. There was also, amid the general fervency, a marvellous effort from Gareth Llewellyn in the second row. England were tactically adrift, hammered when Dewi Morris had a try disallowed in mysterious circumstances.

There was good news, too, from the top echelon of the clubs. Cardiff – not before time – improved, Swansea, until they lost momentum late on, played some superb rugby and catapulted their personable and dedicated coach, Mike Ruddock, to the very top level of coaches in the British Isles. Ultimately, the sensation of the club season were Llanelli. They overpowered Swansea and Cardiff in the run-in to the title in Heineken League Division 1; they also held out against a ferocious effort by Neath in the Cup, helped by an astounding dropped goal from Emyr Lewis after a free kick. The score was allowed by Gareth Simmonds, the referee. Neath, furiously, reminded everyone that a drop-kick cannot be allowed after a free kick until the opposition has touched the ball. After the match, just as Simmonds was about to apologise all around for forgetting the law, the replay found that a few Neath fingers had grazed the ball anyway as Llanelli set it up, so by default Simmonds (along with Ed Morrison, Derek Bevan, David Bishop and Fred Howard, one of the referees of the year), was correct.

Llanelli were an absolute delight. In one sense they had no excuse for a bad season since their catchment area in West Wales is so comparatively huge, but under the inspired coaching of Gareth Jenkins and his team, and the remarkably effective leadership of Rupert Moon, the voluble and irrepressible captain, they played the most entertaining and effective club rugby and beat Australia hands down. In the League they averaged six tries and forty points per match, extravagantly turning the new law to their advantage in a riot of running rugby. Ieuan Evans was in deadly form, as were Moon at scrum-half, almost all the threequarters and, perhaps especially, the rampaging back-row men Mark Perego and Emyr

Lewis, and the blond, wily Lyn Jones, superbly clever and cunning on the open side.

The club's open policy is now actually enshrined in their constitution. 'The philosophy of Llanelli Rugby Football Club will be to try to provide entertainment and excitement for its supporters by playing effective and adventurous winning rugby in a style which will be enjoyable for both player and spectator alike.' Gareth Jenkins, the articulate coach, expressed his own philosophy: 'I have sincerely loved the club and the town. Llanelli lost its heart a decade ago when the steel industry collapsed, and the lifeline that was left was rugby. It is a great privilege to imagine that we are doing something to brighten the lives of so many people.' How droolingly looms the inevitable Anglo-Welsh League programme which must surely arrive soon. Is there a club ground in the rugby world which could hold the people who would come to watch Llanelli play Bath, or Wasps play Swansea, or Cardiff play Northampton?

So there was glorious rugby from Llanelli, a victory over England, and in the close season, an unbeaten national tour of Zimbabwe and Namibia, culminating in a pyrotechnic win over a strong South African Barbarians team, which Alan Davies described as the performance he had been working towards for two seasons. Gareth Llewellyn, as both captain and lock, was vastly impressive. Unfortunately, for me these were all potentially straws in the wind. You can shoot me for defeatist talk if you like, but I believe that as far as any substantive playing revival is concerned we are still waiting.

The remainder of the national team's season was grim. They hammered Italy and they were competitive in Cardiff against Australia and in Paris against the French, although not so competitive as to suggest they were ever going to win. They were barren at Murrayfield and disappointing at Cardiff against Ireland.

What of the clubs, and the Heineken leagues? Their advent has galvanised the club scene overall, driven clubs into gear, made them streamline and improve, given them hunger. It has positively revitalised the status of rugby clubs in the smaller communities, because even in Division 4 of the Leagues, some of the clubs are drawing enormous crowds and have set the towns and villages talking. But as far as impetus for the national team is concerned, the effect is fitful. The truth is that Division 1 began and almost ended with Llanelli, Swansea, bits of Cardiff and essence of Neath. The standard at the middle and bottom and the standard in Division 2 varied from variable to miserable. The evidence lies in the performance of Newport. They were stuck in mid-table, easily able to demolish teams around and below them – yet on two occasions they conceded more than seventy points to Llanelli. Welsh rugby will not recover until there is a minimum of nine competitive teams in Division 1.

And furthermore, it will not recover until a large crop of players of all-round talent can be unearthed. Far too many people in Wales become far too excited by players who can produce the fleeting shaft of brilliance; they can then drool about flair. With the greatest respect, one or two of the younger Llanelli backs who had been carving through at club level were over-praised in that they were ineffective and inconsistent out of that Scarlet context. The Welsh should instead be bemoaning the lack of rounded, quality backs in the country to group around Tony Clement and Scott Gibbs; and while they are at it, the lack of a commanding number 8, of forwards who can play football, and perhaps above all, a man who can stand in the middle of the line-out and cause a little grief to the likes of John Eales, Martin Bayfield, Ian Jones and the other lighthouse jumpers. They should also bemoan the dismal lack of a few cold-eye fixers (as opposed to dirty players), the kind of breed which John Perkins of Pontypool so beautifully describes as 'hairy-arsed forwards'. Disturbingly, there seemed no sign in the Under-21 team last season of a new lighthouse; no indication of a new seam of real and rounded talent behind the scrum.

The national team structure, provided the gripers of the WRU do not decide to cut it back so that a few figures balance, is strong. In essence, the place of the game in Welsh hearts is still secure. Yet inside the strong-boned skeleton there still seems to be too little in the way of flesh and blood.

# CHAPTER 11

# The Death of the Grand Illusions

## SHOPPING AT THE WRONG MARKET WITH RUGBY LEAGUE

On a June evening in 1989, Wigan played Warrington in a rugby league match in Milwaukee. Why they did so has never, to my knowledge, been properly explained. The teams were weeks out of season, organisational aspects of the trip were a shambles. The teams shuffled on and played their game, walked off to a warm ovation. Then they went home. And after all, they were apparently trying to propagate one of the least successful sports on the planet.

'Ah,' said one fervent rugby league man of my acquaintance, 'The National Football League bring two teams over to Wembley every year. They have large crowds. Why shouldn't rugby league try to spread to America and promote the game there?'

Two problems there, old son. First, the NFL are not trying to spread their game to Britain. The whole point of their annual tepid would-be extravaganza at Wembley is to incite every youngster in the country to go to his sports shop and buy NFL goods – satin jackets and caps, sweatshirts and key rings and footballs and fluffy mock-helmets and the rest.

At one time they may have thought briefly about flogging a franchise to London. An NFL team might have played in London but in no other sense would it have been a British team. Top American players would have been employed. But all that was before the balloon of a short boom in interest in American Football in the UK burst so spectacularly – as seen in the short, meteoric and doomed-from-the-start life of the London Monarchs, a team created in a sub-NFL which quietly went out of existence in 1992.

And if the NFL cannot reach people with its vast resources then what was rugby league's idea in Milwaukee? At least some people in the UK have seen American football on Channel 4. When Wigan and Warrington flew home they left, according to the city's leading sports writer, a sneaking admiration for their courage in playing without bulging shoulder pads and helmets, and for the fact that the men they started with, with one or two exceptions, stayed on the field for the whole match, and mucked in with the attacking, defending and kicking duties. Apart from that, the match had no impact.

It was a venture typical of the earnest and deeply misguided efforts of rugby league to transplant itself, to become a bodyless head. There have been other dead missionary games executed or planned around the world and in the vast areas of league desert in Britain.

A more promising development for rugby league is looming. In 1995, the Auckland Warriors, a brand new rugby league team, will take its place in the most significant competition in the world, the Sydney Premiership. The debut of the team has been put back twice but now it seems certain that Auckland will proudly take their place in the competition to find the best team in . . . Australia.

They will not be quite as proud as they might have been. Two years ago, when plans were first revealed, the publicity machine for the team made excited revelations about the space-age backdrop for the new venture. As the *Sydney Telegraph-Mirror* reported, they would play in the Manukau Superdrome, a magnificent, spanking new, state-of-the-art indoor stadium which would accommodate 39,000 people. The first sod was about to be turned at the site near Auckland's airport. By the second half of 1993 the picture had changed slightly. The Auckland Warriors were casting round anxiously for a home. Manukau Stadium, nicknamed Pie in the Sky by Aucklanders, remained resolutely unbuilt and quietly forgotten. Carlaw Park, home of the small operation that is New Zealand domestic rugby league, has been described as a slum. No good for the brash, bright bunch of, er, Australians who are proudly to represent Auckland. Mount Smart Stadium, the other alternative, is a bowl without soul miles from anywhere.

Still, the lack of anywhere to play is a mere detail. The Warriors' marketing manager, Laurie Stubbing, declared some time ago that on the back of the success of the team, rugby league 'will become the best-supported game in New Zealand by the year 2000'. Another hopeful from the camp declared, at the start of 1993, that the All Blacks, the country's rather well-known rugby union team, 'would be second best, blown away by the appeal of league. League could overtake union in popularity terms in New Zealand within five years.'

Even some general sports reporters in New Zealand agreed. 'Do you know,' one of them told me in 1992, 'lots of Kiwi kids now go around wearing league replica jerseys.' So that is the end of the All Blacks. Still, they were good while they lasted.

But wait: take heart, poor All Blacks. In any given country and any given nation, the sports played are part of the culture and tradition. Those traditions have been built over decades and decades and sports have become central to the leisure lives of the population – or not.

It is possible to theorise as to why cricket is not played the length and breadth of the USA, but the simple truth is that it is not, and both cricket and the USA are stuck with it. It is possible to theorise about why the Eton Wall Game has not exactly swept the world. But the only truth is that it has not become absorbed into other cultures and locations.

Ditto rugby league. Did they honestly believe that, after one match, scores of schools and colleges all over Milwaukee would suddenly switch on to a game alien to culture and traditions? The Milwaukee experience was to be the making of the United States Rugby League. There were plans for a follow-up match in Chicago a year later. An excited entrepreneur in that city claimed he could fill a 60,000-seater stadium for a rugby league match. Sure, sure. And with a flypast of pigs against a blue moon backdrop, no doubt.

An account of the Milwaukee occasion stated: 'The story of the United States Rugby League looks set to run and run.' It didn't. In the middle of 1993, I rang the Rugby League and asked for the number of the USRL. 'There isn't one.' What about a contact number for anyone involved in rugby league in the US of A? 'We don't have one.'

And does anyone with his head screwed on facing vaguely to the front seriously believe that in a matter of a few years (or ever, come to that) one team of rootless rugby league players can inspire a country so much towards one code of rugby that the All Blacks, part of the country's fabric, will become a sideshow? The Auckland Warriors will be a major and welcome addition to the sporting fabric of New Zealand, but even if they last the crucial first five years without folding, they will not change that fabric. And what on earth happens to New Zealand's domestic rugby league game if attention switches to one big side?

What about the kids with the rugby league replica jerseys? Anyone investing in a business proposition on the back of a children's fad is in desperate trouble and only Gerry Anderson of *Thunderbirds* can disagree. Even Postman Pat will make his last delivery in the near future, and Fireman Sam will thunder along the streets of Pontypandy in Jupiter only until the kids tire of him.

What of real rugby league occasions? They are a different matter altogether. In October 1992, a real rugby league match took place at Wembley Stadium. Rugby league does not actually figure in the culture of London-born Londoners any higher than it does in Milwaukee, but this was An Event. It was the Rugby League World Cup final between Great Britain and Australia. It was settled in favour of Australia when Steve Renouf, the centre from Brisbane who was winning his first international cap, scored a try in the second half. Renouf burst on to a clever pass from Kevin Walters and completely outfoxed John Devereux, the British defender, on his path to the line. For most of the enormous crowd, it was a memorable occasion.

Yet too many people mistook the ribbons of the occasion for the contents. Afterwards, many rugby league observers were bemoaning the lack of spectacle. Britain had confined themselves in every set of six tackles to five rather uninspired plays, plus one hoof downfield. The whole match was a barrage of tackling with very little expansion in the play. There was an anguished debate in the aftermath. What on earth could rugby league do to ensure that tries came flooding? I read a fair few suggestions. Reduce the teams to twelve a side? Make the defending side stand further back at the play-the-ball? Tinker with the rules at the play-the-ball to get the action restarted more quickly? The same debate threw up the suggestion that league should be switched to the summer (another doomed move as it would take the game out of its own culture).

The critics were on entirely the wrong track. If league's World Cup final is to mean anything then it must be a gladiatorial collision of utter conviction, worth winning at any expense, not simply a gaudy promotional vehicle for a sport in which the winners are incidental.

An article in *Rugby League Week* in Australia once made precisely the same mistake when discussing the fact that fewer tries were being scored in State of Origin games. 'Suddenly, the score reads 5-4 when it used to be 43-22,' the author, Steve Crawley, complained. He did not realise that the low scores and ultra-competitive matches meant that the State of Origin concept had come of age, not diminished. If this means that speculative plays are out, then so be it. You are either a sport or a circus act. It is the essential difference between, say, a serious sport and Hulk Hogan and the ludicrous World Wrestling Federation. Rugby league, far too often, fails to spot the difference. It is a different branch of the same mistake made in Milwaukee and Auckland.

The marketing and promotion of activities in which you wish the paying public and the paying sponsor to be involved are life-giving in global sport. You can use marketing to bring out the best in your sport, to show the best side, to gloss the dodgy bits, to create a benevolent circle in which gate money and sponsorship money and the interest of young children and their teachers and parents lead to a better product and thence to more benefits.

But what you cannot do is promote a sport into existence – in Milwaukee, say – to make it, almost overnight, into part of a culture of which it has never before been a part. Promotion can nurture roots. It cannot create the roots, no matter how big the coffers for your promotional campaign. And what you must not do is change the character of the sport merely to pander. If the object of the game is to score tries then it is a dangerous over-simplification to suggest that you can attract people and keep them by putting on a saccharine try feast. This mistake was the basis of a shambolic set of new union laws passed by the International Rugby Board, rugby union's governing body, in 1992-93. You need roots to grow, and you need to be true to your roots.

In the late 1980s, rugby league believed itself to be in the throes of a massive revival, a boom. There was talk of a new era of magnificent athleticism (which, to some degree, materialised). There was talk of massive expansion in Britain and around the world (which did not materialise). There was some evidence that crowds were becoming larger, although compared to the huge gatherings of the game's old days, not significantly so. There was talk of new spectacle – and indeed, at the top level the era has brought some great stuff. But at first sight, there seemed to me more to this new marketing culture than doomed one-match wonders. At *The Sunday Times*, we were (we thought) on the pace. Together with David Lawrenson, my colleague on the paper and also editor of *Rugby News*, I examined the new-look rugby league.

'The cloth cap hangs, forgotten, on its hook,' we wrote. 'There is a furious urgency as the game works to improve its appeal . . .' We outlined many new marketing exercises, including a nine-a-side event. We outlined the lead from RL headquarters. We pointed out that one of the major planks of the venture was that league should burst the banks of its old localities and surge out into the embrace of the millions and millions who, allegedly, were waiting for the league to arrive with the same eagerness as Jim Bowie and Davy Crockett waited for the goodies at the Alamo.

The article was finished and filed and, as we say in journalism, put to bed. Some time after our masters in the sports department had approved the story but before it appeared on the streets of the nation, I broke into a cold sweat. I realised that during the process of research, we had not been on the pace after all. We were a significant step behind. The story was not that the game had turned over a dazzling new leaf and was determined to promote itself ferociously to an outside world and rid itself of its cloth-cap-and-pigeon-dropping image. The story was that rugby league was already mistaking the gaudy trappings of promotion, the work of spin doctors, for the process of improving the game and the empire of the game itself.

They have wasted time and money. They have wasted time in Milwaukee. They have fretted about major occasions when all they needed was to rest their case on the honesty of the sport itself. They have missed their chance. Our feature duly appeared under the heading 'League graduates to a new ball game'. It was well received in league circles, among people who did not realise that they had lost sight of that ball.

In the middle of 1993, with the code beset by financial problems and reducing by the month in its professional arms, the grand illusions of the late 1980s were quietly being laid to rest. There was a significant statement by David Howes, the Rugby Football League's public relations officer: 'After so many years of optimism and bullshit, reality has come as quite a shock,' he told the *Observer*. How beautifully put.

# CHAPTER 12

# *Thousands Stuck in Traffic Jams*

## THE BOOM, BUST AND BITTERNESS OF RUGBY LEAGUE

When the World Cup final of 1992 was over, a tide receded. Wembley's staff rubbed out the pitch markings, took down the goalposts and prepared the old stadium for the next big attraction. It was a one-off. If youngsters, and indeed, able-bodied men and women of any age, had been electrified by the match then they may well have been, at least till the next fad, infected by the benevolent and persistent germs of the oval-ball game.

Yet if any harboured ambitions to play rugby league and if they lived outside Lancashire, Yorkshire and parts of Cumbria, then their chances of taking up the game were minuscule. There are only a scattered handful of amateur rugby league clubs outside those heartlands, next to no schools playing the game and only one semi-professional club to speak of – a strange, nomadic, mainly Aussie outfit called the London Crusaders. If any other people were attracted to rugby and if they lived between Cornwall and the Wash, Milford Haven and Dover, Anglesey and John O'Groats or Bantry Bay and Derry Quay, then all they could do was take up rugby union.

To generalise only slightly, rugby league has never spread. That is the first characteristic of the sport. Apart from a thriving outpost in New South Wales, it remains largely locked within the same borders behind which it retreated in 1885 when the great schism saw the Northern Union split away, partly because of the insufferable smugness of the richer southern rugby men. It is all very well upholding the principle of amateurism but many of the northern players of that day had to take a full or half day off work to play their sport. It is one of sport's least remarkable events that southern smugness should have driven a wedge between itself and northern economic necessity.

Yet modern day league has the bitter frustration of the prospective managing director of a global food conglomerate who is still stuck serving sprouts by the pound in a corner shop. The lack of progress is staggering, and they blame everyone – bar themselves.

If you study the public utterances of the Rugby Football League itself, of the Australian Rugby League, of the letters columns of newspapers and league publications, of the campaigns of many rugby league writers and, most especially, of the editorial columns of *Open Rugby*, the most famous and the liveliest magazine on the code, you will experience first hand the sheer desperation of many people for their game to spread. Or, as a psychiatrist really should have written, to boost their self-esteem through the knowledge that others love them.

Take a random example of the editorials written in *Open Rugby*. There has, according to a subscriber, never been an issue of *Open Rugby* in the last five seasons that did not make the expansion of the sport a central issue. Here are some of their points:

November 1988: 'London, Cardiff, Bristol, Leicester are just four obvious places where the League could help immeasurably by staging "exhibition" games.'

December 1988: 'For years, we have been urging the game to appoint development officers . . .'

January 1989: 'On the international development front, things, at last, look genuinely optimistic.'

March 1989: 'The future development of the game across continental Europe is something that interests me greatly.'

April 1989: 'We must . . . attract the uncommitted to the sport, by taking top games into new territory . . . at every opportunity.'

June 1989: '. . . Swindon offers rugby league a marvellous opportunity for development . . .'

April 1990: 'Gateshead wants league.'

May 1990: 'League fans have been waiting anxiously for signs that the game would be seriously promoted as the national showcase . . .'

June 1990: 'The world of rugby league has rarely known such potentially exciting times for development . . .'

September 1990: 'National league so important.'

November 1990: 'It is a sad fact that the development of rugby league in playing terms . . . has gone backwards. That trend has to be stopped.'

January 1991: 'There are an awful lot of dedicated enthusiasts out there who are desperately keen to see rugby league expand to a wider audience . . .'

February 1991: 'For as long as anyone can remember, rugby league's major dilemma has centred around its need to expand outside what have become known as its "traditional areas".'

March 1991: 'In worldwide terms, we desperately need the credibility of having more major nations playing our game at a serious level.'

June-July 1992: '*Open Rugby* would like to stand up and be counted and offer all our support to any genuine . . . initiatives to help promote the game.'

League's lack of geographical development would be partly understandable if they wanted to cringe behind their barricades, but *that* sounds like a sport desperate to expand. Throughout history there have been attempts to extend the pro game in Britain. Yet take just the recent casualties of an expansionist dream.

Scarborough Pirates (Scarborough is in Yorkshire, for God's sake) subsided into nothingness in 1992 after a lifetime lasting one season.

Nottingham City were forced out of the league at the end of the 1992-93 season for reasons we shall discuss later. Yet for all but their tiny and magnificent band of followers, it was a merciful release. They were dreadful. In season 1992-93 their record read: P24 W1 D0 L23 F181 A1132. Their victory came at Barrow, by 19-12. They conceded, on average, 47 points per match. Mansfield Marksmen had already folded – or at least, metamorphosed. They had become Nottingham in 1989 after five years of heroic denial of the inevitable. Between them, Mansfield/Nottingham had a career which was not even good enough to be called chequered. They join Kent Invicta, who fell into the dead pool without causing a ripple; and Cardiff Blue Dragons, a failure in passionate rugby country.

Carlisle have passed their tenth anniversary so the struggle availeth them for the moment. Sheffield Eagles, founded in 1984, are a shining light. They fought their way into Division 1 of the Stones Bitter Championship for 1992-93 and are thriving. In Gary Hetherington, chairman, they have one of the game's expansionist heroes. Yet Hetherington stands out in part because, among the new or newish teams outside the old lags of the game, he and his club have succeeded while the others have died or deflated.

London Crusaders, who played at the National Sports Centre at Crystal Palace, certainly have a story good enough for a book, or even a film or even a soap opera. It will probably have a sad ending. Mike Stephenson, BSkyB's summariser and personality, is for me the best league television man in the game. And at the risk of appearing in the *Private Eye* column which monitors sugar praise for BSkyB from cringing employees of News International, I have to say that the station's coverage of the sport is outstanding. So is their magazine programme, *Boots 'n' All*. Stevo, however, was categorical about the Crusaders recently. 'They are drinking at the last-chance saloon,' he said of the club's precarious existence.

When the Crusaders began in their original form (as Fulham at Craven Cottage in 1980) they were a gift from the Great Sports Fan in the sky. For us innocent young Welsh lads, life in suburban

London on slow, grey winter Sundays could be objectionable and morose. So when Fulham were born, my friends and I from London Welsh – where I was still playing – turned out in droves. The early games were heady. Even though I am deeply suspicious of any comparison between the two codes because of the entirely different nature and requirements of each, I am tempted to say that I have rarely seen a more tasty centre partnership than Derek Noonan and Mal Aspey of early Fulham. While the novelty was there and while Fulham were winning, we loved it.

We drifted off, of course. So did London. So did the hosts, Fulham's soccer club. The novelty went. So did Derek and Mal; so did the goodwill of the rest of rugby league, who treated the club not as a welcome child to be reared strong and bold, but as a cuckoo's egg to be smashed for presumption. The wilderness years began. We preferred union.

The nomadic Crusaders have stopped off at various points, desperately trying to flog life into the concept by obtaining a dispensation which, basically, allows them to play scores of Aussie imports. Yet they have slipped further from London sporting consciousness. They ended the 1992-93 season sitting, unremarked, in the middle of Division Two of the Championship. If you find a sports follower in London who can name one Fulham player I would be astonished.

Even Ross Strudwick, the amiable Australian who gave up the coaching reins that season, was often unsure. 'I know his nickname,' he said in response to an inquiry about a player, 'but I've no idea what his full name is.' If and when the last pint is downed at Stevo's last-chance saloon, rugby league will be able to contemplate, in the icy silence of London's league Sundays, why on earth a massive cosmopolitan city, moreover a city with a massive Antipodean population, could not support even a frayed-shoestring operation. The only stronger emotion will be wonder and warmth for the followers of the club who have remained so loyal for so long.

In the early 1990s, when league still believed itself to be on an unstoppable charge, Maurice Lindsay, then chairman of Wigan and now chief executive of the RFL, propounded the view that rugby league must strive to be a national game by 1995 and that it would become so. Others took up the cry throughout the game. 'National by 1995.' A few of those who did so now angrily deny they ever said it. They lie.

No wonder. A national spread was never going to happen. A national game is a game you can play by leaving a house anywhere in the country and walking to the pitch, or rink, or ring or court, or by taking a short bus ride. There are a few park-pitch league operations which are bravely operating, small and vulnerable shoots of amateur expansion here and there (Hemel Hempstead and Aberavon, to name two and most). Every little pocket is lauded in league publications as if the Bastille had been stormed, as if Earth had played Mars and as if the dodo had been discovered in droves, and all on the same afternoon.

There is no problem with the heartland amateur rugby league game – BARLA's amateur clubs still thrive. Yet even league's pessimists must be dumbfounded by the total lack of movement towards fulfilling even the tiniest part of the cry 'National by 1995'.

As far as global spread goes, it would also be inaccurate to say that the sun never sets on the league empire. The code has established a powerful hold on the sporting consciousness of the people of New South Wales, who follow avidly the high-profile Winfield Cup competition centred around Sydney. There have been large crowds for one-off matches in Brisbane, too.

Yet Sydney's Premiership is the only rugby league of any significance played anywhere in the world outside the heartland of Yorkshire and Lancashire; outside Papua New Guinea, small cells of other Pacific Island groups, and parts of New Zealand (mainly the Maori parts); and outside those parts of France not cringing from the avaricious monster that is French rugby union. Around the globe the news is bad, and in many of these locations, the news is getting worse.

What of Wales? Season 1992-93 saw the next step in the attempted re-establishment of the Welsh rugby league team, and if ever a team flattered to deceive, if ever rugby league roped themselves to a doomed concept to fool themselves into visions of global expansion, it was in celebrating the event. Wales thrashed the mighty Papua New Guinea and France, and gave England a decent contest, losing by only 36-11. As one-off matches they were rich in entertainment value. The revival of the Welsh team in itself was a superb if obvious idea, vivid and passionate.

Yet as usual, league drew the wrong conclusions. The Welsh team will have a brief life. There is only a tiny pool of Welsh players, with no spare capacity to ride out injury problems. It can only be sustained with a massive batch of new signings, especially in the forwards. To be brutal on three counts, at the moment rugby league can afford none, Welsh rugby union can provide very few people worth signing, and if they could, they would put together a package to entice the players to stay.

The Welsh team, bursting with pride and with Jonathan Davies and John Devereux, Paul Moriarty and David Young, is withering already. For the return match against France in 1993, when several players were injured, they had to drum up Welsh qualifications for all kinds of people just to field a team. The process became a farce. The concept of the Welsh team will soon become a farce too and then, shortly afterwards, impossible to maintain. You need thirteen players to make a team.

Ah, but what of the promotional value to the game in Wales? Clive Griffiths, the Welsh coach, discussed the prospects of rugby league making inroads. After all, crowds into five figures went along to that Mecca for rugby league, the Vetch Field in Swansea, for the matches. But what game in Wales? There *is* no game in Wales. It was Auckland Warriors all over again. It was all, to borrow the graphic expression of David Howes of the Rugby Football League, bullshit.

The thousands at the Vetch did not go to see rugby league. They went to watch the old heroes of rugby union, to catch the prodigals. To see Jonathan play.

There is no question whatsoever that the attentions of rugby league dynamited Welsh rugby union; did far more than all the other weaknesses of the Welsh game lumped together to ruin results. A combination of disillusion and economic necessity caused the drift. Whenever I hear someone at Twickenham pompously proclaiming that league is a 'safety valve' for union, I feel like petrol-bombing the damn place.

Davies was an incalculable loss to Wales and to British rugby; you have only to examine his successors in the number 10 jerseys of British rugby to realise that none could have laced his boots. The loss of one player sapped much of the self-confidence of the sport.

Devereux, as I once wrote weekly, was on the point of becoming a union centre of world class; Stuart Evans, a failure at league (as I predicted in print the day he signed), would now be regarded as the greatest Welsh union prop of all time had he stayed; David Young, who departed for the north soon afterwards, could have won more than ninety caps. Both Young and Evans would have toured with the 1993 British Lions in New Zealand. It was that sense of frustration, of the boys coming home, that caused people to file into the Vetch Field. Rugby league was entirely incidental.

There is slightly more encouraging yet faintly bizarre news from two countries which were, until recently, perceived as being as far apart in the political spectrum as it was possible to be: the former Soviet Union and South Africa.

A few good ol' league men in South Africa have put together a small-scale competition of sorts and even made noises about taking the game to townships – at least they beat the South African rugby union authorities in that investment. The union body announced plans to invest millions of rand into non-white rugby only because they were largely shamed into doing so by union public opinion outside the country. The league code is hardly established enough to be called fledgling, and could go under at any second, but at least they are trying.

The story of the arrival of rugby league in the Soviet Union is a tribute to the heroic desperation of people involved in British rugby league to persuade someone else in Europe to play the game and to banish their own loneliness. A professional competition began in parts of the old Soviet Union in 1991, and a headquarters office has been established under the guardianship of the Soviet RL's first president, Edgar Tatourian.

In May 1991, both the London Crusaders and Ryedale York made a short tour of the country, with fixtures against each other, against combined teams and even an 'international' in Moscow. Only rugby league could parade a team described as Great Britain Select but which was, in fact, merely a combination of the two lowly British club teams. Still, it was a mighty effort. The crowds attending were disappointing but not negligible – local predictions of a crowd of 40,000 for the 'test' in Moscow proved about 37,000 wide of the mark in the wrong direction. But the tour went ahead, and Soviet teams came on reciprocal visits last season.

It is far, far too soon to speak of a game being established. The disastrous economic climate of the old Soviet bloc would render a rugby league wage an attractive proposition. Unconfirmed reports suggest that some players might even expect 350 roubles per month in the season (the national average wage is around 250). Yet those same economic factors would cripple the ability to pay out those sums in all but the most phenomenally well-connected clubs. No one could put hand on heart and say that rugby league will still be played in the old Soviet Union in ten or even five years' time. But progress and the sheer energy and optimism of the venture are to be warmly praised. Yet by mid-1993 the concept was fading, the officials losing touch, the numbers falling again.

Yet the whole exercise, as are most of the development ventures, is an offshoot of British rugby league. Almost the whole of the Soviet start-up costs, the coaching aids, the admin apparatus, the kit, the office suite, were paid by the RFL. It was the RFL in Britain who discovered Tatourian. He is no long-term league addict, but a disaffected former high flyer in the Soviet Rugby Union, cheesed off for various reasons, who spotted a main chance with league. Why the special interest from Britain? To spend, as they have, so much time developing the sport and donating to it seems well above the cause of duty. Why the extra time and money? Easy. In 1995, the RFL will host the World Cup to celebrate the hundredth anniversary of the split from union.

Previous world cups have, of course, been rampant misnomers. 'Name the losing semi-finalists of the World Cup' was the cruel catch question among some of my mates when the 1992 final took place at Wembley. There were none. Yet the RFL are desperate that the 1995 event should show the game in a good light in its centenary and should reflect a global spread.

As a leading official said to his RFU counterpart at Twickenham two seasons ago, they need eight teams for any meaningful event. They have Australia, New Zealand and, at the moment, Great Britain as established teams; they have France and Papua New Guinea as relatively established but non-competitive teams. They could field separate England and Wales teams, but only if there are no key Welshmen in the Great Britain squad at the time – it is vital that a British team wins the Cup and if they fail to reach the final then it may as well be called off.

'We think we can get the Russians,' said the RFL's man, some years ago. They did not. To get their eight, they have effectively bought in some Fijians, Samoans and Tongans.

That is the impetus behind the anxious efforts to boost fledgling rugby league efforts around the planet. It will be interesting to see how long the RFL's interest lasts when the World Cup is over and they have financial problems of their own. The departure into retirement last season of David Oxley, the chief executive, will not be to the fledglings' advantage. Oxley was, at least in theory, an internationalist. Maurice Lindsay, his successor, appears to be more concerned with the profitability and problems of the British game. We shall see.

Yet if you tour the sporting globe you can come to only one conclusion. The truth about rugby league is that it is an abject failure; if success is judged on the spread of its appeal (and what other criterion is there?), then it is the biggest failure in sporting history.

But why? Why has league had so much difficulty spreading? Why does it have difficulty breaking out? It has some of the same balance of running and gladiatorial contact that is the appeal of union. Why?

At first sight it is desperately difficult to say. When the Northern Union split from the Rugby Union nearly one hundred years ago, both codes had inbuilt advantages in the race to make one code dominant. Union had students and servicemen to spread the gospel overseas. League, especially as it began to develop the shades of the modern game, had two advantages. First, rugby league can often be more immediately viewer-friendly. Second, you can sometimes be paid to play.

In one sense, rugby union probably deserved little of its spread. No one among the major playing nations of the International Rugby Board cared about it, nurtured it. One of the most revealing books I have ever read is *The Guinness Book of Rugby Facts and Feats*, produced by Terry Godwin and Chris Rhys in the early 1980s. The book astounded me because I had had no idea how far the game had spread. The IRB, smugly, never made an effort to find out. Rhys, a tireless researcher, gave details of rugby union in over a hundred countries, of rugby thriving everywhere from Brazil, Denmark, India, Indonesia, Ivory Coast, Martinique, New Caledonia, Sarawak and Trinidad to Zambia. I understood for the first time the feeling of security and vindication that comes with the knowledge that a good few people see things the same way as you.

The Welsh Rugby Union and, to a lesser extent, the Rugby Football Union, introduced some of the lesser-known rugby nations to a wider world, notably in the epoch-making visit of the Fijians to Wales in the 1960s. Smug Brits learned with shock that there was a wide world out there and that in some parts of it, notably Fiji, the game was played a great deal more skilfully and stylishly than it was in Britain. That tour, incidentally, was the start of my full-scale and lifelong admiration for the fervent, maddening, dazzling game that is Fijian rugby.

Nowadays, that over-complicated organisation called Rugby World Cup has set up an International Settlement Trust to disburse to the have-nots, but in general, it is still left to a few genuine internationalists to provide the impetus and encouragement, among them Keith Rowlands, secretary of the IRB, and Chris Thau, an expatriate Romanian living in London, who keeps his

*Bag-snatching alert! Damien Smith attempts to retain his ball as Neath's Rhodri Jones approaches in the controversial Neath-Australia match when the accusations, and the testicles, flew*

*A try for England B against South Africa. It was a match which proved that outstanding games could be played under the new laws. But only just – it was the only decent game in the whole English season*

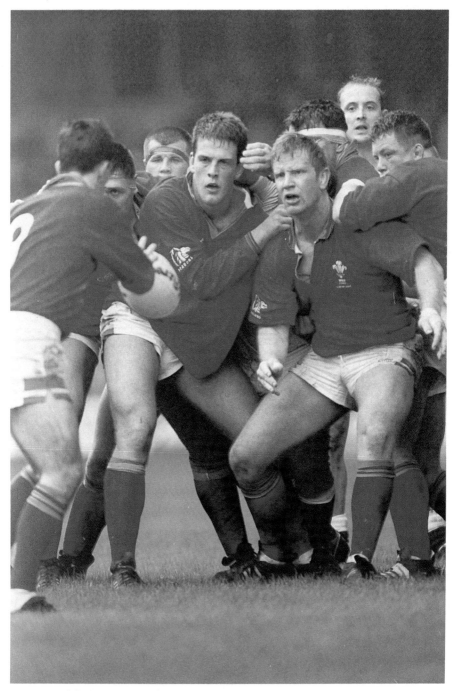

*A solid phalanx of Welsh beef protects possession for Robert Jones during the passionate Welsh victory over England, while Brecon's Dewi Morris peers over the top*

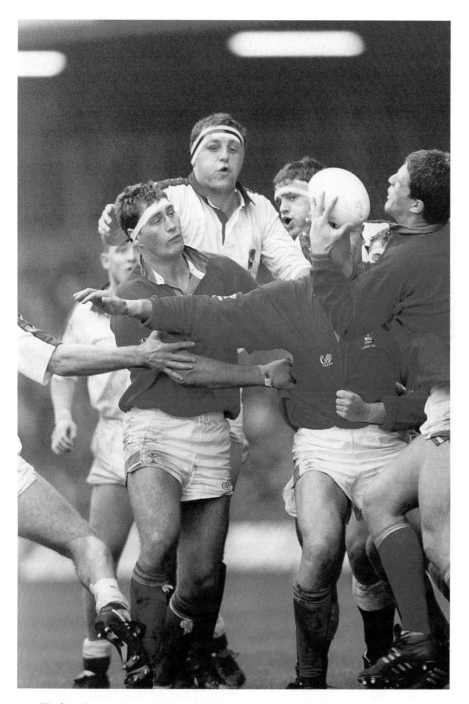

*Wade at bay Dooley was unhappy throughout the season. He dominated rugby so they changed the laws. A magnificent giant grounded by law-making pygmies*

*Stuart Barnes tries to send Will Carling through the gap. For Carling, it was a season marking time, standing back from the summits and the pressures. For Barnes, it was two fingers to the lot of them*

*The tide is coming in and it is coloured emerald green. Michael Bradley, the heroic Irish captain, has received the ball from sundry other heroes in Ireland's tumultuous win over England in Dublin*

*A trophy won through togetherness. Bath's machine, together, celebrate their Division One triumph and Andy Robinson and Jeremy Guscott flourish the Courage trophy*

*The England team celebrate after the World Cup Sevens. They've beaten all comers, they've overcome the organisers, now they're off to get the press. L-R, back row: Chris Sheasby, Justin Cassell, Matt Dawson, Damien Hopley, Tim Rodber; front row: Adedayo Adebayo, Dave Scully, Andrew Harriman, Nick Beal, Laurence Dallaglio*

*Jack Rowell. You want certificates, you want coaches who talk a good game? There are plenty available. But if you actually want your team to win something, you need Jack*

*Bob Lindner of Australia fends off Ellery Hanley of Great Britain as Australia stride towards the then misnamed World Cup of rugby league. In 1992-93, Hanley was a fading force in a fading sport*

readers in *The Times* and *Rugby World & Post* aware, through his tireless travels, of the wide world outside old walls. His contribution cannot be overvalued. Still, union has not embraced its full responsibilities and possibilities. Many of the major member unions give not a damn for anyone outside their confines; would rather take any money going to embellish a spanking new stand with a hospitality box or hundred than hand it on for some impoverished and earnest players to buy a proper ball or a jersey out in the bush of the game.

Yet league has not reached even the stage of such possibilities. Throughout history it has lost out in the race to expand in the most devastating fashion. Rugby union is played now in roughly 107 countries of which nearly ninety have fully-fledged governing bodies and well-established clubs. The union game dwarfs its offshoot at every turn. In Britain, outside the north, there are probably more established teams playing octo-push than league.

As far as spreading the word internationally goes, we have already established in the previous chapter that rugby league missionaries were apparently shot at Dover or Heathrow. The truth is more stark than that. Currently, in these years of union's frantic quantum leaping, the gap is widening at a rattling rate.

Did I say it was desperately difficult to explain? Bob Dwyer, the Australian coach and an outstanding man of rugby union, may have given the nail a good biff straight on the head recently. He wrote in his book, published in 1992, that league's lack of appeal lay in its 'endless repetition'. He meant the interminable chain of run and tackle, run and tackle, run and tackle; the fact that over 250 tackles are made in a game and that the game stops dead with every one. He may be right. Yet I feel that a sport's appeal is simply too basic a matter to explain with stylistic observations. But perhaps there is no need to find reasons. The plain facts of union's victory are posted on the world scoreboard. Whatever strengths, inner goodness, whatever special culture, whatever appeal, whatever chemistry you need to reach people, the facts say that union has them in far greater measure. Full stop.

Yet league needs reasons. It is an outstanding, fervent game to its acolytes and deservedly so. Those people need answers, need their conscience to be salved if only to postpone moments of painful self-revelation. They need, for God's sake, a bloody scapegoat. They have found one, and it is beautifully convenient.

That brings us to the other essential truth about rugby league: the sheer bitterness it holds for union. It cannot forgive union's dominance. If you read letters columns of national papers and rugby league publications, listen to television and radio and follow rugby league's literature – or if you have read the ludicrous columns on league written in the *Observer* by Colin Welland – you will know that rugby union is seen as an evil, malevolent influence, as a sport which exists only to stop the spread of rugby league.

Ray French, the BBC commentator, wrote of stillborn plans to push the game in continental Europe in the 1993 *Rugby League*

*Yearbook*: '. . . projects in the USA, Holland and Germany have been far from successful, the plans wrecked by miscalculation, ill luck and lack of moral and financial support.' I have never heard or read of a single person in the game prepared to admit that the world has voted with its feet, that some people are simply not bothered, full stop.

Some of the distaste for union is well justified. The wellbeing of rugby league in France is central to the progress of the code in Britain. France is the only possible international opposition available to Great Britain in the Northern Hemisphere. If rugby league is to have any meaningful international profile then it is essential that France is strong. In season 1992-93, the two Tests between the countries were simply embarrassing to watch, so miserably abject were France. Yet French rugby league is under remorseless attack from the giant union game in the country. There is an inexplicable and vindictive malevolence in the way that leading French rugby league players are courted by the major union clubs, which are culpable in far more than mere illegal inducements.

The malevolence certainly extends to the top. In the reign of Albert Ferrasse, the old autocratic president of the French Rugby Federation, it seemed as if they were trying to blast league out of existence. They may well succeed yet. French rugby league is one small step above a park-pitch game. Yet even in France, most of the league bitterness is simple jealousy, a reaction to the basic desire on the part of union to beat off all opposition.

In the 1993 season, there was the Pilgrim case. Steve Pilgrim, an able all-round footballer who played on the wing for Wasps, had a trial with the reserve string of Leeds rugby league team. Someone ratted on him. If he had played for an amateur club as a trial for the pro ranks, or if he had not been grassed up, he could have returned to union with no problem. Instead, in an outburst of mock piety, the Rugby Football Union at Twickenham banned him from the code because he had broken a bylaw which forbids union players who have played for pro league clubs at any level, even unpaid, to return to the fold. He could apply for readmission, they said, after a year.

There followed from rugby league quarters, rugby league observers, league apologists and solid sports observers the most fierce outburst. Most pointed out, quite accurately, that Pilgrim had received no money, had hardly stuck a rapier into the heart of rugby union; and that to refuse to allow him to return to Wasps and take up his wing jersey was harsh. At a media briefing held by the RFU, I asked Dudley Wood, the RFU secretary, if he would feel able to grant a one-off reprieve, tell Pilgrim to jolly well not do it again – or at least, to wear a wig and false beard at his next trial. Wood reacted as if I had suggested that Twickenham should be blown up. 'We have no dispensation to do that,' he said in almost incredulous tones. The RFU had a case. We will come to it later. But the case they had was not the one they presented.

People spoke, with just a tinge of pomposity, of appeals to various courts of human rights. David Hinchcliffe, MP, is the secretary of something called the Parliamentary Rugby League Group. He asked that Gerald Kaufman, chairman of the Commons National Heritage Select Committee, should act against the RFU. The prospect of Mr Kaufman arriving at Twickenham would almost certainly have won Pilgrim an immediate reprieve if only Kaufman promised not to stay too long. However, the Parliamentary Rugby League Group turned out to have as much practical clout as the United Nations. Others demanded that all the vast Government subsidies that union enjoyed should be cut off. A swingeing step, too, had it not been for the fact that union receives not a penny from anyone and is entirely self-financing.

Some people, myself included, wrote that a minor rule change was needed to allow non-professional players to carry on. Others pointed out the anomaly that union players could make a fortune by legal means after relaxations in the game's bylaws; that others gained financial advantage under the counter throughout the game. And Pilgrim had never earned a brass farthing. People on all sides had a genuine sympathy for Pilgrim, who was eventually turned down by Leeds and tried to carve out a career at Halifax. Others never gave a damn for Pilgrim. They used him entirely for their own ends. The Pilgrim affair was a heaven-sent opportunity for the ranks of the bitter. All they had to do was to trot out every imagined slight ever perpetrated by rugby union, jump aboard every high horse in the stable and, blissfully, to perpetuate the myth that rugby union's malevolence was the one and only reason why their perfectly formed but small world never expanded. It was very sad. It wasted time. It poisoned minds.

That, to a large extent, is what league has tried to do in its anger at the overbearing code. That anger is manifested in many ways, or at least, in any way they can find to attack union, however spuriously. There are some classic examples of this bitter genre. The first is in false comparisons for self-justification. These comparisons come in many forms. A few years ago, a set of earnest and entirely bogus figures were produced which purported to show that rugby league was, apart from soccer, the best-supported game in Britain and that more people went along to watch it than union.

The figures were convenient, if nothing else. They simply left out about half the numbers who had attended rugby union games that season so that the league figure was above that of union. No spin doctor needed there. Just leave out half the statistics. And if anyone is really suggesting that rugby league is a more popular game in Britain than cricket, then I suggest they are dreaming. In truth, rugby league attendances are, usually, alarmingly poor, considering that they have to pay wages from gate proceeds. Rugby league's switch to Sundays means that they avoid all the other sporting fixtures of the typical Saturday, and do not have to compete with shopping, nor with their own amateur arms. Take a union team like London Scottish, now back in Courage Division One. They have to compete with all the attendant alternatives for leisure time on a Saturday, and also with the fact that within, say, a five-mile radius of their pitch in Richmond, Surrey, there will be as many as a hundred other matches being played concurrently with their own, at all levels.

The finest example of the sheer hopefulness of league's view of itself came when the league 'World Club Championship' took place at Old Trafford in 1989. One report commented on the size of the crowd, a healthy 30,000-odd. 'And there were thousands more stuck in traffic jams outside,' it ended. That traffic jam detaining the missing fans has now lasted around a hundred years.

Then there are eager (and false) comparisons in play. There is much of the playground bully in league. 'Our game's harder than yours, so there', is a constant theme. Probably the best example came from someone who should have known better, Phil Larder, formerly the RFL's national director of coaching and now the coach of Widnes. He produced, quite recently, an article which trotted out many irrelevant non-sequiturs and compared many incomparable situations. It was drivel. It purported to show that, because Rob Andrew, the England union fly-half, had made fewer tackles and been less involved in a match than Shaun Edwards, the Great Britain league stand-off, playing in another match in a different sport, then union was softer, inferior and less physically demanding. Larder is a man, of course, who has never coached, or attended to the mental build-up of a national team facing a Test Match against the All Blacks; or about to undertake what is recognised throughout union as the supreme physical test, a trip to the howling cauldron of the Parc des Princes to play France; or a team under real pressure in a game that meant something to the nation at large, to the sporting world at large.

Edwards, though it did not suit Larder's stance to point it out, merely had to tackle or be tackled, then the play stopped. He had no need, as did Andrew, to sap himself in the aftermath, tackle and ruck and maul in lightning and onerous tandem. It was sad that even a man of eminence could not contain his anger and bewilderment and had to find some specious way of asserting a league lead.

There are other ways. The centenary of the breakaway of the clubs of the Northern Union, the forerunner of the rugby league code, arrives in 1995. There have been a score of calls from officials, writers and followers of rugby league for a top league team to meet a top union team under union rules at somewhere like Twickenham or Wembley. Such a match could mark, say, a rapprochement between the two codes; could provide funds for a worthy charity; could mark the century itself.

There are a few teething problems to sort out before this game goes ahead. Who will insure the rugby league players in the front row against the grave danger of serious neck and spinal injuries which is always a possibility when players with no experience of a rugby union scrum are involved? What on earth will the rugby league men do all day? They will never, ever see the ball. There is absolutely nothing to stop the union men heeling the ball at every scrum, setting themselves and driving it five, ten or a hundred yards for a pushover try.

Certainly, the league team will win nothing in the line-out. The union men could field, say, four men of six foot eight or over; league forwards are comparatively tiny. They would be vastly out-reached and outweighed. How would league defenders fare when to adopt their normal practice of launching three men at the ball-carrier would create the formality of a two-man overlap in every attack? The profusion of specific techniques in union, by definition, makes a switch from league to union a great deal more difficult than travelling in the opposite direction.

Perhaps the biggest fount of bitterness and opportunity lies in the signing of a union player. Whatever he costs, it is worth it. The rigmarole is now well established. The newly arrived player appears at a press conference. He has always, he says, wanted to take on the new challenge of league (he can hardly admit that he is only there for the money). After a game or two, he is trotted out again. 'Would you say,' is the standard opening question for the apologists, 'that league is much harder than union?'

Signing a union player provides two more essential sticks for beating union. The first is that it gives league a window to the outside world, where it revels in a little of union's reflected glory and obtains rich publicity for itself – the signing of Jonathan Davies gave rugby league more publicity in one week than all the other pro players in the whole of the world. The second (hoped for by the game in general rather than by the signing club) is that the new player might not immediately make the grade. Then there are loud cackling noises that league must be a harder and better game because the union man is struggling. It is never mentioned that the difference in the two codes can be unbridgeable for the greatest players, and easily overcome by a relatively poor union player.

Not surprisingly, backlash publicity is not given such a wide airing. It is hardly a closed secret that Jonathan Davies yearns for the pastures of the dragon. He recently expressed, with some vehemence, his views on comparisons. He suggested that prepara-tion of Test teams in league is light years behind that of union teams; that the commercial possibilities are also infinitely higher in union; that league men would struggle to convert if they had the chance. I have never seen those views expressed by a league observer. They do not fit with the need to excuse league's lack of progress. To use *Open Rugby* as a model, a reflection of real life: never an issue goes by without one writer or another setting all the ills of the world at union's door, and some of the bitterness is astonishing. Compare, say, a year of *Open Rugby* with a year of *Rugby World & Post*, the union magazine, in which you will hardly see league mentioned in the whole year, in a good, bad or indifferent light.

Media coverage as a whole is another preoccupation of league men. You will see letter after letter demanding more coverage. We receive them at *The Sunday Times*. We once received four in a week.

The sender, the same man in every case, would have done far better had he disguised his handwriting. All four letters purported to come from different names in different parts of the country, yet strangely they were all posted in the same box in Leeds. The fervent belief of league people is that their sport receives nothing like the coverage it deserves. Yet it is a sport apart. In the north it deserves more; in the south, Scotland and Wales, it probably receives far too much. I have never met a southerner with a blind bit of interest in the sport, and all surveys indicate beyond doubt that awareness of league in the south is negligible.

The only answer for newspapers is 'editionising', changing their pages for different regions. Last season, the arrival at *The Times* of a new rugby league correspondent, the splendid Christopher Irvine, added immeasurably to league coverage. There are far too many reporters around who have never, ever seen a bad game – if you believe their reports, that is. In the final analysis, over a period of time a newspaper covers those matters it needs to cover to satisfy its readership. Otherwise, it changes. With drastically few exceptions, all sports get the coverage they and their appeal deserve.

Yet if rugby league is anywhere justified in its suspicion of union's attitude, then is it surprising? Rugby league is anxious to expand, and to do it quickly. How can it expand outside its heartlands? It can spend decades trying to start the sport in schools, I suppose – an almost impossible task. Furthermore, if a league nut is casting around for players to join him in forming a club, he can hardly wait eighteen years for schools to produce them. Where else can he get his players? There is only one source at amateur and pro levels: rugby union players. It is his only chance. What use are absolute beginners to him? So league is seen as a jackal at the carrion – hardly helpful to the image. Where do they attempt to find their players? In the ranks of the disaffected and the ranks of players with poor day jobs.

The same principle is behind one of their most recent ideas – trying to establish the game in Fiji. The situation is promising in several ways: there is a vast pool of players, kids to adults, bonkers on rugby union; an economic squeeze making the bribe stakes lower; and above all, no development costs. Rugby union has done all the development, the education, for them. It is the same all over the international front. When David Oxley wrote an article for a Wembley match programme in the early 1990s, he detailed the encouraging progress of early rugby league operations in Russia. He briefly mentioned former rugby union players as his source. But, he hinted, the main thrust of the campaign was to draw in some of the outstanding athletes in the Soviet Union.

Was Oxley seriously suggesting that he was going to pay good money to people who had never played any form of rugby before, never held a rugby ball? The truth is, of course, that league can only make fresh inroads by conversion. That is what they have tried to do in Russia. Growing your own takes a generation, a fortune. You have to steal.

Rugby league wants more than a free gangway. It wants a free ride. It is the equivalent of storming the boardroom of a multinational company, demanding that leading directors come and join your own company, and then being miffed when the managing director throws you out of the building. The penny has still to drop that no one owes league a living.

The antipathy of rugby union's leading officials, on the IRB, the RFU and elsewhere, is grossly misplaced. They cannot defend their action over the Steve Pilgrim affair, or, in France, claim defence of amateurism against broken-time hordes. You can earn, occasionally, far more in union.

But if they defended their no-return policy as a protection for their own assets they would be on much firmer ground than they are dribbling about whether or not a player earned a fiver for a trial. In the rampant commercial age in union, to lose an international, or even a top club player, after the years of investment would be a setback. League has a carrot: they can pay money up front. Union has a carrot: the ban on players professionalised by going to league. It is a legitimate weapon.

If the weapon were surrendered, then the likes of Jeremy Guscott, Tony Underwood, Ben Clarke, Scott Gibbs and others could disappear on short contracts (admittedly, they would probably disappear to Australian league – Guscott's agent regards the prospect of her charge departing to British league with horror), disrupting team-building and results and therefore the massive back-up marketing operations. I discussed the possibility of former union players being allowed to return with some of the Welsh Lions living in New Zealand. Tony Clement, Robert Jones and Richard Webster were unanimous, 'They should not let them back', they said.

There is no shame in losing that weapon. Perhaps the supergun could be downgraded, but it must not be dismantled. When the day dawns when league players can simply cross over to union's wider and more lucrative world (and that day is coming), then league will need safeguards to save its own skin, its team-building and commercial profile. At least league men will not toy with the bogus and doomed concepts union showed over the Pilgrim case.

Rugby league men reach a purple peak of apoplexy when they discuss the free gangway. This was something on which they rode round on high horses for years. Put simply, union's law was that you could not switch from league to union and vice versa, whether or not you took money for playing league. At least, that was the high fence with deep moat which was presumed to exist. In fact, around 95 per cent of people who prognosticated on the subject never realised that you could indeed switch – you simply had to end membership of one code. You could switch back every month if you wanted, provided you had chucked in your membership of the other lot. Union had its reasons, none of them particularly vital.

That was not good enough for league. They wanted everyone to be able to play any code at any time, memberships notwithstanding. They trotted out stories of union's abuse of poor deprived youths queueing up in hordes and hordes and desperate to play every code every day. Cyril Villiers, a regional director of the Sports Council, let it be known that he would act against any union club in receipt of a council grant which banned a former league player. He was on the alert for a full fifteen years.

'How many cases have you unearthed in that time?' I asked him.

'Er, none,' he said.

In any case, league had an easy way out of the mess, the perfect retaliation, even before union allowed a completely free gangway. All they had to do was ban from league anyone defecting to union. Then you would have had a straight fight – no crossing over, the more popular code gets the players. They would then have put their faith in their game where their mouth is, so to speak. The truth is, of course, once again that league could not get by in the style to which it hoped to become accustomed without union players.

Still, even today, every issue of *Open Rugby* is piled high with the latest 'do-you-know-what-those-utter-bastards-in-union-have-done-this-time'; occasionally reflecting slightly sharp union practice, more often reflecting a basic frustration at being outdone. As I say, rugby league does not want a free gangway. Rugby league wants a free ride. It stamps its foot when it does not get one.

Yet, in the final analysis, rugby league has wasted as much time and effort on its attitudes towards rugby union as it has on doomed promotions and fuss about its image. A severe blast of realism and self-appraisal would suit them far better. They could start with the realisation that union's hammering of league around the world is based, at least 95 per cent of the time, on greater public appeal, better chemistry and acceptable competition; that to hunt the mythical bogeyman of rugby union is simply to lose direction in a red mist of their own jealousy.

What of league this season and all the other seasons to come? As John Harvey-Jones, the unbarbered boardroom buccaneer ('Yes, Mr Managing Director, I conclude that all you need to do to turn this company around is to piss off yourself') says: 'If you don't expand, you contract.' Rugby league is contracting – Nottingham, Chorley and Highfield were all dumped from the Stones Bitter Championship after the reversion to a two-division format for 1993-94. Severe. Clubs are living things. They should not be murdered. As Lindsay Hoyle, Chorley's chairman, said on learning of his club's possible demise through the new structure: 'I thought they had done away with capital punishment in this country.'

In general, the league game is in desperate financial straits. The RFL itself recently made many of their staff redundant, turfing out Fred Lindop, who was performing a splendid job as refereeing controller, a post which union desperately needs to create. Lindop bashed on about uniformity of interpretation and the game became better as a result. He also helped to clean up the game – league is now, generally, a wonderful example of athletes showing each other proper respect, not head-butting and dribbling about rugby being a man's game. Leave aside the ugly fouls by Eyres and Goulding of Widnes against Wigan in Wigan's 1993 Wembley victory. Parts of union have to learn the same lesson. Yet Fred was cast out.

Among the clubs, the financial situation is very little short of abysmal. There are very few who have not had their problems and a good deal of them were caused by clubs overreacting to the supposed boom in the game in the 1980s, over-investing in marzipan instead of cake. Even Widnes have had to slash payments to players; Leigh and Swinton may well be set to join others on a familiar shoestring existence as wandering clubs, changing grounds, changing names, changing towns just to survive – the route taken, with increasing and heroic desperation, by the likes of Highfield (formerly Runcorn Highfield, Huyton, Liverpool City, Liverpool Stanley, London Highfield and Wigan Highfield). Some clubs share glutinous mud-heaps with each other or with soccer teams.

These are problems which will increasingly afflict union clubs now that the advent of leagues has given them the biggest kick in the seat of the pants for 150 years, has made them splash out in anticipation of future income.

There has been a savage verbal battle between the RFL and BARLA (whose clubs are thriving merrily) about control of the youth level of the game. The bitterness of the verbal exchanges outdoes even those within rugby union; and indeed, by banning BARLA players from pro grounds, by treating the opposition with contempt, and with each side refusing to allow its own men to cross the dynamited bridge between them, they were behaving in precisely the same way as union was supposed to behave towards league. The RFL's scattergun handout on the dispute was hardly moderate in tone: '. . . BARLA's unilateral and disgraceful action in imposing a hateful piece of legislation . . . Betrayal . . . intimidating and poisoning young minds . . . action in the courts if necessary . . .'

There is a lull in household names. Ellery Hanley is, slowly, fading. Hanley, to be brutal, is broadly speaking the only British player raised in league to have become a household name in Britain in the last decade. Consciousness and marketing (as opposed to bullshit) needs famous, brilliant league-raised Brits to send out the rays. Andy Gregory? Not quite. Garry Schofield? Great player, but not a face known country-wide.

There is a lull in sponsorship, too. It is not the fault of the league salesmen, but some of the league's recent major sponsors – Silk Cut, British Nuclear Fuels, British Coal – hardly constitute a state-of-the-art greened-up portfolio, however welcome their backing. And it is a bitter truth, a rampaging anomaly but still a truth, well understood by Welshmen, that the spin doctors of the sponsors and their PR men now blink before they invest in something with a non-

London base, with non-London accents and attitudes; an activity
not splashed across ITV (or, less preferably, the BBC).

The global lull is still causing anxiety. The Ashes series between
the British Lions (Ashes? British Lions? Of course league is not
derivative, perish the thought.) and Australia was magnificent,
beautifully covered by BSkyB, wonderfully competitive and exciting. It was a tragedy that Great Britain could not make the final
leap, straight into the open mouth of Bob Fulton, the Australian
coach, and all the others who do not always, shall we say, give our
rugby its proper respect. The 1993 New Zealand–Australia series
was also colourful, at least until the Second Test at Palmerston
North was stopped because there was no ball to play with.

The fact that New Zealanders have become so prevalent in the
British domestic game – not to mention Tawera Nikau's staggering
haircut – should give a good bite and tension to the 1993 home
series against the touring Kiwis; even New Zealand–Great Britain
series were fading into insignificance, with skeleton crowds in both
countries whenever the teams have met in the last decade. It is
crucial that the tour is a runaway success. Otherwise, international
rugby league boils down to Great Britain versus Australia, full stop.

The World Sevens in Sydney in February 1993 brought the
expansionist dreamers their most embarrassing few days imaginable. There was no global spread to speak of; Aussie played Aussie.
Aussie won. And the biggest story concerned an American VII
drummed up from here and there by phone or fax. They included
one clueless chancer, Mark Gerathy, who turned up for training
and inside thirty seconds proved so conclusively that he had no
ability that he was sent back to the US. 'He talked a tremendous
game,' said one of the coaches. The lack of a British or Welsh team
at the sevens underlined another grievous problem: the British
clubs are so keen on their bread and butter that matters like Test
rugby icing and global spread have to be subjugated.

So woe, woe. All that bankruptcy, all those burned fingers,
decline, tempers. And do not even the kings of the game drag down
the game? Wigan, who won a bagful of trophies in 1992-93 and who
thunder on, are widely supposed to be killing the game by winning
everything. Not fair to the others.

In fact, I believe that the game is far more buoyant than it
appears. Economic depression is not always the same as lack of
interest in the game, not at all. Tempers can cool. Maurice Lindsay,
for all the criticism he has copped since ascending to the secretary-
generalship, for all his lack of Oxley's Oxbridge-meets-Hunslet
manner, has unquestionably steered the game away from silly
global stunts, from promoting fripperies at the expense of the
game; steered it towards a new severity, and a realisation that the
game can creep its way into a wider world by long-term planning
and insinuation and not by bull-at-a-gate fervency.

And the game itself? As usual, when sports burst out on to the
pitch and leave the fuss behind, they galvanise. The marketing men
and the apologists, the bitter and the twisted, may have wasted

league's time and given it a bad name; but the players – they are
something different. Rugby league, for me, still has some of the
essential heroism of team sport as it is meant to be. Your lot take
your players and followers over to play the other lot across the
county; town descends upon town.

There are few barriers between the players and their followers
and between the players and honesty. At least in British league, the
problem of performance drugs is probably minimal; so are the
problems of prima donnas. There is no bottling out, as athletes
bottle out, to protect market value. There are still very few hold-
outs for better contracts. What did the Widnes players do when they
were told in 1992 that to save the club they had to take a pay cut?
They winced, they went out and lifted their season and they
reached the Challenge Cup final at Wembley in May. In league you
take what is coming.

Wigan are a delight. My favourite theory of sporting domination
is that the wheel of fortune always applies, and spares no one. If I
read my Marloweian drama correctly, even the most dominant runs
in life are fated to end. My theory has been borne out by the eclipse
of, say, Steve Davis, Jahangir Khan, England's rugby team – who,
less than a year ago, we were told, would win and win for decades –
and Liverpool FC . . . Wigan, and Bath in union, have come closer to
disproving the theory than any team or individual. Wigan have
done more to push the message of league than 1,000 visits to
Milwaukee and 1,000 hours of babbling about how to change the
laws to bring more tries. Most of rugby league wanted St Helens, the
maddening, occasionally glorious runners-up, to take some titles
last season. Wigan's men said no, at least till the Premiership final.

If there is one sad development that has come with Wigan's
silverware it is probably the advent of the full-time pro. I always
shudder when BSkyB's caption for an individual gives his occupation as 'rugby league player'. Wigan, though not other clubs, could
possibly sustain a fully pro team over a long period. But could the
players sustain a career afterwards? Rugby league's pension arrangements are excellent. But league's men are not famous enough
to live on their names when they retire, and only a tiny minority can
go on to coach. I would rather see a young player take a pay cut
from his club and return to a career path. I have a dreadful feeling
that a sizeable scrapheap, composed of players who have neglected
long-term careers, may form in the next decade. The current crop
of rugby league players, especially those at the top level, deserve
more.

As Brian Moore, England's hooker and one of the hardest-
training union players in history, says: 'I don't particularly want to
sit round in a tracksuit all week waiting to train and play rugby. I
want to get on with other things. Rugby is an important part of my
life. It isn't life.'

Of course, there may well be a day of reckoning which is of far
more significance than the current problems. Rugby union is
drifting, relatively quickly, towards professionalism. If you com-

pare the current situation, the new laws and the new abuses, with five years ago you have some idea of the pace of change. Bastions are falling. Pressure is rising. The players no longer cower, and quite right, too. Union has reached a massive and unscaleable wall. They cannot ask any more of their leading players without paying them. The possibility exists that, even within the next ten years, union will become so lucrative that economics blow away all restrictions to playing any code.

Imagine the choice facing rugby league's top men, and pro players at all levels. Suddenly (once they have mastered the techniques), they can sample the world of union: play all over the globe, in a meaningful, high-pressure world cup; perhaps even dabble in the spring sevens circuit – Hong Kong, Las Vegas, Lisbon, Monaco, Fiji, Canberra; the best could take part in major product launches. Beguiling, and for league, asset-stripping.

League, at the moment, has a Catch 22 dilemma. You hear everyone calling for union to come clean, admit its professionalism, payments legal and illegal, to come out into the open. But if union did so, if it swept away all checks one morning, then it might sweep league away with it. Maurice Lindsay recently came clean, when he announced a blueprint for the future in mid-1993. He stated, categorically, that it was aimed at the encroaching power of union. You always know when a sport is in trouble, they have lots of 'blueprints for the future'. Of course, league is so much part of the culture of its heartlands that it will always exist. The base is not wide, but it is strong and well laid. Union has no culture in some league areas and culture, as we have discovered, cannot be transplanted.

League still just has time to reshape a future to resist some of the attractions that professional rugby union might bring. But surely not all. Today, almost a hundred years since the games split and the new code set off into the world, and with talk in the air of a future rejoining, it is clear that any amalgamation will be conducted entirely on terms dictated by the mother code.

# CHAPTER 13

# The Boys of Kerikeri

## HAMSTRING BATTLES IN THE PHONEY WAR OF THE BAY OF ISLANDS

The Lions left Heathrow in mid-May to begin what is still rugby's greatest adventure, unpatriotically flying the Singapore flag on Singapore Airlines. Some of us flew out on British Airways; there are certain loyalties and standards we British should always maintain – not to mention the millions of air miles you get.

When the Lions boarded they stretched out in comfort in the business-class cabins. All the Test rugby teams now travel near the front even though the cost is more than double the economy-class fare. It is money well spent, every penny of it. It is less than three years since international rugby teams were shunted into cattle class for the interminable flights to the other side of the planet, where six-foot-nine locks folded themselves into cramped seats; it is a mere five years since the Welsh rugby team were boarded in a desperate New Zealand motel of dispiriting tin cabins in a trading estate in the week of a Test match and Jonathan Davies and the others had to wear towels and tracksuits in bed because they were so cold.

The treatment is better now. The 1993 Lions, bar a few low-grade hotels in the redneck districts, were treated well. In Auckland, Wellington and Christchurch they stayed in the top hotels the city had to offer, with fluffy towels and flunkeys to open every door before you had a chance to make a grab for the handle, and they were often entertained royally. But in passing, you still wonder why on earth the culture of treating players like third-class citizens, while rugby's smug officialdom flew in the front, took so very long to disappear.

They landed at Auckland's International Airport. They were 12,000 miles from anywhere that mattered in the global scheme of things, of course. But they were also in one of the capitals of the rugby world. Geoff Cooke, Ian McGeechan and Gavin Hastings – the management – held a press conference on arrival at which they

released the astonishing news that the Lions were hoping to win the
Test series, that they respected New Zealand rugby and that the
Lions were not as slow as their pre-publicity. That's the trouble with
rugby press conferences – you just stagger from one astounding
revelation to another.

Then they transferred to the domestic terminal for the flight to
Kerikeri, the gateway airport (if one shed and a bit of tarmac is an
airport) in the Bay of Islands, the glorious region on New Zealand's
north-east coast where they were to spend a week gearing up. Those
veteran Kiwiphiles among us had already pointed out to newcomers
that the Bay is winterless, a place of blissful and endless calm, of tiny
islands and lapping beaches. As soon as the Lions arrived, the whole
area was struck by violent storms.

It was an apt send-off for the tourists because every single
weather forecast the party received for the rest of the trip was
completely off the mark as well. Whoever you asked – concierge,
knowing sage, official meteorologist, local loony, old bat – they all
piped up with forecasts which proved spectacularly wrong.

And so began life as a Lion, with the stately, unstoppable process
of a rugby tour, the nearest thing in sport to the mega-group rock
tours. You arrive in town, set out your wares and show what you can
do; you pack, you leave and fly on to the next town. There is an
irresistible momentum about a Lions tour: never mind the friendships and enmities and impressions good and bad, as soon as the
match is played and the next day dawns, on you go with hardly a
backward glance, deaf to persuasion. In a sense there is something
sweeping and heroic about the whole thing.

A little way into the tour, I put to Stuart Barnes my favourite
description of a Lions trip. It was written of a previous tour by John
Hopkins, a predecessor of mine as rugby correspondent of *The
Sunday Times*, now golf correspondent of *The Times*. 'A Lions tour,'
he wrote, 'is a cross between a medieval crusade and a schoolboys'
outing.' Barnes, like me, regarded the description as impossible to
better. 'I would totally go along with that. There is certainly the
element of the outing. Whatever we want to do we can do –
shooting, fishing, golf, jet-boating. It is all laid on; everything. The
rugby itself is so much bigger and more significant and intense than
anything else in the game.'

They unpacked. Stuart Barnes took me through the kit. The
Lions were each given, through the official suppliers, two blazers,
one dark blue and one lighter blue as the number one rig; three
formal white shirts, two Lions ties and one bow-tie; one blue V-neck
pullover with Lions badge; one green crew-neck pullover with
Lions badge; two pairs of grey trousers and one belt; two tracksuits,
one red ('horrible', said Barnes) which was used as a kind of day-
time function gear and one blue; two training tracksuits; one pair of
casual shoes ('Unofficial deal. Bob Weighill went mad.'); three
different training shirts, red and white, blue and green and blue;
two casual short-sleeved shirts with a different Lions motif; two
polo-neck shirts; two pairs of casual trousers ('disgusting'); two

pairs of rugby boots, two pairs of trainers and a set of holdalls ('Like Russian dolls. One giant one, one big one, one medium one, one small one').

The players were not likely to retire on the proceeds of their tour. They were each given £22 per day under the IRB regulations for 'communications allowance'. That was not ungenerous in that it bought each Lion roughly 25 minutes of telephone calls to the British Isles per day (if they decided to use the allowance for communicating). Some of the party also claimed the £40 per day hardship allowance, essentially a broken-time payment and a principle which, when it was allowed by the IRB, caused apoplexy at the RFU at Twickenham.

Barnes was on full pay from the Stroud & Swindon Building Society, his employers, so did not claim the hardship allowance. Most of the team were being paid in full for the period of their absence but others did claim. They had to provide evidence to the Four Home Unions' tours committee that they were indeed losing out but the committee, to their credit, did not insist on photographs of starving wives and children before they granted the pay-out.

A player on full allowances would therefore receive roughly £3,050 for the tour. Geoff Cooke doled out the money on a weekly basis, sitting like an old-style ledger clerk with his wedge. The party ran some minor schemes for extra pocket money, although compared to the lavish money-making operations run by the All Blacks and Australians while on tour, which provide everything from speakers for company days to fiercely marketed ticket packages, they bought only small beer.

When the Lions arrived at any hotel the unloading process rivalled that undertaken after a drop in a famine zone by a Hercules. There were hundreds of bags, the medical equipment of Dr James Robson, the young and popular medico on his first major tour, and of Kevin Murphy, the Lancastrian physiotherapist on his umpteenth. Murphy, short and bespectacled, ferociously loyal to the players, has certainly won matches for England and the Lions with his work over the years in dragging injured players back to the pitch. It was Smurf who usually took the players through the warm-up phase of training before handing over to the coaches.

Also on tour were the liaison officers appointed to the party by the NZRU, Merlin Shannon and Peter Burke; the baggageman, a saturnine Kiwi called Milton Floyd, and local liaison officers who acted as local fixers. They helped to arrange the golf and jet-boating and ten-pin bowling and go-karting and fishing and boat trips and school visits. Mick Galwey, the popular Irishman, had the responsibility of contacting Irish bars on arrival in any location to arrange a visit by the team.

Guinness now sweeps the world, even if the standard of the glorious auld brew in Kiwi establishments ranged from passable Dublin to passed water. Stoutaphilia is catching on in New Zealand too: all the big towns had some establishment paying homage to Kitty O'Shea's in Dublin. There was Kitty O'Brien's, Brien O'Kitty's,

Seamus O'Hoolihan's. Some of them featured so-called Irish bands, who rendered 'The Wild Rover' in a kind of mish-mash Irish-Kiwi-Yankee accent.

In the rooming lists for each stop, the management worked extremely hard to break up the large English faction into manageable chunks. The party was further sub-divided into smaller groups for training exercises and also for off-the-field competitions. Scott Gibbs was in the Taxi Drivers, so named after Gibbs' recent court case and conviction for driving away a taxi after a night of celebrating in Cardiff. Barnes' group was called the Densas. 'Like Mensa, only with a D,' said Barnes. Geddit?

The intensity of the fixture list was well publicised. Even Kiwi commentators reckoned that the Lions were bonkers to agree to it. But the alternatives were difficult: modern-day tours are much shorter and more packed; the need to take games out into the hinterland has to be balanced by the need to play in large population centres to draw in the money. Granted, there were powerful fixtures in midweek, two of them against teams from New Zealand's top four in North Harbour and Waikato. But even though all the best Lions teams are those which fall quickly into first and second teams and allow the first team to progress and nurture itself, it was not such a bad thing to have met, say, Waikato in midweek. It meant the midweek team had something to aim for; their own 'test'. The only drawback to the fixture list as a whole was that it never allowed for a decent stop in any location. We travelled every Sunday and every Thursday (Wednesday in Test weeks), and there hardly seemed any point in unpacking your case. Surely tours could be arranged which allow for week-long stopovers here and there with a bus trip to the midweek game rather than a lock, stock, and barrel move.

But it was harsh not only in the matches. The Lions worked ferociously hard between games, too. They trained long and hard; even harder on the Monday and Thursday sessions two days before the games, with a lighter though hardly soft session on Tuesdays and Fridays. They even ran out on the occasional Sunday. When I passed their hotel on the morning of the North Harbour game they were even out then on a nearby pitch. On training days, the outriders and gofers would arrive and arrange the tackle bags and balls and other paraphernalia, set up a table with the isotonic drinks laid out. A van dragging a scrummaging machine puttered around New Zealand following the party, and that would be set up for most sessions. The slight disadvantage was that it needed an electrical power point. Scrummage practice in the club kitchen was always difficult. But all in all, if you tot up the sweat and blood and the hours, the Lions could not possibly have worked harder.

Dogging the steps of the party all the way was the travelling media party, which began about twenty strong and effectively grew to well over sixty as the tour progressed. At some stage of the tour every London paper save the *Daily Star* had their men on tour; so did the Press Association, which services every national and local paper in the UK, and the New Zealand Press Association. ITV, which had outbid the BBC for tour coverage at home, had a sizeable crew who pattered around the place with suitably luvvie gestures. The leading papers in Scotland, Ireland and Wales were all represented, albeit by journalists occasionally doubling up for two or more papers; later, the BBC World Service, BSkyB and the *Manchester Evening News* sent their men. Even the self-styled Beastie Boys arrived. John Etheridge and Colin Price, respectively the rugby men from the *Sun* and the *Mirror*, arrived in time for the Tests. Etheridge admitted privately to me that he intended to cut back slightly on the technical analysis when filing his stories.

There were commentators for Welsh language TV and radio, for BBC Radio; there were the home-based TV and newspapermen; and then there were the snappers: there were eventually seven photographers from the UK. You could tell their rooms on the media floors of the hotels because you would hear the wire machines whirring away as the pictures beamed up to London. David Rogers, the British photographer from Allsport revered among the media corps as one of the best tourists, was shooting for *The Sunday Times*. One cracking colour picture nestling next to your report and suddenly the whole thing can glow. That was the theory, anyway.

The overwhelming majority of the press party from the British Isles had toured together before; some were on their seventh visit to New Zealand. I was on my fifth: I had reported the 1983 Lions tour, the 1985 England tour, the 1987 World Cup and the 1989 tour by Wales. The party was far too big to stay in the same hotel as the team so the two groups, circling each other warily, usually stayed in hotels close to each other.

In the old days, when three or four travelling press constituted a large party, the journalists were part of the main tour, and even went on trips and visits. Now there is the problem not only of sheer numbers but also of ethics – there was not a single Lion whom I disliked but nor do I feel it is ever part of the job to spend ages drooling over their shoulders. Guidelines were drawn up which we had to follow. We had to ask the permission of Geoff Cooke, the manager, to interview a player. We were not supposed to ring them in their rooms. The players were available briefly after training sessions; there was a formal press conference after each game, and every Sunday, dressed in his Sunday best-casual, Cooke would sit on a chair in front of the press and discuss the match the day before, the injury situation and the future of the sporting world as we know it.

Cooke at least had a working knowledge of the operations of the sporting press. He is one of the best officials in European rugby for grasping the media's role, although he is not above a certain testiness – and why should he be? Yet around 80 per cent of the people I have met in the game, even press officers, leading officials and many players, have not even the remotest idea of what the media is, how it operates, what it needs; how requirements and talents differ; how good the job can be and how harsh and pressurised, especially in the loneliness of the empty screen or typewriter sheet.

The most prevalent error of all made by rugby people is to see the media as cheerleaders. A tiny few of the Lions plainly regarded criticism as disloyalty; certainly, in the hostile atmosphere of New Zealand rugby there is an element of all the Brits (and Irish) being in something together. Some remained urbane about criticism; others scowled and grunted. In fact, the team and management would have been surprised at how fiercely most of the media agonised with the team, how much we wanted them to win, how painfully we counted the seconds when they led the First Test until the last few minutes. But thankfully, most of them seemed to understand that you simply cannot let down the people who have paid for you to travel for two months around the country by joining the Lions fan club on an official basis. What you feel inside as a British Isles camp follower and what is your duty to the paper may occasionally, and blissfully, coincide; often, they can be two completely different things.

The patriots flying British Airways reached Auckland a day or two after the Lions. Less than two hours after disembarking from the flying city that is a Boeing 747 we were uneasily eyeing something called a Piper Commanche parked in a bay. It was our transport to Kerikeri in the Lions' wake.

New Zealand is the place where nervous fliers finally crack up. Even after 300 flights I can never quite remain sanguine in severe turbulence. I have no idea what climatic conditions conspire but the average Air New Zealand domestic flight is traditionally a terrifying affair in which the plane bounces up and down, left and right, and bangs and creaks like the old big dipper at Barry Island fairground with the same gut-wrenching swoop. Some of the flights of past tours have become more legendary to the press corps than past games – 'Remember that bastard when we flew to Christchurch after the First Test in 1983?' 'Yeah, but that was nothing compared to the Fokker Friendship flight to Wellington on the '85 England trip. Even the stewardesses panicked.' The Piper Commanche pilot sensed the nervousness, contributed a ludicrous landing man-oeuvre in which he came into the Kerikeri strip at the same angle as a crashing Spitfire, and we were on the ground and on the tour. There was a tingling feeling that had nothing to do with the flight. We were part of a Lions tour, the biggest thing in the players' careers and for me, the biggest thing in mine.

Ahh! New Zealand! Dontcha just love it? Well yes, actually, I do. The country takes a fearful pasting in Paul Theroux's spellbindingly boring travelogue, *The Happy Isles of Oceania*, if only through Theroux's priceless ability to generalise about whole nations – history, demeanour, culture – after two days there. But we young Welsh boys always assumed, or were conditioned to assume, that the country itself was like its rugby players. In my mind's eye, daydreaming about the place as young Welsh boys often did, New Zealand itself was therefore gloomy, harsh and functional, without colour or frills or fripperies; an unfriendly place. Above all, a place of dark, satanic hills. Every Kiwi was Colin Meads, sheep under each arm, glowering from a Te Kuiti hilltop.

So my first day in the country, in April 1983, was as revelatory as Chapman's Homer. We had made a landfall in Auckland and then boarded an Air New Zealand 737 for the flight to Christchurch, where the Lions were playing. From 30,000 feet, the perfect overview, I was staggered by the greenness, the beauty of the place. And also by the size and space. It is a place in which you feel able to fill your lungs. There are around eighteen million sheep but only three million Kiwis.

A few days later, that tour moved from Christchurch to Greymouth and we drove over Arthur's Pass in the Southern Alps, the backbone of the South Island. It was a wonderful experience: hair-raising bends curving out over deep valleys, massive craggy mountain peaks from which the mist descended. Hardly the New Zealand of youthful perception. It is a beautiful country, from Fiordland and Coromandel to Christchurch's orderly brightness.

There is also the sheer approachability of most New Zealanders. On my first-ever night in the country, ten years ago, I went to a function thrown by the Canterbury Rugby Supporters' Association. It was a typical New Zealand rugby gathering – dull, completely male-dominated, a drinking, yarning throng in blazers with wire badges, a room without relief of colour in clothes, wit or speeches. We poured a little of their watery beer into small glasses from a pitcher. 'Oi!' someone called to me from a nearby table. 'Oi! Come over yer!'

He was a bristling squat figure wearing a cap and a voluminous grey pullover, and with the ruddy face of the outdoors. I can still see him now. I looked away. 'Ignore the mouthy bastard,' said one of my colleagues.

'Oi!' he called, and beckoned me. 'Get some of this piss down you.' He pulled up a chair. I sat stiffly at his table. 'You a Pommy journo?' he rudely rasped. 'Reckon the All Blacks'll murder you.' It was just as I was contemplating a night in the cells for ABH when it dawned. This was his welcome. His embrace. We sat and talked, and thawed. He still talked raspingly. He appeared not to have any life outside his farm and his passion for rugby. He never asked if I had a family, where I was from in Pommyland; which paper I wrote for. We downed a pitcher or two and parted. Next day, I saw him in the ground at the Test. He fished into a bag, brought out a creased red Canterbury Rugby Supporters Club T-shirt, and gave it to me. It was far too small, and may at one stage have been used as bedding for lambing ewes. I gave him a London Welsh tie. New Zealand is a graceful country though not exactly full of grace. But the average Kiwi is essentially a friendly, welcoming beast.

A few of them have the same urgent need for national self-justification of the average Australian, the desperate celebration of any sporting achievement to cover the lack of greatness in certain other areas. The lead in the *New Zealand Herald*'s Wimbledon coverage one day during the 1993 Lions tour was the story of the Kiwi who had won a round of Junior Wimbledon, rather than any real Wimbledon news. Agassi? Graf? Sampras? Navratilova? Sorry, they weren't Kiwis. Titanic Sinks! New Zealander Saved!

And on the early visits you could never quite forget the description of the country as Britain twenty years ago. Grim mutton dishes with slapped mountains of pumpkin were all they could pull in from fields of lamb; Elton John's 1970s albums were filed under 'progressive rock'. *Coronation Street* was years behind, so that Ena Sharples was still the core figure; desperate motels lurked to catch the unwary traveller.

Even in 1993, game squadrons of old Ford Anglias and Cortinas chugged on, and here and there, you still found the odd 1970s belting feathered haircut. Tawera Nikau, the Kiwi league loose forward still has one; though Steve Bachop's has gone, to be replaced by a 1980s model.

By the standards of the BBC, the general television service is still something of an insult. During the Lions tour, TVNZ proudly revealed their brand-new programme. It was New Zealand's own version of *Give us a Clue*. As a prelude to the launch, they ran some of the old Brit *Give us a Clue* programmes, featuring Michael Aspel with wedge haircut and ballooning flares. The average New Zealand mid-evening peak-time transmission was three old BBC bombed series in close succession. Their *Last of the Summer Wine* repeats are so old that the three old groaners look young.

Yet the country has grown up twenty years in ten. The contrast between 1983 and 1993 as far as cuisine, hotels, music, and fashion went was marked. Stu Wilson, that sharp right wing who led the All Blacks against the 1983 Lions, has opened a bar in Auckland. It is well appointed, relatively luxurious, with important quasi-antique artefacts and Stu in Mine Host apron. 'You have to educate people here to come out to a place like this,' he says. 'People are so used to standing drinking in a large shed all day, with the women at home.' The body language of some of his clients that night, sipping their drinks in Stu's luxurious surroundings, seemed furtive, as if they were caught perusing the display in a Soho bookshop. But you could see his point, and in 1993 you could sense a culture changing. Compared to 1983 it was as if the twentieth century had come through customs and checked in.

The country appears to be growing still. The wondrous contrasts in nature and backdrop are still the same and along with the odd Ford Anglia, there are still enough reminders that the country is still not, quite, cutting new sods at the sharp end of the definition of modern life and new worlds. But good old New Zealand. It may be 12,000 miles from the head of the world, but not quite so far away from the heart.

The rugby is heartland, all right. In 1993 it was a strange collision, or hybrid, of the old and the new. On the one hand, the old grey macho culture prevailed, the men in blazers, the still, quiet, unresponsive crowds which so bewilder visitors used to high-volume, packed houses in the Northern Hemisphere. The crowds at a club game at Neath, Young Munster, Northampton or Bath would make far more noise at a mid-table league match than would a New Zealand crowd at a deciding Test match. Every time a touring pressman new to the tour and to New Zealand arrived, he would turn to the older hands and ask: 'What the hell is wrong with this crowd? Are all New Zealand crowds this quiet?'

At the First Test in 1983, they made a bid to create a similar world to that of the Northern Hemisphere cathedrals of the game and to boost the atmosphere. They rolled on a movable podium and up climbed a cheerleader to start community singing. 'Right,' he barked. 'We're going to have community singing. And I want you all to join in and sing just like they all do at Cardiff Arms Park and Wimbledon.' Not many of us could recall hymns and arias on Centre Court. But in any case, he was doomed. For a start, the first song on the bill for the communal singsong was that stately old hymn 'I've Got a Luvverley Bunch of Coconuts'. Secondly, it is not in the Kiwi sportswatching culture to go along for extra-mural frolic, to party on down, to do anything other than sit stolidly and watch the match.

And on the other hand in the collision so clearly visible during the 1993 tour, there was the imported-Australiana-imported-from-Americana, the attempted razzmatazz and hype and rock, a good deal of it imported through New Zealand's Sky Television, which shows basketball and baseball from America. Before almost every game on the 1993 Lions tour there were curtain-raiser matches, marching bands, dancing girls, sky-divers, rock anthems on the PA. Sometimes, there were glorious Maori troupes, hot-air balloons, celeb introductions. Fun. And hand in hand with that was rampaging commercialism. In New Zealand, if you wish, you can sponsor the touch-judge's testicles. Almost every home team has another name, that of their sponsor. The Lions played Liquor King North Harbour, Yarrows Taranaki, Hawke's Bay Draught Magpies, Trustbank Southland, Speights Otago, Steinlager All Blacks. The Lions tour itself was sponsored, by Steinlager. The example set by the Foster's Oval has also been followed. Okara Park in Whangarei is now known as Lowe Walker Park, after a local company. The match ball would be sponsored, the sky-divers would be called something like the Joe Soap Furnishing Sky-divers; the dancing girls would be the Radio Something Dancing Girls.

The local sponsorships are teeming. Hawke's Bay went in for individual sponsorships – even their assistant coach was sponsored – by Napier Glass Company. The touch-judges were in fact the Rawcliffe, Plested & Pembrose Valuers touch-judges. It was all very bitty. It was harsh for us northlanders, because for all the Northern Hemisphere's playing inferiority, rugby is far more successful commercially than in the Southern Hemisphere. Here it was unsightly and not easy on the ear because of the constant exhortations to support scores of advertisers. Yet it was essential, part of the battle to float the game in all its aspects, and to push it along.

But it was the incongruity that was striking. Essentially, New Zealand rugby is a conservative sport. It is a sport which has existed on its solid, untrumpeted merits for so long, and dressed itself in dark blazer with wire badge. Now, it is grafting on the colour and the gilt and the marketing punch and the two worlds sometimes co-exist uneasily and incongruously. Colin Meads, after all, was never a walking billboard.

Yet it is the energy of the game that leaves the strongest impression. The blazored ranks never sit and moan about the old days. They bloody well get on with it. If someone thinks they need a marching band or a gang of under-dressed young girls or that a traditional old ground should be renamed after a beefburger, then that is what they will get.

They will re-invent themselves. For example, Laurie Mains, the grim-faced All Black coach, has never been revered as one of the great communicators. Yet he has wound up his best smile, polished off a few phrases, sharpened up the eye contact and he is out there in front of the cameras pushing the game and his team.

New Zealand rugby can have an air of scruffiness, of intrusive marketing, perhaps of a process in the lower registers of soul-selling. It is not, at heart, a game comfortable with American marketing methods. The crowd still, largely, sit in silence, no matter what entertainment you lay before them. But New Zealand rugby has energy, ambition, honesty. It now has rivals for national affection – new pursuits and culture, the impending arrival of the Auckland Warriors rugby league team. But it will never be surprised by a rival tapping it on the shoulder while it is taking a nap.

There are other sides to it, of course. Rough edges on the side of a set of studs, for a start, plus an arrogance that only their philosophies were worth bothering with. Whether it was still strong in playing power was something which we were just about to discover for ourselves, first hand. Onwards to Kerikeri.

The Lions were training at Kerikeri when we landed so we stopped off at the Kerikeri club to watch. It was purposeful and impressive; obviously meticulously organised by Ian McGeechan and Richard Best. It was also obvious that Ian McGeechan would be true to his quiet pre-tour assertion that he would be trying to beat the All Blacks at their own game, not with the traditional British Isles style (whatever that is–answers on a postcard).

All the exercises at Kerikeri, and indeed at training in the first few weeks of the tour, seemed to be aimed at jacking up the pace of the team and the pace at which they thought and acted; more precisely, it was an endless succession of drills and practices to improve play in the secondary phases: to drive into rucks and mauls, how far to drive, when to keep the ball up in a maul, when to put it down for the ruck; when to pop the ball to a forward standing off, how far he should go and at what angle; when the ball should eventually be laid back to Dewi Morris or Robert Jones, the tour scrum-halves. 'It is a matter of individual decision-making, of the players adapting to the needs of the situation and of the referee,' said coach McGeechan. Relatively speaking, there was very little work on the line-outs and even less on the scrum – no massive scrummaging sessions with forty and fifty big ones. The van pulling the scrummaging machine often puttered in vain.

In training and in the whole week that the Lions prepared, looming around the foyer of their beachfront hotel, padding in tracksuits around the streets of Pahia, training and boating, the almost boyish pleasure they took in each others' company was transparent. It was the 'shy liking' of Ralph and Jack in *Lord of the Flies*. The process of coming together, perhaps even the banishment of old scores, was formidably obvious and vitally necessary. The two national captains on tour apart from Hastings were Will Carling and Ieuan Evans, and both played a major part in bringing their men to the feast. Quickly, the feeling grew and the party became one. To the outsider, the process was one step down from an outburst of mass closet-exiting gay awareness. The insiders knew that the Lions were bonding to face a fiery ordeal.

Richard Webster launched his bid to wrest the Test place at openside flanker from Peter Winterbottom. For some reason which I never fathomed, the selection for the tour of the hard-nosed and indestructible Swansea flanker was criticised. He seemed the obvious choice, especially when set alongside the list of unproven and gentlemanly hopefuls that his critics paraded as alternatives. Webster went on a clay pigeon shoot. He fired off a few shots, smashed a few clay pigeons into, well, clay. He whooped and celebrated his success as he lowered his gun and a round still in the chamber discharged and missed Winterbottom's foot by, taking an average from eyewitnesses, one yard.

There were two amazing sights among the Lions. One day, when a few of us were walking through Pahia's shopping arcade, we saw Will Carling. What is more, we saw him in a café, drinking a cup of coffee, and pouring it himself. Phew! I was delighted when Hastings, not Carling, was chosen as captain of the Lions. I was pleased because Hastings has certain inbuilt advantages of compatibility with the Kiwi; I was especially delighted for Carling himself. At the end of the England season I believe he was exhausted, and would gladly have spent the whole summer dodging the spotlight. Here he was in Pahia, in the ranks. It was an indication of the wildness of our perceptions of an essentially good bloke that we should have found Carling and the coffee incongruous.

The other sight was that of Bayfield limping. It was a major story. The first week, before the first match, is always the phoney war. There is sweat and intent, words and threats of war but no war. Effectively, everything happens and nothing happens. Her Majesty's press needs news. Then Bayfield pulled a hamstring. The world ended. The news wires hummed. He didn't pull it badly, and he was soon fit again. One week later, everyone including him had forgotten it, yet in the phoney war in the Bay of Islands, it was drama.

Not that the trip was wasted for the onlookers. At Kerikeri in the sunshine, the locals gathered. Old warriors running to fat leaned on the fences growling softly to each other, 'Jeez, that Dooley's a big bugger.' And young children gathered, most holding hands with a parent. The Lions were brilliant, in Kerikeri and in New Zealand in general. They signed every autograph book, posed patiently with arms around unknowns while unknown's mate fumbled with his camera. Once in Kerikeri Brian Moore, who regards every training session as part of a master plan to dominate every opposition hooker and the other hooker in his own party, broke off training to take some fluids on board and stood scowling by the drinks table. One of the keenest, most star-struck youngsters sidled up to him. 'Christ, not *now*,' we thought. Moore signed the proffered book, shook the little boy's hand, chatted briefly and yet warmly with the lad's parents, reapplied the scowl powder and ran back to the session.

Later that day, another small lad was laid out when fooling with his friends and a tackle bag. Doctor James and Physio Kev raced over, carried him carefully to the pavilion and then took him for x-ray in case he had sustained damage to his neck. At the hospital he proudly waited in line with Rory Underwood, who was having a precautionary x-ray on a cheekbone after colliding with Stuart Barnes in training. All plates were negative, the boy had his picture in all the local papers, festooned with posing Lions. His mother could simply not say enough about the exotic visitors.

No big deal, of course. Yet if a Lions tour is anything then it is a point of contact between tourists and hosts. If it loses the human element, if it wraps up the party in cotton-wool and agents, if all the home people ever see of the team is through a camera, then half the Lions' life is not worth living. Imagine an American football team taking themselves out round the backwoods playing the locals, especially if the locals were fanatically determined to hammer them. And do the real followers get so close to their heroes in soccer, or athletics, or even cricket, except in staged stunts? Of course not. Perhaps rugby and the British Lions are old-fashioned but in this case, I profoundly hope that they remain in the past. No big deal – except for the excited boys of Kerikeri.

The first tour match approached, and the Lions were to drive for two hours south to Whangarei and the meeting with North Auckland. The Lions, in general, were not vultures of culture. Near Pahia is Waitangi, where in 1840 the Treaty of Waitangi was signed, whereby the turbulent Maoris conceded the sovereignty of the Land of the Long White Cloud to Queen Victoria. The Treaty House is a museum of the event. As far as the curator could remember, none of the Lions party had visited. They had other things on their minds.

So the Lions wound up their week of training. From the rooms in the media's hotel you could see right across the Bay, towards the dotted islands. The weather was restored. The sea was so calm the waves hardly lapped, the surface mirrored every light in the surrounding islands. There was no wind. Or even a sound. It was impossibly beautiful and calm and impossibly incongruous, considering what was to come.

# CHAPTER 14

# *The Uncatchable Slow Men*

## NORTH AUCKLAND, NORTH HARBOUR, THE MAORIS, AND CANTERBURY

Whangarei is a comfortable drive down New Zealand's Highway 1 (we'd call Highway 1 a single-track road with passing places down the farm) from the Bay of Islands. The Lions stayed in the Bay until Saturday, with most of the party itching for action – 'I was really bored in the end,' said Scott Gibbs – and then their bus set off towards rugby. After a few kilometres, the sun which had been with us for most of the week suddenly disappeared and a cold and clammy mist descended. Was it a Wagnerian symbolism? Or was it just raining? One of the Lions was desperately trying to keep from others the fact that he was bursting with pride and anticipation. Stuart Barnes had endured agonies of frustration in his rugby career but he had been made captain for the day, he was to lead out the team to start the tour. 'Not bad for a guy on his first Lions tour with only a handful of caps,' he said, with heavy irony. Barnes is outwardly phlegmatic but inwardly probably less so.

It was pointlessly early to look for Test selection pointers. The Lions management had promised everyone a match in the first two games, against North Auckland and North Harbour. But a sharp and accurate send-off for Barnes and Robert Jones at half-back would have set the tone. Jerry Guscott, blisteringly sharp at training, was alongside Scott Hastings in the centre, Ian Hunter and Rory Underwood on the wings and Tony Clement at full-back. In the pack, Mick Galwey had his first outing on the blindside flank and there was massive pressure on him to prove to the Union of Blindside Flankers at home that he was worthy of a Lions number 6 shirt, rumbustious forward though he is. Richard Webster and Ben Clarke completed the back row, Damian Cronin came in alongside Andy Reed to replace the hamstrung Bayfield, who had originally been named for the first match, and Jason Leonard, Brian Moore and Peter Wright were the front row.

Whangarei, friendly and deeply unprepossessing, was similar to many small New Zealand towns in the dreadful barrage of advertising signs and hoardings cluttering many of the streets. The similarity to many places in small-town America was completed by drive-in burger bars and pizza huts nestling next to used-car lots. Another triumph for the town planners.

North Auckland, of course, is Going country. The offspring of Surly Sid Going, Ken and Brian are spread throughout rugby in the area. The three senior Goings used to pull off spectacular double- and treble-dummy scissors movements for North Auckland and when they were winging it together the TV commentator sounded like an auctioneer. Eight Goings – Charles, Adrian, Quinten, Troy, Clint, Dion, Karan and Des – play for Mid-Northern, one of the strongest club teams in the area. Jarad and Milton are coming through nicely while Vaughan is playing in Waikato and Darrell down in Dunedin.

When Sid toured in the British Isles he did more than anyone on the field to give the All Blacks their aura of power and more than anyone off the field to propagate the theory that they were all the biggest bunch of miseries in sport. By 1993 Sid, urbanity bravely peeking through the dark clouds, was North Auckland's selector-coach. Brian was also a selector and the only non-Going on the selection panel was Jim Miller. However, Miller is married to none other than Gloria Going, Sid's sister. It was not altogether surprising, therefore – and far be it from anyone to accuse the Goings of nepotism – that the Lions faced Troy on the wing, the veteran Charles in the centre and Adrian on the flank. Quinten was not selected. What the bloody hell are we going to do with Quinten? Got it. He can sing the anthem. Quinten sang 'God Defend New Zealand', solo, a cappella and very well.

Charles, meanwhile, was on his best behaviour. He was by now 36 and vastly experienced. Indeed, he had played for North Auckland against the 1977 Lions and marked some Jock called McGeechan. Yet Going, allegedly, had kicked a Taranaki player, Andy Slater, in a televised match and he had been cited. The citing procedure, unique to New Zealand's domestic rugby, was a plank of their clean-up campaign. Basically, any Thomas, Richard or Harriet from the terraces or even from the depths of an armchair could cite a player for dirty play – could complain to the NZRU or the players' union if they detected dirty play live or on TV and if the incident had not been seen and dealt with by the referee.

Perhaps the intentions were pure but it was a ludicrously costly and unwieldy practice. Pontypool might have had to install a new switchboard in a past era. The Lions matches were subject merely to the new IRB procedures whereby only members of a participating organisation – opposition team or union – can cite. And since both sides on the tour were determined to bite any bullet fired in their direction there was no way that anyone would be cited. There was no way, either, that any opposition player was ever going to retaliate

against Charles Going. Imagine three hundred Goings walking up
your garden path to remonstrate.

The other local hero and North Auckland's captain was Ian
Jones, the All Black lock from Kamo, near Whangarei. I first came
across Jones at the Sophia Gardens pitches in Cardiff, where the All
Blacks were training before their tour of Wales in 1988. He was
tallish, but no giant, and gangling almost to the point of being thin.
He was impossibly fresh-faced and boyish. I assumed, as he ran
around the training field, that the All Blacks, as they sometimes do,
had invited some junior players to run with them. I simply could not
believe from his outward appearance that he was an All Black lock.
These days he is a little heavier yet still boyish. He is also one of the
most experienced forwards in the squad. The Kamo Kid was an
electrician but in the emancipation-through-sport which rugby can
still bring about, he now works for New Zealand Breweries in their
sales force. He recently made a TV documentary in which he
proudly showed off Kamo's major landmark claim to fame: they
have New Zealand's most northerly set of traffic lights. Who needs
the Taj Mahal or the Hanging Gardens of Babylon?

As kick-off time approached, sky-divers descended with the
match ball. Then there was the premiere of 'Take us to the Top',
North Auckland's own and brand-new rugby song, produced by
those household names of rock, Dave Voyde and Brady Arkel.

> *We're North Auckland rugby watch us fly*
> *And we're going to take them on, we're gonna try*
> *When you put us to the test, you'll find out we're the best,*
> *We can fly like eagles, we can fly.*

Thanks boys, leave your phone numbers at the reception on the way
out.

There was an extra cheer for the Lions from a surprisingly large
group of beflagged British and Irish on the terraces. The group
attended every game. They included a few expat locals but
consisted chiefly of young people busking their way round the
country in pursuit of the tour. Some of them sold T-shirts and
sweatshirts embossed with 'Lions Tour 1993' slogans and itinerary
to pay for some of their expenses. Some people turned up their
noses at the noisy antics. I thought they were great and so did the
players. They never missed a match.

Barnes led the Lions on and the massive gathering cheered. It was
a charged moment, and even though the tour was later to falter I
never lost the sense of thrill as the team took the field. The captain
would always carry on the cuddly toy Lion mascot, a magnificent
beast. Barnes flourished it high above his head, placed it carefully
on the pitch for the duty boy to retrieve as per common practice. In
Whangarei, before the duty boy could retrieve the lion it was
attacked by the home mascot. Some idiot had dressed up as a
*taniwha*, a mythical Maori beast of the seas. The *taniwha* came across
and stamped on the lion. The Lions were furious, and Peter Wright

dashed across threateningly and told the bloke in the costume, if my lip-reading was up to scratch, to leave extremely quickly. There was the brief possibility of a British Lion being dismissed for attacking a *taniwha*, which record-books assure me would have been a first.

The first moments of a Lions tour are more anxious than those for any other touring team simply because of the styles which have to be welded together or weeded out. And the early stages were so weedy that the horrendous thought that they were going to lose the first game and every game after that briefly intruded. Certainly, the scrummage was a mess and continually lurched backwards on the tight-head side. The form improved; the scrummage never did until the closing stages of the tour.

North Auckland's game plan was to wind up the pace of the match to and beyond the point of frantic. Richard Le Bas, the scrum-half, simply tapped the ball and ran and asked questions later whenever the Lions were penalised. North Auckland, deservedly, scored first. Mark Seymour, the bustling home centre, went back to retrieve a loose pass, looked up and saw space and set off. Richard Le Bas joined the move and they sent Doug Te Puni, a typically squat and rampaging New Zealand hooker, on a thirty-five yard touchdown run.

They had scored again by half-time. Tony Clement, at full-back for the Lions, had begun shakily but had also been let down by Hunter. Clement originally decided to run a ball from under his posts, looked up for Hunter and found that Hunter, instead of doubling towards and behind him to form a triangle from the back three, was rooted way out on his wing and in front of him. Clement was scragged. Later, Clement looked for Hunter again and shaped to pass to him but, again, Hunter was too far away and in front. Clement checked his pass but dropped the ball and North Auckland's Glenn Taylor, the flanker, sent Seymour careering over at the posts.

Yet between these two home scores the Lions showed New Zealand a little something. Damian Cronin won some lifeblood line-out ball and Richard Webster and Ben Clarke gradually began to wrest some authority. As the Kamo Kid said after the match: 'Gee, that Clarke is a great player.' The platform was gradually established. Barnes set the line moving and Clement came up running his angles to make an initial breach. He was checked and looked around for support. Barnes suddenly shot on to his pass and blasted the same sort of hole in North Auckland as he had to Scotland at Twickenham. It was as if the match had been thrown into fast forward. Such was the pace of the burst that it seemed as if Barnes might have to hang around for support.

Then, suddenly, Jerry came gliding. Guscott came up on Barnes' shoulder, matching the staccato stride of his friend and fly-half with his own more economical panther stride. He took Barnes' pass. Warren Johnston, the home full-back, came across and began to set himself for the tackle. Microseconds later, after Guscott had swept past him with the most coruscating burst of pace, he was setting himself for the conversion.

Two minutes after that try, the Lions scored again. Robert Jones put up a clever box-kick and Rory Underwood chased it. Rory's policy is usually to allow the defender to catch the ball before hammering him but this time he went for it. He leaped high, snatched it from the cradled arms of Troy Going and ran on. Scott Hastings came up inside to score. Barnes kicked one conversion and the Lions led 15-12 at half-time.

By half-time, Ian Hunter's tour was already over. He moved in to tackle his opposite number, David Manoko, partly caught his man and then tried to grab him again as Manoko took off. The shoulder was at full stretch and dislocated. There was no sight worse on the tour than that of tour doctor James Robson and physio Kevin Murphy leading off a player who had obviously suffered a serious injury, waving frantically to the replacements' bench. Hunter was led off with shoulder hanging and no one needed the post-match press conference to confirm that he was homeward bound.

Gavin Hastings took the field, and amid the tumult of a flawed and fast match he soon began to give off waves of assurance, especially in his punched diagonal kicks. The Lions scored again early in the second half when Clarke and Robert Jones attacked the blind side of a scrum and Clement, now on the wing, came hammering into the cover defence's zone of pain and barged his way over. Hastings kicked a beautiful conversion and a penalty after fifty minutes made it 25-12.

The Lions lost their way a little after that. They were trying to adapt to their new fluid loose game, a game with not so many reference points of scrummage and set plays. They began to fumble a little. They also sat back. When Barnes was in charge the attacking edge of the cutlass glinted. Gavin Hastings preferred to steady the ship. Essentially, the captain was no speculator. It is arguable that Hastings calmed a fraught match but also arguable that one more blast of Barnes and Guscott at 25-12 and the Lions would have pulled clear into the roaring forties.

North Auckland simply went faster and faster and they scored the try they deserved through Troy Going at the end of a furious set of attacks. Rory Underwood scored the final try, seizing on a mistake in the home midfield as they tried to run the ball from deep defence.

The final impression was of a patchy victory in which the most striking individual performance was that of Webster, who was never downed before crossing the advantage line no matter how unpromising the circumstances. 'The important thing was to win. There were some nice bits of play,' said McGeechan. 'And don't forget that some of the players had not played for six weeks.' Fair enough. It was obvious, too, that the Lions were leaden-legged from their training. There was so little time, and certainly no way that they could taper off their heavy training before Whangarei. Frighteningly, there were now just two Saturday games remaining before the First Test in Christchurch. It was roughly half a good performance and there was also a rather comforting glimpse of attacking excellence from the team that was supposed to be obsessed with set pieces.

Sour Sid, speaking for Goings everywhere, had a whinge that the referee, Lindsay McLachlan, had not picked up the Lions backs for offside. Why should he, Sid? No referee in any game in either hemisphere referees the offside line. Why pick on poor old Lindsay?

That night in the early hours, TVNZ showed the final of the Super-10 tournament from Ellis Park. Auckland, a little unluckily, lost 17-20 to Transvaal. The tournament was colourful and controversial. It was definitely yet another twist in the ratchet which will, very soon, make it utterly impossible for leading players not to become professional. The ten teams – Auckland, Waikato, North Harbour, Otago, Queensland, New South Wales, Western Samoa, Western Province, Northern Transvaal and Transvaal – all put in weeks of preparation and had to spend weeks away in one of the other competing countries, often playing warm-up matches, too. The authorities cheerfully hoisted the two fingers to such piffling matters as bylaws, allowing tactical replacements and drinks breaks after quarter-time and three-quarter-time for TV advertising.

New Zealanders, meanwhile, clearly felt that the event was more to the benefit of other countries than their own. Still, it was colourful, high-profile and fascinating – and it showed that the South Africans were learning fast, or to be more precise, re-learning fast. 'There is no doubt that these guys have worked hard to try to catch up,' said Sean Fitzpatrick, who led Auckland in the final.

On the Sunday morning at the Lions' hotel, just before they bused down to Auckland to play North Harbour, Hunter sat in his tracksuit with his arm slung in a crêpe bandage and bravely discussed his overwhelming disappointment – months of training and anticipation wasted, dreams of glory dashed. 'I knew that something was seriously wrong when I felt my shoulder muscle was down near my bicep,' he said. 'The hardest thing will be watching the Tests at home on television. I desperately wanted to play in the Tests. But at least I am a Lion. To run out on to the field wearing a Lions jersey made the hairs on the back of my neck stand up. It was fantastic. I hope I am young enough to experience it all again.'

Next day, Hunter solemnly shook hands with every member of the party and flew out from Auckland for London and home. At his best, Hunter is an outstanding player: strapping, quick and courageous. With Ieuan Evans in such good form, he may not have fulfilled his wish to play in the Tests, but he would surely have been a major asset when the midweek team came under the pressure of its own limitations at the end of the tour. He had lost his way a little in the domestic season, and missed the South African Test because of an injury suffered in a soccer kickabout. That clearly did not impress Geoff Cooke as England manager. He was shunted back and forth from wing to full-back, easily his best position; he was at odds with Northampton in that, for various reasons, he hardly appeared for the club and indeed, attracted some vitriolic letters and phone calls from Saints followers as a result. He has a shot at England's full-back jersey now that Jon Webb has departed. Conceivably, after a full Lions tour he could have gone home as the racing certainty.

The poor man joined a melancholy club of Lions who failed to last their first match of the tour. The members are Wilf Sobey (1930), Niall Brophy (1959), Sam Hodgson (1962), Stuart Lane (1980) and Paul Dean (1989). At least they never suffered homesickness.

There was no mistaking the nationality of his replacement. That night the massed ranks of the Irish media contingent on tour – both of them – burst into the public rooms of the media hotel bearing hot news. Richard Wallace, the Garryowen wing with ten caps for Ireland, was on his way. Ned van Esbeck of the *Irish Times* and Barry Coughlan of the *Cork Examiner* were joyful. There is, after all, a limit to the number of times you can interview Mick Galwey and Nick Popplewell, engaging characters though they were. Wallace, a company director for a Limerick concern, was actually drinking Guinness when the news came through, in Rosie O'Grady's bar – in Moscow.

The Lions drove on down the country to Auckland and their base at the Poenamo Hotel on Auckland's North Harbour, travelling across the harbour bridge built by the Japanese and known as the Nippon Clip-on. The hotel was in Takapuna, just across the road from Onewa Domain, North Harbour's home ground, a small stadium of grassy banks. It could take only 12,000, so the game had been moved out of the North Shore altogether, across the bridge and to the south of the city to Mount Smart Stadium, a soulless concrete extravaganza which hosted Auckland's Commonwealth Games. The media party, swelling all the time, split off to Downtown Auckland and the Regent, a hotel of such luxury that after three days there you had to make a determined and bloody-minded burst for the main doors to stop some flunkey opening it for you as if you were visiting royalty.

'Look son, I can open the bloody door myself.'

'Very well sir, and can I clean your shoes and generally cringe around the place?'

North Harbour, who split from the Auckland mother ship in 1983 with the likes of Wayne Shelford and Frano Botica on board, had since established themselves in the top four of the New Zealand provinces even though their identity among supporters was not yet powerful. And indeed, such is the continuing hegemony of Auckland that there are theories that another chunk should split off to form another union. North Harbour had not played well in the Super-10 series. They lost to Waikato, lost heavily to Transvaal in Johannesburg and by one point to New South Wales at home. They recovered well and beat Northern Transvaal in Takapuna. They had three current Test backs in Ant Strachan, the scrum-half, and

the hard-hitting centres Frank Bunce and Walter Little; they had
the second-string All Black hooker, Graham Dowd, and also Kevin
Boroevich, the former All Black prop who had coached Richmond
in the English domestic season and whose playing style might best
be described as excitable. They also had the remarkable Eric Rush,
who has played top rugby as wing and flanker and who needed a
good game against the Lions to take him into the All Black team –
John Kirwan was not yet back from his Italian club interlude and
Rush was one of the favourites. At least, he was until he met at
Mount Smart Stadium a young Englishman called Tony Underwood.

The Lions management were as hopeful as Rush in another
department. 'Are you going to sit down with New Zealand referees,
or some other body with authority in the laws, to standardise
interpretations?' I asked Geoff Cooke.

'No,' he said. 'We don't foresee too much problem. We may be
able to speak to individual referees but I am sure there will be no
difficulties.' Ian McGeechan added: 'We have drummed it into the
players that they must react and adapt to conditions on the field.' It
was blindingly obvious that McGeechan and Cooke had decided
that they were not going to whine about referees in any specific
context, or even in a general context. There were several press
conferences when it was also blindingly obvious that the management were desperate to get to their feet and damn the whole
philosophy and practice of some of the refereeing that they met.
They bit their tongues.

It sounded fine but I had grave misgivings. I had the suspicion
that interpretations in New Zealand simply ignored some of the
laws. I felt very strongly that any major touring side must, as a first
stop after clearing customs, meet with some body with the authority
to speak for referees in the host country and go painstakingly
through every law which might be contentious and every one which
could be interpreted differently, and that the 'minutes' of the
meeting should be made known to every referee on the tour and all
other referees in the host country. That would be the first faltering
step towards uniformity for the host and touring teams and the first
step to some sort of universal framework.

Otherwise, you are in the utterly ridiculous situation where you
only really know which laws you are playing under – especially in
the line-out, tackle, rucks and mauls – after the match has started. I
felt that Cooke and McGeechan, unusually for them, were leaving
far too much to chance. Before the Second Test, just after Patrick
Robin of France had arrived to take charge, we asked Cooke
whether he had consulted M Robin to clarify the many cloudy areas.

'Not really,' said Cooke. 'I did have a quick word with him when
we met at a parliamentary reception.'

Until the IRB take urgent action to reverse the process under
which the law-book is becoming fragmented, perverted and pil-
laged for local self-interest, then managers and coaches must take

more formal action. The refereeing of the North Harbour match
was to be the perfect case in point.

On the day before the game the Lions took part in a throwback to
past tours when they were farmed out to local schools in an Adopt a
Lion scheme run by the hard-grafting North Harbour Union. On
the longer Lions tours the players would always be adopted
individually by schools around the country. The children would
collect any publicity and cuttings about their charges and at the end
of the tour present them with a scrapbook as a keepsake. Ian
McGeechan received a magnificent work after his tour as a player
with the 1977 Lions and John Taylor, on the 1993 tour as ITV's
commentator, recalled receiving a similar mega-work at the end of
his tour with the 1971 Lions.

In a sense, the 1993 team went through the motions. They had
drastically little free time at this early stage of the tour and so had
only half an hour to spend with their schools before returning on
time to worship the training gods. The programme was enticing:
Stuart Barnes and Martin Bayfield went to Kristin School, where
their programme included a poetry reading. There was a good deal
of haw-hawing when McGeechan and Jerry Guscott departed for
what the programme called 'skills with fifth form girls'.

Wade Dooley and Kenny Milne, panicking, went to Birkenhead
College, where they were to address an assembly and then take
questions. The headmaster met them at the door, gushed drip-
pingly about not taking charge, allowing the kids to express
themselves, etc. So poor Dooley and Milne stood cold in front of a
massive gathering of kids with hardly an intro, let alone a few warm-
up jokes from their hosts. The Lions did well. 'I'd rather play
against the All Blacks than stand here,' said Dooley. But soon he was
off, talking about his life and rugby career, his view on the All
Blacks. The questions were sharp. 'Do you sometimes get intimi-
dated by players in the opposition?' asked one bright spark.

'No,' said Big Wade, 'and I'll see you outside afterwards.'

Why did the All Blacks always win? Was it fair that the Lions were
four countries playing against one? Why did the press in Britain
dismiss the Lions as old men past their sell-by date? 'Ask him,' said
Dooley, pointing to me cowering in the corner.

Milne gave an insight into the time he spends on his rugby. 'I used
to have a job in a bakery which I really enjoyed,' he said. 'But rugby
now takes up so much time. I had to change jobs to become a
representative.' Unfortunately, Wade never did get the chance to
return for his scrapbook.

It was a worthwhile half-hour and when the Lions returned to
camp they had all enjoyed themselves. But perhaps the shrinking
world had removed a little of the magic. In past tours, when the
team arrived they were driven round the host towns in motorcades;
they were farmed out to schools where they were worshipped. The
Lions as a concept is still massively powerful in New Zealand but so
are the arms of television and communications. Still, the Lions were
besieged by youngsters wherever they went. But there is no longer

quite the feeling in New Zealand that beings from another planet are moving among them. They are so familiar. It is a little like the end of a child's belief in Father Christmas.

For the North Harbour match the Lions chose the fifteen players who did not start the North Auckland match. It meant that Gavin Hastings would start, that Ieuan Evans and Tony Underwood were on the wings, Will Carling and Scott Gibbs paired in the centre and Rob Andrew and Dewi Morris at half-back. Paul Burnell was under the spotlight at tight head, given the lack of scrummaging authority at Whangarei, and Ken Milne and Nick Popplewell were also in the front row. Wade Dooley was alongside Martin Bayfield and the three men on whom so many hopes rested, Peter Winterbottom, Dean Richards and Mike Teague, were an old firm in the back row. It was vital that we received early evidence that the older Englishmen still had something purring under the bonnet.

The final preparations took place in private at the Devonport naval base. There was usually at least one private session per week, so that, as Cooke and McGeechan said, no cameras would take back to the home camps details of the Lions' plans. It did seem to approach the outer reaches of paranoia; although to be fair, there was a camerawoman at a session in Takapuna who could easily have been Laurie Mains in a blonde wig and mini-dress.

North Harbour was the day when the tour took off. The Lions won 22-13, playing gratifyingly well in many departments and in some areas, superbly well. Controversy reared its ugly face when a major brawl erupted round Dean Richards and the refereeing of Alan Riley of Waikato was appalling in that he became completely obsessed with the Lions and took charge of only one team. He ripped into the Lions and incensed them, on and off the field. Towards the end, the Lions rose above him and the opposition in a big finish. As Tony Roche of *Today* pointed out near the end, 'The ref's run out of ideas.' Significantly, none of the four All Black contenders in the backs, Strachan, Little, Bunce and Rush, had any influence.

Rush will never forget the day. Tony Underwood, playing a brilliant match, left him standing three times, once on the way to scoring. Whenever Rush tried to run, Underwood hunted him ruthlessly. He once chased him and buried him as Rush tried to break clear across the face of his own posts. Underwood produced a variety of different tackles and generally looked indecently sharp. Rush was quietly crossed off the list of wing contenders for the Test series. To be fair to Rush, he was only just back in the game after injury, but with Timo Tagaloa, the ferocious Western Samoan wing, on the North Harbour bench it was difficult to see why Rush had not waited longer for full fitness.

The Lions were patchy, yet when they put it together they were lightning quick. They scored early on when a lovely kick by Andrew set up the position. Morris and Andrew then set up Tony Underwood, arriving hot-foot from the blindside wing. Gavin Hastings took the move on and when the ball went loose, it bounced off Will Carling and Andrew came nipping round the outside to score. Andrew kicked a long conversion.

Tony Underwood stepped on his own personal accelerator shortly after a penalty from Ian Calder, the North Harbour full-back, had made the score 7-3. Carling, standing in at dummy-half after a move which had caught Morris up among the big men, set the line moving. Andrew found Gibbs, who was launched already into a delightfully sharp match, full of lightning half-breaks and crunching tackling. Hastings then came up and sent Tony Underwood screaming outside the desperate Rush. Underwood chipped the ball past Calder, and although Calder shoulder-charged him off his stride he recovered the balance and dived on the ball in the in-goal area. The Lions set up another outstanding attack just before half-time when Gibbs shipped on an unpromising pass with real sleight of hand and North Harbour infringed. Gavin Hastings kicked the goal and it was 15-3.

In the second half, Frank Bunce was caught on the floor as a frantic ruck developed in centre field near the North Harbour 22. Dean Richards came in raking in the approximate region of the ball but also of Bunce's head. He caught Bunce, although a remote camera suggested strongly that Richards did not deliberately lunge with his boot at the centre's head. The ensuing brawl heavily involved Dowd, the home hooker, who rushed in with petrol for the flames, and Mayhew, the home lock. Both Richards and Popplewell were punched and it took some time for order to be restored as sub-plots came to the fore, fanning the dying flames of the main action. Richards was led from the field dazed and with a swollen jaw, and Richard Webster arrived near the hour. Bunce departed for twenty stitches, returning to the match wearing a turban.

What was the referee doing all this time? He was penalising the Lions. The final count was 20-6. He thrashed the Lions line-out with an endless stream of penalties – nine with none against North Harbour in one sorry period. And if anyone is suggesting that in the jungle warfare of the line-out one team is transgressing all the time and the other not at all then he should be carted off to the funny farm by the first available tractor. Referee Riley also allowed Walter Little to take out Dewi Morris when Morris was still in the air after his clearance kick, an offence which could easily have drawn a sending-off in the Northern Hemisphere.

Not surprisingly, North Harbour came back strongly. Apollo Perelini scored after concerted and well-sustained Harbour attacks. But the Lions reasserted themselves. After Winterbottom and Webster had set off with a misplaced clearance kick, Ieuan Evans scored down the right, giving notice of the clinical brilliance with which he was to finish all tour, and then Webster, the replacement, thundered over for another try. He picked up the ball ten yards out with half the North Harbour team in his way; Webster is a hard man, a square bull. He set off, scattering defenders. Dooley piled in behind and together they battered their way over. Hastings kicked both conversions and, with the smell of gunpowder still in the air, the teams trooped off.

The stamping incident was played down. What was the reaction to the punch-up of Brad Meurant, the North Harbour coach? Brad was not exactly beside himself with righteous indignation. 'Both teams did the right thing by going in to help their mates,' he said, unfathomably. 'I was on the wrong side. It was just one of those things that happen,' said Bunce himself. It was, in one sense, a big attitude to take. On the other hand, it was a dangerous attitude – as is the attitude of all those who allow kicking to proceed in New Zealand – and so, if he really was as careless with the boot as eye-witnesses suggested, was the action of Richards.

None of this was unexpected. New Zealand believe, as does Ian McGeechan, that players hanging round the ball are fair game, that they should be raked out. Some referees go on the difference between standing upfield from a player and raking backwards, so that you can see the studs from behind, and stamping downwards from above. There is nothing official whatsoever in the law-book to allow it, of course. And in any case, the dividing lines are so fine. In the Lions tour, we saw players raked when they were lying near the ball, we saw them raked when they were nowhere near the ball and we saw them indiscriminately kicked and stamped on when the ball was miles away – and all under the protective umbrella of the original philosophy and *carte blanche* from the referees: they were seen to be holding up the game, not being positive, if they whistled up for stamping or dangerous use of the boot.

Lions were kicked in almost every match. When Brian Moore came in, feet upraised, to a ruck under Auckland's posts in the provincial match at Eden Park, no one even mentioned a possible penalty. Moore and the Lions had simply worked out what was allowed. Cooke gave a few 'when in Rome' speeches. The ref gave a loud blast on the whistle all right, as Moore came jumping in – but only to award the Lions a penalty try.

I acknowledge that, especially in the Northern Hemisphere, players linger on the ball. But don't tell me that New Zealand's philosophy of allowing kicking is some sort of exact science, some sort of limited response. The only beneficiaries are those who manufacture materials for stitches and, one day, the bank balance of a brain surgeon. People say that serious injuries after raking are very rare. Big deal. Vigilantes mean anarchy.

While we were in New Zealand, the rugby-loving satellite station showed the French tour of South Africa. We saw the match against Western Province in which Jeff Tordo, the French captain, had his face rearranged by the boot of Gary Pagel, the Western Province prop. 'I have never seen anything like it in my life,' said Ian Borthwick, the New Zealand-born Paris-based writer who was on the tour as the interpreter and press relations man, a long overdue appointment by the French Federation. 'The stud had lacerated Jeff's cheek, hooked in his nostril and split open the nose.'

All Tordo had done was to tackle a Western Province player in open play and he was struck before he had a chance to roll clear. He got to his feet, pouring blood already. He was on his way out of the tour. As he staggered off, he lifted his hands above his head and with bitter irony, applauded in the direction of the home forwards. There was a leading plastic surgeon available so with any luck, the grotesque scar across his face will fade a little as time goes by.

Pagel took the affair to a court of law because of what he saw as the severity of the sentence. (Nine months suspension, reduced to six after, sadly, he won his case.) The French, and hopefully rugby followers everywhere, were sickened. Tordo even had to endure a grotesque charade in which Pagel's lawyers produced a video which did not show the incident clearly. 'They asked him to point out on the screen the exact moment when Pagel kicked him,' said Ian Borthwick. 'Jeff was completely furious. He wondered aloud who was supposed to be on trial.' But fear not, Jeff. According to certain philosophies of the game, the blow which sliced your face was a blow for continuity, was merely a 'reminder', an affirmation that if you are lying helpless on the floor then you are fair game, can be kicked like a dog. It was a 'positive' boot. I'll spread the news to loving mothers all over the rugby world.

Richard Turner, the North Harbour captain, was easier on the ear after the match. Like the captains and coaches of almost every team the Lions met, he was constructive and gracious. 'You all said that the Lions were too old and too slow,' he said to the assembled press. 'Don't try to tell me that again.'

Would McGeechan break his vow of silence over refereeing? 'Are you concerned at the number of penalties you concede and the standard of refereeing?' he was asked. 'No,' barked Geech, too loud, too early and with counter-productive vehemence. The captain was slightly less reticent. 'It is difficult to keep going when every time you attack you are penalised,' he said.

The Lions left Auckland wiser in the ways of their hosts and also having gained new respect. They had not yet put together a complete performance or anything like it, but they had shown steel and they had shown, in the persons of almost every back who had pulled on their jersey, real pace and skill.

There was only one immediate fear. The next match was in Wellington against the Maoris, and on the Thursday after the North Harbour match those of us uninfected by the spirit of Amy Johnson strapped ourselves into our seats for the flight to Wellington, the windiest city in the world with the hairiest airport. The plane duly dived this way and that, and for a period of around thirty seconds dipped and banked and thrashed like a live beast in mortal agony, and soon we were in Wellington, the national capital.

At least three things were at stake at Athletic Park, the Test ground where the Lions were to meet the Maoris. There was the early progress of the tour as it warmed up, there was the whole future of Maori rugby and there was the future of Athletic Park itself. As the Lions hammered away in training, still in endless drills for perfecting their play in and through the rucks and mauls, they were still giving no clues. They had decided, as far as injury allowed, to play two completely different teams in the next two matches, against the Maoris and Canterbury. For the Maoris, they paired Will Carling and Scott Hastings in a punishing midfield, with Rory Underwood and Ieuan Evans on the wing (and both needing a top match to equal Tony Underwood's breathtaking hammering of North Harbour). Gavin Hastings was at full-back, Stuart Barnes linked with Dewi Morris at half-back. Brian Moore was chosen between Nick Popplewell and Peter Wright. Moore's body language was not yet at its most defiantly eloquent. Strictly speaking, he is not anywhere near big enough for the severe new world of giant scrummaging hookers. He gets by on footballing ability, cunning and the indomitable will not to let any giant get the better of him. He was not yet at his angry best on the tour. Damian Cronin, after a promising if not sustained effort against North Auckland, was paired alongside Wade Dooley and Ben Clarke, steaming along in training, was at number 8 with Mike Teague and Peter Winterbottom on the flank.

It was a big match for Barnes. He had impressed everyone, McGeechan included, by the sharpness and the analytical brain he had brought to the tour. In training, it was his facility for making last-minute decisions which marked him out – often, his scrum-halves had to twist around to find him after they set themselves for a pass to the other side.

The Maoris' build-up had been fractured. Unlike the other provincial opposition, they were essentially a scratch team. They had last played against a major touring team in 1981, when they met the Springboks, and they had not met the Lions since 1977. They chose a massive back row with Jamie Joseph and Zinzan Brooke on the flanks and Arran Pene, who was to impress the Lions as a player and a man. Boroevich of North Harbour turned up again, Rush popped up for another encounter with the Underwood family – he was to mark Rory this time, and was to fare little better than he had against the rampaging Tony. After the match, Rush could be heard inquiring as a matter of urgency whether there were any more Underwood brothers. And did Mrs Anne Underwood play at all?

The Maoris were playing for their future as a team, as an entity. There was, according to New Zealanders, a revival of sorts in Maori culture. Certainly, the revival reflected itself in affectation among the *pakehas*. It became *de rigueur* among TV personalities and presenters to litter every place name with the thickest Maori pronunciation that endless practice could make possible. Humble old Whakatane became, to the *pakeha* weather forecaster, Fokkertarney. There has also been, apparently, a turning-point in Maoris' self-regard. A few years ago, a book by a Maori writer was published which castigated what the author saw as Maori under-achievement and laziness and the jealous malevolence of Maori elders in propagating the old lackadaisical ways.

There has always been controversy about Maori rugby – chiefly because, the critics said, qualification was so *ad hoc*, and players became available with only tenuous qualifications. Certainly, and if you go by appearance, Mark Cooksley of the Maori second row looked about as much of a Maori as Michael Heseltine. Some of the players opted for the Maori squad with only distant ancestry. There is a new pressure too, a ferociously ironic development. The new constitution of the South African Rugby Football Union states that neither home nor opposition teams can be selected on a racial basis. Therefore no Maori team can tour South Africa and no Springbok tour can ever accept an itinerary which includes the Maoris.

Yet the contribution of Maori rugby players to New Zealand is staggering. As the Maoris trained and prepared themselves there was no mistaking the pride that they took in their team. And, as it transpired, there was no limit to the admiration the Lions camp felt for their opponents.

The day before the match I enacted the Athletic Park ritual. The forecast was for wind and rain and, foolish me, I had not yet grasped that the forecast was always wrong. The press party had been given free rainwear by our travel operators, Gullivers Travel, who were also handling the Lions and the biggest of the supporters' groups. The raincoat was of wonderful quality – and terminally unwearable. It was coloured red, white and blue in sweeping garish slashes with unfetching olive green detail. I never saw a single pressman wear his coat. One swapped his for a book, another for a vodka and tonic. 'A large one, mind,' he said. But the prospect of Athletic Park was such that I even laid out my clown raincoat.

The stadium itself, dull and piecemeal, stands at the neck of a long valley rising up from the city itself and any game there is usually ruined, or at least turned into a lottery, by the driving wind and torrential rain. I have long felt that the whole place should be damned to hell, left derelict as a bad idea. Others feel the same, because there is now increasing pressure for rugby to retreat into the city itself and for the Basin Reserve, the neat Test cricket ground, to be developed to take other sports and to rehouse Wellington and New Zealand rugby.

The day dawned – sunny, still and almost warm. No tempest. Athletic Park was calm. No coats needed. It was still not much of a rugby ground, however. Perhaps the most famous landmark on the ground is the Millard Stand, the uncovered cliff face which rises steeply opposite the main stand. It is the most exposed, vertiginous sporting vantage-point I have ever seen. Before the kick-off, we decided to check it out. In company with Eddie Butler, the *Observer's* man and former pride of Pontypool, I attempted an ascent of the Millard, without sherpa. I made it about three-quarters of the way to the back row before I gave up with a combination of vertigo and exhaustion. Butler ploughed on courageously and actually reached the summit.

The people at ground level were dots. The stand is so steep that when you sit in your seat you are watching the match between your feet. The gangways are narrow. From the edge seats, you look straight down the valley from where the tempests usually sweep. I simply cannot believe that no one has ever died of exposure up there. The whole edifice would have been condemned in about five seconds in Britain and it brought home just how much more safe and salubrious British sports stadia have become under the Safety at Sports Grounds Act. It will be unbearable if New Zealand has to have an Ibrox or a Bradford or a Hillsborough before they have their own safety act.

Poor old John Taylor of ITV was in the worst place. His commentary box was perched up at the top of the stand, bound by scaffolding over the back edge. 'I've just been talking to someone about the corrosion in the stand,' said J.T. miserably as he munched his midday pie before mounting the scaffold.

There was a splendid massed Maori display of singing and *hakas* by a school group before the teams took the field; there was also a dreadful Maori group which, instead of singing their own tradition-al songs, delivered a cappella irrelevant old rock 'n' roll semi-classics with broad, cloying Yankee accents and then torpedoed the New Zealand anthem by leading it with the same preposterous American intonation. 'Garrrd defend New Zealand.' Gods knows, the anthem is dire enough in tune and lyric. It almost makes 'Advance Australia Fair' sound like a decent song, although it lacks quite the same nonsensicality of lyric as the Australian dirge.

The match was something else. It was brilliant, a majestic spectacle. The Lions won 24-20, and if ever a result told nothing of the match then this was it. They trailed by 20-0 at one stage, could easily have slipped 27-0 down before half-time and were still under heavy Maori pressure in the second half. Some of the crowd – and the press – thought it was all over. It was the most stark illustration of the truth of the tour to date: the Lions of their pre-tour image, strong-armed and slow, did not exist. The Lions were electric and quick, but their arms were weak.

The Maoris began at rare pace, Pene steaming at the Lions, Cooksley winning a stream of line-out possession against Dooley. Stu Forster and Steve Hirini, the little Maori half-backs, played superbly, darting and diving and stoking the driving forwards. Rhys Ellison was a double handful in the centre. For a long time, certainly for the first half, it seemed that only the coolness and resourcefulness of Gavin Hastings at the back was saving the Lions from complete disintegration.

For much of the match, the Lions' tactics were appalling. Yet again, the scrum was rocking and rolling. Wright and Cronin were, apparently, completely sapped by the effort of trying to hold on. Both laboured around the field yards behind the action. It was an alarming sight. 'One or two of the Lions seemed short of a gallop,' said Charles Ferris, the Maori coach, afterwards. Yet from that weak platform the Lions' doomed back row tried peeling moves.

The scoring procession began after eight minutes. Forster chipped to the blind side and Allan Prince, the Maori left-wing, was allowed to escape with a crude leg-raised lunge as Hastings tried to field the ball. Prince regained possession, shrugged off Ieuan Evans and ran on to score. Hirini converted. A poor pass in the tackle by Scott Hastings gave the Maoris another priceless loose ball. George Konia, the centre, hacked it on, chased by Barnes. Konia rewon it and Forster sent it high to Hirini, who scored. Hirini had already kicked a goal when the Lions were offside in trying to stop a Maori attack. He kicked the conversion, added another penalty and it was 20-0. The Lions were playing into a fierce, low sun which certainly disorientated them. But 20-0? No sun is that strong. Even Carling in the centre was unhappy.

Just before the kick which made it 20-0, the Lions' desperate situation almost became terminal. After another glorious set of sustained attacks, Prince was launched for the line with only Clarke to beat. Somehow, Clarke got to Prince and hauled him down. It was a marvellous effort. It certainly saved the match.

There was no substantive change in the course of the match even after half-time. It was still 20-3 into the final quarter, and the Lions had only one Gavin Hastings penalty on the scoreboard. Butler and I looked at each other. The schedule of production of Sunday newspapers is such that feature articles have to be filed before the Saturday match. They can be updated a little later. We had both filed bullish features on the tour to date. 'Lions catch fire, about to storm through the tour', was Butler's theme. 'Guscott and Barnes can beat New Zealand', was mine. Yet the Lions were playing disastrously; Barnes was invisible. 'Might need a little bit of revision here and there,' said Butler, between gritted teeth, of his apparently doomed feature.

By this time, Jason Leonard was on the field for Popplewell. Suddenly, with Leonard's reassuring bulk in the middle of the line-out, the Lions began to win some more ball. Significantly, Leonard made three or four tackles. After sixty-three minutes, the Lions won a line-out and Scott Hastings set it up in midfield. Barnes and Gavin Hastings attacked the blind side and gave Ieuan Evans the ball with still no real space. Ieuan soon changed all that. He came slanting inwards on to the pass from Hastings, went between two defenders, left Sam Doyle, the Maori full-back, clutching great clumps of thin air, and scored. It was a brilliant, Gerald Davies-type, Ieuan Evans-type finish.

One minute later, Ieuan brought out the old magic box again. He caught a dangerous chip ahead from Doyle at full stretch and set off flat across the field from his wing, with onrushing defenders threatening to bury him yards behind his own advantage line. Evans outflanked the hunters, straightened and found Will Carling and Scott Hastings alongside. Hastings delivered a delicious pass in an instant in the tackle and suddenly Rory Underwood had a run. He blasted outside Prince, ran fifty metres in all and scored at the posts. Gavin Hastings converted both these tries. It was, suddenly, 20-17.

With eight minutes left, and with the crowd and Sunday journalists with a feature to save in a fever, Gavin and the Lions came again. Cronin won a line-out, Scott Hastings and Winterbottom set the ball up in midfield and Barnes, now smoothly oiled, attacked the blind side. He handed on to Gavin Hastings and gesticulated furiously for Hastings to feed the men outside him. Hastings, instead, came in off his left foot and thundered for the line. He hammered through two or three defenders, made a nonsense of Doyle's last-yard tackle and scored. Amazingly, the Lions led.

The Maoris stepped up the pace for one last series of assaults. They spun the ball wide through rucks and mauls. But by now, the Lions were waiting. There was some tremendous tackling from Winterbottom and Clarke especially, and also from Barnes and Teague and both Hastings. The Lions held on. 'When the whistle went,' I recorded in *The Sunday Times* next day, 'friend and foe in the stands blew out their cheeks, turned to each other and acclaimed a wonderful game.'

Eddie Butler turned to me. 'Always knew my feature was rock solid,' he said, white-faced. 'Me too,' I replied, knees knocking.

There was some glorious rugby to savour in the post-match evening. There was also so much to chew over. The Lions backs, especially through the brilliance of Ieuan Evans, had posted a warning for all New Zealand teams. So far, we had seen only brilliance from the Lions backs and only head-down crash-ball runs from home backs, a ruck or maul waiting to happen. But we had also seen worrying fallibility in the Lions scrum and line-out, which could by no means be shored up by the burgeoning power of Ben Clarke and the Lions back-row men. We had seen a team which could play brilliantly, but not, at least not yet, for the whole match or even for two-thirds of it.

After the match, the impressive Pene began his summary. 'They fully deserved their win,' he said graciously. 'They are very strong in the set phases.' That astonishing final comment suggested one of three things: either a) Pene was taking the piss, or b) he was being unbelievably gallant to his opponents, or c) he was beginning a propaganda war to try to make the Lions believe their tight-forward platform was a rock.

The Lions glossed over the problems and the obvious discomfort of Wright on the tight head. 'I thought we came back extremely well,' said McGeechan. 'It is nice when you learn some lessons and still win. I am pleased with the character the team showed.'

That was all very well, but to me, the comeback was founded not on the match being wrested from the Maoris by an improving pack, but on the individual brilliance of the backs eventually thrashing the forwards into some sort of life. Until Ieuan made his dazzling dashes, hardly anything had changed, and the Maoris had still dominated.

It was also the day when it became blindingly obvious that Jason Leonard had to play in the Tests. His line-out work and tackling were of a high order; so was his scrummaging. It either meant that they had to go in without the splendid Popplewell on the loose head, or, preferably, that they had to convert Leonard to the tight head without delay. They delayed. It was to be another two weeks before they began the conversion.

They asked Hastings for his views on Maori rugby. He was emphatic: 'They should keep it for years to come.' Cooke held a Sunday school press conference in the Lions hotel next day. When he, McGeechan and Gavin Hastings sat down together for full-scale press conferences during the tour, they always tended to give answers so studiously bland that they could not be used against them, could not come back to haunt them, could give no clues whatsoever to the opposition; and therefore, were hardly worth uttering. McGeechan especially was far less forthcoming and, to the naked eye, far less relaxed than he had been in Australia in 1989 – no doubt it was the added pressure. It was also my impression that they did not exactly harbour overwhelming respect for the noble calling and personnel of Her Majesty's Press.

However, whenever Cooke could be weeded out of the management pack he was far better value. As he mulled over the Maoris game he could keep silent no longer about the nonsensical myth that, while British Isles players were flopping all over the ball, the noble Kiwi was on his feet, being positive, letting the ball flow by sticking to the laws. On the evidence of the tour so far that was garbage. 'We have been surprised by the number of people off their feet on the deck,' Cooke said with understatement. 'We are working like hell to keep the boys on their feet as the law requires while they have bodies flying all over the place. New Zealanders are scathing to the point of arrogance about our game, then this happens.'

It was soon to become obvious that New Zealand referees gave not a fig for the law requiring players to stay on their feet after tackles. Col Hawke, one of the leading home referees, took charge of the final All Black trial at Pukekohe a few days after the Maori game. The players dived on the ball to secure it, dived on each other to set up a wall, even scraped it back with their hands. As Cooke was to say later, 'Hawke told us that he would allow things to go provided the players were positive, were going to the ground with the intent to keep the move going. It is hard to argue with the philosophy, but the law is very specific: the third man in after a tackle must be on his feet when he plays the ball. They are just ignoring it. There are procedures for altering laws.'

What Cooke called 'New Zealand's obsession with continuity' was, we discovered as the tour progressed, to speed up the game considerably and to lead to fewer stoppages. Laurie Mains, New Zealand referees and New Zealand technocrats also felt it led to a better game. I felt it led to a corruption of the game, a cheapening of the game and, in some cases, to a perversion of the game. Still, the Lions were four for four, running at pace towards the First Test.

There was a lap of the South Island to come, with the First Test a fortnight away. 'It'll be bloody freezing down there,' said hordes of

Wellington weather experts. Needless to say, it wasn't. The soup of the day, however, was always pumpkin, whichever Island you were on.

Paul Theroux was bored with Christchurch in no time. Roughly the same amount of time, in fact, that it took me to become bored with his *Happy Isles of Oceania*. To be fair, I have rarely found a hankering to settle in the place, but there is something clean and spacious, open and almost glamorous about it. It had also, like most major New Zealand towns, apparently doubled its size in terms of commerce and cultural distractions inside ten years.

Sadly, there was no Lions match against the West Coast this time, and therefore no match in the frontier towns of Greymouth or Westport – and therefore, no drive across Arthur's Pass, the breathtaking route across the Southern Alps, the backbone of the South Island, from east coast to west. But no time for fripperies. The Lions, installed in the Park Royal, New Zealand's best, announced their team to play Canterbury. By all accounts, the home team were diminished from the old fierce days but had reincarnated themselves as a fast-moving outfit which would try to outpace the Lions from a weak forward base – or, to the cynical among us, had joined the Kiwi bandwagon which is driving headlong towards basketball, emasculating the forwards of their traditional power and strengths.

The Lions again made fifteen changes from the last match – at least, that was the plan. The granite Webster was unable to play because of strained tendons in his ankle. What to do? Peter Winterbottom had played a harsh and taxing match against the Maoris and the great man was of the age when twice a week was pushing it. Easy. The Lions by this time had formed such a high opinion of Ben Clarke that they drafted him to play on the openside flank, completely out of position but by no means beyond his capabilities.

Dean Richards, the reassuring rock of Leicester, was made captain and Mick Galwey completed the back row. Martin Bayfield and Andy Reed were teamed at lock, with Paul Burnell, Ken Milne and Jason Leonard in the front row. Robert Jones and Rob Andrew were paired at half-back for the first time on tour, with none of the four half-backs having as yet pulled clear of the field. Richard Wallace, the dark-haired Irishman, freshly arrived and kitted out and assimilated (and later to be fined by the players' court, Judge Popplewell presiding, for arriving late on tour), was on the wing. He was returning to the ground where, a year before, he had had his jaw broken by a punch from Andy Earl, the Canterbury flanker. He found the Canterbury team Earl-less this time.

Tony Underwood was on the other wing and Tony Clement was at full-back. In the centre were Jeremy Guscott and Scott Gibbs, two men of similar outlook who had been friends since well before the tour. Guscott certainly rated Gibbs highly. By the end of the match, Canterbury rated Guscott highly, too.

The match programme contained echoes of the bad old days when Canterbury's players had no right to be on a sporting field. They played a savage match against the 1971 British Lions which is probably the most publicised outbreak of on-pitch hostilities in sporting history. Sandy Carmichael, the Lions prop, was repeatedly punched when helplessly locked into a scrum. Other Lions were punched and kicked. Carmichael, invalided home with fractured bones in his face, left the dressing-room with both eyes blackened.

The programme for the 1993 clash contained what was comfortably the most fatuous article I have ever read in a rugby programme, and by God, that takes in a few. It was one of the most transparent and nonsensical attempts to rewrite history since the official historian of Iraq was handed a biro by Saddam Hussein and told to take dictation. According to the unnamed author of the piece (presumably, it was someone called Ray Cairns, who was listed as the programme editor), the 1971 Lions were completely at fault for repeatedly diving on to the upraised fists and boots of Canterbury players. Quoting Ian Penrose, the Canterbury captain in the match, the article maintained that it was the Lions management who had drummed up the fuss.

Penrose blithely stated his understanding that the dramatic dressing-room photographs of Carmichael's blackened face and damaged eyes were taken at a later point on tour, 'in a studio with lights full on his face'. Clearly, Carmichael should have been sent home for faking just before he was sent home for having fractured facial bones. Presumably, the doctor faked the x-rays, too.

Lancaster Park is an odd place. As usual on the tour, the crowd for the match was large, but dull, stolid and quiet. The noisiest fans in the ground, as usual, were in the thicket of Union Jacks in the middle of the popular side terrace. As usual, the surface looked magnificent, suitable for Stephen Hendry to ply his trade. It was only when the teams came on, and each boot sent up a flurry of spray, that we realised it was waterlogged, with bogs lurking just beneath the emerald greenery. The cricket square in the middle was ankle-deep. The ministrations of the heavy roller had sealed off the square over the years and the water drained slowly. The ball, streaming water, was almost uncatchable during the match; the pitch hardly provided a foothold. Guscott, however, was to skate over it like Christopher Dean.

The Lions won 28-10 and the display had everything in common with the other three matches to date. In general, it was encouraging. Again, they were glimpses of true class and pace. In this match there were even glimpses of scrummaging power, albeit against the weakest front five the Lions were to meet all tour. But again there was an unsatisfactory lack of sustained excellence in a match which, because of the paddy field beneath, was not a classic experience.

Canterbury began above the speed limit, thrashing away through rucks and mauls, fourth and fifth phases. The early attacks revealed some leaden feet in the Lions back row because both Robin Penney, the home number 8 and captain, and Graeme Bachop made breaks past Dean Richards and Mick Galwey respectively. In the first eighteen minutes, Canterbury made four clear scoring opportunities. And Guscott saved every one. He brought off a superb tackle on Paula Bale (Paul Bale's sister?), three other crucial tackles in a variety of styles and he kept the Lions afloat. The Lions also escaped when Penney was penalised for scrabbling over the line for the touchdown. Jim Taylor, the referee, probably did the Lions a favour, because it seemed that Penney was not being held in a tackle and therefore had the perfect right to run, crawl or tunnel his way to the line.

After all the Canterbury pressure came a lightning Lion riposte. Clarke set off with a loose ball into the heart of the Canterbury defence and it was obvious from the despairing ankle-taps with which they tried to bring him down that he was moving disconcertingly fast. He went storming up to Anthony Lawry, the home full-back, delivered the most perfectly timed pass to his right and there, gliding easily between defensive duties and those of the offence, came Guscott to score.

It was still fitful. Robert Jones found the ball so slippery that he had to give a little flick of the wrists before passing it on to shake off some of the water. Rob Andrew, not surprisingly, made more mistakes than he would normally reckon to make in a month, although he did kick the Lions 8-0 in front with a penalty after twenty-four minutes.

Canterbury had pulled back to 7-8 by half-time, albeit in ironic fashion. They deserved a try, but the one they scored came courtesy of a glaring mistake by the referee. Robert Jones kicked clear from deep inside his 22 but the ball struck Mark McAtamney, the Canterbury lock. It rebounded to Greg Smith, lurking upfield yards and yards offside, and Smith was allowed to proceed and score.

The Lions could never cut loose, even though Canterbury's handling errors reached epidemic proportions. Tony Underwood found more problems with the competitive Bale than he had with Eric Rush. He was almost clear twice but was just caught by Canterbury fingertips. But the match was changing in texture: the Lions scrummage was coming on stronger and stronger. After Tony Underwood had set up a position with a chase and tackle, the Lions simply drove straight through the Canterbury scrum. Andrew obliged with a drop goal.

The Lions secured victory with another series of massive scrum drives, helped by the fact that Greg Halford, the home loose head, was clearly discomforted by injury. Dean Richards missed a golden chance of a try when he knocked on as the Lions scrum rumbled over the Canterbury line and the only possible outcomes were a try or a penalty try. However, Galwey scored soon afterwards to make it 16-7 on the hour. Halford made a rueful departure.

Guscott, still gliding along with tackling and touches here and there, made a try for Tony Underwood soon afterwards, diving and flipping a loose ball towards the wing. Underwood picked up brilliantly on the run and scored, and Andrew kicked the goal. There was a penalty to come from Greg Coffey for Canterbury but Andrew had the last word, seizing on a sneak drop-out by Canterbury and sprinting over.

Then came Guscott's chance of a glorious finish. Barnes came on for Andrew in the last two minutes and almost immediately surged through on an imperious break. Guscott came steaming up outside with only desperate elements of the rearguard anywhere near. Barnes timed his pass superbly, and Guscott . . . knocked on.

Vance Stewart, the old Canterbury lock now coaching the team, summed up his team's fast, furious and deeply flawed performance: 'I would sum up our approach as one of misdirected enthusiasm.' He praised the Lions' defence and he rated their chances of winning the Test series as 'excellent'.

The Lions management were always loth, as they repeatedly droned, to single out individuals, or to give the press the nuggety, quotable nannies (nanny goats, quotes. Geddit?) which some craved. But now, surely, they would make an exception. What did they think of Guscott's brilliant performance?

'He threw away a try at the end,' said McGeechan. 'He has a bit to work on. But I think we can make something of him.' Could they make something of the team, the tour, the series? The portents were better than some of the advance publicity and some of the darker fears. The backs were firing live bullets; the forwards seemed to be waxing. The shadow Test team would obviously be played against Otago in three days' time. But at least, as the tour moved deeper into the South Island, there were four victories in the bag.

Guscott needed no praise. He is the best centre I have ever seen, but is not aware of his own talent either. He can appear darkly aloof, an impression fuelled by his career as a model, his exotic assignments, his agent. People claim he is arrogant – usually, people he has rebuffed. A little investigation reveals not only a glorious player, but an engaging and well-balanced man, a good bloke.

CHAPTER 15

# *Sinking in the South Island*

## OTAGO, SOUTHLAND AND THE FIRST TEST

They joke in the North Island that a trip to the South Island is a trip out of civilisation. Haw, haw. In Christchurch, halfway down the South Island, they make disparaging remarks that Dunedin, nearly 400 kilometres further south, is the end of the earth. In Dunedin, they scoff in superior tones at those end-of-the-world rednecks at Invercargill, on the southern tip. In Invercargill, they probably speak loftily and patronisingly of the bumpkins of Stewart Island. New Zealand is more than half empty. There is even a large herd of wild horses still roaming on the range.

During the long drive from Canterbury to Dunedin, where the Lions were to meet Otago, I hoped to assume the persona of my all-time movie hero, the Driver in the Seventies classic American road movie, *Two Lane Blacktop*. In the film, James Taylor, Dennis Wilson and Laurie Bird, cast as the Driver, the Mechanic and the Girl, race across plains America against another car driven by Warren Oates. But the race is secondary. It peters out before the end, anyway. The brooding, spacious-yet-claustrophobic atmosphere of the film is profoundly removed from the other road movies – the joshing nonsense of Burt Reynolds in a black Trans-Am in *Smokey and the Bandit*; and even from the storming anti-authority cult road film of the sixties, *Vanishing Point*, in which at least the roadside locals are supportive of the hunted man in the car.

*Two Lane Blacktop* is a withering study in alienation and aimless-ness. At the roadhouse stops, all the redneck regulars sit with broad backs to the door, violently suspicious of the intruders and watching them in the mirror about the bar. The car-borne drifters drift on, right through and, by implication, past the end of the film.

Unfortunately, I could not bring the character to life. The road, in patches, was lonely, with only the small-town dullness of Timaru and Oamaru to interrupt the solitude. Otherwise, there was often just a ribbon of tarmac extending to the horizon with only a single-track railway for company and the occasional boxcar train with the mournful whistle. Some of the hamlets by the roadside had the boardwalks and dust and snoozing old-timers of a wild west town. I even attracted the over-cool, sunglassed cop by the simple expedient of driving at 122 km in a 100 km limit.

But the escapism ended, the full scene could not be set. The roadhouses were, at first, unwelcoming. But then the ice would be broken. The genteel waitress doled out toasted sandwiches and coffee instead of summoning her pa and ten brothers to run us out to the town limits. That wasn't the plot at all. It shattered the alienating, lonesome effect. That and Eddie Butler snoring in the passenger seat.

If they turned the world upside down, Dunedin would just about pass muster as Edinburgh. Half the population of the city seems to have Scottish ancestry. Carisbrook, home of hard-rucking Otago, even has a Scotsman's grandstand. You can watch the action on the pitch from up on the railway bank outside the stadium. There is a Princes Street, and bagpipe bands. Paul Theroux, in *The Happy Isles of Oceania*, and after intensive research lasting a whole day or even longer, calls Dunedin 'cold and frugal, with its shabby streets and mock-Gothic university'.

He addressed the students of Otago University. I beat him by five years. On a long-forgotten England tour of 1985 they asked me to speak to an old students' section of one of the faculties. It was one of the most sensationally, dazzlingly appalling functions ever, so much so that it remains a full chapter in the book of legends of media rugby touring.

It was a buffet-style affair. When they announced that the buffet was served, hordes of the guests stormed up to the trough. I joined the queue near the end. When I reached the top there was a lettuce leaf and a single circle of cucumber left.

I took my hungry seat in the place of honour on the top table. No one remarked on my unpiled plate, or slipped me a spam slice. All over the room, fellow guests – including three other invited Brit journos, Taylor of the *Mail on Sunday*, Newcombe of the *Express* and Norrie of the *Screws*, were downing their wine.

'Is there any wine?' I asked my host, the chairman of the dinner.

'Yeah. Over there by the bar,' he said.

'Shall I get some?' I asked.

'May as well,' he said.

I bought four pitchers of white wine, plonked them down at intervals along the top table and sat down. No one said thanks; no one appeared to find it a little odd that the guest speaker had purchased the wine.

The dinner droned on. Finally, the chairman got to his feet. 'We would like to welcome here tonight,' he said, pausing to study his notes for the name he had completely forgotten, 'er, er, Stephen Jones, of the travelling press.'

I shuffled my notes and prepared to rise. 'But before we hear from him, I would like to declare open the annual general meeting of our association.' It was true. We had to sit through about an hour of motions, elections and points of order before I said my piece.

But the ordeal was by no means over. After I had spoken and the applause had risen to a whisper, the chairman was back on his feet. He declared that everyone in the room now had to tell a joke. You had to give your name, the year you had studied at the university and your funny. The chairman started the ball rolling with an interminable tale, ideal for the mixed audience, which involved sexual relations with a cow.

It may not have been the worst dinner of all time. Mike Burton told me that he was once halfway through a speech in a south London rugby club when they told him to sit down. A scarlet lady had been hired to perform a surprise sexual act with a club member whose 21st birthday was on that day, and she had turned up early. When the birthday present was over, Burton was asked to stand up and continue his address. It never happened at the Oxford Union.

The forecast for the four-day Dunedin stop was abysmal, real highland winter stuff. When we arrived it was glorious. It stayed glorious. We never saw a cloud, not even a long white one, at any time. When we left it was still glorious. The only dark clouds were stationary over the head of Stuart Barnes. The Friday before the match was the first day of the Otago Racing Club's winter carnival meeting and Barnes, a noted judge of horseflesh (self-styled) and keen racegoer, led a raiding party of Nick Popplewell, Ben Clarke, Mike Teague and Ken Milne to the track at Wingatui.

It took around three races for the other Lions, and a few press lurking for the Barnes betting nuggets, to work out that Barnes was having an off day. He became gloomier and gloomier. The wedge, he admitted, had shrunk disastrously.

By the final race we had a system. Number 1 had won almost every race. All the press and all the Lions save Barnes invested on number 1, Almost A Princess. Barnes stuck doggedly to those quaint assessments which take in form, jockey, how well the horse looks in the paddock, what the trainer and the jockeys whispered in his ear, all that rubbish.

Almost A Princess came storming home and the TAB, the New Zealand equivalent of the Tote, paid out at 8-1. We all queued happily at the pay-out desk, a newly enriched Clarke holding winning tickets for the group and Godwin of the *People* gloriously in the black to the tune of $1,000.

Then, a siren sounded. 'What's that?' we asked an official. 'Stewards' inquiry,' he said. It was a devastating moment. Clarke's face crumpled. He looked more taken aback than he had been by any New Zealand tackle. After a few queasy moments, they announced that the result stood.

Otago had not had a season to remember. They had been crushed by Auckland in the Super-10 series by 63-22, the sort of result typical of those in New Zealand domestic rugby in the season which made the game sound a whole lot more exciting and satisfying than it actually had been. They had lost heavily at home to Natal and been beaten comprehensively in Western Samoa and Queensland.

On paper, they did not seem to be too technically challenged. Stu Forster, the scrum-half, Jamie Joseph and the splendid Arran Pene were to meet the Lions again after their success in Maori colours. John Timu, who had played so gloriously for the All Blacks in South Africa in August, was at full-back after recovering from injury, and Marc Ellis, who had played in the senior side in the recent final trial, was in the centre. Steve Bachop, one of the cleverest footballers in the country and more yer traditional Brit fly-half in style, was to partner the nuggety Forster.

A good deal of the pre-match ballyhoo surrounded Josh Kronfield, the twenty-one-year-old openside flanker with fire in the belly. Otago had, by all accounts, an inspirational figure in their captain and hooker, David Latta. Of course they did. Every team the Lions met had as standard gear a rampaging hooker. Otago's proposed game plan was not exactly a revelation, either. They intended to play the game as fast as they could. What a surprise. Cut the heads off fifteen more chickens, farmer.

The Lions selection was eagerly awaited. Cooke and McGeechan stated firmly to a packed press conference that the team to play Otago was not necessarily the shadow Test team. Of course not, lads. Stuart Barnes was at fly-half in a no contest because Andrew was unfit; Ben Clarke, although not officially injured, was injured.

The big deals were the choice of Carling in the centre and Milne at hooker. Carling had not played well on the tour; or to put it another way, he had played reasonably well but not as well as Guscott, Gibbs and Scott Hastings, who were all steaming along. This was to be his first make-or-break game, but his selection was an indication that McGeechan wanted him to make the big time in the Tests because it was not strictly on the merits of his tour to date.

As for the Milne-Moore conundrum, one of the players described to me the scene when the team had been announced at a team meeting. The players seemed to spend all their time in team meetings. They were either in one or rushing to one, or leaving one. What on earth did they talk about all that time? Apparently, the expression on Moore's face when his name was not on the list for the Otago match was terrifying to behold.

The rest of the team was routine – Gavin Hastings was at full-back, Evans and Rory Underwood on the wing, Guscott alongside Carling and Morris was at scrum-half. Popplewell had held off Leonard, Burnell was on the tight head and the English veteran trio of Winterbottom, Richards and Teague had to try to keep up with the headless Otago chickens in the back row. Dooley and Bayfield made the lock positions and Dooley needed a major Wade game, too.

By this time, another powerful incentive for the Lions was growing. The sporting news from home was disastrous. England's soccer shambles was in full swing. They had just lost to Norway and we eagerly tried to predict the tabloid headlines. The *Sun* did not let us down. 'Norse Manure' was their effort. We tried to imagine the scene at the *Sun* sports desk as, hours before the match, they sat round chewing pencils and tossing around insulting one-liners. Marvellous.

The Test cricket team was similarly disastrous. So much so that the Welsh among us were to be heard loftily dismissing the latest savaging at Aussie hands and demanding news from Superglam. Glamorgan were chugging along nicely, not like those English. There was the chance for the British Lions to storm into the starved affections of the public back home.

There was also a vested interest for the media. If the Lions could buck the trend, could start winning, then our own tours were galvanised; we would be asked to file more and our sports editors would be more tuned in to what we were doing. That is far more satisfying than ringing the office from 12,000 miles away to discuss your work at the centre of the sporting world, only to be asked: 'Ah yes. Where are you again, old boy?'

So much for Otago being useless. This was the day when the Lions tour train, chugging along nicely if with the occasional misfire, fell off the tracks and down the embankment. Otago won 37-24, scoring five tries in a riot of movement and playing true to their promise to beat the Lions by playing them off their feet, by turning up the pace just when the Lions wanted to put their hands on their knees and suck in the air lost in what must have seemed like half an hour of continuous action.

There was worse to come. After the departure of Hunter in the first game the tour had provided no more extra fares for Singapore Airlines. This match threatened to reserve a whole row of seats. Carling departed with a thigh strain after nine minutes. He had spent his short time on the pitch obviously bristling with intent.

Scott Hastings arrived as his replacement. After fifty minutes, he took a blow on the side of the face in a tackle. It was a snap tackle on Kronfield, the charging flanker, and Hastings was too pushed for time to set himself properly. He had to station his head in front of Kronfield as he drove in with the shoulder, rather than behind the thighs of his quarry, out of harm's way. Kronfield's knee caught him. He stayed around for a few minutes then was led off by Kevin Murphy. His face was already swelling. It was later that we learned that Hastings had suffered a depressed fracture of the cheekbone and that his tour was over.

For some time, it seemed that there was far worse in store. Bayfield had been a storm force for the Lions in the match. In the last few minutes he went up for the ball in a line-out and when Nick Moore, the Otago prop, burrowed under the Bayfield jump, Bayfield was flipped over and came crashing down to the ground on his upper neck and back.

Whenever any player on either side was injured in any tour match, a horde of eager St John's Ambulancemen rushed on to attend. The Lions' medical men, despite polite pleading, could never dissuade them. This time, Robson and Murphy, with their man felled and still, sprinted on like Olympic athletes, beat an anxious path through the St John's men and almost literally dragged them away.

'I know how well-meaning they are,' Robson was to say afterwards, 'and they do a good job. But they do not have the experience for many of the more serious injuries and I had to stop all attempts to get Martin to his feet. I thought for some time that it was at least possible that Martin had suffered a serious spinal injury.'

It was a dreadful moment because Bayfield lay deathly still. Murphy supported his neck as he was strapped to a stretcher and the Northampton giant, a very nice man and advancing over the borders of genuine world class as a forward, was carried off by a horde of medicos and would-be medicos.

Thank heavens, Bayfield was moving by the time they reached the dressing-room, and although he was taken away in a slow-moving ambulance he was soon on his feet and discharged later in the evening. He had some minor ligament damage and some stiffness and would obviously struggle to make the First Test.

On the evidence of Carisbrook, that Test was looming like something very peckish and very nasty escaping from *Jurassic Park*. The Lions led 18-8 near half-time and were apparently well established, and they had the crowd noise down to a murmur. But Otago came steaming back, began breathing life into their movements and eventually refused to let the ball die until they had scored. In one sense it was acceptable because everything, simply everything, went for them. They played so far above themselves and all known form.

The Lions, on the other hand, shrivelled under the pressure and the pace. Otago seized every fifty-fifty ball. They seized most of the twenty-five-seventy-five balls too. They even grabbed a few ten-ninety balls. Whereas Barnes and Morris struggled desperately at half-back, Bachop and Forster played the games of their dreams for Otago; sharp, fierce and focused. Morris's service was looped and lobbed.

The match ended any hopes that the veteran English back row had of playing in the Test as a unit. It showed how essential to the team the presence of Clarke had become. It also illustrated that the years were now beginning to take their toll on the mighty Mike Teague, so gloriously powerful in Australia in 1989 but by now, with the hammering of the years and the drag of injuries, no longer so close to the ball and to the meat of the match. The Lions' back row and, indeed, their whole pack in the loose, were not so much beaten as circumnavigated. Joseph, Pene and Kronfield were omnipresent.

There was a taste of Otago after nineteen minutes, with the Lions leading through an early Gavin Hastings penalty. Pene and Joseph drew in some defence with a drive, and the ball was set up again towards the right. Andre Bell appeared to knock on but he was allowed to proceed to set up a try for Paul Cooke, the other Otago wing.

The Lions settled and hammered in two memorable tries inside six minutes. A high kick by Barnes was deftly recovered by Scott Hastings and Winterbottom. Teague worked Rory Underwood through down the left of a ruck and Richards went storming over the line. Shortly afterwards, Rory set up the ball in midfield after another incursion from his wing. Morris sent Barnes away, Barnes made a half-break and Ieuan Evans, yet again, made a try from a half-chance. It must have pleased McGeechan – a set-up in the middle of the field and a lightning attack was his favourite play. Hastings kicked both conversions, and although Bell had kicked a penalty when Dooley was offside at a ruck, it was 18-8 and sweetness and light.

Yet Otago re-imposed themselves before half-time, just when the Lions should have been working like dogs to protect their lead. Cooke scored again after a concerted attack and it was 18-13.

The second half will certainly go down in the history of rugby in the deep south. Otago were superb. They had the perfect referee, too. Col Hawke had already demonstrated to the Lions when he refereed the final trial that when he read the law-book, some of the pages must have been stuck together. He fed Otago's continuity. He allowed Otago to throw the ball in direct to their inferior line-out men, allowed them to recycle it from a scrabbling position. And Bachop led them along like a popular conductor. They went ahead after he made a glorious side-stepping run of which even Jonathan Davies would have been proud, past Winterbottom and Barnes, to set up a try for John Leslie, the centre. Bell kicked the goal.

And after fifty-six minutes came one of those tries which will have Otago forwards nodding their heads until their dotage. They won a line-out, piled in and drove the whole thing thirty-five metres to score. They made subtle little touches on the tiller, faithfully coming round again if their effort had driven them out to the fringes. Latta had the ball under control as the pile drove over the Lions' line. It was, of its type, a try to compare with the Barbarians' 1973 magic. Bell converted and it was 27-18.

Hastings did kick two penalties for the Lions in the second half, but by then, Timu had found himself after a grim start. He scored after wondrous sustained attacks, Bell converted and Bachop signed off with a flourish and a dropped goal near the end. Phew!

'It was a costly exercise,' said McGeechan afterwards. 'If you allow New Zealand teams to play two metres over the gain-line, they'll play pretty well.'

The first item on the inquest agenda was the casualty count. As we were to discover later in the evening, Bayfield was up and about, sore and stiff but walking. Carling's injury was neither serious nor negligible. But poor Scott Hastings was detained in hospital, where he had a complicated operation to repair the depression of the fracture. It took four and a half hours and involved the insertion of a small plate in the cheekbone. His face was swollen badly after the operation. He would remain in Dunedin after the party left,

eventually rejoining in Invercargill, the next stop, and was to leave
for home after the First Test.

It was a deep sadness for the Hastings family, some of whom were
to arrive later in the tour and had hoped to see both their heroes in
action. Scott Hastings had been in some of the best form of his life.
As ever, he was tackling with a tremendous thump yet he was also
showing in parts of the pitch which Scotland's game rarely reached.
To be frank, Scotland's back play in the last decade has hardly
threatened to burn Europe's stadia to the ground. His sleight-of-
hand in working away Rory Underwood for the try against the
Maoris was evidence of an all-round game beautifully well oiled.
The players missed him, too. He is a live-wire tourist, far less aloof
in body language than his brother. He is part of the soul of any
party. All four of the Lions centres would have walked into the All
Black team, especially since Frank Bunce had a season which was, by
his standards, eerily quiet.

The obvious replacement for Hastings was Phil de Glanville, the
Bath centre who would have made my original selection. Like Scott
Gibbs, there never seems much to him, yet he is one of the hardest
tacklers and shrewdest midfield operators in the game. But de
Glanville had already been invalided home from England's tour of
Canada and was unfit.

Suddenly, rejoicing Irish journalists were among us again. The
replacement for Hastings was to be Vincent Cunningham, the St
Mary's College man who had played thirteen times for his country.
Bloody Irishmen everywhere, we complained to our Irish colleagues. Especially when they kept the three outside lines in the
press hotel tied up all Saturday evening, seeking the reaction of
every living member of the Cunningham family wheresoever in the
world they lived, while the rest of us were trying to file a few
thousand words to an impatient Wapping.

On every tour, there is a day when everything kicks up a notch,
when everything becomes deadly serious. When you realise with a
shock that nothing light and easy, nothing relaxed, is to come. A day
which marks the end of the early optimism; a day which marks the
end of innocence. That day dawned in Dunedin.

Invercargill can be hospitable. But Bluff oysters were off the menu
due to some sort of offshore pollution and it is – well, a long walk.
There is a set of signposts at the point at Bluff, the southernmost tip
of the country, like the one at Land's End. London 18848 km, it
said, inducing instant homesickness. As Paul Theroux says, 'leave
the southern tip of New Zealand and the next upright mammal you
are likely to see is an emperor penguin'.

Yet the stopover was doomed from the start. It is utterly
impossible to convince anyone who has never made a major tour of
how they can sink occasionally into dark and depression and
homesickness. A Sunday travelling day after the Otago disaster was
bad enough; Invercargill was gloomy, cold and wet. The hotel was,
well, gloomy, cold and non-palatial. For the only time on the tour,

the massed ranks of the press were to share a hotel with the Lions. A religious convention had commandeered the only other large hotel in the town.

There was a large and unprepossessing bar, packed daily, of course, with scene-making locals and travelling fans as well as the guests. The Guinness was on draught, but shocking. Cooke's Sunday school conference soon put that all into perspective, too. We thought we were gathering for a bulletin on morale and on Bayfield's back. The trouble was elsewhere in the second row. 'We have some very bad news,' said Cooke gravely. 'Wade Dooley received the news this morning on arrival at the hotel that his father had suffered a heart attack and passed away. He will leave tomorrow to fly home.'

So the big man departed. 'The New Zealand Rugby Union have already invited him to return if and where he wishes to, but that will be entirely up to Wade,' said Cooke. Many of the players knew Mr Dooley senior very well. By all accounts, he was as popular a figure as his son. It was a numbing moment for everyone.

Cooke did not immediately announce the name of the replacement. It was a fair bet that he had asked the Four Home Unions back in England to pore over airline timetables for Canada, where Martin Johnson, the massive and massively promising Leicester lock, was winding up England's tour. Soon, Johnson and Cunningham were on their way. 'Not the worst replacement,' McGeechan said of Johnson. Quite.

Cooke also offered some decidedly pertinent thoughts on the tour to date, criticising the lack of refereeing of players on the ground and also, in what amounted to a call to arms and feet, declaring that the Lions 'had to get more aggressive and vigorous in the rucks. New Zealand teams kick you to bits on the floor. Some of our players have difficulty adjusting to that mentality'. It was a stark when-in-Rome speech.

But Dooley and Hastings homeward bound? Carling and Bayfield injured? A packed, claustrophobic hotel on a dark and wet Sunday evening in a place which is not so much the middle of nowhere as the end of anywhere? As we left for a walk round the deserted streets, a taxi pulled up bearing a bleary Gareth Charles, the BBC Radio Wales man, hot-foot from an endless journey from Zimbabwe, where Wales were touring. 'Don't send that taxi away, Charlo. Get back in and ask for the airport.' Little Andrew Jones and even littler Rosanna Jones seemed a world away.

Things didn't improve in Invercargill. Southland went on to Rugby Park, another of those imaginatively named New Zealand grounds, to fulfil most of Cooke's observations about kicking people to bits. It was a Tuesday match, as tour matches usually are in the week of the Tests. That gave everyone an extra day in which to expunge from the memory banks the efforts of the Southland rugby team. Not to mention those of Mick Fitzgibbon, the referee from Canterbury.

The Lions selected a team with several people still firmly in the running for the Test. Bayfield and Carling had done only light training since Dunedin, and Dooley had departed, so lock and centre were up for grabs for the Test. Tony Clement was chosen to fill in in the centre alongside Scott Gibbs, who was desperate to carry on a rich vein of form. Gavin Hastings had to play at full-back and Wallace and Tony Underwood were on the wings. Andrew and Jones at half-back were both still in the running.

Leonard, Moore and Wright were in the front row because even though the Lions management had mooted the switch of Leonard to the tight head they were still mooting and not doing. Reed and Cronin were in the second row and were competing for one place in the Test, assuming that Bayfield made it and assuming that not even Johnson could step off the plane straight into the Test arena. Webster, Teague and Galwey were the back row, with Galwey at number 8. Clarke was absent again. He would fry bigger fish later in the week.

Southland were led by Paul Henderson, a fine and fierce flanker. They have an excellent record against touring teams. For a small side from a small town they had a history. They blackened that history. The match was awful. The Lions won 34-16, but their play was annoyingly fitful. 'When are we going to play an eighty-minute game?' asked Cooke. We were still asking that question at the end of the tour. More than that, there was enough bickering, pushing, shoving and swearing to fill a season. Not forgetting that you need a partner to tango, I still thought that Southland were a disgrace.

They had limited ability. They saw their chance to upset the Lions through misplaced aggression. They may have thought themselves terribly fierce, but they came over as a bunch of gauche rednecks. Rata Smith and Chris Corbett, the number 8 and the tight head, were particularly mock-hard and posturing. Some of the press were watching end-on and confirmed afterwards that Southland's forwards put the boot in continuously. Some of the Lions, notably Teague and Cronin, were also too fractious and angry.

Mark Tinnock, the Southland lock, once performed such a preposterous tap dance on Richard Webster, raining studs on the prostrate Lion from above, that it was difficult to know which was the more nonsensical, Tinnock's action, or the failure of Fitzgibbon to send him off.

The blows were coming in clusters. Andrew had bravely played on under severe punishment at the bottom of rucks. He departed after sixty-six minutes, having taken a blow on the nose, and there seemed a chance that it was broken. Barnes came on as replacement, and yet after ten minutes' action, he was led from the field holding a towel to a major cut on the side of his head, obviously in great pain. It was one of the supreme ironies of the day that the cut was caused by an accidental swipe of the studs from Robert Jones. 'Thanks a lot, Jonesy,' said a beturbanned Barnes later in the evening.

Yet a potentially thunderous blow fell just before Barnes had arrived. Scott Gibbs, playing another superb match all over the field, was felled in an attack. He lay writhing and the stretcher was brought on. Kevin Murphy was paying urgent attention to his ankle. By the time Barnes left, Guscott and Morris were on the field.

The only shaft of light on a dark day was the news that Gibbs had suffered only a bad sprain. 'Tony Clement's foot took my legs away from under me,' he said later. Everyone in the stands would have bet a pound to a penny that Gibbs' tour was over as he was carried off, thanks to a fracture or at least a severe ligament injury.

'He could be fit inside a week or ten days,' said Cooke afterwards, after leaving the hospital ward which the Lions dressing-room had become. Now, with the First Test snatched away from him but still hanging in on the tour, Gibbs was entrusted to the care of Robson and Murphy and their medicines, potions and magic touch. They had quickly become the most successful members of the party. They did not let Gibbs down.

The Lions led 24-0 at half-time. Gavin Hastings' boot set them up with four penalty goals in the first half, all beautifully struck on a windy day. They were awarded a penalty try when Bobby Murrell, the Southland scrum-half, flicked the ball away from the feet of Galwey as the Lions went for a pushover try. Andy Reed scored after half an hour from a drive initiated by Galwey from a scrum near the Southland line. Hastings kicked one of the conversions.

A smashing try finished by Tony Clement opened the gap further in the second half. Tony Underwood and Scott Gibbs conjured an opening and Clement, playing beautifully out of position, cut through the last lines. Hastings kicked the conversion and Clement dropped a high goal near the end.

Yet Jimmy Cormack and Phil Johnston, the Southland wings, each scored tries in the final quarter. Culhane kicked a conversion and a penalty. A team harder of heart would not have allowed Southland the satisfaction of those points on the board, and there were worrying early signs of what was to become a collapse of the midweek forward effort. In even the most united parties, there comes a time on tour when the midweek games stop being part of a general tour shakedown and a fascination in themselves, and start to become second XV fixtures. It can be difficult for those players who sense that they will not play in the Tests to re-motivate themselves to the same degree.

Reed easily won the battle with Cronin and played himself into the Test team. Cronin had a fitful game. He was transparently ineffective just when he was expected to give it a real blast. As usual, the right-hand side of the scrum gave ground with almost every scrum, and the original selection of Wright was shown in a light ever more grim. Jeff Probyn was probably tending his greenhouse at home.

Robert Jones, needing form and security of possession to bid for the Test team, found the possession slowing, the ball so untidy and so festooned with Southland harriers, that he could never make an impression. He was furious afterwards. He felt that Test jersey slipping away. Only Webster really impressed in the second half. Home forwards posing as potential gunfighters at high noon on the main street were meat and drink to the pride of Swansea.

At least there would be a newsworthy blast from the press conference: condemnation of Tinnock's stamping attack and of the game in general. The tabloid representatives, not to mention the rest of us, craned forward. What of the incident? Paul Henderson didn't see it. 'I had my head buried,' he said. Keith Robertson, the Southland coach, unfortunately missed it as well. 'I didn't actually see the incident,' Robertson replied when asked if he felt that Tinnock had been lucky to stay on the field.

The Lions management took their seats. Gavin Hastings had seen nothing to make him think that someone should have gone. Cooke and McGeechan, apparently, were similarly unsighted. Strange. Every single pressman saw the incident. So did all 18,000 people in the ground, judging by their loud reaction (generally supportive) as Tinnock stamped. So did the nation, because the TV cameras showed the incident graphically.

I admired the Lions management on tour. They did a good job. They knew as well as anyone that New Zealanders (along with Australians, the world whining champions, incidentally) seize avidly on any whining from the British Isles. But I was profoundly unimpressed by the wise monkeys of Invercargill, for the disservice they did the game in refusing to condemn or even acknowledge. The row rumbled on. The London tabloids, correctly, tore into Southland and were duly quoted back to New Zealand. Predictably, all parts of the home media picked up the story. Significantly, however, they spent all their time pillorying the tabloids and none at all investigating Southland's behaviour.

That evening, the Lions bravely socialised in the public rooms of the teeming hotel. Brian Moore delivered four hours' worth of wisdom and crystal insight into the tour and into rugby in general in about twenty minutes. His body language was definitely becoming louder. The talk in the bar was that Leonard would soon be transferring to the troubled tight-head side. Moore, although he did not say so, was clearly resoundingly unchuffed at having to bid for a Test place from the weak base laid down by the midweek front five. That base was eventually to disintegrate utterly.

Next morning, it was time to check out of Invercargill. No one looked back. The rain was lashing down when we reached the airport to fly to Christchurch. The aircraft was buffeted even when stationary as the wind howled around the fuselage. The captain taxied to the end of the runway. 'We are going to hold here for a few minutes,' he said over the tannoy. 'There is a severe thunderstorm crossing the airfield with winds gusting to sixty knots.' Take all the time you like, old son.

The Lions settled back into civilisation at Christchurch for the Test, the most crucial game in which many of them had ever been involved. The agony of tension rose for those who hoped to be in the Test side. The match was critical because I felt strongly that no team could win a series in New Zealand after dropping the First Test, that the next few days would see the tour achieve lift-off or die on its feet.

By now, the party was back up to strength. Johnson and Cunningham had arrived, Johnson after a fifty-six-hour marathon from Ontario. Or was it? By the Wednesday, Carling was still moving gingerly in training. Bayfield was gradually healing but was he really a proposition for the Test and would he have recovered inside? Would the crashing fall be in his mind when next he had to leap for the ball? Richards had also, surreptitiously, joined the casualty list with a calf tear. And how deep would be the inner wounds caused by Otago and Southland? We reckoned without the healing powers of Dr James and physio Kev.

The press party was reaching its full complement and the vast ranks of travelling package supporters were arriving in droves. Each of the travel companies that brought them had doled out distinctive tour gear: pullovers or anoraks with garish logos. So distinctive, in fact, that you could see them coming three miles off. The celeb tour leaders included Gareth Chilcott, Alan Phillips, Les Cusworth, Barry John, John Dawes, Mick Quinn and Mike Burton. The travel market was ferociously competitive. Any item of news revealing that something had gone wrong in another company – maggots in the beds, aircraft going lame, match tickets behind the dead-ball line, etc. – was greeted gleefully by all the competitors. The whole tour was reaching a peak of tension and expectancy.

The All Blacks themselves gathered in a hotel across the city. It was their first camp since their tour to South Africa. 'It's great to be back together. It's great to be part of something like the All Blacks,' said Ian Jones, the Kamo Kid. And in Christchurch on the Wednesday, they had one of their trademark public training sessions. The numbers who turned up to watch, on a sunny and clear day, would certainly have kept happy the treasurer of a Second Division rugby club in any of the four home countries.

It was the usual odd New Zealand session – great steaming drives and real urgency but all in the false field of unopposed training. The tough stuff would come in the next two days when the sessions went underground. Along with Laurie Mains, the coaches were Peter Thorburn and Earle Kirton, the former Harlequins and New Zealand fly-half and, ironically, a close friend and confidant of Richard Best. How were they getting on, we asked Earle, now that he and his mate were on opposite sides of a high wall? 'The bugger's hardly speaking to me,' he said.

The All Blacks, as they loafed around or stood to attention in front of camera crews, seemed surprisingly small. In fact, they usually are. People used to speak in awe of the giant Colin Meads. In fact, Meads was probably less than six foot three and even his programme notes, traditionally to be taken with a pinch of salt, used to weigh him in at less than 16 stone.

The props, Craig Dowd and Olo Brown, were squat and square and heavy; so was Fitzpatrick, surely the prototype hooker for the nineties. Yet Ian Jones and Robin Brooke, the locks, were small by Dooley-Eales-Bayfield standards; Zinzan Brooke, the number 8, was strong but not appreciably taller than, say, Mike Teague. Joseph was the ideal build for the blind side – six foot three and 16 stone, and Michael Jones was long and lithe on the open side. But there was no real mega-tonnage there.

The half-backs were Grant Fox, his career revitalised, and Ant Strachan, the neat and yet non-explosive scrum-half. Frank Bunce and Walter Little were in the centre and Eroni Clarke, a utility back of military medium pace, was on the wing. He was keeping a place warm for John Kirwan, back in the country after his stint in Italy. The massive, bicep-flexing Va'aiga Tuigamala was on the other. John Timu was at full-back and the selectors had decided to take his match fitness on trust and not to draft in Matthew Cooper instead.

It is always the same with the All Blacks. You can gouge out large holes in the team. We sat down over a beer in Christchurch and thrashed them without breaking sweat. Let's see. Strachan is no threat with the ball and his service is dodgy. Fox is a brilliant kicker, but as for the rest, forget it. Clarke is slow, Tuigamala will go through you if he gets up steam but he hasn't got much football in him. Timu can creak and groan under the high ball, Bunce is off form.

What of the pack? We murdered them. You hardly ever see Brown in the loose; the locks are small and Robin Brooke really looks like a fugitive from the blindside flank. Zinzan Brooke is a conspicuous player, but is he really conspicuously effective? Michael Jones? All-time great, of course, but is he any longer so great? Auckland had been leaving him out in favour of Mark Carter.

And the assessment would always end the same. Individually, how do we rate the All Blacks? Fair only. Who do we think will win? Er, the All Blacks. No matter how limited some of the components, you always underrate the team itself, the ferocious collective with the weight and momentum and confidence of history on their shoulders, at your dire peril.

It was obvious, too, that the All Blacks had fitted a new face. The face smiled. In the 1991 World Cup, especially when they were set directly against the Australians as the semi-final in Dublin approached, they realised that their austere, forbidding and mercenary image ('We'll speak to anyone if the money's right') had misfired badly; that the senior members of the team had become smug and exclusive and forbidding. The Australian PR machine, gleaming, oiled and slick, took them to the cleaners. Who cares about the PR? Those who recognise the power of public opinion.

The team had reacted well. Rick Salizzo, a former TV newsreader, had been appointed PR consultant. He confessed that the team and management was nervous of the British papers, especially of the tabloids – every actual or alleged excess of the *Sun* and *Daily*

*Mirror* in any field is reported wonderingly back to a wondering New Zealand public. They wanted to establish a relationship.

The fruits of the new openness had already been seen. Near the start of the tour, we were invited to an audience with Sean Fitzpatrick, the New Zealand captain, at the bar on Auckland's North Shore owned by Stu Wilson. Fitzpatrick had arrived back from South Africa after the exhausting Super-10 final on the very day of the meeting. He had learned his PR lines. Fitzpatrick worked the room like a master, stopping for a chat; there were a few questions for and some eye contact with everyone in the room. He excused himself skilfully from each group so that he could move on to another. Fitzpatrick also fished a little deeper: 'To meet the Lions is a milestone in my career of special significance,' he said. 'As a boy, I watched them. Every child in New Zealand follows them.'

In Christchurch, the All Blacks held open house in their team-room, little knots of people clustered round little knots of All Blacks. There was art in their method as well. There was money in their profile. The All Blacks had almost a monopoly when it came to advertising. Fitzpatrick and the wide, beaming Tuigamala especially had cornered so much of the market for celebrity ads and endorsements that there was hardly anything left for the traditional glitterati and poseurati of the grade two celebs to do. They had to content themselves with appearances on *Give us a Clue*.

In that week, the All Blacks Club was unveiled. Membership was open to every individual and corporate entity and apparently conveyed certain privileges. No one really explained what they were, but it was hinted that youngsters would receive mailings and gifts and souvenirs, while companies would receive commensurate corporate benefits and even flesh-pressing visits by the players themselves. Any the wiser?

The money would go to the players, full stop. It would be part of the final annual share-out from All Blacks Promotions Limited, which doles out the proceeds of all team commercial activity. Eddie Tonks, president of the New Zealand RFU, declared that the plan would not be referred to the IRB for legal green lights. It was legal, decent, honest and truthful, was his gist. Under some projections, individual All Blacks could receive up to $100,000 (more than £36,000) per annum.

'Many All Blacks have their education interrupted, and lose out on career training and scholarships, and proper job training. Others are forced to go abroad to subsidise their income. The proceeds of the All Blacks Club will help out in times of difficulty, will ensure that no one loses out materially from playing rugby.' Apparently, even though Jamie Joseph was a student at Otago University, he never had the time to attend lectures. What with his commitments with the Maoris, Otago and New Zealand, it was a wonder that he remembered where the university was.

Laurie Mains was a leading light in the formation of the club. His particular beef was the large number of potential All Blacks travelling abroad, especially to Italy, Japan and France. 'If the club stops any player departing overseas before the next World Cup then it will have been valuable,' he said. Particularly so, he might have added, now that stringent qualification periods imposed by overseas unions mean that players bound for some countries have to leave halfway through the New Zealand season to become eligible for their new clubs.

My thoughts turned up the world to Twickenham. I could imagine Dudley Wood, the secretary of the RFU, hiring a grave so that he could turn in it.

The Lions announced their Test team. Gavin was at full-back, Evans and Rory Underwood on the wing. Carling was fit enough to resume alongside Guscott in the centre. Barnes was ruled out – his cut was still sore and not fully healed and the advice of James Robson was that he was not ready for a Test. Morris, doubts about the snap in his service glossed over, and all credits such as heart and soul and physical presence and elasticity safety banked, was at scrum-half, inside Andrew.

The pack selection surely took less than five minutes, once Bayfield was restored and Dean Richards had shrugged off the calf injury he had sustained in training. Clarke had not even played on the blind side on tour, or much at all. But the old Lions selectorial shunter nudged him neatly into the number 6 jersey alongside Winterbottom and Richards.

Following his selection alongside Bayfield, Andy Reed gave everyone a warm interview which detailed his meteoric rise from the Bath third XV to the Lions Test team in less time than it takes to eat a Cornish pasty. Burnell, Milne and Popplewell were the front row. McGeechan reported that the Thursday session, held at the Linwood club in secret, was the best of the tour.

There was one participant whom no one mentioned much, and from the Lions' point of view that was unquestionably because they did not want to dare the devil. Brian Kinsey, the Australian, was the match referee. It was a pure guess, but I guessed that Cooke would rather that just about any other referee in the world take charge. The Englishmen in the party held Kinsey in low esteem as a referee, and had done so ever since he had officiated in the England Tests in Argentina in 1990.

Cooke did mention a few areas which the Lions wanted cleared up with Kinsey before the match. Did he want the ball thrown in straight in the line-out; what movement into the gap would be allowed? Did you really have to join a maul behind the rear feet, or had everyone already patted the IRB on the head and told them to stuff their new law? Was Kinsey in the slightest bit interested in keeping the third man at the tackle on his feet, or would he allow a swallow dive on to the ball, with two and a half twists, like every official in New Zealand? The whole process of clarification underlined the barmy truth that, in matches of real magnitude for which players had prepared for months, they effectively only discovered the laws under which the game would be played as they went along. To think that Dr Roger Vanderfield, chairman of the IRB's laws

*Gavin Hastings batters his way to score the try which sealed the astonishing comeback against the Maoris as Barnes and Carling celebrate*

*Wingatui Racecourse, Otago. Mike Teague, Stuart Barnes and Nick Popplewell have invested unwisely. Optimistically, they scan the horizon for the lost nag*

*Will Carling nailed by North Harbour. His early form was a degree under, and he narrowly lost the race of four superb centres*

*Coach Geech gives a special clinic – Lions giants only*

*McGeechan announces the First Test team to an encircling horde of the Fourth Estate at Christchurch*

*He played number 8 and blindside flank at world class. Here, Ben Clarke is about to impress Canterbury's Greg Smith with his play on the openside at Lancaster Park*

*Ieuan Evans apparently coming between Frank Bunce and a try in the First Test. The camera angle is misleading – referee Kinsey is miles away. He gave the try anyway*

*The blockbusting Va'aiga Tuigamala needed some tackling. Ben Clarke and
Ieuan Evans combine to stop him in the First Test*

*Rory Underwood about to fly back in time in a Tiger Moth at the Wigram Air
base, Christchurch*

*The midweek team crumbles: Stuart Barnes in trouble from half of Hawkes Bay as the trickle of poor possession from the shambolic pack becomes a torrent*

*Rory Underwood has left John Kirwan and John Timu for dead. He dives for glory in the Second Test in Wellington, and the Lions will not be caught*

*Nick Popplewell perfects the ear-to-ear Irish beam as the celebrations begin on the final whistle at Wellington*

*Scott Gibbs caps a brilliant personal tour with his try in the Third Test at Eden Park*

*Defensive formations break down and John Preston, hardly the Gareth Edwards of Kiwi rugby, scores with ease as Gavin Hastings dives in vain*

*Smiling Sean Fitzpatrick nudges the facial muscles of Laughing Laurie Mains into action, and the series is won*

committee, expressed quite recently his view that there was no worldwide problem of interpretation.

On the night before the Test, the Chieftains were playing the Christchurch Town Hall. The Irish six-piece ensemble, which has been together since the dawn of time, has found success piling upon success later in their career with Grammy Awards and cameo appearances on the albums of everyone who is anyone in world music. The Irish maestros were on majestic form. Their musicianship was pyrotechnic. They were a joy. The crowd sat gawping like the average New Zealand rugby crowd – dull, with all the sense of occasion of a limp lettuce.

Three days later, the tours of both the Lions and the Chieftains had moved on to New Plymouth. One night, Paddy Maloney himself came into our hotel bar. The veteran chief Chieftain sat, gnome-like, munching his toastie. The man had played with Van Morrison, for God's sake. I conferred with fellow Van man Steve Bale of the *Independent*. Should we go up and talk to him, like vulture punters? Or should we leave him in peace? Maloney made up our minds. 'How yer going, boys?' he called across.

We swapped old music yarns and anecdotes – well, he gave us his, we didn't have a lot to swap – and we retired glowing to bed. Laurie Mains and Paddy Maloney in one week. You meet all the stars in our job.

Every Kiwi fear about bad first-up form and every Lion fear about Kinsey's refereeing was borne out in spades. The All Blacks won a nervous, halting match at Lancaster Park by 20-18, and the Lions' disappointment was savage. They played below par. The Lions, in fact, played even worse – they had the match snatched away from them in the closing seconds but they could have been out of sight anyway. It was a desperate afternoon, an unpalatable defeat.

Inside the last minute of normal time, with the Lions leading 18-17, Dean Richards grabbed Bunce just as Bunce was trying desperately to initiate one saving attack from a back line which had been utterly blotted out by Lions defence and by lack of imagination. Richards wrapped up his man, turned him round in textbook fashion and freed the ball. It was glorious defensive play, and as Dewi Morris saw the stolen ball come back on the Lions' side, he ran excitedly up to the ruck pointing animatedly into the Lions' side. Almost instantaneously, bodies dived on top of the tackled player and the tackler, trapping them both, and it seemed clear that at least one All Black simply dived in yards in front of the ball just to make a desperate effort to re-secure the ball.

Kinsey allowed play to proceed for a few moments, stationed on the Lions' side of the ruck to supervise, by his gestures, the emergence of the ball. Then he stopped and penalised Richards for, as he explained to a furious Gavin Hastings, 'holding on to the ball'. As Hastings said later, 'Why would he be holding on to the ball in that position at that time?'

It was a shocking decision, a random shaft of illogicality. I never found a referee in New Zealand or, via the telephone, at home who agreed with it. 'It should have been a penalty to us or a scrum to us for a turnover,' said Ben Clarke. 'When the whistle went,' said Dewi Morris, 'I assumed it was a penalty to us. I could not believe he gave it to them.' I could not, quite, go along with some of the people who had far, far stronger things to say about the decision.

As I wrote in the following day's *Sunday Times*: 'The biggest irony is that for the whole of the tour to date, the interpretations of the referees have been so unbelievably lax that it seems the only way in which teams can be penalised in a ruck is if they take a firearm in with them – and even then the penalty would be indirect.'

There was only one matter not in question: that Grant Fox would kick the goal. He was kicking down-wind, the ball was placed forty-five metres out and he struck it nervelessly. Over it went. Even the dull old Lancaster Park crowd reacted with excitement. Earlier in the match, Fox had reached 1,000 points for his country. 'I don't care so much about the other 1,000,' said Fitzpatrick afterwards. 'It was the last three I liked.'

The Lions were not exactly jumping for joy at Kinsey's decision to award the All Blacks their try, either. It came right at the start after Fox had hoisted a perfect, steepling kick. Bunce and Evans jumped for it together. Bunce seemed to grab the bigger chunk but Evans appeared to hold Bunce and also to grab his share of the ball, and they both crashed down together over the Lions' line.

The day before the match, an Australian acquaintance of mine and of Kinsey had described him as 'not one of the quickest referees around'. As the players crashed over and the All Blacks claimed a try, there was a pregnant pause. Kinsey was struggling well behind play, attempting to make a judgment from a long way away and from behind the play. He came puffing up, by his own account received some sort of unofficial nod from his touch-judge, then he awarded the try.

The debate raged afterwards. One TV camera, shooting from almost directly behind, suggested that Bunce had scored. A still photograph delivered to me in the hotel the day after the match indicated strongly that Evans and Bunce touched down together. The only certainty was that the issue was cloudy. Law 12 is categorical about instances such as these: 'Where there is doubt as to which team grounded the ball in-goal, a scrummage shall be formed five metres from the goal-line opposite the place where the ball was grounded. The attacking team shall put in the ball.' Kinsey could not possibly have been certain and he clearly should have awarded an attacking five-yard scrum.

The Lions were feeling bad enough about their own performance in the first quarter, let alone that of Kinsey. If ever in their sporting lives they needed an assured start it was in this match. They were playing with a wind so strong that one of the pre-match skydivers had landed on the back pitch outside the stadium and another had

had to dive forward seconds before touchdown to avoid landing on the heads of a section of the crowd.

It was vital that the Lions began powerfully. Yet they conceded the stunning early try and their early play was dreadful. They were nervous and faltering and, sadly, the first seven tactical kicks with which they tried to turn the screws of pressure were all mishit. Andrew, Guscott and Morris were the offenders. What a contrast to Fox – he could nominate the blade of grass on which he intended to land the ball.

Yet the Lions steadied. Bayfield, showing no inner scarring from his mishap, played beautifully in the line-outs. It was evidence of inner steel. The back row generally out-pointed their illustrious opposite numbers, and the defence was something else – the All Blacks started in thunderous mood, moving the ball on through millions of rucks and mauls, whipping it to and fro.

And going nowhere. It was movement in a vacuum and a vacuum sealed by intelligent, well-organised and courageous tackling. They scored their one try from what was to be their staple play for the series – a giant hoof by Grant Fox – and never looked likely to score another.

By the seventeenth minute, the Lions were ahead. Gavin Hastings kicked two excellent penalty goals, the first after line-out barging from the All Blacks and the second when they had killed the ball after a burst from the tail of the line-out from the storming Clarke. Fox had kicked two more penalties by half-time and Hastings one more, so it was 11-9 to New Zealand.

The Lions turned to play against the wind with many parts of the All Black team already neutralised, and it was a position from which the Lions should have won.

Fox put his men 14-9 ahead at the very start of the second half. Tuigamala thundered through Evans' tackle, and Strachan and Brown took on the move. The Lions' tackling held, but then they lost a ball they were setting up, came up offside to try to save and Fox did the rest.

The Lions were in control of much of the rest of the match. An eerie silence enveloped the ground and the Lions', followers, in swathes around the stands with noisy knots on the terraces, grew more vocal with the nudge of growing expectancy. The Lions lacked the springboard of quick possession and alacrity at half-back to strike out for the win that was there for the taking. Significantly, even though they twice worked Rory Underwood away, the second time after good work on a counter-attack by Andrew, Richards, Winterbottom and Guscott, he could not escape Timu, who twice drove him into touch down the left. Probably, Rory the Rocket would have reckoned to have scored from at least one of those chances.

Yet Hastings kicked another goal, Fox replying after a high tackle by Hastings on Timu, and then the Lions captain scored his fifth penalty with seventeen minutes remaining after taking a late hit by Michael Jones. During the series, there were one or two ill-disciplined nudges off the ball from Jones, perhaps a few signs that the maestro is losing a little snap and crackle in his game.

Nine minutes from the end, Brown fell offside far out on the Lions' left-hand touchline. Gavin Hastings came up with the same confidence of body language as ever. He cleaned the ball, placed it carefully and kicked a beautiful long goal. The strong wind never dragged it off course by an inch. He allowed himself a small, token punch of the air. As he did so, I turned to Bale of the *Independent* on my left. 'I bet you anything,' I said, 'that Kinsey gives Grant one more kick.' At the end they were calling me Gypsy Rose.

The last nine minutes were an eternity, almost an ecstasy of tension. Yet there were clear signs of fumbling and exasperation in the All Blacks ranks and audible impatience as Fox simply hoisted ball after ball into the air. In the last sixty seconds of normal time, Bunce was wrapped up by Richards and Brian Kinsey and Grant Fox did the rest.

The Lions were stunned. No one spoke in the dressing-room afterwards for the best part of half an hour. Clarke stood outside the giant tent which housed the post-match function, shaking his head in a near desperation. 'How did we lose? I can't believe we lost.'

There was one item of good news, one revealing and sustaining shaft of light. The Lions had proved that the All Blacks were beatable. Despite all the bravado of pre-match talk, until they had actually met New Zealand in the middle they could not really weld hope and conviction. They knew that the All Blacks were bound to improve and they knew that they would have to work like fury on and off the pitch to have any chance of saving the series. But they also knew that they had come close without support from the referee and the fates, and when much of their own game was several degrees under.

As the evening wore on, most of the team partied on down in a room set aside in their hotel for them and their guests. Across the city, Sean Fitzpatrick spoke of a game 'that we were possibly lucky to win. It showed the strength of the Lions and the work we have to do. The series is still very much alive.'

Brian Moore's reflections from the stands were revealing. 'The match resoundingly confirmed our theories about what we have to do to beat the All Blacks. We have to take heart from the fact that New Zealand never looked like scoring a try in the last seventy-eight minutes of the match. When we left the ground we were defeated but we were not depressed.' There was a gleam in Moore's eyes which suggested strongly that he intended to be around on active service for the Second Test. And he was.

# CHAPTER 16

# *The Bull and the Lambs*

## TARANAKI, AUCKLAND, HAWKE'S BAY

From a distance at the start of the tour, the next week had looked a waste of time. The Invercargill experience had already established that midweek games in bucolic areas involving tour supernumeraries losing their tempers could be of mixed value. That put the prospect of New Plymouth under a long, dark cloud. And, from the same distance, what did the Auckland game prove at that juncture of the tour? Sure, they had a magnificent record (helped artificially by the massive drift of population to the capital, of course. They are not exactly home-grown). But what a pain. Why not get straight on with the Tests? And pumpkin tastes the same whenever they serve it.

But suddenly these games appeared heaven-sent. Taranaki were a First Division province, though not awesome. It was just the type of match to allow Martin Johnson to acclimatise and launch his bid for meteoric Test stardom; just the match to switch Jason Leonard to the tight head and to test the fitness of Scott Gibbs.

The Auckland game was suddenly inch-perfect, too. It provided the ideal chance for those players bubbling on the fringes of the Test team to test themselves in Test conditions but not in an actual Test, if you see what I mean. That meant that if the Lions chose well, and if everything went swimmingly at New Plymouth, Scott Gibbs could be given a run against Auckland in the centre, Stuart Barnes at fly-half, Jason Leonard at tight head, Johnson at lock, Brian Moore at hooker. With the sole exception of Stuart Barnes, that is exactly what did happen.

On the Saturday evening after the First Test I caught the weather forecast for central North Island – New Plymouth is on the central west coast. Some showers, but mainly bright; winds light, was the gist. When the team and media arrived at Christchurch Airport on the Sunday morning to share a 737 charter to New Plymouth, we found that the light winds had freshened somewhat. Indeed, the whole of central North Island was in the grip of such a tempest that all flights were grounded. 'We might take off and try to get into New Plymouth. We can always pull out if it looks dodgy. We may give it a shot,' one of Air New Zealand's ground-staff chiefs told us after a few hours hanging around. Quite all right, old chap. Don't strain yourself. We'll just sit here till the wind goes.

Various plans were formulated by the air powers that be: we could possibly get into Hamilton then drive for four hours to New Plymouth; or get to Auckland, and wait for another connecting flight. McGeechan and Best grew restless. The delay was cutting into training time, the god of the tour. Eventually, Air New Zealand decided to try for New Plymouth. The Lions, bleary after a night of consolation festivities (they were not the most abstemious party ever to leave the shores of Britain and Ireland), boarded, strapped themselves in, stuck their Walkman leads in their ears and sat back. After a pregnant pause, the captain piped up to reveal that a few bits and pieces had fallen off already. Everyone filed off again. Late in the day, the British Lions and the mended aircraft dipped and yawed and bumped into New Plymouth. En route, Flight Lieutenant Underwood gave a lecture on various types of turbulence.

The pride of the area is Mount Egmont, the visual focal point. 'It means as much to us as the white cliffs of Dover mean to English people,' said someone from the home union. 'When you see the mountain you know you are home.' As the Lions checked into their rather humble motel, there was no sign of the mountain. The clouds were down to base level, and it was thrashing down with rain. It rained so hard that the Lions had to abandon plans to train at the main stadium, Rugby Park.

At Oakura Beach, the rollers came in mountain-high and only the nutcase surfers ventured out. At the remarkable Pukekura Park, an amazing cricket ground aspiring to Test status, where the pitch is surrounded by vast natural banks with seats cut along the contour lines, the outfield had sunk. In the town, the Lions took part in desultory ten-pin bowling, complained about damp beds and also that a huge group of supporters had been booked into their hotel. It was nothing personal, and Gavin Hastings always publicly thanked the followers for the astonishing level of support the Lions received. But by the time you have picked clean the bones and chewed the fat of the tour for the twenty-fifth time on the way from your room to the lobby, you can tire of it a little.

Some of us drove up the slopes of Mount Egmont to look-out stations. We looked out on mist. Of the mountain, we could see not one bit.

But something was stirring in Taranaki. It was called interest, and also admiration, excitement, sense of occasion. New Plymouth was unprepossessing.

'Where's the main street?'

'You're standing in it.'

But what are surroundings? The city was Lions-mad. They had been missed off the itinerary altogether in 1983 and they rolled out the brightest, longest, reddest carpet of welcome of the tour. Indeed, the Taranaki stopover almost harked back to the days before TV made every far-flung sporting hero as well known as your own brother.

Every business had a Lions promotion; the home union ran kiddies' coaching alongside the tour; every radio show did Lions interludes. The *Daily News* of New Plymouth issued easily the outstanding special supplement of the whole tour, and kept up a stream of articles until well after the Lions had departed. It was the sort of welcome and the sort of mutually rewarding experience that underlines the essential greatness of Lions tours as boldly as any Test match. You take your tour round, you meet a few new people; you leave an impression, a boost for the sport, a longing for the next time.

Taranaki's name had almost disappeared. They were sponsored by Yarrows, a local bakery, and never was the team name used without 'Yarrows' preceding it. I had the distinct impression at the match that a few people were shouting 'Come on Yarrows', a triumph for sponsor penetration and awareness if hardly for the old ethos. Under IRB law you are not supposed to call your team after the sponsor. There was a fuss in England when Rugby wanted to call themselves Rugby Cement. Rugby Cement was the name of their sponsor. The RFU tut-tutted, it was not on. The trouble is that in the Southern Hemisphere no one seems to have got round to printing up the IRB regulations. Not one. Lost in the post, I suppose. I'm sure they'll come out soon.

Even the grim bits were more fun in New Plymouth. The average rugby function in New Zealand is a dark and heavy affair with warm beer from small pitchers; regimental ties from disgraced regiments. Every press conference on the tour took place in a dungeon spare dressing-room, and every post-match function bar none took place in a slightly bigger dungeon into which the players were crammed like tinned pilchards alongside every rugby man in captivity for a hundred miles around. There would be a rather frugal burst of speech-making in which both teams thanked the other for such a clean and open game, even when the game had been dirty and dreadful, and thanked the referee, even when the referee had been a nightmare. Then Geoff Cooke would dole out a few ties and pin badges and everyone would scuttle for the sanctuary of the team-room.

Yet at New Plymouth even the functions seemed a little lighter. We attended one where the chairman promised that there would be 'none of those long bloody speeches like you have in bloody London'. He then introduced a succession of monster speeches. We had the managing director of Yarrows discursing about his bread. We also had a major oration from J.J. Stewart, the All Black coach of the 1970s. His reminiscences rambled a little, but were mostly satisfyingly sharp. Then he unveiled his master plan for the game. If I understood him correctly, it was that you should be able to pass to a colleague who was upfield to you. At last someone had admitted it. New Zealand are trying to turn our game into basketball.

At full-back Taranaki had Kieran Crowley, a greying figure who
had flown over during the World Cup for the semi-final, played
palpably below his old form and gone back to Taranaki. They also
had a crew-cut, square, fierce loose-head prop who had impressed
with some mighty, bullocking charges in the junior side in the All
Black trials earlier in the tour. Mark Allen, known throughout the
country and especially in his adoring locality as Bull, was the most
astonishing character the Lions met on tour. Imagine a cross
between Gareth Chilcott, Merv Hughes and Terry Wogan and you
just about had Bull. He was everywhere. There were massive
profiles of him in the papers, Bull hugging a Queen impersonator
to promote the match, surrounded by enough kids to swamp the
Pied Piper; Bull fund-raising for charities, Bull revealing his
dreams of playing for the All Blacks.

You could buy Bull T-shirts, Bull horns, Bull mugs. Everytime he
took the ball for a charge the crowd erupted. There was something
in his character, his fearlessness, his ferocity, his approachability
and, yes, his humanity, which galvanised them.

The Lions selection was routine. Clement was at full-back,
Wallace and Tony Underwood on the wing. Vince Cunningham
was chosen for his first match as a Lion in the centre and Scott Gibbs,
just eight days after suffering a serious ankle injury, was fit to
resume in the centre. Barnes and Jones were at half-back. Jones was
having a fraught time. His form was suffering and he had
contracted a sore throat. Apparently, the neat Swansea scrum-half
suffers from recurring sore throats. He was only just able to take his
place on the replacements bench for the First Test.

There was even a report that he was suffering from symptoms of
ME, the strange and supposedly viral affliction known as Yuppie
Flu. He would have been the first Swansea yuppie if so. He was sent
for blood tests in New Plymouth and Andy Nicol, the Scottish
scrum-half, was asked to drop in on New Zealand en route from
Scotland's tour round the South Seas. He arrived in New Plymouth
and revealed that his Lions call-up had cost him a stopover in the
sun in Hawaii. He might even return home without playing,
because Jones' blood test proved negative and he was fit to play.
Nicol was promptly fined at the Players' Court for arriving late.

In the pack, Leonard began his conversion and Wright switched
to the loose head, where he had played in the Five Nations. Cronin
and Johnson teamed up in the second row and Webster and Teague
flanked Galwey.

Despite the dull weather, Rugby Park was full and excited. There
was a mobile tannoy man dressed like a wasp in Taranaki yellow and
black who stoked up the crowd. 'Givvus a wave at the Steinlager
tent! Start a Mexican wave by the 22!' A coach and horses toured the
perimeter throwing out sweets and giant Yarrow's loaves. Being
dive-bombed by a flying sliced Mother's Pride is never my idea of a
fun day out at rugby. There was a troupe of Radio Taranaki
dancing girls who danced as if they meant it. And, if truth were told,
they were watched surreptitiously but avidly through forty-seven

pairs of binoculars in the benches of the, er, temporarily deprived media.

There was electricity in the air when Barnes led on the Lions, still wearing a rather fetching white turban to protect his cut. It was a cracking match and a cracking atmosphere. The Lions won 49-25, there were some splendid tries, some glorious play by the Lions, some thundering charges from Bull and a maestro effort from Crowley at full-back. His footballing skills illuminated the whole match.

The Lions once again slipped in periods of the match, revealing the inability to fashion glorious patches into a full quilt. They trailed 13-6 at one stage, led for the first time near half-time and eventually blasted off near the end. But Leonard held up well, scrummaging against none other than Bull. Barnes, a few mishit kicks apart, brought electricity to the moves; Gibbs was restored, Tony Underwood needle-sharp and Wright happier on the loose head. Moore was barking round the fringes, throwing beautifully.

Johnson is something else. It is something in his body language and body position. He has the gloomy, fierce, challenging look about him that Colin Meads had. His body positions were drummed in when he was on a sojourn in New Zealand, in King Country, with Meads as his chairman of selectors. 'He was a very good lad,' growled the Pine Tree. 'I was very disappointed when he went home.' Johnson did briefly contemplate staying in New Zealand, and began to work his way into national age group teams. If he had stayed he would unquestionably have played for New Zealand in the Tests.

When he was first summoned to the party, there was a good deal of publicity given to wounded reactions from Alan Davies, the Welsh coach. Davies and his men had completed a successful tour in Southern Africa in which the tour captain, Gareth Llewellyn, had played splendidly. Davies roundly castigated the choice of Johnson over Llewellyn. If he was complaining that Llewellyn deserved original selection over Cronin, Reed and, conceivably, Dooley, then he was on firmer ground, but if he meant that Johnson did not deserve to be on tour then he was wrong. Johnson is unquestionably the best young lock in the world.

I first saw Johnson playing for England Schools against Scottish Schools in Glasgow some seasons ago. He seemed a foot taller than anyone on the field; seemed from the side a little languid and diffident, just as a giraffe can seem diffident among smaller beasts. I wondered in print if the fires of battle really burned in him. I need not have wondered. Against Taranaki, the shock of Cronin's blond hair often bobbed up high in the mauls, Johnson was busy driving low. It took about twelve seconds of the game to decide that the new young lock would play every major match for the rest of the tour.

Taranaki charged from the whistle. Crowley kicked a penalty and Taranaki tried to establish a high-pace game (ready with the chicken-head chopper, farmer). They most certainly deserved a try when a splendid movement sent Feleti Mahoni, the young Tonganborn flanker, diving for the line. He was grounded short, extended his arms and touched down. The ref penalised him. 'Double movement,' shouted sages who forgot that in certain circumstances you can make that movement. Mahoni played brilliantly, and within weeks he had been secreted back to Tonga to join their tour of Australia.

Yet Taranaki were not long denied. A superb move, integrating backs and forwards as one, launched Bernie O'Sullivan, the lock, over. Crowley kicked the conversion and a penalty to two penalties by Barnes for a 13-6 lead.

On the half-hour, Galwey departed injured and Clarke arrived. A ripple of comment greeted him. Here was a tour hero. Things began to change in the Lions' favour as soon as he came on. What a coincidence. Scott Gibbs was the first to poke his head above the parapet. It never mattered how unpromising the ball and the situation, however populous the onrushing defence, he could always get the Lions over the advantage line. After thirty-five minutes, he picked up a dead ball yards behind the gain-line, blasted through the defence and Cronin came up on his left and powered over to score.

Six minutes later, Gibbs made another superb run to bale out Wallace, who was caught in around fourteen minds in possession. Gibbs gave a brilliant pass to Clement, who passed inside to Teague, who scored. The score was lucky in that the Lions were awarded the previous scrum when it should clearly have gone to Taranaki. Bull was not amused. Barnes kicked the conversion and it was 20-13.

Cunningham had been gradually finding his feet and he scored a try to finish a lovely movement. Clarke and Webster set up a ruck, Jones passed flat to Barnes, so flat that Barnes was at and through the Taranaki defence almost instantaneously. Cunningham came up alongside and scored. Ah, the burst on to the flat pass. How it opens up the other lot, if you choose to use it. Barnes kicked the conversion.

It was all over bar the roaring soon afterwards, especially after Clement stopped a smashing Taranaki attack with a tackle in the corner on the ageless Crowley. Taranaki may not have fielded a bunch of backs with household names, but they were among the best sets of backs the Lions met.

The Lions made a hash of a pushover attempt. Someone had made the wrong call because as some of the pack set themselves for the drive, others detached and disported themselves as if pulling some other move. The ball went loose towards Tony Underwood, who flicked it back inside, and Jones scuttled over to score.

Leonard had his moment of glory soon afterwards. Taranaki won a five-yard scrum, heeled it and every Taranaki player bar one dashed in alongside Bull and his mates and went for the pushover. It was typical of the inventive approach they brought to the whole match. It also made you yearn for the Lions to steal the ball to see how Crowley coped with all seven Lions backs. However, the Lions

held, Jason gave himself ten out of ten, a gold star and, probably, a
Test jersey.

Andrew Slater, the flanker, did score for Taranaki at the next
attack. It was a profoundly chilling moment because it made the
score 32-18. The press ran a five-dollar sweep at every match in
which you had to guess the exact score. Over forty people were in by
this stage – from photography, television and serious journalism –
and the pot, rolling over, had risen to well over $1,000.

It was difficult to win because of the high scoring on the tour, but
David Hands of *The Times* had 32-18. People began to sweat. 'Come
on, Kieran my son,' we shouted as Crowley tried to wipe out Hands
with his conversion. He missed. Then, shortly afterwards, another
splendid Lions attack sent Wallace away down the right wing. The
entire press box stood up – with the notable exception of Hands –
and cheered him over the line. Nothing personal, David, we said.

By the very end of the tour, everyone was in a fever lest the
winner be someone who would not bung half the proceeds behind
the bar – and there were a few of those – for his colleagues. But the
pot was never won. Some was invested in some champagne for the
Lions to celebrate a rather important victory. The bulk went to
charity.

The feast of scoring never abated. Clarke made another storming
run, Barnes another darting break and Cunningham was in for
another try. Shane McDonald, the nuggety, driving hooker (like all
the others) scored for Taranaki and then Webster set off at the
heart of the Taranaki defence from the tail of a line-out. He
ploughed on massively and when he was held up the play paused
for micro-seconds. Suddenly, Gibbs came up at the perfect angle on
a lightning supporting run. Webster flicked a pass and Gibbs
scored. Sundry goals took it to 49-25.

By this time Andy Nicol had become a Lion. Jones departed four
minutes from the end with a shoulder injury. Some of the Lions
suggested coyly that it was a staged withdrawal to give Nicol his
Lions status. I doubt it. Jones had another difficult match. He was
trying to find himself and challenge for the Test team, and would
surely not have been in the least inclined to wander off with the
game at its height. Nicol fired a few quick passes and disappeared.
'It was marvellous to get on,' he said. 'It would never have been the
same flying home without becoming a proper Lion.'

When the match ended, Bull was swamped by more kids than you
ever saw. When he eventually resurfaced he was shepherded to the
public address system. He blessed the house, thanked everyone for
their support. Soon he was in the dungeons facing the press. How
had Leonard shaped up against him? 'He is very strong and difficult
to move,' said Bull. He went on to express his pride in his men. He
was justified. Watching him chatting away, a street-level regular
bloke elevated by his talent for playing rugby, watching him
revelling in the spotlight, beaming and joking, you wondered if he
ever would become an All Black. Are All Blacks not supposed to

hold a grimness and gravitas? Or will they let the Bull loose on an unsuspecting world? I hope so.

Barnes paid tribute to the occasion. 'There was a buzz in the crowd and Taranaki played at high pitch. It was one of the best occasions of the tour,' he said. Cooke explained that Nicol was departing for home, his period of cover now over. He also announced that Dooley was to return to the tour now that his father's funeral was over. It seemed unlikely that Blackpool's second most famous tower would make the Test team, but his presence was warmly sought.

That was Taranaki. The Lions moved on for a short flight to Auckland. Anyone who toured with his head up would have left with happy memories.

Some of us drove out of Taranaki early in the morning. The wind had died, the rain had stopped, the sun was shining. And there, standing majestically above the town, snow-capped and clear, was Mount Egmont. It looked beautiful.

That evening in the Lions' hotel in downtown Auckland, Cooke and McGeechan announced the team to play Auckland; the men, therefore, in whose hands the remainder of the tour would rest. From the First Test team, Paul Burnell was stood down and Jason Leonard was chosen at tight head. Moore was at hooker in place of Milne, who had been disappointingly low of profile. Johnson took over from Andy Reed, who had by no means let down the Lions in the First Test.

'The new people have the chance to stake a claim,' said Cooke. 'The experiment of shifting Jason worked reasonably well against Taranaki. Brian Moore has been going well. Andy Reed has been struggling a little bit lately and Martin [Johnson] did enough.' Those were the selections the Lions intended. However, Leonard had a leg injury and was unable to play. It was a severe frustration. Richards had his calf injury so he withdrew as well. Burnell returned for Leonard, Clarke moved to number 8 and Webster came in for the big match he deserved.

Webster was by no means quick around the field – indeed, his weight had mushroomed to over 17 stones during the tour. He was not the complete flanker because he was not as quick as Winterbottom to the ball and did not, quite, have Winterbottom's brilliant gift of anticipation and running the most economical lines, a gift which took Winters to the action yards ahead of people who had more basic speed. Webster was also a little short to convert to the blind side, because there you need to be a factor in the line-out. But around the fringes he was as good as anyone in New Zealand, and anyone in the Lions party. In any case, the simplistic pre-tour assessments that the whole battle in the loose would be settled purely by the openside flankers racing to the loose ball were not borne out. As McGeechan had said, around a thousand times, 'I want all our players to be adaptable and interchangeable. If they are the nearest man to the ball it is up to them to win it, whether they are forwards or backs.'

Webster was also one of the core figures off the field, a life-and-soul man, a target for banter and something of a contrast to the more scientific members of the party. He was deemed, apparently, to be rather missable company in the long evenings. 'Are we going out for a drink tonight?' he asked Best, with whom he had established a fierce double act of deprecating banter.

'Webster,' drawled Best, 'I would rather stick needles in my eyes.'

There was one other change for Auckland, and it was one which was forced on the Lions selectors. Will Carling was left out and Scott Gibbs came in. It was forced simply because Gibbs was playing like a dream and had bounced up from the Southland stretcher so quickly. Carling had not begun well, particularly against the Maoris. 'I was not as sharp as I wanted to be in the early stages,' he admitted. There was no shame in being left out, but because it was Carling the icon and not Carling the bloke, it made big news. I took part in a radio interview on the evening the team to play Auckland was announced, in which the first question was: 'Is this the end of Will Carling's career?'

'I should think so,' I replied. 'I would have thought that, apart from winning another thirty caps for England, probably leading them to the Five Nations Championship at least twice and more and then playing at his peak during the 1995 World Cup and the 1997 Lions tour, he has just about had it.'

What of Gibbs? Did the management now regard him as one of the leading centres in the world? Because that is exactly what he had become. The question was too lively for the management dead bat. 'It is another chance for us to compare progress against top-quality opposition,' they boringly said, through their muzzles.

'Scott has gone well,' said Cooke. 'Some of Will's performances have been fairly unspectacular but solid. He is a solid member of the tour party.'

The original selection for the Auckland match also revealed in all its starkness the abject disappearance of the Scottish contribution. Apart from Gavin Hastings, there was no longer a single Scot in the first team (Burnell did return, but for one match only). Of the original party chosen, Gary Armstrong withdrew before departure; Scott Hastings was invalided home; Burnell had paid the price for a lack of all-round surging in the loose; Wright was simply not of the required class – he tended to stand around blowing like a shot buffalo in the fast matches. For his hands-on-hips stance he became known as Teapot. Milne and Reed had lost their edge and Cronin had never mounted any challenge for the Tests.

It did not reflect at all well on the original selection, especially on the Scottish selectors, who included McGeechan. As I said before the tour began, the major anxieties were that there might prove to be too many old English and too many Scots who had never shown the capacity to dominate international matches. The first anxiety was not borne out; the second came fluttering home to roost. Many of the British newspapers sought reactions from Jeff Probyn, the discarded prop who was left at home and who had received a letter from Geoff Cooke before the Lions departed consoling him but stating that the tour had come a year too late for him. And now the Lions were trying to gerrymander a team as they went along, converting a tight head. The All Black front row must have often found it difficult not to cackle whenever they went down for a scrum, such is Probyn's standing in the game.

Auckland, on paper, were a mighty force. John Kirwan was on the right wing, playing for a recall to the Black colours (he had lost over a stone in weight) and Eroni Clarke on the left, as Tuigamala was not fit. The full All Black front row of Brown, Fitzpatrick and Dowd were on parade and Lee Stensness, the blond and clever young back, was in the centre alongside Waisake Sotutu. The world's leading right foot was at fly-half. Sotutu is a Fijian, and seeing his name on the sheet made you aware yet again of the fantastic fortune of New Zealand and Australia in that they can so easily import Fijians, Samoans and Tongans for their domestic and representative rugby and, at a deeper level, in that the relative economic conditions exist which tug the islanders across in the first place. If all the three island teams could select and train all their available nationals for a World Cup, the rest of us would be playing to make up the numbers.

On the day before the Auckland match came a distraction. Cooke announced, with a face like thunder, that the Four Home Unions were preventing Dooley from rejoining the party. It was one of those asinine administrative howlers that rugby is so addled by.

On the press side, we all tore up our articles in preparation and started again. This is what *The Sunday Times* would have printed on the Sunday were it not for the overriding need, in the public interest, to run instead a piece on the European Vegetarian Pie-Eating Championships.

> On Thursday, the tours committee of the Four Home Unions – the body which organises Lions' tours and which must now, as a matter of urgency, be relieved of the responsibility – declared that Wade Dooley, the Lions lock, should not be allowed to rejoin the Lions on their current tour. Dooley had to leave the tour due to a family bereavement and was replaced by Martin Johnson, the Leicester lock.
>
> The New Zealand RU were prepared to welcome Dooley back with warmth. They said so when he departed and they said so at New Plymouth, when his decision to return was announced. So were the players. 'A great guy,' said Peter Winterbottom. 'An inspiration,' said Gavin Hastings. The Home Unions effectively told Dooley to stay at home. You see, in the fine print of the tour agreement, a document which is never put into the public domain, it states in broad terms that you must not have more than the quota of thirty players on the tour.

'We are very sorry,' said Ronnie Dawson, the chairman, 'but that is what the tour agreement states.' There was no provision, he said, for Dooley to return. It was not covered in the agreement. The secret bureaucracy would not allow it. No doubt, it was more than Dawson's job was worth, etc.

They should redraft that agreement. There should be a clause which reads something like this: 'If a great player who has given his heart and soul to the game, who has flogged himself endlessly to prepare for the tour, who has been an inspiration to every member of the party, should have to go home because the father to whom he was so close dies suddenly, and if that player has the fervent wish to honour his late father by playing on, and also wishes to retire from the game, not in bed with his boots off, but out with the Lions on the field of play, then that player should be allowed to join the tour; and not even the most pernickety and pompous pronouncement from a faceless and, to the general public, unaccountable rugby bureaucrat should stop him.'

Perhaps my proposal needs a little tidying here and there. Perhaps it is not quite in the requisite garbagese of the average rugby rule-book. But it will do for me. And I have thirty Lions, all three members of the team management and the two medical people to second the proposal for me as well.

Friday training sessions are nervous affairs in which the Lions, tension gnawing, usually wish to be left alone. On Friday the travelling media group were besieged with players demanding that their support for Wade Dooley be communicated back to the British Isles. It is to the eternal credit of Geoff Cooke, the manager, that he was prepared to speak out so forcefully at the 'lack of sympathy' of his masters back at home. Cooke handed out a fearsome pasting at what he saw as the totally unsympathetic attitude of Dawson and the unhelpful actions of Bob Weighill, the Home Unions secretary.

'The whole squad is incensed. It is an appalling way to treat a person who has done so much for the game. We are always talking about the amateur ethos in our game and if ever there was a case for that ethos then this was it.

'For our own people to raise objections when the New Zealand Rugby Union has been so considerate is staggering. It started with Bob Weighill, who was very negative in his approach.'

Gavin Hastings joined the battle. 'It is nonsense. It shows no compassion. It totally destroys the ethos which everyone says is great about rugby.' John Dowling, of the New Zealand RFU council, said: 'What a kick in the teeth for someone who has just lost his dad.' Dooley himself was quoted down the line from Blackpool. 'All sorts of obstacles have been put in my way. I would love to have come back. Now I am staying at home.'

So Dooley stayed at home. It was a disgraceful episode. He had to finish his career in bed with his boots off, so to speak. He may believe that he was denied the opportunity to end his career in a British Lions Test jersey.

Would he have made the Test team? Probably not. He almost certainly would not have dislodged Johnson, who had thrived since joining as his replacement. However, had he not had to leave in the first place he may well have won the final fulfilment. Even though he was nowhere near as effective as he was in his greatest days, he was still more of a proposition than Cronin or Reed for the place alongside Johnson, for his flinty attitude alone. As it turned out, his attitude would have served the tour party wonderfully well, because the second string were to come spectacularly to grief.

But if Wade feels as much as a teaspoon of unfulfilment then he should forget it. For me, he was one of the best forwards of his generation, at his best the premier lock in world rugby. Of England's locks in history, only Paul Ackford could challenge him. The engine-room they stoked was the most powerful in English history. Their attitudes were harsh – the punch Dooley landed on Phil Davies at Cardiff, the blow he struck Doddie Weir at Murrayfield were unacceptable. Yet he was in jungle warfare, and he stuck by the statute-book of jungle law. The white headbands of Dooley and Ackford, toppling forward to drive on the next ruck or maul, were the most inspiring sight. They were also the signature of the remarkable recovery of English international rugby in the last five years.

Throughout the 1992-93 season, there was talk that Dooley had declined: a season too far, a tour too far, should bow out gracefully, all that stuff. I believe that his declining effectiveness had only a little to do with his own power loss. It was not Dooley who drifted away from the game, it was the game which drifted away from Dooley. His overwhelming strengths were in the thrashing hurly-burly of the line-out; in holding off the spoilers in the opposition with his inside arm and reaching the ball with the outside arm. He was a master in the unseen world; and also as the second wave into the loose. In the days when you had to shift the whole ruck or maul forward, he and Ackford provided the bulldozer drive, the most irresistible injection of power.

Now, with the misguided tinkering and sanitisation of the line-out and the unnecessary outside arm law, the environment has changed. In the loose, now that ball-winning and recycling depend on pure luck and a few moments of scrabbling at the tackle, his other spheres of operation were taken away as well. Forward play, by comparison with a season ago, had become soft as melted butter. The real hard men were left with no role. He and some of the other hard-core forwards around the world were giants reduced by law-making pygmies.

So he did not end his representative career in the red jersey of the British Lions, alongside players who still had an enormous respect and affection for him, players who were there partly because, in the years of his pomp, big Wade had driven them onwards and upwards.

The Auckland match was a bitter disappointment. Auckland won 23-18 and yet again, even after hours of training and team meetings and nine matches, the Lions could still not extend their periods of classy and powerful rugby into eighty minutes; they did not have the hinge at half-back to drag them out of fifty-fifty matches into victory because neither Andrew nor Morris had the pace and touch to give Guscott and company the extra foot of space and time.

Auckland had not lost to a touring team for twelve years, and they have held the Ranfurly Shield since 1985. Good for them. But the truth is that at Eden Park, before a large and yet muted crowd, they were boring, fitful and quite eminently, rampagingly beatable. And yet they could concede seven points for a completely unjustified converted penalty try to the Lions and still win with some ease, could still win from 15-8 down when, as they did in almost every match, the Lions mystifyingly turned off the taps just when they were gushing. The major matches had arrived, and they were being lost. Panic stations.

As ever, there was clear evidence of sharpness behind the Lions scrum. Guscott and Gibbs played well off each other, Gibbs making his familiar short bursts, appearing omnipresent in support and tackling. Johnson did enough to sew up his Test place and Burnell held on well in the scrum. It was never his courage which could be faulted. Everyone did their bit, but only a bit. The tactics were also lamentably poor.

There were anxieties for the Second Test. Hastings suffered a freakish hamstring injury just before half-time – freakish in that it was an impact injury, not one caused by over-stretching the muscle. Hamstrings, traditionally, take at least two weeks to clear up. Poor Carling had to play the second half at full-back, where the inch-perfect kicking of Fox taunted him unmercifully.

The Lions were off to their traditional start. They were behind in less than a minute when Johnson was penalised by David Bishop, the referee, after the kick-off. Hastings brought the Lions level with a penalty soon afterwards, and after twenty-three minutes, most of which the Lions had controlled, came the penalty try.

They set up the position after Guscott and Gibbs had made space through the midfield, and Andrew set off with Evans outside him. Andrew ran on bravely to draw the defence but that lack of an extra yard in his legs held up Evans just enough. Evans was still able to run outside Eroni Clarke, but Kirwan came dashing from the opposite wing to bring off a superb tackle. However, the next attack was driven on in turn by all three of the Lions back-row men, and as Morris waited for the ball, Eroni Clarke helped to kill the ruck set up by Webster by diving garishly into Lions' ranks. Brian Moore came jumping in from way back to try to rake him out, an action which, as Moore well knew, would have given away a penalty in any other country.

However, even though the ruck was taking place only a few yards from the Auckland line, it was most certainly on the floor and stopped. To say that a try would probably have been scored from that particular attack, as the law requires, was pushing it too far. But Mr Bishop sauntered to the posts, Hastings popped over the conversion and those were the luckiest seven points the Lions scored on tour. Afterwards, Zinzan Brooke had no complaint, which was as surprising as the original decision.

The Lions spent one minute too long on self-congratulation. Auckland drove on the kick-off, worked the ball to the right and Stensness, even though running at full pace, was able to steady and put through a glorious, controlled little chip for Kirwan. It travelled only a few yards, but it wrong-footed Rory Underwood and Kirwan seized it and scored, rising to gesticulate with a variety of gesticulations to whoever he felt needed gesticulating unto.

But the Lions scored again after half an hour and this score was beyond carping. Bayfield and Popplewell set up the ball and Morris, Gibbs, Webster, Guscott and Hastings, handling beautifully, sent Evans away. It was time for a trademark Ieuan try. He cut inside two and outside one to score. It was clinical finishing, and it was also, to be frank, a bold reminder that the Lions had stopped investing sufficient of their destiny in their brilliant outside backs.

At the start of the second half, Ben Clarke made a storming burst down the left wing, carving through in what seemed suspiciously like an outside break. He dived for the line, reached it in a tackle as he bounced on the ground. The try might well have been allowed in Britain. Mr Bishop, practically the only official in the Southern Hemisphere who has the respect of European rugby players after the untimely death of Kerry Fitzgerald, gave a penalty to Auckland. 'That would have made it 23-11,' said McGeechan. 'Auckland would not have come back.'

But they did come back. From the thirty-fifth minute to the seventieth minute, Fox kicked five penalties for Auckland. The Lions' only reply was a penalty from Andrew. Fox may be the least compelling rugby player on the planet to everyone else, but his own forwards gain sustenance from his brilliant kicking. Most of the penalties were awarded under New Zealand's continuity obsession. If the other team poaches the ball in the line-outs, scrums or loose play, the referee is encouraged to assume that skulduggery is afoot. Don't these defending teams realise that in the warped Kiwi scheme of things, one team is supposed to have the ball until they score, unhindered by such matters as the other lot's right to have the ball too?

While Fox hoisted his kicks to rain down on the Lions' emergency full-back, another emergency full-back hung around in trepidation on the Auckland side. Shane Howarth had departed injured after only thirteen minutes and Sotutu, on the evidence of the day not the world's most accomplished all-round footballer, donned his tin hat and waited for his bombardment. It never came. The Lions should have tested his nerve and talent rigorously, to the point of vindictiveness. He was allowed to escape almost untroubled.

Afterwards, Graham Henry, the Auckland coach, had favourable words for the Lions. He was asked to compare them with Transvaal, who had just beaten Auckland in the Super-10 final. 'My gut feeling is that the Lions are a better side than Transvaal. I thought Scott Gibbs had an outstanding game.' In fact, the Lions were easily a better team than Transvaal. Basically, they were in a different league altogether. But how was Henry to know that? Against his team, they had played only half a match.

'There is no need for gloom and doom,' said Gavin Hastings. 'We showed that, basically, we are a good side,' said Cooke. 'We should have won,' said McGeechan, 'but there were too many errors under pressure.'

This sort of reaction at this stage of the tour was all very well as long as the Lions management did not actually believe a word of it themselves. Many observers had grown restive with the lack of booming proclamations at these press conferences that the Lions were fading on the scoreboard and that they had bloody well better get their backsides into gear. I pointed out that the public face was acceptable provided that behind the closed doors of the team-room, the Lions were told that their tilt at history was passing them by. At least all this focused the mind. If they also lost the Second Test then the tour would end in shambles. They had one chance left. Those of us who were convinced that they were a far better team than their results were also growing restive.

The Lions moved on to Napier, the curious resort diagonally across the North Island on the lower east coast. It is a remarkable place – the nearest equivalent in outward appearance is probably Portmeirion in North Wales. Large parts of Napier were levelled by a powerful earthquake in the 1930s. In the quake and a subsequent fire, 250 people perished. When the architects sat down to begin planning the rebuilding, art deco was in, so today Napier is a shrine to art deco. There are art deco hotels, art deco massage parlours, art deco Chinese restaurants and shops and homes. The art deco then evolves in places into Striped Classical and Spanish Mission (it says in the guidebook). It made you wonder about similar accidents of history. If much of Britain had been levelled in the 1960s then everyone would now be cooped up in ghastly jerry-built tower blocks.

Hawke's Bay itself is in a premier wine-growing area, one of the places which have jacked up even further New Zealand's well-deserved reputation for wines. The Lions made a few vineyard visits but, given the stage of the tour, they could hardly let their tastebuds loose on vast quantities.

The Lions checked into their seafront hotel, where the soup of the day was pumpkin. Around the corner at the media hotel, the soup of the day was pumpkin. The Lions sat down on the Sunday afternoon to watch the New Zealand rugby league team narrowly fail to land the biggest prize of the international game when a dropped goal by Australia levelled the First Test of a three-Test series seconds before the end at Mount Smart.

More to the point, they also heard that the closeness of the First Test had nudged the All Black selectors into life. They chopped Strachan at scrum-half and replaced him with Wellington's Jon Preston, who had impressed way back in August when coming on as a replacement at Ellis Park; they removed Ian Jones and replaced him with Mark Cooksley, who had played so well in the line-out for the Maoris. And, since Walter Little had not recovered from his ligament injury, they nudged Eroni Clarke inside to the centre and John Kirwan made his ceremonial return to the wing.

None of these selections bothered the Lions in any way. They respected Jones more than Cooksley and, since Rory Underwood had caught Kirwan without the least trouble when he'd made a break in the Auckland match, they doubted whether Kirwan was anything like the force of old. Clarke was simply a bread-and-butter threequarter, and more sliced cottage than Mighty White. But for the Lions, there was the nagging sight of Hastings limping and taking very little part in training.

He did far better when some of the squad made a flying personal appearance at a training session for hundreds of young children at McLean Park (what was wrong with calling it Rugby Park the same as everywhere else?). He addressed the young troops with inspiration and humour and he and the other Lions made a fine impression as they moved among the children, dispensing advice and autographs.

The dirt-trackers were to be led again by Stuart Barnes. 'I haven't come here to be captain of the midweek team,' he had said with feeling. But there he was. The rest of the team was standard (or below standard, as it turned out): Clement was at full-back, Wallace and Tony Underwood on the wings and Carling in the centre alongside Cunningham. Barnes and Jones were at half-back. The Leonard experiment continued at tight head and Milne, Wright, Cronin and Reed made up a mostly Scottish front five. Galwey, Webster and Teague were in the back row.

Hawke's Bay were not having a fantastic season. On the day of the Lions match against Otago they had challenged Auckland for the Ranfurly Shield at Eden Park (you can rarely accuse Auckland, so their rivals say, of putting the Shield on the line against anyone they might not beat). The Bay had lost by 69-31, one of those pointlessly ludicrous and unsatisfying scores. They had scored five tries, one of them a glorious length-of-the-field effort, but they had conceded a few as well.

On paper, their team lacked celebs – though not sponsorships. Every single player, and the touch-judges, were sponsored. Marketing activity in the Bay was frenetic. Apparently, Norm Hewitt (Napier Textiles Ltd) was as big a hero to the Bay followers as Bull Allen was at Taranaki. Simon Tremain (Bay Motors), son of the celebrated Kel Tremain, the glorious All Black who had died at Christmas, was at number 8.

George Konia (Onekawa Automotive Services) was a clever centre who had appeared in the All Black trials. The powerhouse consisted of two Englishmen, Bill Davidson (McMillin Craig Ltd) and John Fowler (Liquor King Napier), who had long been useful but not stratospheric members of that strange brotherhood called London club rugby. They were both playing for the Celtic club in Hawke's Bay. Jarrod Cunningham, the full-back, was sponsored by the local MP, Michael Laws. A general election was due later in the year. I hope that the voters of Hawke's Bay have short memories: poor Jarrod was to have such a miserable match that otherwise, Mr Laws might poll fewer votes than Screaming Lord Sutch in a non-Loony area.

The weather forecast had underlined that we should take a raincoat to McLean Park for the match. We sat sweating in the stand in our coats on a most beautiful day. McLean Park is a delightful ground, bright and spacious, and when the Lions came, packed to the rafters. It has various snazzy stands and a massive bank on which the travelling punters hoisted their Union Jacks. We sat watching the tumultuous pre-match entertainment. The sky was a glorious blue, and from our seats you could look out beyond the streets of art deco to the Pacific, lapping in the distance on Napier beach. In the programme, there was an article by Steve Lunn, a local referee. In it he denied that there were differences in law interpretations round the world. 'I wonder whether different interpretations between countries really exist.' Welcome back, Steve. You have obviously spent the last decade on Mars.

It was an afternoon of almost cringing embarrassment. The Lions lost by 29-17, and against a team which in the first half were almost entirely clueless, and in which Jarrod Cunningham and the other kickers had missed eight kicks between them. Furthermore, the Lions had led 17-5 at half-time.

The Bay forwards were splendid. Storming Norm Hewitt already stood out, as did the splendidly named Orcades Crawford on the tight head. In the first half, the Hawke's Bay performance constituted the biggest letting-down ever recorded of one department of a team by another. The forwards won the ball; the backs were nervous, their judgment was appalling and their kicking was atrocious. And this was the team that beat a Lions outfit which, second-string players or not, was composed entirely of international rugby players, men who had represented their countries.

As the match wore on, the Lions forward effort amounted to Richard Webster. The concerted forward action was impossible to criticise. How can you lambast something which does not exist? Cronin, the pack leader, was simply not up to it. He came storming up to try to recover the drop-outs and kick-offs. When he arrived he took his eye off the ball and flapped at thin air. The front five forwards never figured. Their work-rate was a disgrace. Some of them walked around the field. It meant that the backs took a fearsome hammering when they were rucking and mauling without support. As the forwards never bothered to tackle, Robert Jones, Stuart Barnes, Will Carling and Vince Cunningham spent most of their afternoon tackling rampaging forwards head-on.

Once Hewitt was at full steam he was irresistible. He went storming at poor Tony Underwood on four occasions. Underwood was embarrassed (though not half as embarrassed as Hewitt would have been had anyone bothered to give Tony the ball to run at Norm), but he was entitled to look around and wonder why his forwards were standing with hands on hips in the middle of the field rather than tackling their opposite numbers.

Surely you have to assume that something was affecting some of the Lions. The only other conclusion that could possibly be drawn as Hawke's Bay swarmed all over them in the second half was that they were not trying, had given up. I have to say that, unpalatable as it may be, that is certainly the overwhelming impression I received sitting in the safety of the stands.

Thank goodness that, even though Cooke tried to smooth over any question of lack of effort and pride afterwards, McGeechan finally came out of his shell. Was he satisfied with the commitment of some of the Lions forwards, I asked him?

'No,' he said. 'Some of them did not do justice to the jersey they were wearing. Some of them have got to look good and hard at themselves.'

The scoring had started with a collector's item – a Carling dropped goal. Vincent Cunningham had set up the position. Barnes took the score to 6-0 with a penalty after a period of Hawke's Bay pressure in which Hewitt was heavily involved. However, Jarrod Cunningham could not give his team the sustenance of points on the board. But Hawke's Bay did score the first try. They drove the ball to the Lions' line, Reed stood out on the fringes awaiting developments and, when the ball came back, Hewitt simply buried straight through his tackle to score.

In the second quarter, with the Hawke's Bay backs in such a mess it was inconceivable that they had ever met before, the Lions scored the points which should have set up a 40-point victory. The impressive Carling rewon the ball after a Hawke's Bay midfield shambles for a Webster try and Barnes kicked his second and third penalties. It was 17-5.

In the second half, you felt as sorry for Carling and the Lions backs as you had for Hewitt and the Hawke's Bay forwards in the first. There was no excuse in the refereeing for what happened, even though Paddy O'Brien of North Otago was quite appalling. Imagine a boat race crew which has trained together for months, but towards the end of the race three of the eight stop rowing, and it will give you some idea of their performance. Some of the driving and rucking by Hewitt and Crawford of Hawke's Bay and even some of the line-out work by the unconsidered Davison and Fowler was outstanding. It just shows what the hardness of New Zealand rugby can do for under-achievers in the soft south of England.

This is absolutely not to say that at any stage Hawke's Bay became an irresistible force. It was just that they were playing a movable object. Jarrod Cunningham started the ball rolling by managing a penalty. Neil Weber, the scrum-half, burrowed over for a try after a drive led by the Hawke's Bay front row, and Simon Kerr, the fly-half, kicked a goal to make it 16-17 as the crowd grew increasingly feverish.

After sixty-four minutes, Hawke's Bay took the lead. The Lions lost their own line-out throw and Kerr dropped a superb goal. Four minutes later, after Hawke's Bay had swarmed through on to a desperate line-out tap from Reed, they catapulted Simon Tremain for the line. It was a lovely moment for him. He spoke afterwards of honouring the memory of his father, that wondrous flanker. Kerr kicked the goal and added a penalty later, by which time the body language of the Lions had developed laryngitis and the likes of Clement and Carling were staring about themselves in disbelief.

The crop-haired, squat Norm Hewitt shyly addressed the press afterwards. He must have been staggered, as a fierce man but also a realist, at how easily his bunch of game triers had overturned an illustrious touring team. McGeechan found nothing in the performance. 'Possession slipped away. The set pieces fell away badly. We took contact at all the wrong times. I don't think Hawke's Bay were any better than Taranaki and we blew them away.'

There was something of a shocked silence later as a bunch of Brits waited at Napier Airport, some for the short hop down to Wellington, others, on the supporters' packages, for an attractive few days in Queenstown, the ski resort. For many of the thousands of visiting fans it was the first game of their package. The final midweek match was to be against the mighty Waikato, a piece of planning which only the Four Home Unions could have achieved. The only Saturday matches left were Tests. There seemed a chance that they might have shelled out a hard-earned grand or two and were not even going to see their heroes in victory.

# CHAPTER 17

# *Day of Thunder*

## THE SECOND TEST

It was a relief for everyone to be back in Wellington. The team hotel was in the busy downtown area and close to a waterfront development with some lively restaurants. And, at least for the Test, the first team would be playing there.

A press function thrown in the ballroom of another hotel by the Wellington press club brought back vivid memories of the 1983 Lions tour. In that very room, I and some of my colleagues had attended a disco and dinner on a slow night on that ill-fated tour. One of the lads soon struck up a promising relationship with a ravishing dark girl with long, black hair. We left them to dance the night away and turned back to our chilled and fizzy New Zealand beer.

People began to sidle up to our table. 'Is that your mate?' they asked, pointing to our hero about to enter full snogging mode. 'You'd better tell him that the person he's dancing with is a transvestite.'

We contemplated letting him stew, contemplated the little surprises in store for him later. Then we decided to tell him. We tried to catch his eye but he looked away, engrossed. We waved. He waved happily back, assuming we were being matey. Eventually he/she went off to the gents/ladies. We rushed on to the dance floor, grabbed our man by the lapels and took him to a quiet spot at the back of the bar. He was taken aback. 'What the bloody hell's the matter?' he said anxiously.

'That woman you're with.'

'Yes?'

'Prepare yourself for a major shock.'

'What the bloody hell's the matter?'

He/she was returning. 'It's a bloke. It's a transvestite!'

'Oh, that. I know *that*.'

We made a contemplative withdrawal back to our fizzy stuff.

In 1993 both camps withdrew from the public gaze, emerging only briefly into the TV lights of the world. The city was gradually gearing up, becoming alive with rugby people from all parts of the globe.

Laughing Laurie spoke warmly of the contribution that the Lions had made to New Zealand rugby. 'They have been a tremendous boost, far more so than any other tour in the last five years. It would be a major tragedy for the game here if they stopped coming. It would be a sad loss. It is also a tremendous learning experience. Both the All Blacks and the provincial teams have learned a lot. They are teaching us heaps about the line-out, especially.'

In the Lions camp the atmosphere was building to a fever. They announced a twenty-three-man squad of players for the Test instead of a final selection. To the team which began the First Test were added Clement, Gibbs, Barnes, Jones, Moore, Leonard, Webster and Teague. It was portrayed as a major psychological coup. It wasn't. It was a sign of anxiety that Hastings and Richards were struggling for fitness.

At the end of the week the team was announced. Gibbs duly took over from Carling, Moore from Milne, Johnson from Reed, Leonard from Burnell. Nick Popplewell pronounced his delight 'at being part of the English pack'. By the time the team had its public run-out on the Friday before the game, it seemed as if Richards was running freely.

Hastings, however, was not running freely. He hardly executed a single kick. At one point in the session, Hastings stood aside and went over to talk to Geoff Cooke. They were joined by Ian McGeechan and Dr James Robson. After a while, they called over Tony Clement, the reserve full-back. There was some earnest discussion. They dispersed. Was Gavin having problems, the management were asked? He was completely fit, they said. It doesn't look like it, we said.

They also said something even more curious. Geoff Cooke revealed that he expected Ian Jones to appear in the match. But Geoff, we said, the All Blacks have dropped him and say that Cooksley is completely fit. Apparently, Jones had packed down in a number of scrums in secret training. 'Only a little test to see how the shove compared,' Mains had said. 'The Lions might play little games but we will have no part of them.' No Jones then? Hmmm.

On the night before the game we listened to the weather forecast. We had watched the second rugby league Test at Palmerston North on television. It was a shambles as far as the staging went, with punters on the touchline hiding the match from the cameras and a long delay towards the end as the players stood in the torrential rain while someone found a ball. Palmerston is not so far from Wellington. It looked likely that a filthy day was blowing down for our Test. The weather forecast, amazingly, declared that it would be a sunny and calm day. Yeah, yeah.

The day dawned. It was glorious, sunny and warm and with only a fresh blow. The forecast had been right. Was it an omen that things were changing? Some of us ate a nervous lunch before the match. Even the hardened pros were affected by the magnitude of the day, the tightrope the tour was treading.

'What is the soup of the day?' we asked, almost rhetorically.

'Cauliflower,' said the waitress. Cauliflower? The correct forecast? Pumpkin soup off the card? Something was in the air. At the ground, the tension wrapped itself around us. The Kiwi/Yankee singing troupe was there to sing the New Zealand anthem in the style of a third-placed entrant in a Japanese Elvis soundalike contest.

Then came Inga and Ieuan and their staring competition. Tuigamala puts all he has into the *haka*, all the tongue-flicking and eye-rolling he can muster. In the First Test, Evans had stood opposite and stared back. Inga won – Ieuan looked away first. At Athletic Park, after the *haka*, Ieuan and Inga stared at each other for so long that it seemed possible that the match would have to carry on around them. Unless my binoculars were mistaken, Inga turned away first.

Glory days. It was like nothing I have ever seen. The Lions won by 20-7, a thrashing every bit as painful for New Zealand as it looked on the scoreboard, and then some. It was a victory played to the incessant, galvanising exhortations to the Lions from the travelling thousands who drowned out the rest of Athletic Park, and afterwards, besieged the tunnel, the dressing-rooms and the team hotel in rapture.

This was the All Blacks shattered. It was a glorious victory, and day, which shook all the smug people who always assume that the Kiwi way is the best. At the press conference the day before, one of the New Zealand journalists had prefaced a question to Laurie Mains with: 'When we win tomorrow. . .'

It was a performance of massive character and courage, of talent and ability. And, the Lord be praised, it was sustained. The Lions kept it up for eighty minutes, no long dips or lapses, nothing left to chance. It was unquestionably one of the greatest days in the history of Lions tours. It was also a rare and welcome victory for a success-starved nation 12,000 miles away. 'At last we have a winner', was the back-page headline in *The Sunday Times*.

It was impossible at the time, and it is still impossible, to drag Lions heroes from the whole pride. Perhaps Andrew and Morris for their tenacity, and for their control of events; Bayfield for the line-out riches he mined; the back row for their domination of their opposite numbers; the square, thundering Popplewell.

It was also the day when New Zealand's obsessions burned them. Laurie Mains, the loudest proponent of the new ruck/maul law and one of a series of New Zealand coaches to put the cause of continuity higher than any other aspect, found so many pigeons coming home to roost that they would have choked Trafalgar Square. .

Here was real continuity. The All Blacks, although beaten in the primary phases, especially in the line-out by Bayfield and Johnson, won a massive 46 rucks, twice as many as the Lions. They would set the ball up through Fitzpatrick or Tuigamala or Bunce, then off it would go again through another series of rucks and mauls, to dead-end after dead-end. For a start, the Lions defence was quite wonderfully well organised and the Lions forwards, as Laughing Laurie's lovely new law allows them to do, stood out on the fringes, where Clarke, Richards and Winterbottom were unbreachable.

And New Zealand found that continuity in itself means nothing; that you can win the ball through three or through 300 phases and the defence can still be there, no longer sucked in to the focal point of the old-style driving mauls and rucks. It meant that the New Zealand backs had to show some imagination. They had none. They put their heads down and ploughed on. There was never a flash of brilliance, nothing sublime and nothing inspired.

After the match Mains complained about the Lions' approach. 'What did the Lions do with all the ball they won?' he asked. They scored a whole lot more points than your lot, Laurie, we thought. In any case, Rob Andrew was absolutely correct, down the wind in the second half, to larrup the ball vast distances down the field. What, pray, would Grant Fox have done with a useful lead and the wind behind him in a crucial Test? Whizzed the ball across the line like a hot potato? I rather doubt it.

There was another bonus for the Lions in the refereeing of Patrick Robin, the French referee. He applied the laws. He pulled up the Lions for throwing the ball in crooked, he did not allow the All Blacks to dive on and over the ball. This was by a distance the best refereeing effort of the tour (the Third Test was a similarly praiseworthy effort from Robin), and it also paid regard to some of the contents of the law-book.

There were also two turning-points that did not involve scores for the Lions but which gave that inner sustenance which even tries are pushed to provide. There was a stupendous tackle. John Kirwan had tried to initiate a move after bursting on to a short inside pass and he ran into Ben Clarke. By the time Clarke had completed the tackle, Kirwan was yards and yards back up the field. At one stage it seemed that Kirwan might be dumped over the back wall of the stadium. It was a king hit, a tackle from the same bracket as the one with which Mick Skinner broke French hearts when he hammered Mark Cecillon in Paris in 1991. Clarke later discovered that one paper had apparently attributed his wonderful tackle to Dean Richards. 'Charming!' he said.

The other seminal moment was a goal-line stand by the Lions scrum. Early in the second half, a set of massed All Black attacks, led by Jamie Joseph, established a five-yard scrum on the Lions line – albeit with M Robin's one howler, when the scrum was awarded to the All Blacks even though the dying ruck into which they had taken the ball, was nowhere near the Lions in-goal area, as the law requires. The All Blacks heeled and went for the pushover. 'We could feel them getting themselves together for the big effort,' said Brian Moore afterwards. At first, the Lions' scrum held steady. Then they drove forward a few precious, life-giving inches, perhaps only two feet altogether. Two feet on the pitch, a world in the mental state of the players. 'They were never so tight again after that,' said Moore. It was a great moment for Moore and Popplewell, and for the new Lions tight head. Leonard stood like a rock.

And all this was achieved after the traditional Lions beginning. Hastings, despite rumours that he would not even start, trotted out at the head of a line of Lions thirsting for the Test. When Fox tested him with a low raker, coming at him out of the wicked low sun, he moved stiffly and without conviction towards the ball and scrambled it away. When, after thirteen minutes, Fox hoisted a superb garryowen to the Lions' line, Hastings dropped the ball and Eroni Clarke seized it and scored at his leisure. Fox converted and the New Zealand downwind leg had the perfect send-off.

Hastings began to flex the hamstring and found that his problems, as had been hinted at by the medical men, might have been in the Hastings head rather than the Hastings leg. He kicked two fine goals around the half-hour, the first awarded when Fitzpatrick drove into a maul halfway up instead of from behind the rear feet; the second when the Lions won a line-out, made two lightning drives and the All Blacks swarmed over the top to kill the ball. Already the Lions were in control. Already, there were signs that the All Black weaponry amounted to a loud and enthusiastic pop-gun. That was what the Lions' tackling had wrought.

Near half-time, the Lions took the lead. Morris, having one of those indomitable, gymnastic days, barking and harrying, chipped to the corner and Timu panicked with his clearance kick. Bayfield won the line-out and Andrew deftly flicked over a dropped goal with his left foot. It was 9-7 to the Lions, and could have been more had not Michael Jones brought off a crunching tackle on Morris in the All Blacks' left-hand corner. But now the Lions were turning to play with the wind.

At half-time, there was activity on the New Zealand bench. Ian Jones was seen removing his tracksuit and Cooksley walked off down the tunnel. Jones ran on to prove Geoff Cooke's inside info correct. 'Let's say that we weren't exactly surprised to see him,' said Cooke later. With the tactical substitutions completed, the game resumed. Six minutes into the second half, Andrew lifted a high kick to the New Zealand 22, the Lions rewon it and Zinzan Brooke and Fitzpatrick clearly dived over the top. They were penalised, Hastings slotted the kick and it was 12-7. The noise from visiting enclaves grew.

After nineteen minutes of the second half, the All Blacks tried to set up a driving maul. Fitzpatrick, having the non-game of his life, knocked on. Morris was on to the ball in an electric flash and set off down a relatively narrow blind side. He fed Guscott, who swayed in and held on just long enough to draw in Kirwan. Afterwards, McGeechan enthused long and loud about Guscott's carving out of the extra foot of space for his wing.

Rory Underwood duly set off, still with Kirwan almost alongside him – for about three strides. Underwood blasted past the diminished former wonder wing. 'Like a Porsche going past a Lada,' said an excited brother Tony up in the ITV commentary box. Rory raced on outside Timu and scored in the left-hand corner with what the players later described as one of the worst dives ever seen in international rugby.

There was pandemonium: the TV monitors showed McGeechan in raptures, the Lions bench on its feet. The wedges of Lions support all around the ground went stark, staring bonkers. The long-serving terrace terrors punched the air. They had a song for every occasion on tour: if a Welshman scored, they had 'Cwm Rhondda' in their repertoire; they had 'Molly Malone' for an Irish try and 'Flower of Scotland' for a Scottish try. Now they broke into a lusty 'Rule Britannia'.

There was a whole lot of All Black huffing and puffing after that and it came to nothing. Hastings kicked a final penalty and the whistle went. It was 1-1 in the series.

As Mains and Fitzpatrick sat glumly in the press conference, talking about the lack of line-out possession, the need to recover and to keep their heads up and the fact that the Lions had won so much more ball (the stats said that the Lions had won 26 rucks, the All Blacks 46), the strains of a bellowed 'Rule Britannia' could be heard from the hordes which besieged the tunnel to the dressing-rooms.

'We were so confident on the ball,' said McGeechan. 'We made them try to force the ball and that is never easy to do. We had to win a Test match for credibility. Now New Zealand will believe that we are a very good side.'

Hastings, something of a veteran of New Zealand rugby, looked drained and only quietly delirious. He could not believe the level of support the team had had from the stands and terraces. Brian Moore confessed that while everyone was in a singing heap in one corner of the dressing-room, he sat alone and cried in another.

It was so difficult to leave behind the excitement round the hotels and the streets to grind away on the laptop with the story for London. Large knots of Brits, dazed, were still shaking their heads in wonder. For those of us brought up on All Black domination, to be on hand when old orders are reversed and when on the near horizon comes sailing the possibility of a Test series victory, something we might not have the opportunity of ever seeing again, was a profoundly moving moment, impossible for New Zealanders and other outsiders to understand.

The first time I ever saw the All Blacks in the flesh, on a grey October day at Rodney Parade in 1963, they lost, lost to a single dropped goal by dear Dick Uzzell, a student who had skived off for the day. But after that, I had seen them lose precious few times in many years, and had grown to respect their boundless facility for squeezing out of close games, sometimes with luck or cynicism, more often with sheer, indomitable will. The Second Test in Wellington in 1993 reversed a trend of a generation and more; it drew respect, R-E-S-P-E-C-T, as Aretha Franklin once spelled it out. It meant that no journalist would open a question to Laurie Mains with: 'When we win . . .' in the preamble to the final Test in

Auckland in a week's time. It meant that at home, sports editors and news editors and TV executives would be drawn into the excitement, and the rugby followers in the home countries, and even the non-rugby followers, would tune into the spirit of the tour.

The Lions attended the after-match function, repaired for a riotous few hours in their team-room, then dispersed around the city's nightclubs. Many of them effectively went direct to the airport for the next day's flight out. The Sunday dawned sunny in the windy city. It made you anxious to find a witness to the match of the day before, just in case it had all been a rather delicious dream. I met Chris Rea in the lift. 'Did we win?' he asked.

'I think so,' I replied.

# CHAPTER 18

# *Eden's Bitter Fruit*

## WAIKATO AND THE FINAL TEST

Oh, the heavy change. Before the party could devote themselves to the final and fateful Test there was a minefield of a trip to Hamilton, in terms of population the fourth-largest city in New Zealand – and God help them, said one non-lover of the featureless place – to play Waikato, the team which had beaten Auckland in the previous season's national championship and had gone on to win it.

Even worse, Waikato men were raging at their treatment at the hands of the national selectors, and had something to prove. At least half of their team were contenders, and yet for the Second Test, Matthew Cooper, who was on the bench, was the only Waikato man needed, even though Duane Monkley and Richard Jerram, the explosive flankers, were having wondrous seasons, as were Warren Gatland and Graham Purvis, the experienced and fast-moving front-row men.

Richard Loe, the forbidding prop, was still serving his long and controversial suspension for alleged eye-gouging (surely, if he was innocent, as he claimed, he should have been allowed back and surely, if he was guilty, as the TV replay hinted, he should have been banned for life. Is any result worth a player being blinded?). There seemed few other holes in the team – especially since they were not to meet the new respected Lions team but the team which, in some of its component parts, had completely lost respect.

At Cooke's Sunday school in a desperately dreary and wet Hamilton, the management addressed the Test victory with the benefit of a little more perspective. 'It was their greatest performance as a group, quite obviously. Dean Richards told me that the lads were buzzing. They were brave – someone told me that Rob Andrew made twenty-two tackles.

'For a change we sustained the performance. Everything went right. Dewi's passing was spot-on, whereas before he might have thrown a couple off-course. We have had our difficulties but to put in a record performance like that was a great achievement.'

How did the final Test pan out in the inner battle, now that the crushing nature of the Lions' win had ostensibly installed them as favourites for Auckland?

'I suppose we have a slight edge. But they will use all week to analyse us, to find where they can stop us. And to play the All Blacks at Eden Park, to achieve something which the Lions have only once achieved before . . . it is going to be incredibly difficult.'

They revealed that one of the staples of the previous week's build-up had been a meeting which McGeechan called of 'a small group of senior players'. This had set the agenda for the match, set the plans and the tone for the final days of preparation. Which players had been involved, we asked McGeechan? It was hardly asking for a carbon copy of official secrets and the plans for Her Majesty's Dockyards, but he refused to say. 'It was a cerebral session,' said McGeechan. 'So that rules Richard Webster out. That leaves you twenty-nine to guess from.'

How far would the victory influence the Five Nations in style? 'Good question. I don't know,' said McGeechan. 'To succeed here we have had to take on board the whole experience: referees, the commitment, the knowledge of what New Zealand rugby means; we had to compete entirely in their environment. Much of it is different to the way we play at home. And it is also different to the way we are allowed to play at home.'

I know McGeechan would cheerfully import that whole experience. I must confess that if he tried I would be at Heathrow with a detachment of the Special Air Services, because the New Zealand style, in parts, appealed to me not at all.

The team to play Waikato contained all the players who had not played in the Test, with Will Carling as captain. I was surprised not to hear some raging exhortation to the midweek team for their forthcoming battle. This was their Test, in effect. It was a wonderful chance for them to recover the respect that they had lost, by giving it every last drop of sweat and blood and tears against a very powerful team. As Brian Moore had said in the aftermath of Wellington: 'The whole party needs a strong performance by the midweek side to keep the momentum going.'

Instead, Cooke simply expressed his fears that if one of the team had to leave the field, then one of the Test team might be exposed to injury. The final training session, on a wet Monday morning at – yes, you've guessed it – Rugby Park, home of Waikato, seemed desultory. Some of the midweek players had, by their own admission, slightly left the rails when they realised that they would not play a part in the Tests. Concentration dropped, bedtime grew later. There was no shame in that; they deserved a chance to relax. But there is no question that much of the old, almost fanatical loyalty and unity had gone, and that some players lost the respect of their peers.

There was also, unquestionably, the problem of exhaustion. A few days before the Wellington Test, some of the press took a few of the players to dinner. The French restaurant chosen in deference to the nifty wine nose of Stuart Barnes proved just a little rich. Before every course, the chef would steam in with the nosh, go into a long and detailed explanation of, say, where the sole had actually been caught, by which boat; how it had been lovingly conveyed, still flapping, into his kitchen, how the sauce had been created, how old the china was.

The wine waitress would follow with a wine for each course. She would nominate the vineyard, the hillside and the vine row number; the exact date on which the grapes were plucked, whose feet had trodden them; what delights awaited our palates. The effect of her seminars was slightly spoiled by Richard Webster asking for another Steinlager whenever she had finished.

But when the joking ended it was quite obvious how utterly drained the players were. It was, in a sense, worse for the dirt-trackers because they did not have the impetus of the tilt at history to keep them going. It had been a frighteningly harsh tour, every bit as bad as the pre-tour scare stories had suggested. The travelling was fierce, the training was endless and the matches were relentless. Added to that, some of the Lions round our table had been playing for two and three years with hardly a break. Webster is no whiner, still less a quitter. 'I'm knackered,' he said.

'Everybody is completely exhausted,' said Robert Jones. 'But look what happens when we get back. Swansea will be starting the serious training and suddenly, we're off on the treadmill again.' It was true. In the old days, Lions used to return from tour and ease their way into the new season. They used to reappear at training, say, six weeks into the new season and return to active service at the start of November. That easing-in process is no longer available to the 1993 Lions. The club leagues were to start in all four home countries at the start of the season. There were sponsors to please, members and followers to entertain; there were cups to hunt. There were the avaricious demands of the individual national coaches to satisfy. Not to mention those ancillary issues – you know, going to work, spending time with your family, all that stuff.

The Hamilton experience was depressing. The weather was foul, there was no spring in the step of the Lions' midweek team. I was well into the second week of a fierce spasm in the lower back, aggravated no end when the Hamilton motel allocated me a room with a water bed. I killed some time reading Steve Gaines' book on the Beach Boys, those surfing heroes who transported us teenagers through some of the most stunningly glorious pop songs ever crafted, to a world of endless summer where girls queued for you. The Beach Boys spoiled all our summer holidays because they never worked out like the records, with love on the sands.

And so who were the Beach Boys? Gaines dismantled every myth. They hated surfing, they bickered all the time. Brian Wilson, the sublime genius (could even Lennon and McCartney have written *Good Vibrations*?) was a drug-crazed lunatic who went to bed for seventeen years, brother Dennis was a wreck who associated with Charles Manson and who drowned, drugged, under a boat. Most of the others were petty self-seekers. The whole thing was a shambles, the book tore away chunks of the adolescence of a generation. Outside, Hamilton dripped on.

It was probably as bad as anyone had feared. Waikato won 38-10. They began like raging bulls, going on to play a superb sustained match in which they hardly allowed the Lions a pass or a kick. Were it not for the paucity of the opposition I would certainly have said that Waikato were the best team the Lions met on tour, including the Test matches. They were unquestionably a better team than Auckland.

Some of the Lions played heroically, others seemed utterly shattered, unable to run or even to attempt a tackle. Carling, who along with most of the backs had to do his tackling and also the tackling of all the forwards too, played a massively courageous match, remaining on the field with a badly bruised shoulder so that none of the Test players would be exposed. Tony Clement remained unruffled, the morale of Robert Jones did not suffer even though Cronin, Reed and Galwey flapped line-out possession at his toes or over his head, and he took the ball and the storming home forwards at the same time. Barnes kicked badly, the back row were completely overrun, the scrum creaking and the line-out oblit- erated. At one of a series of scrums on the Lions' line in the second half – a series in which the Lions in fact did rather well not to concede a try – Wright detached from Milne, toppled out of the scrum altogether and had to pick himself up and stand guard on the blind side. It was not an edifying experience for him.

In the loose, even when the Lions set it up they were often driven off the ball or had it stolen away. It was astonishing to see how little they had learned during the previous two months about body positions: some of them were bolt upright in the mauls and rucks. The backs showed a little, but otherwise, it was a painful, almost brutal experience. It was the biggest margin of defeat in the history of Lions provincial tour matches and it was a maddening, saddening way for them to mark their last appearance as Lions in 1993 and, for the vast majority, as Lions full stop. It was the last stop for the tour within a tour.

The conviction of the Waikato forwards on the drive bordered on the frenzied. All the forwards could storm around but they could also play football. Gatland was yet another marvellous home hooker and the balding Brett Anderson a wonderful, sweated hard-core man at lock. John Mitchell, the captain and number 8, was inspirational and clever. Mooloo, the ceremonial bull parading around the park, was so excited that he fell over.

Waikato established themselves in fifty-four seconds. They switched the kick-off, won the first line-out and Anderson went thundering at the Lions' midfield on the peel. The ball was rucked and moved to the right and Doug Wilson, the right wing, scored. Monkley had a try after ten minutes as a result of a brilliantly sustained Waikato drive. Cooper kicked the conversion and two penalties, and on half-time, Monkley scored again after a Waikato counter-attack led by Mitchell and Monkley. It was 26-3 at half-time. The referee blew a little early for the break; was he trying to spare the Lions further punishment, as Harry Gibbs might have done?

The next Waikato try came after 54 minutes and was scored by Aaron Collins. Again, there was some splendid driving and setting up and recycling of the ball by the home team, but again, you had to view the efforts of some of the Lions to nip the move in the bud with disbelief. Reed had been hanging around behind the action for long minutes and when it came his way he could not make the tackle.

I suppose it signified an improvement of sorts that Waikato scored just one more try – from Gatland, and a well-deserved one. The Lions made some late attacks and after a drive from Webster and an inside pass from Wallace, Carling scored and Barnes converted. After that, Wallace was clear near the Waikato line. He fell over. He was neither the best-balanced nor the most effective of wings. The large and noisy crowd gave their heroes a warm reception.

Kevin Greene, the Waikato coach, and captain Mitchell quietly summed up the match afterwards. As ever with New Zealand team hierarchies, they were focused and sensible, knowledgeable and fair. I felt sorry for them. They had been shunted out into the wilds of the tour when their superb team deserved to play the full Lions team, and had they found the same form, they could well have beaten them. 'It was unfair to the Waikato team and their supporters,' said McGeechan.

'We came back a bit in the last five minutes,' he said grimly of the match. 'At least they were trying.' I felt this latter observation to be something of a generalisation. How is your shoulder, we asked Carling? 'Sore, but not as sore as my pride.' Had he stayed on to protect the Test players? 'Certainly not,' said a man who coveted the Test place he had lost.

It did not affect the Test match, but Cooke was still at a loss. 'It has been particularly disappointing to see the midweek team perform so badly in the past two weeks.' How did McGeechan explain the loss of form of his Scots forwards? 'I just don't know. I can't explain it,' he said sadly.

On to Auckland, to destiny, and to a city where the Lions meant Ben and Ieuan, Gavin and Scott and Winters, not the dishevelled remnants of the retreat from Napier and Hamilton.

The last few days of the tour were entirely different in tone to all the rest. There were no boat trips or golf. The last Test is, on any tour, fiendishly difficult to win. McGeechan, on both his Lions tours as coach, worked hard to stop the intrusion of home thoughts from abroad, even to the extent of delaying departure for London by a day so that the players need not worry about shopping until after the Test itself. But it is impossible not to have a whirlpool in your mental build-up, carrying along all the inner jetsam of the trip, the glories and disappointments and the memories, the knowledge that the adventure which has dominated your life is soon to be over and above all, that the collective in which you have worked for two months will soon be dismantled and you will be dumped, suddenly alone, to walk through the green channel into Britain. You have to learn to think for yourself all over again.

The training sessions, held in secret, went well for both teams, so they said. The All Blacks had made further changes. Ian Jones returned, this time to start the match in place of Cooksley. Eroni Clarke disappeared and in his place came Stensness, the British-style Auckland back. Zinzan Brooke, a chequered career as an All Black behind him, was dropped and replaced by Arran Pene, who had impressed the Lions during the tour whether in the colours of the Maoris or of Otago. It was a mark of the Lions' strength. The All Blacks reckon two changes is a clear-out. There is no doubt that Kiwi rugby was in a panic.

The Lions kept the Second Test heroes together, as they had to. They drafted Carling for the replacements bench and nudged off Barnes. This meant that Tony Clement did not have to understudy so many positions. Without Carling alongside he was the replacement wing, centre and full-back. Now, he was only the replacement full-back and fly-half. Enough to be going on with, though.

The Thursday session had gone incredibly well, according to McGeechan. 'It was the best session of the tour. Dean Richards came up to me worried that it was going so well. He said that we should make some mistakes so that there was still some improvement to make for the match itself.' On the Friday session, roughly the forty-fifth the players had staged, give or take the odd extra dirt-tracking run, the players made a funnel as they took the field to applaud Peter Winterbottom on to the pitch, to show respect and to mark the last official session of his career. Winterbottom, predictably, was embarrassed.

It was a week of biting anticipation. The next Lions tour of the country would not be for eight years at the very least, so it was very doubtful indeed that any of the current party would get another chance to play in a winning Lions team in a New Zealand series. It was impossible to predict if we would ever again get the chance to report one. There are far more important aspects to the reporting of rugby than that your favoured team should win. On the other hand, it is utterly impossible for anyone warm of blood and heart to divorce himself completely from the fortunes of the Lions. They were mostly driven, dedicated, nice men; some of them were, well, friends; unavoidably, considering all the professional contact over the seasons. In your head you had to work for complete objectivity. In your heart, you had to agonise with them.

Predictably, our leaders at home had thrown a fit. Every call brought more instructions to myself and to Dave Rogers, snapping on behalf of *The Sunday Times* along with Anton ('War on') Want, his young protégé. Rogers had to provide a pic for the front page of this shape, a pic for the back page of that shape. I had to produce a 1,200-word report of the match; had to ghost a Brian Moore column of 700 words, had to dredge up a 1,000-word colour piece for the front page of the paper (which would unquestionably have been the biggest sports piece ever carried by the paper in its news pages, had they actually run the damn thing), plus 650 words to round up the tour for our special Scotland sports section. Should we also include an overall assessment of the tour itself in all its aspects? We had a think. Nah, let's leave it until next week. The daily newspaper reporters were already sending reams zinging down their Tandy lines to London, Dublin, Edinburgh and Cardiff, profiling and predicting, sermonising and colouring in the bare bones of the tour news. The *Sun* and the *Daily Mirror* took major chunks.

When the Lions were settled into their downtown hotel and when they were all rubbed down and administered to by Dr James Robson and Kevin Murphy, we persuaded Robson down to the media hotel and even to a fish restaurant beyond. It was a gesture of thanks. If Robson expected to confine his ministrations to the rugby players then he was disappointed (in fact, he didn't and he wasn't). By the end of the tour, he had been consulted by, and he had treated, all the Lions, all the management, a grand total of twenty-two media people, a large number of players' parents who had arrived, and had even, over the telephone, given advice to relatives of the players at home.

We found a man of fearsome dedication. Robson, from Dundee, had begun his working life as a physiotherapist and had upgraded to doctor later in his career. He had been attached to the Scottish Rugby Union for a few years and by all accounts was vastly popular with the players. He was almost painfully shy but was sure of his ability. It was obvious that McGeechan trusted him to the ends of the earth. 'I think it started during the World Cup,' said Robson. 'Craig Chalmers was injured before the quarter-final match against Western Samoa. The general opinion was that he would not be fit. Ian said: "I want him". I told Geech that Craig would be fit. We got him ready.'

Robson and Murphy soon realised – and they did not entirely blame the Four Home Unions for the situation – that the normal outlay on medical equipment would not buy them everything they wanted. 'We knew that only the state-of-the-art drugs would do and the best equipment. For example, we were anxious to take an interferential machine, which is expensive. It puts an electrical field into the injured tissue and is useful for relief of pain immediately after the game and treatment later on.' The two had to raise their own sponsorship for the equipment. They went to the Pfizer company and, to the company's great credit, they were generous enough to make a sizeable donation. Smith & Nephew donated some of the heavy drugs Robson knew they would need. And as for credit where credit was due, there was none. The Four Home Unions never included Smith & Nephew or Pfizer in the list of acknowledgments which went into every tour programme; staggeringly, they never even insisted that Robson and Murphy should be listed and profiled in the official party, which was a scandal. It was only local liaison officers who insisted upon recognition of two people who unquestionably did as much as any player to boost the tour. Incidentally, it cost both Robson and Murphy thousands of pounds to make the tour as both had to employ locums – Murphy for his own physiotherapy practice, Robson for his partnership in Dundee. At least they could look forward to a holiday after two months of hard work, we suggested? 'This is our holiday,' said Robson.

The pair were no shrinking violets. If they thought that foul play had endangered a player or that referees were missing something, they did not hesitate to say so, as was their right and their duty. They were also given the final say in any decisions over the fitness of players, a heavy responsibility if both the management and the player himself were desperate that he should make a big match. Robson had photographs taken of many of the injuries the players suffered, and had prepared case histories and other notes which would help the field of sports medicine as well as the lectures he would give at home.

What was the effect of all his industry and sacrifice? Robson revealed that Dean Richards would unquestionably have been invalided home after his calf injury in training at New Plymouth, were it not for the equipment and the drugs they had brought; that Rob Andrew had developed a nasty eye infection that the basic drugs would not have cleared up. They revealed the extraordinary efforts they had made to hand back Scott Gibbs to the tour selectors after his injury in Invercargill, including hours spent in the swimming pool. When Gibbs returned, his feet were webbed. He revealed the long process of mending the Hastings hamstring for the Second Test, which included four treatments per day. 'There was the initial treatment at pitch-side. Then there was ice, ultra-sound, interferential, rubs. And also the job of persuading Gavin that he was fit. The normal period for that sort of injury would be three weeks.' Within a week, Gavin was out there. So who said that Gavin, Scott and Ben were the tour heroes?

The tension grew and there was also a late burst of money-making from the Lions. They set up photo opportunities at which individuals and small groups could pose with the whole party; they sold some of the training kit, sold autographed balls and posters. The tour fund swelled after a slow start.

The supporters' groups descended on Auckland from their various sightseeing trips. Gareth Chilcott returned from Rotorua with a story to tell. He and some of the Gullivers supporters in his flock had gone white-water rafting on the river near Rotorua. They were warned that conditions might be a little lively but elected to go anyway. What neither they nor the two supervisors aboard realised was that a dislodged tree-trunk had rafted down the river by itself and had wedged itself tight across the main channel. Chilcott and the fun-seekers came careering down the river, struck the tree and the boat overturned in a violent stretch of the water.

'I went under for what seemed ages. Then I came to the surface and hung on to a branch underneath the river bank.' One of the instructors had floated, concussed, to safety. The other had been trapped under the boat and had to cut right through the bottom with his knife to escape to the surface. The other passengers managed to scramble to safety even though they were badly shaken. The only one who did not was a Spaniard, Isaac Borrego from Asturias. Isaac, following his first Lions tour, could not swim and he had also lost his life-jacket, which had been torn off in the accident.

Chilcott managed to grab him as he hurtled by, dragged him towards the bank and held him there in the tumult of white water until help arrived around forty minutes later. There seemed very little doubt, even allowing for the exaggerations of the onlookers, that Chilcott had saved Isaac's life. 'Don't make me to be a hero,' said Coochie, as, with mock-irritation, he sat through his fifth impromptu press conference.

When they write the book about rugby characters, Coochie will be in it. Indeed, he will be on the cover. The former tearaway, violent on the field, reformed so well that he played rugby for England and the Lions, became the foundation stone and focal point of Bath, a TV pundit, a larger-than-life figure (which was difficult) and, despite the aggressive edge which always remained, a man of real compassion, a hero. In 1991, a denizen of the RFU coaching staff was discussing him. The coach was one of those people under the utterly mistaken impression that all of England club rugby exists simply to satisfy the beck and call of the national squad. 'He's over the top now. He should retire. He's keeping back some young props. Bath should tell him to move over.'

'But if you were Bath,' I replied, 'would you cut out your own heart?' Chilcott played on, was still rumbling when Bath won the 1992 Pilkington Cup after extra time, was still the foundation as they won the 1993 Courage Leagues Championship. As Isaac would no doubt agree, great men like Gareth Chilcott are not to be put out to grass.

On the night before the match, the Lions had a team meeting in which both McGeechan and Hastings spoke with emotion. 'It is the ultimate achievement,' Hastings had said earlier in the day at his final press conference in the Lions' team-room. He had just addressed a massive gathering of Auckland businessmen, leaving them mightily impressed with his authority and maturity. 'It is important not to let all the history and the significance get ahead of you, because that would cause pressure, but this is the biggest match of my life. There is another pressure, because we know we are good enough to win and that all our families and friends will be watching, both here and on the TV at home, we have a responsibility to everyone in British Isles rugby.'

The idea of everyone setting their alarm clocks back at home to rise in the dark to watch was curiously poignant. In the team-room was the video recorder which McGeechan and his cohorts had almost worn out on the tour. There were three videos lying around: *Terminator 2 – Judgement Day*, which seemed apt; *How to Beat the All*

*Blacks*, which was incredibly apt; and *Viz, including Sid the Sexist and the Fat Slags*, the significance of which escaped me.

The calm weather stayed until the end. Saturday dawned less glorious than the rest of the week but it was dry and bright. There was an overwhelming sense of history in the making. I felt the tension rising inside like a live thing so God knows what the players felt as they boarded the bus to Eden Park. Cleaning the lenses of my binoculars I briefly had the image of cleaning a gun for battle. The truth was, of course, that the Lions were favourites. It was a truth that the Lions camp and camp followers were afraid to articulate. It was too dangerous to believe it. But they had won one Test and were unlucky not to have won the other, and in those two matches they had neutralised much of the All Blacks' armoury.

An elongated programme of pre-match entertainment flashed by. And then, led by Peter Winterbottom, who was playing his last match of a career of unbelievable courage and effectiveness, the 1993 British Lions took the field for the last time.

It was a bizarre match to end a bizarre tour. New Zealand won by 30-13 and the Lions, despite shaking New Zealand rugby to the core in the series, were left with a record of real mediocrity: they won only seven of their thirteen games. It was, for British and Irish, a desperately disappointing occasion, leaving them with a sense of unbearable flatness. Even more disappointing, and bizarre, was the fact that the Lions had ridden out what was expected to be a monumental early black storm with ease and had pulled clear to 10-0 after twenty-four minutes.

The All Blacks played well, were sharper on the fringes and were given a wonderful focal point in Arran Pene, who added strength and steam to the loose. Robin Brooke won some useful line-out balls and the All Blacks were far more aggressive in the line-outs than they had been in Wellington. The back row showed for the first time, Bunce was a little more like the Bunce of old and Stensness brought a refreshing glimpse of all-round talent and balance to the team. They scored three tries to one and they were hugely relieved at the end.

The popular opinion at the time was that they had saved themselves with a performance of typical authority and All Black excellence. In part, it was true. Yet I am inclined to believe that they did not play an awful lot better in Auckland than they did in Wellington. They were more focused, but they were simply not irresistible. The Lions' effort simply fell away. We had a re-visitation of the forty-minute team and we were not at all pleased to see them. It was an unfathomably flat effort, easily the least of the three Test performances.

There was also something in the body language of the Lions either side of half-time, and after the game; something which I may or may not have imagined, which suggested that they did not quite have the solid inner conviction that they could win.

Sadly, Hastings had a poor day, misfiring with his kicking and his defending. If he has one fault – and generally, one is all he does have – it is the lack of the extra yard of foot when coming up into the line and, allied to that, a conservatism of perception, which means that he feeds his wing quite rarely. With that and the lack of devil at half-back the Lions had to leave the Rolls-Royce in the garage. They paid the penalty for not trusting their threequarters as a primary force, they hung around waiting for a beautifully constructed platform for which the All Blacks had refused planning permission. No one was asking them to run ludicrous ball, dead ball, slow ball. But they had to strike, speculate a little, both when they were 10-0 and when they were overhauled.

Furthermore, there was less than the expected return from Bayfield and Johnson, because even though Robin Brooke is a fine forward he is simply not a dominating Test lock; no man his size should be. The back row battled bravely, and there were some achingly brilliant touches from the threequarters, especially from Guscott. Yet it was not enough. Nothing was sustained, nothing lasted so long that a platform could become a major series of attacks. There was nothing like the buzz of Wellington.

Hastings had already missed two kicks at goal, and left a few All Black punts to bounce alarmingly in front of him, when Joseph climbed all over Richards in a line-out and Hastings obliged with a penalty after nineteen minutes of squeezing tension. One of the misses had come when the All Blacks had illegally dragged down a Lions driving maul after Clarke, Richards and Winterbottom had hammered away from a line-out.

Still, it was 3-0. After twenty-four minutes Preston, not the next Sid Going, was caught in possession by Winterbottom round a scrum and Clarke, Richards, Morris and Andrew attacked down the left. Winterbottom set up the ball and Underwood came in from the blindside wing on to an inside pass from Andrew. Underwood's pass bounced off Bunce and Gibbs, lightning quick of foot and reflex, grabbed it and barrelled to the posts to score. Hastings kicked the goal and it needed sixteen minutes of the biggest and most concentrated effort in the career of the Lions team to ensure that the lead stayed until half-time.

Yet they seemed to sit back, to lose for the first time in the series the extra thump in the tackle. Eight minutes after the Lions' try, Joseph won a line-out, Pene set the ball up with a charge down the right and when the ball was switched back to the left, Stensness chipped to the Lions' line. In the defence, there was no one at home. Bunce rushed up and scored.

Shortly afterwards, Kirwan set up a driving ruck, Joseph battered his way onwards and Fitzpatrick scored a richly satisfying try. Fox kicked both conversions and it was 14-10 to New Zealand at half-time. It was a baffling, depressing concession of a hard-won initiative.

The All Blacks could easily have added a killing try in the third quarter when they cleared a path and launched Fox towards the line. It seemed as if Fox had only to stretch and stride over, but when it comes to the running game, Fox on the ball is about as comfortable as Tom used to be when Jerry gave him a badly wrapped parcel that was ticking. He flung the ball to his right where it evaded a Kiwi pair of mitts and Underwood knocked it down. It really was an astonishingly poor piece of rugby. Yet Fox had already put over two penalties as the Lions infringed in a fading dream. For the first, Clarke was penalised for going over the top after Bunce and Joseph had combined in a major attack. Hastings did sandwich three points for the Lions between the two Fox kicks, but thirteen minutes from the end of normal time, just after Fox's adamant refusal to score the try, the All Blacks sealed the series. Preston ran over unopposed to score after constant pressure, bursting easily between Richards and Hastings. Fox kicked the conversion and added a penalty near the end.

By this time, the crowd were cheering. Afterwards, the All Black hierarchy was full of praise for the support of the Eden Parkers – even though it seemed to me that in the strange way of Kiwi crowds, they only began to wake when their team was sure of winning.

Lions' attacks in the second half had an air of desperation. Hastings once held on when Underwood had a foot of space (all he needs) outside; Evans was overwhelmed a few times when put outside his man. It was the same air of desperation as that with which the All Blacks had played near the end at Wellington.

The whistle blew on the tour and the All Blacks celebrated mightily. Both Fitzpatrick, a vindicated captain, and Hastings addressed the crowd over the public address system, Hastings thanking the country as a whole for their hospitality. Most of the Lions wandered to the far stands where their supporters sat. They were cheered generously to the echo. Then they walked to the end of the ground where the loyal knots of long-serving bludgers waved back frantically. But the Lions knew that the place in history which had been reserved for them would now go to someone else, to another team on another tour.

The relief on the face of Mains and Fitzpatrick afterwards was palpable. 'That was a week I would not like to go through again,' said Fitzpatrick of the pressure of the days of build-up. Both he and Mains tore into the Lions for what they saw as negative tactics throughout the series, both ignoring the fact that in every Test of the series the Lions had harvested points and yards of ground because the All Blacks had been penalised. Yet for the truths of the tour you had only to look at the scoreboard. The scoreboard said that, after all the sound and fury, New Zealand had won.

All the thousands of words to be filed back to London suddenly became a massive chore; we were merely messengers to be shot, not the harbingers of history. People back in the office spoke about cutting back the coverage – after all, it was the day of the Wimbledon ladies' final, old boy. 'Leaden Lions trip over history's hurdle', said the headline in *The Sunday Times* the next day.

The final Saturday ended for the touring party at the official dinner, the only formal bunfight of the tour. The teams mixed socially, and suddenly, players who had merely been weaknesses to be exploited or supermen to be curbed took on a personality of their own.

On the Monday, after speeches of thanks and commiseration, and drinks of commiseration aplenty, after protestations of blood brotherhood from the members of the party, the Lions embarked for the journey home and on a summer dawn at Heathrow Airport, the tour party landed and then ceased to exist.

# CHAPTER 19

# *Falling for the Culture Gap*

Right! Everyone up on their high horses! The epitaph to every Lions tour ever made, apart from those to New Zealand in 1971, to South Africa in 1974 and to Australia in 1989, carries the title 'what went wrong'. Traditionally, this epitaph bemoans the appalling management, appalling selection, appalling coaching, low standards of fitness compared to the opposition, and, depending on which tour is involved, the dreadful back play letting down the forwards (1977, 1980 and 1983) or the dreadful forward play letting down the backs (every tour up to 1968).

The tradition is to see the tour in pompous terms of global trends and movements in the game – even though the defeat may have come about simply because the key man pulled his muscle getting out of the bath or the ref was a rampant homer.

Amazing to contemplate, practically none of this applied to the 1993 British Lions. Horses back in the stables. Their management team could not have been improved upon to any significant degree. Geoff Cooke was the best manager available. He may not be quite the mystic guru suggested by some of his publicity during England's revival, but the standard of management and man-management he brought to the tour was of an altogether higher class than that achieved by the ranks of blazered buffoons and time-servers who comprise much of the history of Lions managers.

McGeechan, with the exception of Bath's Jack Rowell, was unquestionably the best coach available to the British Lions. He did, in almost every respect, a noble job. He retained the high respect of the squad; as did Richard Best. The post of assistant coach is not coveted. You tend to feel like something spare at a wedding, but Best coped superbly well. The medical men, Robson and Murphy, were exceptional. The state of their art was such that players who should have withdrawn tended to play on and play well.

Gavin Hastings established a world first in that he is the first admired captain of a losing Lions team. His form fell away in the final Test but he was still a tower of the tour. He was usually the archetype of a Lions captain: detached, calm, authoritative and a Test player to his studs.

The selection? Some of it *was* appalling. If the tour was picked again today then either eight or nine of the squad would be discarded. In particular, there was a complete lack of understanding that the Scottish forwards chosen were all very well in a certain context, the Murrayfield context, to be exact; but that they were not, as individuals, likely to dominate New Zealanders. They duly blew up. The experiment of choosing Mick Galwey as tight flanker was a nonsense. Galwey was an excellent tourist and a decent lock. But remember that at blind side they left at home Jon Hall, Emyr Lewis, Tim Rodber, Dean Ryan, Steve Ojomoh and Derek Turnbull. Neither of the Irish back replacements was a bolter, and Peter Clohessy and Jeff Probyn, my original choices, should have been the tight-heads.

But while the fact that some of the air tickets went to the wrong address was eventually to hammer the midweek teams, it never *really* affected the series. The All Blacks would have suffered grief had Jeff Probyn propped against them on the Lions tight head – but not too often. In some matches there were hardly any scrums. None of the rest of the Test team would have been improved by any player left at home. It is as simple as that. Any high horsemanship on the subject offers nothing more than a sore backside.

There were other reasons for the defeat. On the face of it, to stagger the All Blacks in the Second Test and to keep the series so competitive was a praiseworthy achievement, considering the mediocrity of the 1993 Five Nations tournament. And also that, as McGeechan said before the tour, the Lions had to take on the All Blacks at their own unique style, and by emulating that style to the letter, and in their backyard under sympathetic referees, in the harsh environment of a Lions tour in the Land of the Long White Cloud. They had to take them on at their game in the absence of anything which could be called a British Isles style. It meant that McGeechan had to spend ages and ages explaining the new controls before he could tell them to drive faster.

And yet despite all that, despite a few selectorial holes, despite the awful home internationals, the enormous local difficulties and the sheer psychological barrier, even despite the decision which robbed them of the First Test, the Lions unquestionably should have won the Test series. Why? Because they were emphatically the better team. They had a better line-out through Bayfield, a better balanced back row and the outstanding Clarke. They were not strong at half-back, but then neither, as link-men, were the All Black halves. And the Lions backs were vastly superior.

The post-tour baggage which the Lions will have to check in when they board the final flight to meet that great coach in the sky is that they missed a glorious chance to come back with at least a 2-1 series victory. Potential is one thing; but as we have seen, their achievement never matched their potential. They were quite unable to sustain a level of performance through more than two-thirds of each game in twelve of their thirteen tour appearances.

But why? There are no glib answers. That was the essential bizarre nature of the tour. Bloody maddening it was, too. Was it because of lack of mental hardness or because, under pressure, they could not handle a style of game which, despite all the endless sessions, they were not used to. Maddening. The Lions were a one-half team.

And for me, the Lions ultimately made the same mistake as have England, occasionally, over the past few years. They saw that their backs were so vastly superior, that Guscott, Gibbs, Evans, Rory Underwood and indeed, Tony Underwood and Carling, needed just a few inches of space and it was Goodnight Vienna to the home defences. And yet they did not implicitly trust the evidence of their own eyes.

As I say, both Hastings and McGeechan had a basic instinct of caution. This meant that they entrusted the half-back positions to Andrew and Morris, two men guaranteed not to falter under even screaming pressure but who lacked, in the case of Morris, the pass to kick-start the backs, and in the case of Andrew, the speed and vision on the ball to do so. Barnes' form declined on the tour, but especially when he saw the lie of the land and realised that it was not he who would be making his bed on it. Yet his attitudes were more guaranteed to drag the Lions from the large number of fifty-fifty games on a fifty-fifty tour.

No one is suggesting that the Lions should have chased lost causes by stringing the ball along the line, 'shovelling shit', in the charming phraseology of the Backs' Union. But there were periods in all three Test matches and against Auckland, where the Lions were sent on to the field with neither the personnel nor the orders to really let their backs fly. There were times when, even though the situation might have been upromising for steady-Eddie backs, the Lions could have slashed the home teams to ribbons given the chance, and the yard. It was not speculation. How can it be speculative to entrust your dreams to a player like Jeremy Guscott or Ieuan Evans? Evans may have been worried by the power of Tuigamala but not half as worried as Tuigamala might have been with the incisiveness of Evans, had Evans been given the chance to run at his man in Tests.

The truth is that when it came to the crunch, and even allowing for the infuriating inconsistency of the team as a whole, there were final steps which McGeechan and his lieutenants seemed reluctant to take, times when you mentally urged the Lions to strike out. The Lions drew in their sharp horns just when they could have charged. As I said before the tour, the All Blacks have never been beaten by teams trying to absorb and outlast them, only by teams attacking them.

The All Blacks are never an easy proposition in New Zealand. Anyone who believes that there is anything free on offer in the country is fooling himself and has no conception of the inner mental baggage which has to be shifted out of the way before you actually start to play them in a rugby match – the weight of history, the mental barriers.

Yet they never did much more than front up, breathe fire, whip the ball around this way and that to very little effect. Otherwise they waited in anxiety in case the Lions unleashed the level of performance which would have taken the series away without them having any answer. Fitzpatrick is still a marvellous focal point, Jamie Joseph potentially a tight flanker of world class and Grant Fox's kicking was nothing short of brilliant.

It brought home forcibly that in the British Isles, kicking is one of the lost arts. Neither on the tour nor in the rest of British and Irish rugby was there anyone who could turn the screw as Fox can. The standard of kicking from fly-half in the British Isles is absolutely appalling. Remember when Ollie Campbell, Tony Ward, Phil Bennett and the marvellous John Rutherford projected such a range of kicks – short stabs, huge diagonal boomers, steepling garryowens – and every one would cause the maximum amount of grief it is possible to cause with a rugby ball? Barnes and Andrew can kick as well, but not nearly as consistently. Many of the fly-halves who have appeared for the home countries and France over the last four years have been, by those standards, unable to kick. Tony Clement is probably the best kicker of a ball in the British Isles, yet he is exiled to full-back through his own wishes and those of the selectors.

Yet the All Blacks had no real forkers of lightning apart from those dependable and focused footballers and sinew-straining standard-class forwards. The Lions had more class in more key positions. And yet ultimately, for their tenacity and for the fact that they maintained their concentration and their level of performance, the All Blacks deserved to win the series. Having the ability to win by a street is by no means the same as winning, or even deserving to.

On the evidence of this tour, the old gaps in conditioning and unit and team skills between the hemispheres has disappeared. So, just perhaps, has a little of the old aura, because in the Second Test we saw an All Black team, outplayed, begin to fumble and panic. They suddenly seemed to be fifteen human beings.

Most important, there is still, unquestionably, a culture gap between New Zealand and the home nations, something which goes deeper than mere rugby ability and techniques and interpretations. It can easily be summarised. New Zealand take it more seriously; it means more to the psyche. They want it more – just as, deep down, Tests mean more in the psyche of an Australian cricketer than his English counterpart, more in the psyche of a German footballer than in that of an English player.

Rugby means more in the scheme of things to the average New Zealand player. There are still fewer distractions, even in a country growing up. He is far more focused on his goals for the game, personal, fitness and collective. He understands the game better (he should, his game is simpler). He is far more sure of his ground, how to proceed in a given situation, how to step things up or change things around if it is all going wrong. He is sharper, more aware,

than his counterpart in the British Isles. As I have said before, the
post-match press conference involving the captain and coach of the
home side always underlined the quiet, analytical, focused practical
nature of their game. Coaching in the British Isles, by comparison,
is staggeringly, lamentably poor. Never mind the lack of freshness
and original thought. That focus is absent in all but the very top
strata of teams.

It will be absolutely fascinating on their tour in the autumn of
1993 to see how All Blacks cope with the British game, how much of
their will they can impose on the opposition and on the referees;
whether they find the game as alien to them as the Lions found the
game in New Zealand in so many of its aspects.

What of their style of play? I hated it, hated what they have done
in their domestic rugby to the rhythm of the game and even the
ethos. I filed these thoughts to *The Sunday Times* after the First Test
Match but they ran instead coverage of the World Underwater
Darts Championship:

> When Brian Kinsey, the Australian referee, made the appall-
> ing decision which robbed the British Lions of victory in the
> First Test in Christchurch, he at least brought referees back
> into the spotlight. Down in New Zealand's winter, we had
> almost forgotten they existed. Who is that guy out there? And
> why does he never blow his whistle?
>
> New Zealand have a vision of the game that simply does not
> include the referee. They worship at the altar of continuity.
> They do not want to stop. They do not want some old guy
> whistling some bloody concerto. They even, in an unfathom-
> able paranoia, are anxious about the arrival in New Zealand in
> 1995 of a ten-second wonder called the Auckland Warriors,
> ostensibly a Kiwi team which will play in the Australia rugby
> league premiership.
>
> Non-stop rugby: ah, doesn't it sound great? It isn't. It is
> eventually a corrupted bore and like most corruption, it is
> brought about by anarchy, by unilateral abandonment of the
> laws. They believe they have created a glorious game. They
> have made a monster.
>
> This is how they do it. The Northern Hemisphere season was
> ruined because of the new ruck/maul law where the buried ball
> was turned over to the opposition and the game stopped. In New
> Zealand, turnovers are rare, due in part to the fact that they are
> better at recycling the ball, better in rucks. To save the ball
> becoming buried, New Zealand authorities have given referees
> *carte blanche* to turn blind eyes – after the tackle, players are often
> allowed to dive illegally on the ball to resecure it; are often
> allowed to scrape it back illegally with their hands, to dive over
> the ball illegally to set up a human wall.
>
> And what of the poor devils in the opposition who are
> caught on the ground on or near the ball, or indeed, yards
> away from the ball? They are sacrificed on the continuity altar.

They are, as Cooke puts it, 'kicked to bits'. New Zealand's philosophy is that if a player is lying near the ball, he should be given a 'reminder', a tickle of the studs, so that he moves away and the ball emerges. Ian McGeechan, the Lions coach, subscribes to this view. At first, you can see the point. Ultimately, it is a charter for nutcases. Anyone who claims there is no fine line between scraping players delicately away and standing on them is dreaming.

So where is the referee? Enslaved to continuity, enslaved by New Zealand's trendies. Stamping, even the grossest examples, is never penalised. That would, in the eyes of the trendies, be a decision in favour of the (largely imaginary) ranks of players trying to kill continuity.

When Southland's lock, Mark Tinnock, performed a nonsensical violent tap-dance on a Lion, the managements of both teams were asked for their condemnation. None gave it. In Europe, a courageous referee like Fred Howard would have had Tinnock in the dressing-room where he belonged. In New Zealand, they have decided that the threat of violent physical assault is good for keeping the game going.

So the game rolls on in front of you, with hardly a check. As I say, if you forgive the sheer arrogance and anarchy of New Zealand deciding on their own laws and interpretations then it sounds great. As Cooke says, 'It is difficult to argue with some of the philosophy though there are formal ways of changing the laws.' Quite right.

Yet it has been deadly difficult to enjoy the results as well. Sometimes, you get continuous processions of scoring. As in basketball, you get a score one way then a score the other way. While the Lions were in New Zealand the satellite TV showed the NBA play-offs from America, between the Chicago Bulls and the Phoenix Suns. The teams contained some of the 'dream team', that obnoxious bunch of overpaid prats who won the Olympic gold medal. The basketball action looked familiar. Of course, we were seeing games of that structure, pace and boredom on New Zealand rugby fields, especially in the domestic stuff.

It becomes difficult for even a mediocre team to lose possession, hence the 55-45 scores. All very well, but nothing to do with top-class rugby. Even in the better games, tries are cheapened. The Maoris-Lions game was a classic, so was the midweek riot against Taranaki; otherwise, basketball scores abound. 'Rugby is becoming closer to basketball every minute,' says Bob Dwyer, the Australian coach. 'One lot score, then the other lot score.'

The continuity of play means nothing if most of the passages of play are taken up with short forward drives battering away in a vain attempt to draw the defence, time and again. In the opening passage of play in the First Test, the All Blacks, at first sight, seemed irresistible. They won the ball, drove and drove and rucked and rucked. Back the ball would come – and there, waiting and filing their nails, would be the Lions defence. As we discovered very early in the British season last September, the new law removes the need to commit players to stopping the drive. The All Blacks, for all their drive to what they see as attacking rugby, scored one try from a dirty great hoof up into the air. In the Second Test, they won a grand total of 46 rucks against 25 won by the Lions – and scored one try from a dirty great hoof into the air. The continuity was pointless, and Laurie Mains, the loudest proponent, was hanging from his own yard-arm.

You have only to be in New Zealand a week to grasp the clarity of purpose and devotion in their rugby, and the grip rugby union has on the national psyche. If they keep winning – and they hammered Australia in the Bledisloe Cup after the Lions departed – then they will believe that their vision of rugby is vindicated. It emphatically does not mean that their vision is the only one under which rugby can be played or enjoyed by spectators. I can only say, of this vision, that they are welcome to it.

There was one thing that all sides agreed on in New Zealand's fascinating winter. British Lions tours are the summit of the game. They are the freshest anachronism in the sport. The concept is thriving wonderfully. Even in defeat, the heroic, crusading feel of the tour remained.

Lions tours are accessible, whereas the World Cup is a step towards the polarisation of players behind a wall of commissionaires and marketing men and sponsors. The players love them, revel in them, despite the onerous demands made on them. The hosts covet them – all over New Zealand people flocked to the matches. And they are part of the essential finishing school for players, coaches, media and followers of the game on all sides. They must continue if rugby is to be maintained as a one-world brotherhood.

The organisers in the British Isles must step up their act. The management should be appointed before any arrangements are made, so that the people who will be at the sharp end can be involved in all aspects of the organisation, especially the itinerary, the other major appointments, the tour agreement. They must step up the funding for medical and other matters, and continue to ensure that the tour party is treated like visiting royalty at every leg. They should market a little more of the Lions aura and personality, and some of the proceeds will, in the near future as Britain catches up with New Zealand, go to the players. They should also rule that the manager and coach should, if at all possible, take a year off from their duties with their own individual countries to assume the global perspective as soon as possible.

Mere details, these, but important to ensure continued success, and perhaps even the odd Test series victory, in what is still the ultimate sporting adventure. Long live the Lions – and next time, let them live for eighty minutes.

# Guards on the Borders

And so rugby's winter never did end. It simply ran into the back of its new self. One year after South Africa hosted the New Zealanders they were again on tour themselves, on a slog through Australia. When they finished their tour the Northern Hemisphere season was blasting off. Effectively, rugby never ended. It was a colossal year. Technically, standards were mixed but the game continued to grow and to change with astounding speed.

I found the soul of the game. I did not have to hack through its jungles. I found it, not on some obscure trip, late in the second half of some godforsaken game, after an anxious search. I found it largely unscathed, pervading everything, hovering around almost every pitch in the packed season, enveloping every man and woman I met with an association with the sport. It hung around, as well balanced as ever. You still had to love it.

Sean Fitzpatrick, the captain of New Zealand, was probably the most fierce competitor I met. He stood, snarling over his gumshield, blasting his way around for Auckland in the onerous Super-10 series and for the All Blacks as, shaken, they tried to reassert themselves against the Lions. For Fitzpatrick, the stakes were incredibly high. He had to live up to a whole history of All Black superiority and the blessed memories of his predecessors. He would go to any lengths to win.

Or would he? Certainly, Fitzpatrick played with ferocity, tweaked the edges of rugby's laws, berated referees and angrily refused to give any quarter. But there were lengths to which he would not go. He would not take drugs to enhance his performance or his training, or take or offer bribes to throw a match; or assume the airs and graces of an icon divorced from the common herd of rugby followers; or cheat blatantly, or perform any rugby equivalent of a handball over the head of the goalkeeper; or instruct his men to injure deliberately the Lions' key men; or savage the referee in the bitter hour of his defeat in the Second Test; or shrink from fair competition to preserve his market value; or do anything other, at the end of the series, than exchange jerseys with Gavin Hastings, sit down with the Lions at the post-Test dinner and shake hands on a promise to meet again, once more in severe physical combat, when he led the All Blacks to England and Scotland in the autumn of 1993.

And yet none of this was worthy of reporting. It was simply a
natural course. Fitzpatrick, give or take a few twists of the ratchet of
pressure in stratospheric rugby, was merely performing all the
same functions and adhering to all the essential inner goodnesses of
rugby captains of teams of all standards in more than a hundred
countries in the world.

My conclusion is that in the playing of the game, the stakes are
incalculably higher, especially with the new competitions and
revolutions in attitudes in the British Isles, and particularly due to
the World Cup. The number of high-pressure games is phenomenal and terrifying, but remarkably, the game is now cleaner and
less violent than it has ever been. The endless winter of 1992-93
contained satisfyingly few incidents. In a harsh new world, players
respected each other and their heritage. Those outbursts which did
happen were, I am proud to say, highlighted by the media. That is
evidence of a problem addressed and therefore, a problem being
solved. There are victories which still cost too much. But the balance
is there, and, among the followers, the bystanders from all callings
and roles, the ambience unquestionably remains.

The one qualification is this. From now on it may not be enough to
wallow in it. We may have to go out and guard it. This was a
watershed season. During this season, we finally reached the point
where we could not ask any more of the leading players, not one
scrap, simply because rugby is now full. If any unions wanted
another competition in any of the major countries, or if they wanted
another tour, or another series of training sessions, there is simply
no window in which to schedule them. Finally, rugby is choked.

And, allied to that, we finally crossed one of the last Rubicons.
The advent of the All Blacks Club in New Zealand and of a
spectacular dinner in Australia, the proceeds of both going directly
to the players in those countries, swept away any vestiges of the
notion that commercial activity should not be directly related to the
game. All checks were off. Please don't bother me with semantics.
Everything, absolutely everything, is now, sometimes unofficially,
allowed in the game bar straight wage packets. All bylaws have been
evaded. And I can now see the day – still distant, but on its way –
when, at the top level, the rush of earning evolves quietly into direct
payment and the game becomes semi-professional. Bob Dwyer, the
Australian coach, is already calling for retainers for national squad
members.

The Northern Hemisphere unions, drowning in the incoming
tide and with no recourse to the helpless International Rugby
Board, have a savage problem. If they capitulate to the powerful
threats, they are ditching their own ideals; if they do not they
immediately divide rugby into two camps (if it is not already in those
camps), hostile and, from the point of view of players in the
Northern Hemisphere, jealous. And, indirectly, it is their fault. The
headlong rush away from amateurism derives from within. I know
we live in a commercial age, I know that rugby is big business, I
know that players want a slice. But the rush has been caused because

we have finally gone beyond the bounds, because rugby authorities
have made the idea of maintaining the principle completely fatuous
through their own demands.

What will be the fall-out as the rush into harshness and quasi-
professionalism, already well established, picks up even more pace?
And as the famous and treasured amateur foundations finally
disappear? In his excellent book *Betrayal: The Struggle for Cricket's
Soul*, Graeme Wright, former editor of *Wisden*, quotes Lucretius:

> 'Whenever a thing changes and alters its nature,
> at that moment comes the death of what it was before.'

Rugby will have to be vigilant for the excesses and the abuses which
follow the scent of money like a faithful Labrador follows its master,
just one step behind. Such as hiding from fair competition to
preserve market value; such as commercial wide boys – they are
already circling the fringes of rugby's World Cup; new breeds of
athletes motivated by rewards other than the glorious intangibles
which rugby offers; coaches who might, just, stoop to conquer and
deny the heritage maintained by Sean Fitzpatrick which protects
the game from violence and the drug culture. There is no doubt
that performance drugs are creeping into the South African game,
and that the authorities there are fatuously mealy-mouthed in
acting gainst them.

   From more salubrious yet still problematical sources, there will be
calls to prostitute the game more to television; to sell bits and pieces
of the game's ethos to a sponsor's logo, to leave the game covered
like the client of a tattoo parlour who fell asleep in the chair. To
make the allocation of World Cup venues into the crooked circus of
Olympic Games voting. To enter, in fact, what people involved in
some of the appalling excesses in other sports call, erroneously, the
real world. If that is the real world then I would prefer rugby to stay
in its smug vacuum.

   In July 1993, Dudley Wood of the RFU came under attack after
he made some ill-judged comparisons between rugby and other
sports at a lunch in London. In a condemnation of Wood in the
*Observer*, the paper's sports editor declared that it was time for
rugby to come clean about the shady payments in the sport, 'just as
athletics had done'. It was a remarkable statement. The example of
athletics 'coming clean' is the best possible ammunition for Wood in
his fight to keep rugby amateur – it is precisely the tawdry, drug-
infested, over-hyped world, the extremes of individual posing and
wealth and collective poverty of athletics, that Wood and others
believed will descend on rugby should the game go pro.

   Furthermore, even though under-the-counter action in rugby
continued at high pace throughout the season, the truth is that,
whatever the unstoppable processes moving the game away from its
roots, as yet the vast majority of players, even at the top level,

showed not one farthing of profit from the sport all year. The explosion has, substantially, not yet come.

The steps into the unknown must be better guided. Rugby's administration is dangerously poor, as the shambling small minds of the Welsh Rugby Union have proved so beautifully in 1993. The International Rugby Board must, immediately, open its doors and its books so that the anxious rugby world can know what protection is offered to their game. The ludicrous self-seeking of all the members at the moment – passing laws, both playing and bylaws, simply to suit their own houses and family – must be replaced by global policies. There must be actual help, not promises of it, to other nations around the world, because while the whirlpool of commerce in rugby affects some of the nations, there are hundreds of others who will not have the resources to change the nature of their game.

The funereal pace of the IRB must be replaced by a quick, counter-punching outfit which can react on a weekly basis, can drum some universality of interpretation into all its regulations on and off the field, can guard the key to the safe containing rugby's balance. At the moment, anarchy is ruling and no one in the IRB will admit it. Every member union has the improvement at its voting fingertips.

Rugby World Cup Ltd, guardian of the major competition in that month when non-rugby people turn up at the gates in wonder, must be utterly reformed, run by younger people: people who can communicate, people who are more accountable, less self-serving, more commercially minded but also more careful with rugby's birthright. On all those points, Rugby World Cup falls down flat on its face.

And if the impetus towards the danger zones is caused by too many demands, why doesn't every union take out a red pen? They could sit down with the itinerary of any of their leading players over the last three years, read it and weep. Take the RFU in England. Why not strike out the Divisional Championship and two of the national sessions not directly before Test matches? They are just gilding the lily. Work back towards a reduction of league games; keep one summer in four fallow – completely fallow, no B or Under-21 tour, either – maintain a total ban on rugby on a Sunday . . . Either do it now, or stop whingeing about the death of amateurism. There are no more options. And there is no alternative to vigilance from every observer, especially those who are paid to report on the game.

So *is* it possible that rugby can change substantially in tone and ethos and maintain its inner calm? It will be painfully difficult. But it can be done. As I say, the interim news is good. A revolution has been in operation in all parts of the game for some years and in my experience there is no change yet. It is a sign of basic power. Some of the nightmares raised by those fighting for amateurism have simply not come true. They said that hordes of amateur officials would decamp, unwilling to be simply a conduit for the new game. I know of none who has left – the game is still too attractive. There was the fear that all the lower levels of the game would turn away in jealous pique at the antics of the privileged few. Garbage. Did soccer on Hackney Marshes end when soccer stars were earning £1 million? Of course not. As far as I can see, the more humble rugby men all over the world still worship their high-class heroes with all the old fervency. Of course they are two different games, but still the same brotherhood and sisterhood.

The main battles will be fought over the next few years. That is when we will find out whether rugby and all its essential glories does depend on amateurism or whether, after all, that concept was incidental.

Rugby's defensive team, however, is strong. We have on our side all those millions of people who, in all their different roles, have toasted their feet at the warmest point in the sporting world and who would simply not tolerate the fires being allowed to die.

# Index